Fodor's

E X P L O R I N G

BRITAIN

FODOR'S TRAVEL PUBLICATIONS, INC.
NEW YORK • TORONTO • LONDON • SYDNEY • AUCKLAND

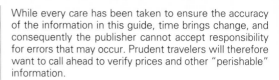

While every care has been taken to ensure the accuracy of the information in this guide, time brings change, and consequently the publisher cannot accept responsibility for errors that may occur. Prudent travelers will therefore want to call ahead to verify prices and other "perishable" information.

Published in the United States by Fodor's Travel Publications, Inc.
Published in the United Kingdom by AA Publishing.

Fodor's and Fodor's Exploring Guides are registered trademarks of Fodor's Travel Publications, Inc.

ISBN 0-679-02662-2
First Edition

Fodor's Exploring Britain

Authors: **Tim Locke, Richard Cavendish, Barnaby Rogerson**
Series Adviser: **Ingrid Morgan**
Joint Series Editor: **Susi Bailey**
Cartography: **The Automobile Association**
Cover Design: **Louise Fili, Fabrizio La Rocca**
Front Cover Silhouette: **Catherine Karnow/Woodfin Camp**

Special Sales
Fodor's Travel Publications are available at special discounts for bulk purchases for sales promotions or premiums. Special editions, including personalized covers, excerpts of existing guides, and corporate imprints, can be created in large quantities for special needs, For more information, contact your local bookseller or write to Special Markets, Fodor's Travel Publications, 201 East 50th Street, New York, NY 10022.

MANUFACTURED IN ITALY
10 9 8 7 6 5 4 3 2 1

Goldfinch is a dry slightly sparkling Cider, fermented and matured in oak vats. It has a taste that reflects the art of real Cidermaking. Made in the heart of the West Country by the Sheppy family whose traditions of Cider making go back nearly 200 years. This Cider is best enjoyed within 24 hours of opening.

Tim Locke is the author of two books on walking in Britain, *The Good Walks Guide* and *Town and Country Walks*, both published by the Consumers' Association. He has also contributed to *Thailand* and *Germany* in the *Fodor's Exploring* series, as well as other guides on Britain. Richard Cavendish has had numerous books and articles published on Britain, including *The Complete Book of London,* and has contributed to *Where to Go in Britain*, published by the AA. Barnaby Rogerson, an experienced travel writer, is the author of *AA Essential Scotland*.

Bassenthwaite Lake lies on the northern edge of the Lake District, Cumbria

How to use this book

This book is divided into five main sections:

❏ Section 1: *Britain Is*

discusses aspects of life and living today, from politics to pubs.

❏ Section 2: *Britain Was*

places the country in its historical context and explores those past events whose influences are felt to this day.

❏ Section 3: *A to Z Section*

is broken down into regional chapters, and covers places to visit, including walks and drives. Within this section fall the Focus-on articles, which consider a variety of subjects in greater detail.

❏ Section 4: *Travel Facts*

contains the strictly practical information vital for a successful trip.

❏ Section 5 *Hotels and Restaurants*

lists recommended establishments throughout Britain, with a brief description of each.

How to use the rating system
Most of the places described in this book have been given a separate rating:

▶▶▶ **Do not miss**

▶▶ **Highly recommended**

▶ **Worth seeing**

Not essential to see

Map references
To make the location of a particular place easier to find every main entry in this book has a map reference to the right of its name. This includes a number, followed by a letter, followed by another number, such as 176B3. The first number (176) refers to the page on which the map can be found, the letter (B) and the second number (3) pinpoint the square in which the main entry is located. The maps on the inside front cover and inside back cover are referred to as IFC and IBC respectively.

Contents

Quick reference   6–7

My Britain   8
by Brian Redhead
by Bel Mooney

Britain Is   9–22

Britain Was   23–41

A to Z
London   42–59
The West Country   60–85
Southern England   86–109
The Heart of England   110–33
Eastern England   134–49
Wales   150–71
Northwest England   172–89
Northeast England   190–209
Southern Scotland   210–33
Northern Scotland   234–62

Travel Facts   263–74

Hotels and Restaurants   275–84

Index   285–8

Picture credits and
contributors   288

Quick reference

This quick-reference guide high-lights the features of the book you will use most often: the maps; the introductory features; the Focus-on articles; the walks and the drives.

Maps

Regions and 3-star sights	IFC
London	42–3
London walks	52
The West Country	60–1
Bath walk	66
Thomas Hardy country drive	76
Southern England	86–7
The Weald drive	106
The Heart of England	110–11
The Cotswolds drive	121
Oxford walk	127
Eastern England	134–5
Cambridge walk	139
Constable country drive	148
Wales	150–1
Snowdonia drive	170
Northwest England	172
Lake District drive	180–1
Northeast England	190–1
York walk	205
Yorkshire Dales drive	207
Southern Scotland	210–11
The Borders drive	217
Edinburgh walk	224–5
Northern Scotland	234–5
Loch Ness and the Black Isle drive	243
Map of Britain	IBC
Transportation routes and nationally protected areas	IBC

Britain Is

Variety	10
The Government	11
The British people	12–13
The economy	14
The pub	15
Gardens	16–17
Events	18–19
The industrial past today	20–1
The semi-detached house	22

Britain Was

Man and the landscape	24–5
Castles and manors	26–7
Churches and monasteries	28–9
Domestic architecture	30–1
Kings and queens	32–3
A maritime nation	34–5
Writers and places	36–7
Artists and places	38–9
The Industrial Revolution	40–1

Focus on

The north Cornish coast	68–9
The south Cornish coast	70–1
English place-names	81
Seaside resorts	94–5
Houses of the Weald	102–3
The Cotswolds	118–20
Ironbridge Gorge	123
The canal system	128–9
The north Norfolk coast	142
Threats to the landscape	144–5
East Anglia's artists	149

The Valleys 156
Welsh culture and politics 160–1
The Lake District 178–9
Inner-city Britain 184–5
Port Sunlight 188
The Brontës 198
Clans and tartans 233
Bonnie Prince Charlie 246
Highland land use 262

Walks

London 52–3
West Country walks 64
Bath 66
Southern England walks 92
Oxford walk 127
Cambridge walk 139
Wales walks 158

Northwest England walks 175
Northeast England walks 193
York walk 205
Southern Scotland walks 214
Edinburgh walk 224–5
Northern Scotland walks 238

Drives

Thomas Hardy country 76
The Weald 106–7
The Cotswolds 121
Constable country 148
Snowdonia 170
The Lake District 180–1
The Yorkshire Dales 207
The Borders 217
Loch Ness and the Black Isle 243
Mid-Argyll 249

Brian Redhead
Journalist and broadcaster Brian Redhead has been a presenter of BBC Radio 4's *Today* program—a national institution—since 1975. His background, however, is in newspapers, having been a features editor and assistant editor of the *Manchester Guardian*, as well as editor of the *Manchester Evening News*. He made his first broadcast in 1942, playing the clarinet on *Children's Hour*.

He is a long-standing defender of the countryside, and a passionate champion of northern England.

My Britain

by Brian Redhead

"Wherever you are in Britain, you have only to travel for ten miles in any direction, and you are somewhere else." The speaker was my geography teacher 50 years ago, and, after a lifetime seeking to explore and to explain this country, I can testify to the truth of his observation.

There is no more interesting place on this planet.

Britain is a monument to nature and to mankind. It is a lived-in, lived-on, and much loved landscape; from high level to sea-level.

The beautiful parts of Britain are no more unoccupied territory than are the industrial conurbations; wherever you go, someone has been there before, and enjoyed being there.

The country is a testimony to good works, to the patient labour of men and women over the centuries, cultivating the land, caring for their homestead, proclaiming their enthusiasms, their ingenuity, and their faith. You can see their achievements and enjoy their treasures, not least the many churches which punctuate the landscape.

Nowhere in the world is the truth more evident that history is what we make of our geography.

I tell every visitor to this country whom I meet, "Stand on any piece of high ground here in Britain, and you will see the then, and the now, and the always."

I think my geography teacher would have agreed.

My Britain

by Bel Mooney

In August I usually travel to southern Europe in search of sun, to escape from the often disappointing British summer. At the beginning of September I rejoice to be back, aware that my restlessness was not the heat, but something as simple as homesickness. Wherever I go, no matter how beautiful and interesting, deep within me is the conviction that my Britain can match anywhere for beauty and interest. I think of the great cultural cities: London, Edinburgh, Glasgow, Manchester, Durham, Liverpool, Bristol, Newcastle. Then the architectural jewels: for example Bath, York, Canterbury, Harrogate, Cheltenham.

On this small island you can travel in a short time from the austere beauty of Scotland and Northern Ireland, along haunting coastlines, by the lakes of the Northwest and the mountains of Wales, to the lyrical rolling beauty of the Southwest. But a country is more than its physical beauty. When I watch tourists in London or Bath I am profoundly aware of what they are seeing—British history still alive in spirit. This is the land of Shakespeare and Milton as well as Elizabeth I and Winston Churchill. We have a proud, tolerant history, and if we work hard to preserve what is best about us, from ideas to landscape, my Britain will be the pride of my grand-children too.

Bel Mooney
Bel Mooney was born and raised in Northwest England, moved as a teenager to Wiltshire, gained a degree at London University, and now divides her time between Bath and London. A former journalist, she is the author of 16 books, including four novels, nine children's books, and a personal guide to Somerset. She is also a regular contributor to BBC Radio 4.

BRITAIN IS

■ **Britain is by no means a uniform entity: the more you travel around this compact island, the more there is for you to see and enjoy. Within the boundaries of its 88,000 square miles Britain shows an astonishingly rich variety of landscape, architecture, climate, regional accents and cuisine, cultural traditions, social make-up and economic activity.....■**

10

This is the land of William Shakespeare, Thomas Hardy, William Wordsworth, Beatrix Potter and Winnie-the-Pooh; the land of Edward Elgar, Benjamin Britten, Gilbert and Sullivan, the Beatles and the Sex Pistols; the land of Scotch whisky, Yorkshire pudding, real ale, fish and chips, Scottish haggis, Welsh cakes, and Chinese and Indian take-out restaurants; the land of seaside piers, cricket, greyhound racing, heather moorland, the early Industrial Revolution, stately homes, lawns and herbaceous borders, porches, chimney pots, village fêtes, the Royal Family and, last but not least, the Loch Ness monster.

The diversity Many newcomers to Britain are constantly surprised by how abruptly the urban scene gives way to beautiful rural landscapes. Significant factors include the compactness of many urban centers, restrictive zoning laws and the constant variations in the natural environment: low-level arable fens, rolling hedgerow-lined pastures, craggy dales, blustery moorland tops, post-glacial mountain scenery, rugged cliffs and shingle shores. This in turn has given rise to numerous types of local architecture: sometimes the bedrock itself supplies the building material as can be seen in the Cotswolds, Cornwall, rural Wales, the Scottish Highlands and the Pennines, while elsewhere timber and/or bricks predominate.

Twentieth-century progress has inevitably eroded some of the finer distinctions in various locales (high-tech agriculture today blankets vast tracts of farmland, and chain stores dominate small towns' main shopping streets), but in spite of this, much has either been carefully preserved or has survived. Regional accents, for instance, continue to thrive to a surprising degree: a well-trained ear can distinguish from which side of the Pennines, of Scotland or even of London the speaker comes.

Britain's greatest assets for the visitor include its sense of history and wealth of variety, all of which are packed into one accessible island country where the driving distances are never too long between distinctively different landscapes and cultures.

Market day (this one is Norwich)—a colorful experience in every way

■ **The British system of government is that of parliamentary democracy, based on principles of common law—there is no written constitution. The system has developed gradually over many centuries and is still evolving to this day. Every adult person, except peers, lunatics and certain criminals, has the right to vote in the elections, although this is a comparatively recent development—universal male suffrage in Britain dates only from 1918 and women did not get the vote until as recently as 1928.....■**

❑ Let not England forget her precedence of teaching other nations how to live.
John Milton (1644) ❑

Britain has a confusing variety of names. The British Isles are the two islands of Britain and Ireland. Britain, or Great Britain, means England, Wales and Scotland. Wales was conquered by England in the 13th century. The King of Scots succeeded to the English throne in 1603 and the political union of England and Scotland dates from 1707.

The United Kingdom is England, Wales, Scotland and Northern Ireland, the latter being the six counties of Ulster (predominantly Protestant in religion) which refused to join the rest of Ireland when it broke away from Britain in 1921. The United Kingdom is a highly centralized state. Scotland, Wales and Northern Ireland are ruled, like England, from London, though Scotland has its own legal system.

The seat of power The head of state is officially Queen Elizabeth II. Much of the ceremonial of British life revolves round **the monarchy**, dating from a time when the monarch actually ruled the country. Today, however, actual power rests with the government, a set of officials appointed by whichever political party controls the most seats in the Parliament's democratically elected **House of Commons**, the chief legislative body. The unelected **House of Lords** is primarily a revising chamber. The country's relationship with the European Community, however, and the consequences for British sovereignty and the supremacy of Parliament is a matter of debate in the 1990s.

❑ Great Britain has lost an empire and has not yet found a role.
Dean Acheson (1962) ❑

The British people

■ **Class distinctions are still profoundly important in British life. They involve the most acutely discriminating judgments—about people's houses and furnishings, clothes, cars, jobs, education, manners and personal tastes. The simplest clue to someone's class is usually gained by listening to their accent—as George Bernard Shaw once remarked, an Englishman cannot open his mouth without making some other Englishman despise him.....** ■

The population of Great Britain numbers about 56 million. A small and thickly populated country, it would fit neatly inside the American state of Oregon, which has a population of only 3 million. Or, keeping the comparison within Europe, the country has about the same number of people as France, in an area less than half as large.

Early ancestry The British are a nation of mongrels, principally a mixture of Germanic and Celtic strains. The original English, or Anglo-Saxons, came across the North Sea in their dragon-prowed longships

from northwest Germany and southern Denmark some 1,500 years ago. They subjugated most of the native Celtic people, whom they dismissively called Welsh, meaning "foreigners."

More Germanic invaders came from Denmark and Norway in the Viking Age. Then the Norman Conquest of England in 1066 eventually gave all areas of the British Isles a new and initially French-speaking ruling class. From the 16th century to the 18th, thousands of French Protestants, known as Huguenots, came to England to escape religious persecution. The 19th century brought substantial Irish immigration to Britain and an influx of Jewish families fleeing from persecution in Russia and Eastern Europe. After World War II fresh waves of immigrants came from the West Indies, the Indian subcontinent, Cyprus and Commonwealth countries. All these

arrivals over the centuries have enriched the British national mix and the British way of life.

Ethnic and religious mix Despite the presence of many ethnic and religious minorities, statistics show that more than 80 percent of the U.K. population is still classified as English, about 10 percent as Scottish, 2.5 percent as Irish and 2 percent as Welsh. Britain is 95 percent white, with West Indians, Indians and Pakistanis numbering about 1 percent each. There are also tiny percentages of Bangladeshis and Chinese. Of the ethnic minority population, close to 50 percent was born in Britain.

The population is overwhelmingly Christian, or thinks of itself that way. More than 85 percent of the British people regard themselves as Christians, but fewer than one person in five goes regularly to church or chapel. The Muslim population is about 2 percent and practising Jews total 1 percent.

Males and female members of the population are nearing equality in numbers. All through this century the British birth rate has increased extremely slowly and in the 1970s

the U.K. population actually fell for a time.

A national character? Whether there is anything that can be called a British national character is open to question. The Scots, the Welsh and the Irish have retained their separate identities despite (or because of) English domination. Even in England itself, people from London, Yorkshire, Lancashire, the Northeast, the West Country and other areas cherish their regional identities.

As seen by outsiders, at least, qualities of the typical Englishman (there is no such thing as a typical Englishwoman) include reserve and politeness, helpfulness, a gift for understatement and awkwardness with women and children. The English pride themselves on fair play and a genius for compromise. Profoundly conservative by temperament, they suspect intellectuals and ideologies, change, professionalism, fads and fancies, and foreigners. They like sports, gardens, dogs and horses. And although they love the countryside, most of them do not actually live in it.

Perhaps the most fundamental trait that the British have in common is an ironic sense of humor which lets them poke fun at themselves with good grace.

❏ Arthur Koestler, a notable foreign writer who lived in Britain for many years, described the average Englishman as an attractive hybrid between an ostrich and a lion: keeping his head in the sand for as long as possible, but when forced to confront reality, capable of heroic deeds. ❏

The economy

■ **If anything causes the British more complaint, anxiety and frustration than the weather, it is the economy. In the Victorian Age Britain was the most powerful industrial nation on earth, with a mighty economy based on coal, iron and steel, heavy machinery, textiles, shipbuilding and foreign trade. Queen Victoria ruled the largest empire in history. This commanding position has since been lost, however, and with it the vigorous self-confidence of Victorian Britain.....■**

14

The British economy today is based on private enterprise; in the 1980s many of the nationalized industries were restored to private ownership. Heavy industry has steeply declined while the service sector has grown. Britain used to import raw materials for its factories. Now it is a net importer of manufactured goods from countries that make them better and cheaper. The once flourishing fishing industry is hampered by European Community and government restrictions. The balance of trade, along with unemployment and inflation, is a perennial problem.

Trade and resources On the other hand, the U.K. has rich energy resources—coal, North Sea oil and natural gas. A strong financial sector brings in more wealth from overseas. Less food is imported these days and more grown at home, though only 2 percent of the working population is employed in agriculture. In 1973, belatedly, Britain joined the European Community, which now accounts for more than half of Britain's trade.

The U.K. was the sixth richest country in the world in 1950, while in 1980 it was only the 22nd richest. All the same, by the early 1990s, with two-thirds of British households owning their homes and two-thirds owning cars, Britons had a higher standard of living than ever before.

❑ The change which has come over Britain can be observed in the mining valleys of South Wales, where King Coal once raised his grimy scepter above teeming pits and slag heaps. Today not a nugget of coal is mined in the Rhondda Valley, and the valleys are being extensively "greened." ❑

The Bank of England, at the heart of the City of London

■ **Pubs are much more than simply places to drink in. They are enclaves of laughter and gossip, arenas for playing games, and havens of sympathy in times of trouble. A good pub has its own distinctive atmosphere and comes complete with its own resident cast of characters.....■**

❏ When you have lost your inns drown your empty selves, for you will have lost the last of England.
  Hilaire Belloc (1870–1953) ❏

Some pubs are dedicated to thoughtful imbibing and peaceful conversation, others to deafening taped music and clattering slot machines. There are venerable half-timbered Tudor hostelries, leaning at an angle and apparently held up as much by the strength of the ale on tap as they are by their massive black timbers. There are broad-fronted Georgian coaching inns, glittering Victorian gin palaces and dubious little backstreet taverns. There are pubs with romantic tales to tell of smugglers and highwaymen, rose-wreathed pubs idyllically set by rivers and canals, lobster-potted inns gazing over picturesque fishing harbors and patronized by blue-sweatered sailing types, while weatherbeaten pubs perched high on remote moors are frequented by ramblers in thick boots and waterproof anoraks.

Then and now
Today's neighborhood pub is descended from the local alehouse of Anglo-Saxon and medieval England, an ordinary house whose occupants brewed and sold ale. In the 12th and 13th centuries inns began to open up, providing overnight accommodation for travelers. In recent years, the traditional pub has found a new identity: serving food—"pub grub"—has become more important, and there has been a comeback of real ale,

There are town pubs, village pubs country pubs . . . and boaty pubs

meaning old-fashioned beer, once threatened with extinction by the big commercial brewers. Most pubs have become less aggressively masculine, and women can now feel more comfortable in them.

What's in a name? Pubs have picture-signs hanging above their doors, illustrating their names—a custom dating from days when few people could read. Some names are derived from heraldry, like the White Hart and the Red Lion. Others are named for royalty, as in the Crown or the King's Head. Other names reflect country life – the Plough or the Fox and Hounds. There are New Inns that are centuries old, and there are strange and enigmatic names: the Pig and Whistle, the Cat and Fiddle. All are part of the richness and variety that keep the British pub a vital institution.

■ **Gardens and gardening are a national passion. Whether they possess the tiniest cottage garden or live on the grandest estate, the British have always found opportunities for self-expression and creativity. This selected list of gardens that are open to the public gives you an idea of the vast scope and diversity of the nation's "backyards".....** ■

The British garden dates from Roman times, when every upwardly mobile villa-owner aspired to an atrium with a small garden. Monastic gardens were merely practical affairs for growing food or cultivating herbs and plants for dyes or for medicinal purposes. With the first great houses of the 16th century came the first true pleasure gardens, with their knots of herbs and flowers. In the next century the aristocratic classes toured France and Italy and saw the formal creations of Le Nôtre; topiary and water parterres were the rage.

The classical age of English landscaping in the 18th century saw formality rejected in favor of the naturalistic contrivances of Lancelot "Capability" Brown and others, who designed green expanses fringed by woodlands, interrupted by lakes and punctuated by classical follies. Victorian times saw formal rockeries, ferneries, roseries and other horticultural extravaganzas back in fashion.

Meanwhile the working classes tended small plots in allotment gardens where they grew their own vegetables, and middle-class suburban villas sported lawns and herbaceous borders. In their back garden, Mr. and Mrs. Everyman found a private haven from the outside world, and whether it be to satisfy a creative urge or as an antidote to the stresses of daily life, toiling in the garden is a national pastime.

The West Country Subtropical species thrive in the gardens of **Tresco Abbey**, in the Isles of Scilly. On the mainland of Cornwall **Glendurgan** (NT), **Penjerrick** and **Trebah** are neighboring subtropical havens; **Trelissick** (NT) is noted for rhododendrons and azaleas with color all year round; paths wind down to the waterside with glimpses of Pendennis Castle. At **Trewithen** magnolias and rhododendrons and rare shrubs surround a Georgian mansion. In Wiltshire, **Stourhead** (NT) is a splendid example of 18th-century landscaping.

Southern England and London
Kew Gardens in London is the king of all botanic gardens. The collection of rare specimens from all over the world owes much to the 19th-century botanist Sir Joseph Banks. Don't miss the elegant Palm House and the Princess of Wales Conservatory. **Wisley Garden**, Surrey, was set up in 1904 as experimental gardens for the Royal Horticultural Society: it has

Stourhead, the quintessential landscaped garden

Late spring at Sissinghurst

many scarce species and an excellent garden center. **Winkworth Arboretum**, Surrey, is a great tree collection, splendid for spring and fall colors. In East Sussex, **Sheffield Park Garden** (NT) enjoys lakes, azaleas, rhododendrons and more, while **Wakehurst Place** (NT) has rare trees and shrubs in a lakeside setting. In Kent the gardens of **Hever Castle** are strongly Italian in feel and those of **Scotney Castle** (NT) are of the picturesque-romantic style in a lake and island setting. **Sissinghurst Garden** (NT) is the wonderful 1930s creation of Harold Nicholson and Vita Sackville-West.

The Heart of England and Eastern England Barnsley House, **Hidcote Manor** (NT), **Kiftsgate Court**, **Miserden Park**, **Painswick Rococo Garden** and **Westonbirt Arboretum** are all in the Cotswolds, each offering something different (see panels, pages 118 and 120). **Rousham House**, Oxfordshire, is an excellent example of an 18th-century romantic rural idyll by William Kent. **Anglesey Abbey** (NT), in Cambridgeshire, has a charming Georgian garden.

Wales Powis Castle in Powys is set amid fine 18th-century terraces. At **Bodnant**, Gwynedd, is a garden of sublime inspiration based on five Italianate terraces with the mountains of Snowdonia behind.

Northern England Chatsworth in Derbyshire is a masterly marriage of parkland, landscaped by Lancelot "Capability" Brown, and gardens full of surprises that owe much to Joseph Paxton, head gardener from 1827. **Studley Royal** (NT), North Yorkshire, is an ultra-romantic creation around Fountains Abbey.

Scotland Culzean Country Park, Strathclyde, is landscaped park and woodland. At Edzell Castle, Tayside, is a 17th-century "pleasaunce," while Branklyn, Tayside, is a modest-sized, amazingly stocked suburban garden. Crathes Castle, Grampian, is enchanting and innovative. In the wilds of the Highlands, Inverewe is a spectacular oasis in a mild gulf-stream climate.

> ❏ The National Gardens Scheme is an umbrella organization for gardens throughout Britain. Included are many private gardens whose owners open them to the public just one or two days a year, offering the chance of a peep into their personal Edens. Details are given in the booklet *Gardens of England and Wales*. ❏

■ The national calendar of events ranges from the local customs of Mayday dancing and Shrove Tuesday pancake-racing to the royal pageantry of Trooping the Colour and the great sports events at Wembley Stadium, Royal Ascot and Lord's Cricket Ground. Local tourist information offices stock details of what's on where and when.....■

18

Pageantry and spectacle Trooping the Colour, the celebration of the Queen's official birthday, takes place in June in Horse Guards Parade in London and shows off the best of royal pageantry. The Lord Mayor's Show in November features the new mayor of London in procession in a gorgeous golden coach. Among other spectaculars are Cruft's Dog show (March, Birmingham), the International Air Show (September, even-numbered years, Farnborough, Hampshire) and the Chelsea Flower Show (May, London).

The Randwick Wap, a Cotswolds mayor-making ceremony

Arts festivals The major arts festival of the year is held in Edinburgh in August/September; other sites include Aldeburgh, Bath, Brighton and Glasgow, plus Gloucester, Hereford or Worcester for the Three Choirs Festival (see page 117) and Llangollen for the International Eisteddfod in Wales (see page 163). The Promenade Concerts ("Proms") at London's Royal Albert Hall take place from July through September, with classical music old and new being performed.

Sports Professional soccer matches are held every Saturday between August and April; the FA (Football Association) Cup Final in May is the big match. Cricket, the gentle summer game played with bats, balls, and wickets, is subtler than it looks at first sight; try a one-day game first. Wimbledon lawn tennis tournament is held in London late June to early July. As for horse racing, the Grand National is a notoriously tough steeplechase run at Aintree near Liverpool in April, and the ultra-fashionable Royal Ascot takes place in June. Regattas are rowed at Henley and Fowey, and a round-the-island yacht race takes place at Cowes in the Isle of Wight. In March the University Boat Race (Oxford versus Cambridge) is rowed on the Thames in west London.

Numerous traditional sports get an annual revival: variants of medieval football are played in the streets of St. Columb Major in Cornwall and Ashbourne in Derbyshire, while Cumberland Wrestling takes place in the Lake District. In Scotland the summer Highland Games at Braemar and elsewhere feature caber-tossing, mountain races and pipe bands.

Shows and fêtes County shows have an agricultural emphasis with livestock and horticultural competitions drawing in the farming communities, but also include sport and entertainment. Village fêtes are in many ways miniature versions of these, with tombolas, cake competitions, produce and bric-à-brac stalls, and sometimes sheep-dog trials—essential for anyone wanting to see the real rural Britain.

Folk and religious customs The only nationally celebrated event unique to this country is Guy Fawkes Night, on November 5, when fireworks are set off and crowds burn effigies of Guy Fawkes, the anarchist caught attempting to blow up the Houses of Parliament in 1605, are burnt on the top of big bonfires.

Locally, an amazing variety of folk customs is celebrated. Some of the oldest owe their origins to Mayday fertility rites, including maypole dancing around the country and, in Cornwall, the Furry Dance in Helston and the 'Obby 'Oss festival at Padstow. Elsewhere, you can take your pick from such oddities as oyster-blessing at Whitstable (Kent), a pancake race at Olney (Buckinghamshire) or face-pulling through a horse-collar at Egremont (Cumbria). Church customs include rush-bearing (dating from times when churches needed rushes to cover earthen floors) and, in the Peak District, well-dressing, when wells are decorated with elaborate pictures made of flowers etc.

The 'Obby 'Oss festival, Padstow

■   **The Industrial Revolution began in Britain, in a phenomenal burst of innovation in the late 18th and 19th centuries. In the late 20th century, even as Britain's heavy industrial base continues to decline, museums that explore this aspect of the national heritage are a boom industry—and you don't have to be a fan of rusty sprockets and cogwheels to appreciate and learn from them.....■**

Listed here is a selection of the best museums to visit. Though they haven't been turned into museums as such, you can also see evocative reminders of Britain's industrial past in the textile mill towns of West Yorkshire, the valleys of South Wales, the factory villages of Port Sunlight and Saltaire, and numerous abandoned mining landscapes such as the tin mines of Cornwall and the lead mines of Swaledale. Many of the sites mentioned below are described more fully in the A to Z section of the book.

The West Country Coldharbour Mill at Cullompton in Devon is an old wool mill that recalls the heyday of the Devon woolen industry; the processes of carding, drafting and spinning are shown, and there are some fine old machines. At **Geevor Tin Mine**, Pendeen, and **Poldark Mine**, Wendron, both in Cornwall, visitors can tour the old tin mines. At **Wheal Martyn**, St. Austell, Cornwall's still-surviving china clay industry is explained, with a tour around an abandoned site and a fine view into the eerie cratered landscape that results from the extraction process.

Southern England At the Chalkpits Museum at Amberley, West Sussex, visitors see craftsmen at work in a former chalk pit, while the **Royal Naval Dockyard** at Chatham in Kent has the country's longest brick building (the rope works) and the world's oldest corrugated iron structure.

The Heart of England The Black Country Museum, Dudley (West Midlands), is a skillful reconstruction of an industrial Black Country community of yesteryear, with a colliery, redbrick cottages, a canal where you can try "legging" along the tunnel in the time-honored fashion, and an old-style fairground. The **Ironbridge Gorge Museum** (in Shropshire), considered the birthplace of the Industrial Revolution, is the undoubted star of Britain's distinguished industrial museums.

Wales Visit the **Big Pit Museum**, Blaenavon, Gwent, to get the full experience of going down into a coal mine in the heart of the Welsh valleys. **Sygun Copper Mine** in Beddgelert, Gwynedd, and **Llechwedd Slate Caverns** in Blaenau Ffestiniog, Gwynedd, offer imaginatively conceived tours of the old mines, and the **Welsh Slate Museum**, Llanberis, is an evocative semi-abandoned slate quarry.

The Museum of Iron at Ironbridge Gorge, a World Heritage Site

A look inside a chainmaker's cottage at the Black Country Museum

Maesllyn Woollen Mill Museum in Llandysul, Dyfed, gives a complete picture of every stage of wool production. Adjoining is a museum with an entertainingly miscellaneous collection of unrelated bits and pieces.

Northwest England **Cromford Mill**, Cromford in Derbyshire, is an exciting monument to Richard Arkwright on the site of his first water-powered cotton mill. At **Chatterley Whitfield Mining Museum** in Stoke-on-Trent, colliery tours are enlivened by excellent guides, while at **Gladstone Pottery Museum**, also in Stoke-on-Trent, craftsmen give demonstrations of traditional methods (numerous Staffordshire pottery factories can also be visited, see page 189). The **Paradise Silk Mill and Museum** in Macclesfield, Cheshire, gives the story of the town's heyday when anyone who was anyone wore Macclesfield silk buttons. **Quarry Bank Mill**, Styal, Cheshire, is an excellent restoration of an 18th-century water-powered cotton mill in a fine verdant setting. Authentically clanking old machines can be seen, and heard, at the **Museum of the Lancashire Textile Industry**, Holmfirth, Lancashire, in the heartland of the former Lancashire cotton-making country. At **Stott Park Bobbin Mill** in Finsthwaite, Cumbria, former mill workers explain the process of one of the last bobbin mills to be operational in England.

Northeast England At **Abbeydale Industrial Hamlet**, Sheffield, South Yorkshire, a courtyard is surrounded by 18th-century workshops, where scythes were forged in the River Sheaf. The sense of period and sheer atmosphere are most impressive. The **North of England Open Air Museum, Beamish**, Co. Durham, is a clever evocation of the early 1900s.

Southern Scotland New Lanark Mills, Lanark, Strathclyde, is a remarkably well-preserved factory village; there is not much in the way of working machinery, but further work is in progress; the village has a dramatic setting near waterfalls. At Newtongrange, Lothian, the **Scottish Mining Museum** has a fine working steam engine used for winding. Ambitious displays cover the lives of the miners and some of the colliery buildings can be visited; its sister site at Prestongrange features a beam engine and locomotives.

21

The semi-detached house

■ **Although it is often taken for granted, the "semi" is a major component of British cityscapes. Rapidly and cheaply built during the 1930s, semi-detached houses were laid out street after street in neat rows, avenues and crescents. A major component in the suburbanization of the British countryside, the semi may never have been particularly chic but over the years it has adapted well for modern living, and is still going strong today.....■**

Mention the word suburbia in Britain and it is the semi that springs first to mind. The length and breadth of the country, semi-detached houses stand in single lines beside the roads that lead into every major town. To the passer-by, each may look superficially the same as the other, but closer inspection will reveal certain marks of individuality. For an Englishman's home is his castle, and never more so than his semi.

Rise of the "semi" The terraced house, similar to the American row-house, had been the dominant feature of 19th-century popular housing in England and Wales (Scottish cities specialized more in tenements); inexpensive and quick to build, the terrace provided housing for the artisan classes. Wealthier folk aspired to semi-detached or detached properties.

The semi-detached was a feature of the urban scene in Victorian and Edwardian times but it was in the 1930s Depression years that it was really to come into its own. Labor was low-cost and plentiful, cheap materials readily available. Speculative builders were creating new subdivisions in the verdant fringes of London and other major cities and improved rail and road links made commuting more feasible. House advertisements promised a rural idyll.

The building boom With this boom came the mass-produced "semi": a square plan, a common pitched roof, one party wall, a front and back garden, often a garage built on to one side. Since only a modest down-payment was needed, the semi was available to virtually anyone with a reasonable income. Rustic and fanciful flourishes were added to the basic design: leaded windows, gables sporting Tudor-style half-timbering, tile-covered walls, stained-glass windows, sunrise-motifs. Interior plans varied little: three or four bedrooms and a bathroom, a living room and a small kitchen (in the new labor-saving age of convenience foods, after all, who needed a big kitchen?). Three-piece suites (a sofa for the children, an armchair for each parent) in the living room exemplified Edwardian solidity.

And more than half a century on, the semi has shown itself readily adaptable, with new porches, picture windows and extra rooms over the garage being frequent alterations.

A typical semi, in Basingstoke

Man and the landscape

■ England's "green and pleasant land" is not a natural phenomenon, but the product of 200 generations of hard work. To oversimplify matters, imagine Britain's underlying geology as dividing the country into a highland zone in the north and west, including Scotland, the Pennines, the Lake District and Wales, and a lowland zone in the south and east. No matter what the geology, however, hardly any part of the landscape is unaltered by human hand.....■

The first people to make a mark on the landscape were the mesolithic people, nomadic hunters who burned forests and cleared large areas of land in order to gather herds of wild animals together. This lifestyle gradually became more settled over the years as neolithic peoples introduced crops, farming and domesticated animals. In order to make the necessary cropland and pasture for their cattle, sheep and pigs, they made permanent clearings, creating landscapes that were not unlike those we see today, although the actual use of the land was substantially different. Generally, small groups lived in hamlets of a few huts, surrounded by an earth bank or a wooden palisade, with fields outside. These were the forerunners of subsequent centuries of village life.

A well-preserved Roman road on Wheeldale in the North York Moors

❏ The stone axes with which neolithic farmers cleared the land were far more effective implements than is generally realized. Experiments indicate that one man working alone could have cleared a half acre a week. ❏

The earliest communities Villages grew up where there was fertile soil and an adequate water supply. The "typical" English village of houses clustered round a village green and duckpond is only one of several types (in Wales and Scotland the green is not a common feature). Other villages are stretched out along a road or have more than one center or sprawl about in a congenial muddle.

Each village was a service center for the surrounding countryside, providing a church, a drinking house, craftsmen, a market for produce. The more successful ones usually had some geographical advantage—they were located at a ford or an important road junction, for instance—and they grew into towns. Other towns were founded by landowners looking for profit.

Tracks and roads The earliest roads were created by farmers and their livestock, and many of today's country lanes, lying deep between high banks, may be thousands of years old. Trade also had its part to play and a network of prehistoric "high roads" can still be traced. It was the Romans who introduced the first

❏ Britain's human history stretches back over a vast period of time to the arrival of manlike beings more than 300,000 years ago. It is conventionally divided into the periods shown here, but the dates should be taken only as extremely rough approximations.

Period	Dates	Outstanding example
Palaeolithic (Old Stone Age)	to 12000BC	
Mesolithic (Middle Stone Age)	12000–4500BC	
Neolithic (New Stone Age)	4500–2500BC	Belas Knap tomb
Bronze Age	2500–750BC	Stonehenge
Iron Age	from 750BC	Maiden Castle hillfort
Roman invasion of Britain	AD43	Baths, Bath ❏

Oak woodlands near Butts Lawn in Hampshire's ancient New Forest

Forest and woodlands As well as clearing forest for agriculture, neolithic people managed woodlands very successfully. Coppicing is a good example: the tree is cut down to ground level so that it throws up several shoots to replace the lost one. Over several years this produces a crop of poles of just the right size for whatever use the woodsman decides upon. And coppiced trees live on almost indefinitely so long as coppicing continues. It is a perfect self-regenerating system. After World War II men were still using and refining skills such as these, first learned over 4,000 years ago.

Today, however, most woodlands are unmanaged since management is seen as expensive, and the skills are nearly lost. Wildlife actually suffers as a result: flowers are shaded out, butterflies have lost the glades that they need.

Landscape today Intensive agriculture ("agri-business") has changed the look of Britain's landscapes. Since the 1950s and '60s more woodland, heath, down and wetland has been obliterated than throughout the whole history of agriculture in Britain. Despite rhetoric from many sides, the destruction continues. Outrage is expressed over ill-considered road-building schemes, but much less is said about the day-by-day destruction caused by agriculture and industry. Britain's landscapes and habitats are unique and irreplaceable—but this is a notion that politicians pay lip service to but show little real sign of doing anything about.

centrally planned road network—dig a few feet beneath many a long straight stretch of today's highway and you'll find Roman road. The Roman network sufficed until a new era of road building began in the 1700s.

❏ The great charm . . . of English scenery is the moral feeling that seems to pervade it. It is associated in the mind with ideas of order, of quiet, of sober well-established principles, hoary usage and reverend custom. Everything seems to be the growth of ages of reverend and peaceful existence.
Washington Irving (1820) ❏

■ **Gaunt and gray in the British countryside, the shells and ruins of formidable medieval strongholds still defy time and weather. They were sited at strategic points—to control a river crossing, a hill pass or a harbor, for example. Many of them saw little or no action, which is testimony to their effectiveness. They were not built to provoke attack, but to deter it.....■**

The Norman Conquest of England made 1066 one of the key dates of British history. The triumphant William the Conqueror—known in his own time, though not to his face, as William the Bastard—divided England out among his Norman, French, Breton and Flemish followers. The more important built castles to secure their grip on their new estates, and by 1100 there were some 500 of these strongholds in England. The early ones consisted of a mound of earth (the motte), built by conscript labor, with a yard (the bailey) round its base, enclosed by an earth rampart and ditch. Wooden buildings housed the castle's lord, his family and his small private army. The local villagers could take refuge in the bailey in time of danger.

Bastions of stone Many of these primitive fortresses were soon replaced by daunting strongholds built of stone. A hulking keep was erected on the mound, its walls as much as 100 ft. high and 20 ft. thick

Stark and strong, Corfe Castle in Dorset was built by the Normans

at the base, pierced by tiny windows through which archers and crossbowmen could fire. The living quarters were in the keep, with the ground floor used for storage and dungeons. Outer walls kept besiegers at a distance, and around them might be a water-filled moat, crossed by a drawbridge. Castles became ever more elaborate as time went by. The

> ❏ The rich man in his castle,
> The poor man at his gate,
> God made them high and lowly,
> And ordered their estate. ❏
> **19th-century hymn**

Tower of London, originally built for William the Conqueror himself, is a particularly impressive specimen.

In Wales, both Norman and native warlords built themselves castles. When Edward I of England conquered the country a chain of powerful fortresses, which could be supplied by sea, cemented his hold. **Caernarfon**, **Harlech**, **Conwy** and **Beaumaris** castles still testify to the skill of his military engineer, James of St. George. Scotland, where central authority was never as strong, bristles with ferocious and romantic strongholds, led by **Edinburgh** and **Stirling**, high on their lofty crags.

The manorial estate Castles were extremely costly and only the richest nobles could afford them. In medieval England the basic landholding unit was the manor, ruled by its lord, who lived in the large manor house. Often a manor was a village with its surrounding countryside, but some manors contained more than one village, while others covered

Harlech Castle, impregnable monument to King Edward I

only part of one. The villagers cultivated the land, while the lord's function was to protect them and to keep order. Above the lord, in what is now called the "**feudal system**," a chain of greater lords led up to the king himself, each link in the chain owing support to the one above it and protection to the one below.

The lord's manor house was at first just a bigger version of the timber-and-mud hovels of his villagers. By the 13th century, though, manor houses were being built of stone and the fortified manor house appeared—cheaper and more comfortable than a castle, but defensible. They centered on one main room, the hall, where the household ate and slept, while the dogs gnawed bones on the straw- or rush-covered floor and smoke from a central hearth drifted out through a hole in the roof.

Over the centuries the medieval lord of the manor became the less omnipotent though still dominant figure of the country squire. Just as the power of kings has ebbed away, so the title of lord of the manor has become a picturesque but empty honor.

❏ Perhaps England's best example of a fortified manor house is Stokesay Castle, near Shrewsbury in Shropshire (see page 124), which has preserved its medieval atmosphere to a remarkable degree. ❏

■ However beautiful they may be, churches are not art galleries. They were built as earthly houses for God, what their congregations saw as symbols of the God-given order of the world. In them down the centuries generations of Christians have worshipped, have joined in the community's spiritual life, have been baptized and married and finally, after life's fitful fever, laid to rest in the peace of the churchyard.....■

From the humblest parish church to the most sumptuous cathedral, in country and town alike, churches are an essential element of the British scene. Almost all of them have been altered, enlarged or rebuilt many times over.

Styles of architecture A few Anglo-Saxon churches are still standing. Small and plain, they are the oldest English ecclesiastical buildings to survive. The **Normans** built on an altogether more massive and powerful scale, with thick round columns supporting the roof and round arches above small doors and windows.

Movingly simple, the Saxon church at Greensted is built of split logs

The **Gothic** style, which arrived in Britain in the 12th century, was lighter, airier, more slender, more uplifting to the spirit. Its earliest phases, Early English and the more ornate Decorated, introduced the pointed arch, the flying buttress and the tall spire that directed worshippers' eyes and thoughts heavenwards. These churches were alive with elaborate decoration, carvings in wood and stone, stained-glass windows, statues and wall paintings—the religious textbooks of an age that could not read. (Much of this decoration, however, was destroyed or painted over by the Puritans when they took over the government in the 17th century.) In the 14th century came the Perpendicular style, named after the strong vertical lines that carry the eye up to the roof. Tall, soaring shafts support a web of fan-vaulting and enormous windows of the most delicate tracery, while graceful towers rise to a riot of pinnacles. The style reached its apogee in the astonishing stone cobweb of **King's College Chapel**, Cambridge.

The monastic movement Among the most haunting legacies that the Middle Ages left to Britain are the now ruined monasteries—**Fountains, Rievaulx, Glastonbury, Tintern** and many more. Medieval abbeys and priories ran a virtual welfare system for the poor, treated the sick, kept scholarship and art alive, and gave hospitality to travelers, but their primary function was as centers of prayer and worship. At eight services a day, from matins long before dawn to vespers at sunset and compline at bedtime, the monks paid humankind's tribute of devotion to God.

The church was always the biggest and finest building in a monastery, usually standing at one side of a quadrangle. Around the other sides were the domestic buildings—the refectory for meals, the kitchen, the dormitory, the infirmary. The monks themselves took vows of poverty, but monasteries accumulated large estates, ran farms and raised sheep. Fountains Abbey in Yorkshire, for example, was the

The soaring ruins of Tintern Abbey

North of England's biggest wool producer.

In the 16th century the **Reformation** created the Church of England as a separate body, no longer owing allegiance to the Pope, and in the 1530s the monasteries were all closed down (the church, however, was often retained by the community as a parish church). Most of the monastic land ended up in the hands of the aristocracy and the country gentry, not only enriching them but making it quite certain that the Dissolution of the Monasteries would never be reversed. Today empty, roofless shells stand quietly where generations of monks once lived and prayed.

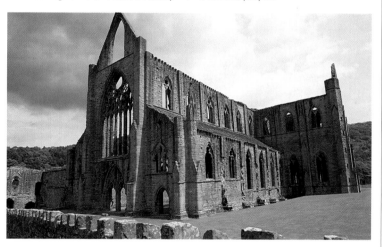

❑ Guidebooks often use the following terms for early and medieval styles of architecture in Britain. The dates should be considered as rough indications only.

Style	Dates	Outstanding example
Saxon	650–1066	Church of St. Andrew, Greensted-juxta-Ongar, Essex
Norman (or Romanesque)	1066–1190	Durham Cathedral
Gothic: Early English	1190–1275	Salisbury Cathedral
Decorated	1275–1375	Exeter Cathedral
Perpendicular	1375–1485	King's College Chapel, Cambridge
Classical	17th–18th centuries	St. Paul's Cathedral, London
Gothic Revival	19th century	Truro Cathedral ❑

■ A long era of peace on British soil since the 1500s has left Britain virtually without equal in the number of grand historic houses open for visitors to enjoy. They're packed from floor to ceiling with treasures of art and triumphs of decoration—paintings, sculptures, furniture, carpets, porcelain, books, clocks. Surrounded by exquisite gardens and sumptuously landscaped parks, they testify to five centuries of wealth, taste and social prominence.....■

30

Ordinary people's houses in the Middle Ages were made of sticks, mud and thatch, easily built and, when they fell down, easily replaced. The comparatively few medieval buildings which have survived are the important ones—castles, churches, monasteries—constructed massively of stone.

Tudor Chenies Manor House, near Amersham in Buckinghamshire

The Elizabethan age The Tudor era was one of peace and prosperity in which the rich Englishman's home no longer needed to be a fortified castle. The wealthy built ostentatious houses, Cardinal Wolsey and Henry VIII leading the way with the huge brick palace of **Hampton Court**. Capacious bay windows gazed out upon the countryside, while the fantastically elaborate chimneystacks of grand houses of the 16th and 17th centuries joined the gables, turrets and balustrades that enlivened the

roofline to impress the neighbors with the owner's wealth.

Much Tudor building was in brick, but in areas where there was plenty of timber—as in the Southeast and the western Midlands—houses were half-timbered, with rectangular wooden frames enclosing panels of whitewashed plaster or brick. The most lavish examples, like **Little Moreton Hall** in Cheshire, are a riot of zebra-striped patterns.

❏ The stately homes of England,
How beautiful they stand,
To prove the upper classes
Have still the upper hand.
Noel Coward (1899–1973) ❏

The classical ideal Outside these houses, a formal symmetrical garden was evidence of the Renaissance enthusiasm for classical Greek and Roman ideals. The first really famous individual British architects—**Inigo Jones** and **Sir Christopher Wren** in the 17th century—were influenced by classical architecture.

The typical house of Queen Anne's reign was a simple, symmetrical red-brick mansion with large sash windows and a four-sided roof behind a parapet. As the 18th century developed, **Sir John Vanbrugh** piled the colossal baroque palaces of **Castle Howard** and **Blenheim** upon the groaning earth, with their splendid domes and porticoes. Most of the English upper class, however, preferred the restrained elegance of the Palladian style of mansion, with its straight lines and pleasing proportions, its classical pillars and pediments. Around the house would stretch a noble park, where smooth lawns escorted the eye to carefully positioned groups of trees, an artificial lake, a bridge, a temple.

Georgian elegance The same style, imposing a calm order upon unruly Nature, created some of Britain's most satisfying townscapes in Bath, London, Edinburgh and other cities. From the 1760s the interiors of Georgian houses were opulently enriched by the genius of **Robert Adam** and his many imitators, who reintroduced color and glamour into mansions like **Syon House** in Middlesex, in rooms never intended for living in, but for entertaining, intrigue, gossip and politics.

Victorian exuberance A powerful enthusiasm for medieval Gothic Christian architecture gave many Victorian houses an ecclesiastical look, with turrets, pointed windows and stained glass, while Scots magnates built themselves mock baronial palaces. Victorian architects and their patrons took the whole past as their province. They adopted whatever architectural style took their fancy and blended characteristics from different styles to romantic and sometimes wildly over-the-top effect. In the Edwardian period came a revival of the Queen Anne style and traditional English "vernacular," or coun-

❑ All through the 19th century the Gothic and the classical styles vied for supremacy. In Yorkshire, for instance, the city fathers of Leeds built a magnificent classical temple as their town hall, while rival Bradford erected a Gothic town hall of mammoth proportions. ❑

tryside, styles, led by **Richard Norman Shaw** and **Sir Edwin Lutyens**.

Changing ideals A fierce reaction against Victorian and Edwardian "pastiche" followed in the 20th century as the modern movement in architecture adopted an austere simplicity of straight lines and concrete, often resulting in totalitarian brutishness. A reaction has now developed against these high-rise concrete egg-boxes, as unpleasant to occupy as to look at, with a return to a more romantic approach.

The vernacular Just as fascinating as the range of styles displayed in Britain's great houses and public buildings is the variety of regional style seen in the country's vernacular buildings. These—the houses of the ordinary people in particular, but also their agricultural and industrial buildings—were constructed following local traditions and in whatever material was readily to hand, be it stone, flint or cob, thatch, slate or pantile.It is perhaps these buildings above all that give Britain such an excitingly diverse architectural heritage.

Kiftsgate Court, Gloucestershire: a Georgian house in a lovely garden

■ **Few Britons today know much of their medieval rulers. The kings and queens whose memories still live are those of the Tudor, Stuart, Hanoverian and Windsor dynasties, which have reigned for the last 500 years. Figures such as Henry VIII, Elizabeth I, Mary, Queen of Scots and the Young Pretender are remembered in a popular mingling of history and romance.....■**

The modern history of Britain is usually reckoned from 1485, the year when a shrewd Welshman named Henry Tudor seized the throne of England by force to make himself king as Henry VII. His son, **Henry VIII**, he of the massive frame and little piggy eyes so famously depicted in the Holbein portrait, is known for his six wives. Two he divorced, two he executed, one died in childbirth and the sixth outlived him. He has been an object of intense fascination ever since.

Elizabeth Tudor It was typical of Henry's daughter, **Elizabeth I**, that when a deputation arrived at Hatfield House in Hertfordshire in 1558 to tell her she was queen, the 25-year-old princess was found sitting under an oak tree demurely reading a book. She always had a genius for public relations. A consummate politician, with her father's physical and intellectual vigor combined with grace and charm, she steered her country safely through 44 dangerous years.

Henry VIII, with Anne of Cleves

Elizabeth I, "Virgin Queen"

❏ Mr. Speaker, we perceive your coming is to present thanks to us. Know I accept them with no less joy than your loves can have desire to offer such a present, and do more esteem it than any treasure or riches; for those we know how to prize, but loyalty, love and thanks, I account them invaluable. And though God hath raised me high, yet this I account the glory of my crown, that I have reigned with your loves.
Queen Elizabeth I, the "golden speech" to her last Parliament, 1601 ❏

The Stuarts Scotland, meanwhile, had seen a long succession of kings of the Stuart dynasty, who since 1371 had struggled to impose their authority on their turbulent aristocracy. The beautiful **Mary, Queen of Scots** was forced to abdicate in

A Van Dyck portrait of Charles I

1567. She escaped to England, where she was politely kept prisoner for 20 years until executed at Fotheringay Castle in 1587.

Her son, **James VI of Scotland**, succeeded the childless Elizabeth I in 1603 as **James I of England**. The house of Stuart fared little better in England than in Scotland. **Charles I**, attempting to uphold royal power against Parliament, was defeated in the **Civil War** and executed on a cold January day in London in 1649. **Charles II** was restored to the throne in 1660, after an interregnum of republican rule that proved deeply unpopular. He is remembered for his charm, his cynicism and his sex life. His brother was **James II**, who was dethroned for his Roman Catholic sympathies in 1688 and whose daughter, **Queen Anne**, was the last Stuart ruler.

The Hanoverians On Anne's death in 1714, the Elector of Hanover became king as **George I**. Although he was a German who could not speak a word of English, as a Protestant he was preferred to the Stuart claimants, who made a dashing but unsuccessful last bid for the lost throne in 1745, led by Prince Charles Edward, sentimentally known as **Bonnie Prince Charlie**.

Poor mad **George III**, who was much liked for his hearty geniality, was king when the American colonies broke away to become an independent nation. His granddaughter, **Queen Victoria**, enjoyed the longest reign of any British sovereign, 64 years from 1837 to 1901. A dumpy little person, clad invariably in black after the death of her beloved Prince Consort in 1861, the Widow at Windsor was ruler of the largest empire in history. She became immensely popular as a symbol of British power and influence at their peak.

The House of Windsor Victoria's grandson, **George V**, sensitive during World War I about the dynasty's German connections, decided to change his family's name to the House of Windsor. Windsor Castle remains the favorite residence of **Queen Elizabeth II**.

> ❏ Walk wide o' the Widow at Windsor,
> For "alf o' Creation she owns. ❏
> **Rudyard Kipling** (1892)

■ **The fact that Britain is an island has formed and colored its whole history and character. Britain's greatness was built on seaborne trade and the British Empire rested on the Royal Navy's command of the sea, celebrated in popular patriotic songs from "Rule Britannia" to "All the Nice Girls Love a Sailor". The sea and seafaring are in Britain's blood.....■**

Nelson's flagship, HMS Victory

The sea has played contradictory roles in British history, as both barrier and bridge. Britannia has always needed her "towers along the steep," coastal fortifications against attack by sea. They can be seen bristling along England's southern and southeastern shoreline, ranging from Roman forts of the Saxon Shore to medieval and Tudor castles, Martello towers and Palmerston forts against the French, and World War II defences.

Overseas trading At the same time, while the sea has served Britain as a defensive moat, it has also been by sea that people, ideas and trade have moved between Britain and the rest of the world. Far back in prehistoric times, ships from the Mediterranean came to Cornwall for tin. In Roman days, Britain exported slaves, oysters and hunting dogs to the Continent and imported wine.

The great medieval "wool churches" of England stand as testimony to the wealth generated by the export trade in wool and cloth. It remained a major factor in the economy into the 16th century, when merchants forged thriving trade links with the world beyond Europe—Asia, Africa and the Americas. The piratical **Francis Drake** sailed away in 1578 in a cockleshell of a ship, which was only the second to circumnavigate the globe. Gleefully plundering Spanish possessions on the way, he returned in 1580 with loot estimated at $37.5 million in today's money.

In command of the seas The British navy can trace its history back ultimately to **Alfred the Great** in the 9th century, the first English king to lead his own squadron in battle, against the Danes. In medieval times, ships and crews were supplied for the royal fleet by the **Cinque Ports** of southeast England—Dover, Sandwich, Hythe, New Romney and Hastings. The Tudor and Stuart kings built up a more effective and powerful force. Along with two other formidable Elizabethan seadogs, Hawkins and Frobisher, Drake

❏ Britannia needs no bulwarks,
No towers along the steep;
Her march is o'er the mountain waves,
Her home is on the deep.
  Thomas Campbell, "Ye Mariners of England" (1800–01) ❏

helped send the ponderous Spanish Armada packing in 1588.

Between 1700 and 1780 Britain's foreign trade almost doubled. The port of Bristol took a leading part in the slave trade, which shipped millions of Africans to the American plantations. Meanwhile Britain became the world's leading colonial power in a struggle against the French in which command of the sea was of paramount importance. The French were driven from India and North America, and the British built up the empire on which the sun never set. The "wooden walls"—the Royal Navy's implacable three-deckers—kept **Napoleon** at arm's length. "I do not say they cannot come," said Admiral Lord St. Vincent of the French invasion barges, "I only say they cannot come by sea."

Illustrious names The navy was the guardian of British liberty and a succession of naval heroes etched their names on the British consciousness—Anson, Rodney, Hood, Howe, St. Vincent, Collingwood, Cochrane. The most admired and loved of them all was **Horatio Nelson**, killed at the battle of Trafalgar in 1805 as the *Victory* bore down upon the foe. The great ship is lovingly preserved in Portsmouth.

A Martello tower on the south coast, one of many built against the threat of Napoleonic invasion

❏ A willing foe and sea room. The Royal Navy's Friday night toast ❏

The British Empire eventually covered a quarter of the land surface of the globe, stretching across the world's heaving waters from Canada to India, Australia, New Zealand and remote islands in the Pacific. It could not be sustained in the end, and World War II demonstrated that command of the sea had passed from Britain to the United States.

■ **English is the language of one of the world's great literatures and many places in Britain are linked with writers and their work. The Hampshire village of Chawton shelters the modest house where Jane Austen wrote, hiding her papers when any of the household came in. Not far away at Selborne is the home of Gilbert White, the dean of English nature writers. Each year Rochester, Kent, honors Charles Dickens, who lived nearby. You can explore George Bernard Shaw's home at Ayot St Lawrence in Hertfordshire, both Lord Byron's and D.H. Lawrence's near Nottingham, Rudyard Kipling's at Bateman's in Sussex, and Samuel Johnson's in Lichfield and London.....■**

No writer in English is more admired than **William Shakespeare**, and the town of Stratford-upon-Avon in Warwickshire is the most visited British tourist destination outside London. The Bard's birthplace attracts more than half a million visitors a year.

Literary shrines In West Yorkshire the once-grim little town of Haworth is thronged with pilgrims to the parsonage where **Charlotte**, **Emily** and **Anne Brontë** and their brother **Branwell** lived. Out on the desolate moorland is the ruined farmhouse that may have been the original "Wuthering Heights."

The Lake District also draws literary pilgrims, to **William Wordsworth**'s homes at Dove Cottage and Rydal Mount and the Lakeland scenes which inspired his poetry. **John Ruskin**, the Victorian art critic and social reformer, owned a house with a magical view over Coniston Water. **Sir Hugh Walpole**'s romantic "Herries" novels were set in the Derwent Water area, as was **Arthur Ransome**'s *Swallows and Amazons*. **Beatrix Potter** lived at Near Sawrey.

At Laugharne in South Wales the most famous Welsh poet of this century, **Dylan Thomas**, is fondly remembered at **his studio**, the Boathouse. Scotland's national poet, **Robert Burns**, is cherished at the humble cottage where he was born

in the outskirts of Ayr, and also in Dumfries, where he spent his last years. **Sir Walter Scott**'s engaging collection of historical curios— Rob Roy's sword, a lock of the Young Pretender's hair and so on— can be admired at Abbotsford, his home in his beloved Borders, while at Kirriemuir is the birthplace of **Sir James Barrie**, author of *Peter Pan*.

John Bunyan's iron violin is on show in the museum in Bedford devoted to the author of *Pilgrim's Progress*. At Coxwold in North Yorkshire is the house where **Laurence Sterne** wrote *Tristram Shandy*, and **Milton** completed *Paradise Lost* in a cottage at Chalfont St Giles in Buckinghamshire.

> ❏ Selborne, Nov 22, 1777
> This sudden summer-like heat was attended by many summer coincidences; for on those two days the thermometer rose to sixty-six in the shade; many species of insects revived and came forth; some bees swarmed . . . the old tortoise . . . awakened and came forth out of his dormitory.
> **Gilbert White** (1720–93), *The Natural History and Antiquities of Selborne* ❏

Resting places Interesting literary connections frequently lie in church-yards. **T.S. Eliot** is buried at East Coker in Somerset, **John Buchan** at Elsfield near Oxford. The country churchyard of **Thomas Gray**'s famous *Elegy* can be found at Stoke Poges in Buckinghamshire. The memory of the evil Count Dracula, **Bram Stoker**'s creation, vampirishly haunts the Yorkshire graveyard of Whitby. In London, Westminster Abbey's south transept is affection-ately known as **Poets' Corner** because Chaucer, Edmund Spenser, Tennyson, Browning and many other famous poets are buried or have memorials there. Monuments to Shakespeare, Milton, Wordsworth, Burns, Keats and Shelley cluster

❏ The curfew tolls the knell of
   parting day,
The lowing herd winds slowly
   o'er the lea,
The ploughman homeward plods
   his weary way,
And leaves the world to
   darkness and to me.
      Thomas Gray (1716–71),
      *Elegy in a Country
      Churchyard* ❏

close to memorials to Byron, T.S. Eliot, W.H. Auden and Dylan Thomas.

" ... my country still" Some writers are associated with a whole area of countryside, seen through their eyes and peopled with their characters. **Thomas Hardy** Country extends over much of Dorset and the muse-um in Dorchester has an excellent Hardy collection. The "blue remem-bered hills" of Shropshire are insepa-rably linked with the melancholic poetry of **A.E. Housman**. Tennyson is particularly cherished in his native county of Lincolnshire and there is a noble statue of him outside Lincoln Cathedral. The center of the **George Eliot** industry is Nuneaton in Warwickshire; the southern part of Tyne and Wear calls itself **Catherine Cookson** Country in homage to the best-selling romantic novelist.

❏ The first fire since the
   summer is lit, and is smoking
   into the room;
The sun-rays spread it through,
   like woof-lines in a loom.
Sparrows spurt from the hedge,
   whom misgivings appal
That winter did not leave last
   year for ever, after all.
      Thomas Hardy (1840–1928),
      *Shortening Days at the
      Homestead* ❏

Sometimes it is the characters more than the author who cast the spell. It is hardly possible to explore Exmoor without recalling Lorna Doone, Cornwall without thinking of the heroes and heroines of **Daphne du Maurier** and **Winston Graham** or Dartmoor without memories of Sherlock Holmes, Doctor Watson and the hound of the Baskervilles.

Thomas Hardy's statue at the top of the high street in Dorchester, the "Casterbridge" of his novels

■ **Britain's most characteristic contribution to Western art lies in a long tradition of landscape painting, which inspired such artists as Gainsborough, Constable and Turner. It is this tradition which created the British idea of what the landscape looks like—or at least of what it ideally ought to look like. Visitors enjoying the British countryside today still tend to see it through the eyes of the great painters of the past.....■**

The British tradition of landscape painting was founded by **Richard Wilson**, who was born in Wales in 1714 and was deeply impressed by the work of the French painter Claude Lorraine. Unappreciated and poverty-stricken, he struggled to convince the British eye that wild scenery could be beautiful; his paintings of his native Welsh mountains looming above limpid lakes have a classic grandeur and serenity.

The great names Far more successful financially was **Thomas Gainsborough**, who came from Suffolk. He made his money as a fashionable portrait painter in Bath and London, but his passion was for landscapes—often generalized and idyllic, rather than depicting a particular place. The great Victorian critic John Ruskin said of him: "His touch was as light as the sweep of a cloud and swift as the flash of a sunbeam."

John Constable, arriving on the scene 50 years later, came from the Suffolk–Essex border and his paintings of hayfields, church towers, river scenes, carthorses and wagons have remained hugely popular ever since. Salisbury Cathedral, Stonehenge and the South Coast were also favorite subjects of his. He believed in the most minute study of Nature, to render, as he said, "light—dews—breezes—bloom—and freshness" with loving accuracy, and he broke free of the formal Claude-inspired landscape.

Constable's contemporary, the prodigious **Joseph Mallord William Turner**, traveled all over Britain, painting romantic landscapes, castles, cathedrals and great houses. He followed in Richard Wilson's footsteps in Wales, painted extensively at Petworth in Sussex and in the Thames Valley, and rejoiced in the scenery of the Lake District and Wharfedale in Yorkshire. As he grew increasingly fascinated by effects of light, in his paintings of Norham Castle in Northumberland the ruined fortress and the grazing cattle almost disappear into abstraction in the glowing sunlit mist.

> ❏ He saw that there were more clouds in every sky than had ever been painted, more trees in every forest, more crags on every hillside, and set himself with all his strength to proclaim the great quantity of the universe.
> **John Ruskin** (1819–1900), on Turner ❏

Places of inspiration Other painters drawn to the Lake District included **Philippe de Loutherburg** and **Joseph Wright** of Derby, and much later, oddly enough, the German Dada artist **Kurt Schwitters**, who settled at Ambleside after World War II. **L.S. Lowry** painted Lake District scenes, too, though better known for his northern industrial townscapes.

Some areas have inspired groups of artists, like the **Norwich School** of painters in the early 19th century. **Bristol**'s flourishing school of artists was dominated by **Francis Danby** in

Above: the young J.M.W. Turner. Top left: from Stanhope Forbes's "Fitting out, Mousehole Harbour"

the 1820s. The **Newlyn School** of artists, based in Cornwall's premier fishing port, was led by **Stanhope Forbes** from the 1880s, while **St. Ives** in Cornwall was later a base for **Barbara Hepworth**, **Ben Nicholson** and the great potter **Bernard Leach**.

The mystical painter **Samuel Palmer** settled at Shoreham in Kent in the 1820s to explore his "Valley of Vision." **John Singer Sargent** painted Worcestershire landscapes in the 1880s, **Graham Sutherland** painted in Pembrokeshire before and after World War II, while Cookham in Berkshire owes its fame to the paintings and parables of **Sir Stanley Spencer**. In every generation since the 18th century, artists have found inspiration in the British landscape.

Flatford Mill in Suffolk, still recognizable from Constable's paintings

> ❏ There was not a picturesque clump of trees nor even a single tree of any beauty, no, not a hedgerow, stem or post in or around my native town that I did not treasure in my memory from earliest years.
> **Thomas Gainsborough** (1726–88) ❏

■ Crowded, noisy, dirty, pulsating with life, Manchester was the archetype of the new cities created in Britain by the Industrial Revolution. Instead of a skyline of church spires, hundreds of factory chimneys belched out smoke and fumes. Though horrified by the city's abominable slums and its turbid rivers crawling with filth, many visitors saw Manchester as the symbol of a dawning new age of intense creativity and vitality.....■

40

The Industrial Revolution was revolutionary not in its speed, but in its consequences. The century between 1750 and 1850 ushered in the machine age of factories, mass production and the assembly line, the industrial town and the industrial working class. Why it should all have started in Britain is a disputed question, but the country had certain obvious advantages: ample resources of coal and iron, and a growing empire overseas that provided a captive market for British-made products.

The textile industry The industries most affected in the early stages were textiles, iron and steel, coal mining and pottery. In textiles, a succession of inventions made it possible to increase output while using less human energy. This transformed the making of cloth from a small-

scale operation, carried on by skilled workmen and their families at home, to large-scale production in factories where unskilled workers, many of them women and children, toiled as acolytes of the insatiable machines. In 1765 **James Hargreaves** patented the spinning Jenny—he named it after his wife—for spinning several threads simultaneously. Four years later a formidable Lancashireman named **Richard Arkwright**, who became the first great industrial tycoon, patented a spinning frame powered by water. He built a cotton mill and company town at Cromford in the beautiful Derbyshire valley of the Derwent, where his workers labored in 12-hour shifts as the machines clattered on day and night.

Titus Salt's vast 1853 mill and his model village at Saltaire, Bradford

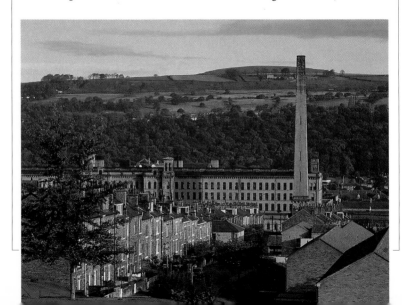

> ❏ And if here man has made of the very daylight an infamy, he can boast that he adds to the darkest night the weird beauty of fire and flame-tinted cloud. From roof and hill you may see on every side furnace calling furnace with fiery tongues and wreathing messages of smoke.
> **Arnold Bennett**, *The Potteries* (1898) ❏

The power of steam Arkwright's machinery was powered by water, but in 1779 **Samuel Crompton** invented the mule, a spinning machine that could be powered either by water or steam. Steam was the driving force of the Industrial Revolution and the most important figure in its development, the Scottish inventor **James Watt**, patented the first modern steam engine in 1769. Steam was used to drive all manner of machinery in factories and mines, and later to propel railroad locomotives and ships, as a transportation revolution developed in the 19th century.

> ❏ Since the introduction of inanimate mechanism into British manufactures, man, with few exceptions, has been treated as a secondary and inferior machine.
> **Robert Owen**, *A New View of Society* (1813) ❏

Coal and iron Steam required coal. Britain's coal production doubled between 1750 and 1800, and then grew by 20 times by the end of the 19th century. **Abraham Darby** initiated the mass production of iron ore at Ironbridge and new industrial regions grew up close to the principal coalfields in the **Midlands**, the **North of England**, Scotland's **Clydeside** and **South Wales**. The flow of coal from the valleys turned sleepy little fishing villages like Cardiff, Barry and Swansea into busy, blackened ports. At the entrance to the Great Exhibition of 1851 in London's Hyde Park there stood, appropriately, a towering 24-ton block of coal.

Towns like Manchester, Birmingham, Glasgow, Leeds, Bradford and Sheffield covered their surrounding countryside with terrace upon terrace of back-to-back workers' housing. Many a lush valley became an inferno of blast furnaces, slag heaps and Satanic mills. A new Iron Age introduced iron buildings, iron machines, iron bridges, iron boats, even iron tombstones—as well as the iron regimentation of the assembly line.

Victorian Britain was "the workshop of the world," but other countries took the same path and began to pass it by, notably Germany and the United States. In the 1880s Britain enjoyed 37 percent of the world's trade in manufactured goods, but by 1913 the figure was down to 25 percent. A new phase of the Industrial Revolution had opened, based on steel, chemicals and electricity, and Britain was unable to keep up.

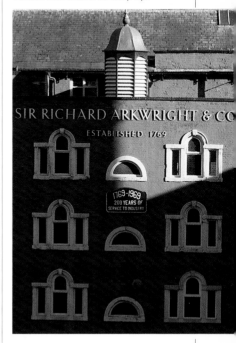

The cotton mill built by Richard Arkwright in Cromford, Derbyshire

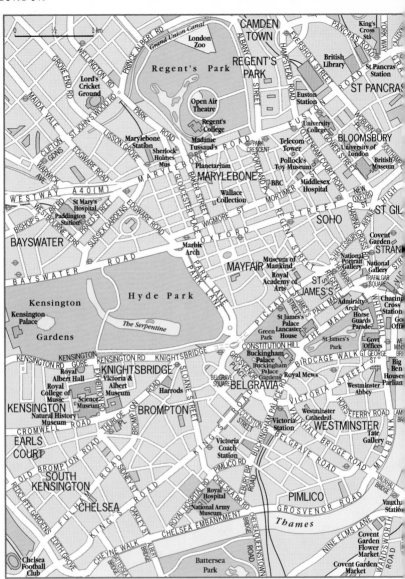

London With a population of over seven million, London is not an easy city in which to get your bearings; even many Londoners think of the capital in terms of the Underground (subway) map, and have little idea of how one neighborhood leads into another. Stand on Hampstead Heath and you get an idea of the city's sprawling form, across a great basin dissected by the meandering River Thames. Nevertheless, it is a highly rewarding city for exploring on foot.

The West End The bulk of the capital's attractions are to be found in the West End▶▶▶. Trafalgar Square is the undisputed center of London, where a statue of Nelson

A to Z LONDON

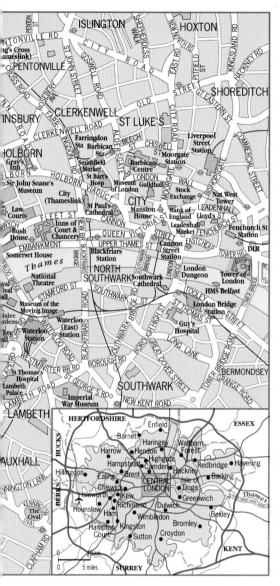

stands high on a column guarded by lions modelled by artist E. H. Landseer. **St. Martin-in-the-Fields▶** and the **National Gallery▶▶▶** take up two sides of the square; Admiralty Arch leads through the third into The Mall, the grand entrance to **Buckingham Palace▶▶** (begun 1825), the chief residence of the Queen. In August and September a series of 19 rooms is open to the public, including the Throne Room, Picture Gallery, State Dining Room and Music Room (tickets on sale in the morning for afternoon only). **St. James's Park▶▶** is an alluring expanse with a lake and bandstand concerts in summer.

The hub of **Westminster** is at Parliament Square, domi-nated by the clocktower housing the huge Big Ben bell.

Taking a break by the fountains of Trafalgar Square

**London: A concise history
Part 1: The Romans to Wren**
Becomes the Roman settlement of Londinium after the Roman invasion of Britain in AD43; London Bridge built across the Thames (not until 1738 was a second bridge built across the river, at Westminster).
Hit by the Black Death in 1348–50 and the Plague in 1665–6. The Great Fire in 1666 destroys four-fifths of the city, taking the slums, rats and plague with it. Sir Christopher Wren rebuilds St Paul's Cathedral and a host of city churches.

This is London's most photographed building, and the symbol of the seat of government. The magnificent Gothic Revival **Houses of Parliament▶▶▶** (remodelled by Charles Barry and Augustus Pugin after fire destroyed an earlier building in 1834). When Parliament is in session, the Strangers' Gallery is open (from 5:30PM to about 10:30PM, Monday to Thursday, and from 9:30AM to 3PM Friday). Across the square is **Westminster Abbey▶▶▶**.

To the west, some of the best addresses in London are in **Mayfair**, chic **Chelsea**, elegant **Knightsbridge** and **Kensington**. Here there is a preponderance of 19th-century stucco in addition to the familiar yellow-gray London stock brick. South Kensington is the primary **museum quarter**. Hyde Park and adjacent Kensington Gardens constitute a green swath north of the Royal Albert Hall and the mildly preposterous Albert Memorial (currently swathed in long-term scaffolding).

Covent Garden▶▶, the former fruit and vegetable market hall, has been imaginitively revamped into a lively piazza, with boutiques, street musicians and craft stalls, while **Soho▶▶**, further west, is the center of London's Chinese community (around Gerrard Street even the street names are printed in Chinese) as well as a lively amalgam of Italian delicatessens, high-class restaurants, night clubs and sex shops.

Bloomsbury▶ represents intellectual London: blue plaques (placed on buildings throughout London) indicate the former houses of the famous, including the homes of Charles Dickens (a memorial museum is at 48 Doughty Street) and Virginia Woolf and her "Bloomsbury Set." Bloomsbury still has a gracious atmosphere, and is a good illustration of how residential London developed into formal squares and terraces in Georgian and Regency times; Bedford Square continues to be as fashionable as when it was first laid out in 1775. Landmarks include the **British Museum►►►**, within whose former reading room Karl Marx wrote *Das Kapital*, and the **British Telecom Tower**.

Regent's Park► is a gracious tract laid out by Regency architect John Nash in conjunction with the supremely elegant stucco terraces on its east side; within the park is London Zoo, a boating lake and an open-air theater, a memorable stage for summer productions.

Legal London revolves around **Holborn**, with its Gothic Revival High Courts in the Strand and the Central Criminal Courts in the Old Bailey; both have public galleries within the courtrooms. Barristers (lawyers qualified to plead cases in court) are attached to chambers within the **Inns of Court►** (Lincoln's Inn, the Temple etc); aspiring lawyers are trained within these.

The City The "square mile" of the ancient city of London, the **City►►►** is where the major financial institutions are concentrated; it retains its medieval street pattern, and though the city wall has largely disappeared its gateways live on in place-names (Ludgate, Aldersgate, Moorgate etc); these gates, plus plinths bearing the City griffin (holding the flag of St. George, patron saint of England) still mark the City boundaries. It is best approached from London Bridge, which has a picture-postcard view of **Tower Bridge►►** and the **Tower of London►►►**. The **Monument►**, designed by Sir Christopher Wren to commemorate the Great Fire of 1666, is a good viewing platform for those fit enough to manage the narrow steps up. The **Lloyd's Building►** in Lime Street is London's most innovative contribution to high-tech architecture. The **Bank of England** (museum inside), the central bank of the UK, stands at an intersection of seven streets opposite the Mansion House, the official residence of the Lord Mayor; Lombard Street, leading east, is London's Wall Street.

The choir of Wren's St. Paul's Cathedral, in the City

London: A concise history Part 2: World War II to today
Enemy air-raids in World War II culminate in the Blitz, in which much of central and suburban London is destroyed. Influx of Commonwealth immigrants, invited from the West Indies and Asia in the 1950s and 1960s to help solve a labor shortage. 1990s recession is accompanied by a slowdown in major building projects in the City and Docklands. Political debate surrounds the future of London's traffic management and public transportation policy, as traffic problems intensify.

45

Whitehall
Linking Trafalgar Square and Parliament Square, this street contains grandiose 19th-century government offices. London's main royal residence was Whitehall Palace until it was destroyed by fire in 1698; the Banqueting House (designed by Inigo Jones in 1622), with its superb painted ceiling by Rubens, is the sole survivor. The archway at the Horse Guards is the former entrance into the palace: picturesquely uniformed soldiers still keep watch; the Changing of the Guard occurs daily at 11am (Sunday 10am).

LONDON

Canary Wharf

Close by **St. Paul's Cathedral**►►►, the somewhat bleak-looking **Barbican** complex comprises 21 high-rise concrete apartment blocks and a confusing maze of walkways; within is the Barbican Arts Centre, home of the London Symphony Orchestra and London base of the Royal Shakespeare Company, and the **Museum of London**►►►. To the west and outside the City proper, the quiet streets of **Smithfield**► are a different world, with an endearingly workaday look. The Smithfield Meat Market is an outstanding example of a Victorian market building; adjacent Cloth Fair has a rare wooden house, a survivor of the Great Fire, while the **Church of St. Bartholomew the Great**►► has enormous charm.

The suburbs **Docklands**► is Europe's biggest urban development area. Once the heart of the docklands of the East End, it is now a futuristic cityscape of gleaming office blocks and somewhat Dutch-looking waterside housing. But the recession has hit hard and many houses and offices stand vacant. The best way to see it is by taking the toylike Docklands Light Railway (closed at weekends) from Island Gardens, by the Greenwich foot tunnel, to **Canary Wharf** (Britain's tallest building).

Greenwich►►► The former center of the maritime world (see also panel, page 47), Greenwich Park occupies a hillside above the Thames, and within it are the Greenwich meridian line, **Wren's Royal Observatory** of 1676 and the **Greenwich Planetarium**►►; just below, the **National Maritime Museum**►► and Queen's House (begun in 1616) together form a supreme early classical composition by Wren and Inigo Jones. To the north of Romney Road is the Royal Naval College, designed by Wren; the **painted hall**►►, open in the afternoons, has a superb painted ceiling by Thornhill. At the river, the *Cutty Sark* and *Gipsy Moth IV* can be boarded; a riverside walk extends eastward to the Cutty Sark Tavern.

Hampstead and Highgate►► Hampstead Heath remains pleasantly countrified, with hollows, glades and grassland. Parliament Hill Fields, in the southeast corner of the heath, attracts kite-fliers and has a wonderful view over central London. Hampstead village developed as an 18th-century spa and is one of the most fashionable residential districts; artist John Constable and poet John Keats number among its former residents. **Highgate Cemetery**► has a spectacular derelict portion (guided tours available) where many rich and famous Victorians are buried.

Richmond and Chiswick►► These charming riverside villages, now affluent suburbs, are best seen by taking the summer boat service (piers at Putney Bridge, Kew Bridge and Richmond Bridge) or by walking along the river, for example westward from Hammersmith Bridge along Chiswick Mall and on to **Chiswick House**► (see page 51) or from Kew to Richmond, where there is a handsome green next to the remains of the palace of Henry VII. The towpath continues westward past **Ham House**► (see page 51). **Richmond Park**► is a former royal hunting park, fenced in by Charles I in 1635 and still inhabited by deer; within is the renowned Isabella Plantation, famous for azaleas and heathers. For **Kew Gardens**►►► see page 16.

Getting around
Forget the car and use public transport. Day travelcards can be purchased at Underground and railroad stations, and from many newsagents, and entitle you to unlimited travel by train, Underground and bus (but not night bus services); Zone 1 tickets cover the center. The Underground (or "tube") is easiest to understand, but the double-decker buses give excellent views (route 11 is recommended); free bus maps are available from tourist offices.
For organized tours see page 271.
The A–Z Street Atlas is especially useful for exploring the center and suburbs.

Museums and art galleries

The principal museums and galleries to be found in central London are listed below, grouped together in geographical areas. Those outside the central area are described in the side panels on pages 47–9. Admission fees are charged unless stated otherwise.

Piccadilly Circus and Trafalgar Square The Museum of Mankind▶, Burlington Gardens, W1, an offshoot of the British Museum, deals with ethnic culture outside Western Europe (free). In Piccadilly Circus itself are the **Guinness World of Records**, Trocadero Centre, a fun look at the world of extremes, and **Rock Circus**, London Pavilion, where Elvis, the Beatles and many more are brought to life with animated mannequins and music.

The National Gallery▶▶▶, Trafalgar Square, WC2, has a superb collection of paintings, many of which will be instantly familiar, from the early Renaissance to the French Impressionists (free). Excellent free guided tours take place at 11:30AM and 2:30PM (2PM and 3:30PM Saturdays) from the foyer of the new Sainsbury wing. Around the corner, in St. Martin's Place, WC2, is the **National Portrait Gallery▶▶**, as complete a collection of faces of British history as you will find.

Travel through time at the London Transport Museum

Covent Garden and Bloomsbury The art gallery of the **Courtauld Institute▶▶**, Somerset House, Strand, WC2, contains Britain's finest selection of French Impressionist paintings. The **London Transport Museum▶▶**, in the Piazza, Covent Garden, WC2, traces the development of London's buses, trams, trains and "tubes," with exhibits you can climb aboard. Nearby, the **Theatre Museum▶**, 1e Tavistock Street, Covent Garden, WC2, is a home for stage memorabilia appropriately located in London's theaterland. See Houses, page 50, for **Sir John Soane's Museum▶▶**.

The **British Museum▶▶▶**, Great Russell Street, WC1, is one of the greatest collections in the world (free). The most famous of its artifacts ancient and modern include the Rosetta stone (which helped historians to decode hieroglyphics) and Egyptian mummies, the Elgin marbles from the Parthenon in Athens, and the Mildenhall and Sutton Hoo treasure hoards. **Pollock's Toy Museum▶**, Scala Street, W1, has tin soldiers, mechanical curios and toy theaters in a varied collection for children of all ages.

Greenwich
Greenwich Pier, SE10, is home to the "tea-clipper" *Cutty Sark*, launched in 1869 and the last of her kind to survive, and *Gipsy Moth IV*, a ketch in which Sir Francis Chichester sailed around the world single-handed in 1966–7. Both vessels can be boarded. In Greenwich Park the *National Maritime Museum*, Romney Road, SE10, celebrates Britain's long maritime history, with a fine array of nautical clocks, sea paintings and ship models. Also here is the *Old Royal Observatory*, designed by Wren, with astronomical and navigational exhibits. Adjacent are the *Greenwich Meridian* (0° longitude), where you can have one foot in each hemisphere, and the *Greenwich Planetarium*.

Excursions
The number of possible day-trips from the capital is endless. Here we highlight some recommended excursions that can easily be made by train.
Castles: Dover, Windsor.
Historic cities: Cambridge, Canterbury, Oxford, Salisbury, Winchester.
Industrial, railway and naval interest: Amberley Chalkpits Museum, Bluebell Railway (near Haywards Heath), Chatham Dockyard, Portsmouth, Watercress Line (Alton to Alresford).
Roman remains: Fishbourne Palace (near Chichester), Lullingstone Villa (near Eynsford), Verulamium (St Albans).
Seaside: Brighton, Broadstairs, Eastbourne, Hastings.
Small towns: Arundel, Rye, Lewes, Sandwich, Tunbridge Wells.

Museums and art galleries

Changing exhibitions of art and design
Major sites for art exhibitions are the *Hayward Gallery* on the South Bank, SE1, the *Royal Academy* in Piccadilly, W1, the *ICA* in the Mall, SW1, and the *Barbican Centre*, Silk Street, EC2 (Moorgate subway). The latest aspects of design are on show at the *Design Centre* in Haymarket.

The ever popular Natural History Museum

Wembley Stadium
The FA Cup final (the highlight of the domestic English soccer season) and most England internationals are held at Wembley Stadium in northwest London; it is also a site for major pop concerts. The guided tour around the stadium takes visitors into the changing rooms, hospital, TV studio and up the hallowed 39 steps to the Royal Box where they can lift a replica FA cup; tours take place daily (10AM–3PM in winter, 10AM–4PM in summer); take the subway to Wembley Park (Metropolitan and Jubilee lines).

Regent's Park and Baker Street London Zoo►► in Regent's Park, NW1, is one of the world's great animal collections and an important research center. Threatened with closing, it now looks as if it will survive lean times.

In Marylebone Road, NW1, **Madame Tussaud's►** tops the charts as a paying tourist attraction; be photographed alongside politicians, pop stars, murderers, sportsmen and sportswomen. Lines can be long—some may feel the wait and steep admission are not quite worth it. Its annex, **the Spirit of London►** is a "sight, sounds and smells" journey in replica London taxicabs through 400 years of London: experience the Great Fire, the swinging sixties and more. Next door, at the **Planetarium►** the sky at night is projected onto a dome; a commentary guides you around the constellations.

The **Sherlock Holmes Museum** at 221b Baker Street, W1, displays memorabilia of the great sleuth at the address used in Conan Doyle's stories. In Hertford House, Manchester Square, W1, the **Wallace Collection►►** is a treat for the eye: the 18th-century house contains a dazzling collection of paintings and furniture, bequeathed to the nation in 1897 (free).

South Kensington The Victoria and Albert Museum►►► (the "V & A"), Cromwell Road, SW7, is a treasurehouse of applied art, displayed by theme (musical instruments, costume, furniture etc) and by civilization (Japan, China, India etc). There is something for everyone but too much for one visit (free, but donation requested). Meanwhile, across the road at the **Natural History Museum►►►**, Cromwell Road, SW7, dinosaurs, evolution, blue whales . . . just about everything is here in this splendid Victorian building. Transferred from antiquated glass cases to high-tech displays, the collection is popular with enthusiasts, semi-enthusiasts and children. The **Science Museum▶▶▶**, Exhibition Road, SW7, is suitable for most tastes and interests, despite the obvious technical bias of many exhibits. Children can conduct their own experiments at the "Launch Pad." There is space technology, air transportation and much more. The **Geological Museum**, Exhibition Road, SW7, offers rocks, gems, landform models and an earthquake simulation.

In Kensington High Street, W8, at the **Commonwealth Institute**, an odd tent-like structure has displays on the Commonwealth countries and their peoples. It's fun for children, and free.

Chelsea and Westminster The National Army **Museum**, Royal Hospital Road, SW3, tells a 500-year story of soldiers through the ages (free). The **Cabinet War Rooms▶** in King Charles Street, SW1, was the subterranean emergency accommodation for Winston Churchill and his cabinet in World War II; the Map Room and the Transatlantic Telephone Room remain intact.

The **Tate Gallery▶▶▶** on Millbank, SW1, is the greatest collection of British and modern art to be found in Britain. Free entry but admission charged for special exhibitions. **The Queen's Gallery▶** at Buckingham Palace, SW1, has items from the royal collection on display.

South of the river The Imperial War **Museum▶▶**, Lambeth Road, SE1, covers the wars that Britain has been involved in since 1914. There is a Blitz reconstruction and a trench dug-out, in addition to weapons, memorabilia, uniforms and a distinguished collection of paintings by war artists. The **Museum of the Moving Image▶▶** on the South Bank, SE1 (by the National Film Theatre), has entertaining high-tech displays and hands-on exhibits on everything to do with film and TV.

In Southwark the **Bear Gardens Museum**, Bear Gardens, SE1, commemorates Elizabethan theatrical history, with models of the Rose and Globe theaters of Shakespeare's day, while the **Design Museum▶** at Butler's Wharf, 28 Shad Thames, SE1, is a stylish riverside building housing an exhibition of the best of 20th-century design. At the **London Dungeon▶** in Tooley Street, SE1, gloomy vaults reveal the dark stories of punishment, torture, witchcraft and more in times past. Moored on the Thames close by (reached from Vine Lane, Tooley Street, SE1) is **HMS Belfast▶**, the last of the Royal Navy's big World War II gunships, launched in 1938.

Tower Hill and the City The **Tower of London▶▶▶** on Tower Hill, EC3, is the greatest Norman castle in the kingdom, standing silent sentinel in the shadow of adjacent Tower Bridge; the "Tower" has a long and gory history from Roman times on. Traditionally dressed Beefeaters still patrol the grounds. The White Tower is the main Norman feature, housing St. John's Chapel and the Armouries. The Crown Jewels are in the Jewel House.

At the **Museum of London▶▶▶**, London Wall, EC2, a time-walk display begins with Roman London, passes a cell door from Newgate prison, a panorama of the Great Fire, and a street of Victorian shops (free).

The East End
The *Bethnal Green Museum of Childhood*, Cambridge Heath Road, Bethnal Green, E2, is an entertaining offshoot of the Victoria and Albert Museum (free). Toys of all ages and countries are here; among the exhibits are a wonderful collection of dolls' houses, a surreal display of dolls' heads and a group of puppet theaters. The *Geffrye Museum* occupies a row of early 18th-century almshouses in Kingsland Road, Hackney, E2. Each of a series of rooms is furnished in a different period style from the Elizabethan era to the 1960s. It is a succinct summary of furniture styles through the ages.

49

Off the North Circular
Sited on the former Hendon airfield, the *Royal Air Force Museum*, Hendon, NW9, (free) has over 60 aircraft and galleries about military aviation and the RAF. Adjacent, the *Battle of Britain* and *Bomber Command* museums cover related themes. The *Musical Museum*, 368 High Street, Brentford, houses a large collection of musical instruments, with hour-long demonstrations.

The White Tower, the Tower of London

LONDON

Houses

A suburban overview: Commuterdom
Most Londoners live outside the center; commuterdom extends far into the Home Counties (that is, the counties adjacent to London). The suburbs are much-expanded villages, joined together for the most part by somewhat anonymous 19th- and 20th-century fill-in, but seen from the air it is the greenery that really stands out: several ancient commons (originally common grazing grounds) have been retained as public open spaces, and there are literally millions of trees in back gardens, suburban roads and parks.

Where the famous lie at rest
Inner London's churchyards were so crowded by the early 1800s that they had become revoltingly unsanitary. To relieve pressure, massive cemeteries were created further out, which are the resting places of some of London's most famous dead. Emmeline Pankhurst, the Suffragette leader, is buried in Brompton Cemetery, the music-hall queen Marie Lloyd in Hampstead Cemetery, Isambard Kingdom Brunel and Anthony Trollope at Kensal Green; George Eliot and Karl Marx repose in Highgate Cemetery.

Hampton Court: the Tudor Pond Garden

London has a wide range of houses open to the public, from grand palaces built for monarchs to the more personal homes of the famous or eccentric. Some are listed below.

Hundreds of buildings in London carry blue plaques. These mark houses where famous people lived and died, such as 25 Brook Street, W1, where Handel lived for 25 years until his death in 1759, or 45 Berkeley Square, W1, where Clive of India cut his throat in 1774. The plaques add an extra piquancy to a stroll in London's streets and squares.

Central London Sir John Soane's Museum►►, 13 Lincoln's Inn Fields, WC2, is a wonderfully eccentric house, designed by Soane, the architect (1753–1837), to contain his collection of artifacts. The house is full of inventive lighting effects, mirrors and quirky details, and some great treasures, in particular the paintings of *A Rake's Progress* and *An Election* by Hogarth, and the sarcophagus (from ancient Egypt) of Seti I. Free admission; tours on Saturdays at 2:30PM.

Dr. Johnson's House, 17 Gough Square, EC4, hidden away in an alley off Fleet Street, is the house where Dr Johnson lived between 1749 and 1759, and where he completed his celebrated dictionary. Now it is a museum, with mementoes of Johnson's life and work.

Apsley House►►, Hyde Park Corner, W1, was the London home of the Duke of Wellington, built in 1778 by Robert Adam with 19th-century alterations by James Wyatt. Its grand interior houses mementoes of the Iron Duke and his campaigns, as well as his impressive collection of paintings.

Kensington Palace►►, Kensington Gardens, W8, was remodelled by Christopher Wren and William Kent. It was

the birthplace of Queen Victoria; today it is the residence of the Princess of Wales and of Princess Margaret. On show are the royal collection of pictures and furniture, a display on the Great Exhibition of 1851 and a set of magnificent court costumes. Hunt out the famous statue of Peter Pan nearby in Kensington Gardens.

Leighton House►, 12 Holland Park Road, W14, is the charmingly offbeat Victorian house of Lord Leighton, former president of the Royal Academy, who installed antique Islamic tiles into the Arab Hall. Pre-Raphaelite paintings, William de Morgan ceramics and Leighton's own canvases are on show (free).

Hampstead Kenwood House►, Hampstead Lane, NW8, is handsomely situated on the edge of Hampstead Heath, the quasi-rural oasis in north London. Robert Adam gave the house its classical proportions; within is a collection of old masters and portraits, including works by Reynolds and Gainsborough. Outdoor summer concerts, often with fireworks, attract big crowds on Saturday evenings. Free admission to house. Hampstead's oldest house, and one of the grandest, is **Fenton House►** on Windmill Hill, NW3. Now owned by the National Trust, it contains a collection of antique keyboard instruments, paintings and furniture.

South and west Hampton Court►►►, East Molesey, Surrey, is best reached from London by river boat from Westminster pier. The palace was begun in the early 16th century by Cardinal Wolsey and later presented to Henry VIII; it is an enjoyable potpourri of styles and history, with a hammer-beamed hall, Wren's Fountain Court and carvings by Grinling Gibbons. The grounds contain a famous maze. **Ham House►**, Ham Street, Ham, which stands by the Thames towpath close to Richmond Park, is, for London, an outstanding example of Jacobean architecture, built in 1610 (NT).

Kew Palace►► was built in 1631 for a London merchant and subsequently leased by George II for Queen Caroline. Since its purchase in 1781 by George III, the house has changed little, and retaining its old panelling and portraits. A visit here ties in nicely with Kew Gardens (see page 16) and a walk along the Thames towpath to Richmond. On the other side of the river is **Syon House►**, Isleworth. Founded in 1415 as a monastery, the house underwent a remodelling in the 18th century, being given crisp interiors by Robert Adam and grounds by Capability Brown. Adjacent in Syon Park are a major gardening center, a butterfly park and a collection of historic vehicles. **Chiswick House►**, Chiswick Park, Chiswick, is a small, formal Palladian villa (1729) once used for soirées and as a library rather than as a house. Modelled on Palladio's Villa Capra in Italy, it stands in delightful parkland, naturalistically landscaped in what came to be regarded as the English manner.

Osterley Park►►, off Great West Road (A4), Osterley, is a gracious manor house set in parkland, all but engulfed by the suburbia of London's western fringes, Osterley provides an excellent opportunity to see Robert Adam's interiors at their richest. Adam's work dates from 1761 to 1780; the house itself has Tudor origins (NT).

The gilded gates of Kensington Palace

51

LONDON WALKS

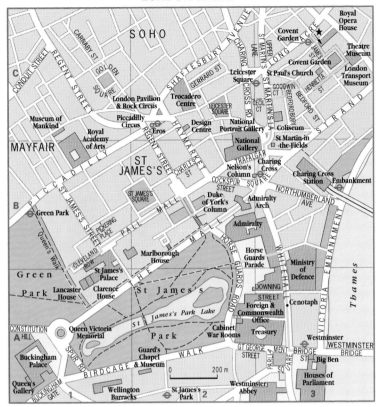

Walk **Covent Garden, royal London and Westminster**

Start from Covent Garden tube station. Walk down James Street to Covent Garden►►, the former fruit and vegetable market, now transformed to a stylish shopping piazza and cheerful meeting-place. The **Theatre Museum►** and **London Transport Museum►►** are close by. From Henrietta Street, an archway on the right leads into the churchyard of St. Paul's, the innovative design of Inigo Jones. At the heart of London's theaterland, St. Paul's is known as the **actors' church►** and its interior walls are covered with plaques in memory of stars of stage and screen. Leave the churchyard via a gate into Bedford Street; off the next street to the west, Bedfordbury, an arch leads

into Goodwin Court, where bow-windowed houses have changed little since the 18th century. Reach St. Martin's Lane; opposite is Cecil Court, part of the secondhand bookshop quarter. Enter Trafalgar Square, the great pigeon-populated piazza fronted by the church of **St. Martin-in-the-Fields►►** and the **National Gallery►►►**.

Cross over to the Admiralty Arch and enter the Mall. Steps lead up to the right past the Duke of York's column. Walk along Pall Mall; a long-established concentration of fashionable gentlemen's clubs is here, distinguished by unobtrusive signs at the entrances. Detour to look at the east side of St. James's Street with its

Big Ben, Britain's most famous timepiece, and Parliament Square

trio of old-fashioned shops—Lock's the hat-makers, Berry and Rudd's wine merchants, and Lobb's, makers of custom-fitted shoes. Adjacent Pickering Place was once used for sword duels.

Cleveland Row skirts **St. James's Palace►**, residence of Prince Charles and others; leave by gates into Queen's Walk, along the edge of Green Park. Return to the Mall: **Buckingham Palace►►**, the residence of the Queen, is to the right; the Changing of the Guard takes place daily at 11:30AM. Cross the Mall and enter St. James's Park, keeping left and to the near side of the lake. Leave by the gate and pass through the arch into **Horse Guards Parade►►** and into Whitehall; Downing Street to the right, permanently guarded, has at No. 10 the house of the prime minister. Reach Parliament Square, presided over by the clocktower of Big Ben, part of the **Houses of Parliament►►►**, the seat of British government. Across the square is Westminster Abbey. Return from Westminster subway station.

53

Walk Along the South Bank to Tower Hill

Start from Westminster Bridge. The above walk can be extended by following the South Bank (which has a walkway for much of the way) from Westminster Bridge to the **Royal Festival Hall►**, where the **river bus** can be taken to London Bridge. The walkway continues east of Waterloo bridge past an impressive modern office complex, with outstanding views of the City. At **HMS *Belfast*►** it is necessary to detour away from the river to Tooley Street, but a path leading through a small park takes you to **Tower Bridge►►**, which can be crossed (a museum inside the bridge explains its workings and history); to the right you can see Canary Wharf, Britain's tallest building. On the other side, circle around the moat of the **Tower of London►►►**. Signs to the World Trade Centre lead you to **St. Katharine Dock►**, a yacht haven with a collection of historic boats. Return from Tower Hill subway station.

St. Katharine Dock

Southwark Cathedral is noted for the many monuments that survived from its days as a monastic church. That of poet John Gower, above, is dated 1408

Sir Christopher Wren (1632–1723)
Wren, one of the most celebrated of English architects, was responsible for the rebuilding of St. Paul's Cathedral (in which his monument appears as *lector, si monumentum requiris, circumspice* – "reader, if you seek my monument, look around") and the City churches. He drew up an ambitious plan for the rebuilding of London with Continental-style avenues, but the complexities of land ownership prevented it from being carried out. M.P. for Weymouth in Dorset, he used the local Portland stone liberally in his buildings. The other great architect of the day was Inigo Jones, who designed Covent Garden piazza, the first piazza in London.

Although the Great Fire of 1666, the Blitz of 1940 and constant rebuilding have changed London's face repeatedly, it still has an impressive legacy of church architecture, dating from Norman times. There are particularly fine examples of designs of the master architects of the 17th and 18th centuries: Wren, Hawksmoor and Inigo Jones. Here we list only the undoubted masterpieces.

The earliest churches The only large-scale church of the Norman period in London is **St. Bartholomew the Great►►** in West Smithfield, EC1. It is the survivor of a 12th-century Augustinian Priory and although the apsidal east end is a 19th-century rebuilding, the atmosphere is one of great antiquity. **Southwark Cathedral►**, Borough High Street, SE1, the cathedral for the South Bank, was founded as the Augustinian priory church of St. Mary Overie in 1106. Although much renovation was carried out in the 19th century, it is the most substantial medieval artifact in Southwark, a district now inextricably part of inner London. The building attained cathedral status in 1905.

Sir Christopher Wren Wren's domed masterpiece, **St. Paul's Cathedral►►►**, Ludgate Hill, EC4, replaced an earlier Gothic cathedral that perished in the Great Fire of 1666. It no longer dominates the skyline as it did until the mid-20th century, but when seen close up the proportions are overwhelming. Inside the dome, the Whispering Gallery plays acoustic tricks (whispered sounds carry around the great void). There are tombs of Wren, Nelson, Wellington, Turner and Reynolds in the crypt, views from the Golden Gallery, woodwork by Gibbons and ironwork by Tijou.

After the Great Fire, Sir Christopher Wren graced the City with 51 churches (some restored after World War II bombing). Among the most celebrated of **Wren's City churches►►** are St. Bride's (Fleet Street), St. Margaret's (Lothbury), St. Martin Ludgate (Ludgate Hill), St. Mary Abchurch (Cannon Street), St. Mary-at-Hill (Eastcheap) and St. Stephen Walbrook (Walbrook).

Other great churches St. Martin-in-the-Fields►, Trafalgar Square, WC2, is an 18th-century rebuilding by James Gibbs, and a particularly satisfying example of the temple-like architecture of the period, with a characteristic galleried interior.

Westminster Abbey►►►, Parliament Square, SW1. Here British sovereigns are crowned and many great men and women are buried, among them monarchs, statesmen, poets and scientists. It also has a cloisters, treasury, brass-rubbing center and the oldest garden (open Thursdays only) in the country.

Westminster Cathedral►, in Ashley Place, off Victoria Street, SW1, is Britain's premier Roman Catholic cathedral, a vast Byzantine brick creation, finished in 1903; incense fills a gloomily cavernous interior.

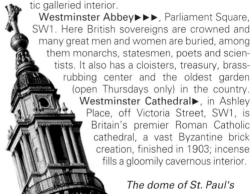

The dome of St. Paul's

Nightlife

Theater There are dozens of theaters to choose from, offering everything from Shakespeare to Andrew Lloyd Webber musicals; the capital has an impressive legacy of Victorian theater architecture. Discount tickets for the day of performance are available from a booth in Leicester Square (see panel).

Nightspots Soho and Covent Garden constitute the heart of the disco and nightclub land with such youth-oriented establishments as the Hippodrome and Empire Discotheque by Leicester Square; The Wag in Wardour Street draws in young trendies. Nightspots come and go, but Ronnie Scott's (47 Frith Street, W1) is a well-established jazz spot, and Heaven (under Charing Cross Station) is a leading gay club. Cabaret and alternative comedy is performed at The Comedy Store in Leicester Square. Out of the center is the highly esteemed Fridge, at Town Hall Parade, Brixton Hill, SW2. Watch listings (see panel) for pop concerts at the Hammersmith Odeon and Brixton Academy.

Classical music London has five resident orchestras. The Royal Festival Hall on the South Bank (plus the smaller Purcell Room and Queen Elizabeth Hall, both scheduled for rebuilding) and the Barbican Hall, Silk Street (Moorgate subway) are major concert halls. The old-fashioned Wigmore Hall in Wigmore Street has Sunday morning coffee concerts and often hosts performances by up-and-coming artists. Summer visitors should try to take in a performance at the Promenade Concerts ("the Proms," see page 18), Europe's biggest music festival. Operas at the Royal Opera House in Covent Garden are performed in the original language with "surtitles" projected above, while the English National Opera in the Coliseum in St. Martin's Lane gives performances in English.

Movies The big first-run movie house is the Odeon at Leicester Square, with a huge main auditorium, still boasting an organ. The National Film Theatre (NFT) on the South Bank near Waterloo Bridge is the leading repertory cinema; programs change daily and one-day memberships are available.

Listings and bookings
The weekly magazine *Time Out* gives listings for all London's entertainments, events and exhibitions, and has excellent previews. The *London Theatre Guide*, updated every two weeks, lists theatrical events and is available free of charge from West End theaters, libraries and tourist information centers.
Buy tickets directly from the box office to avoid paying commissions. Ticket agencies include Ticketmaster (tel: 071-379 4444) and First Call (tel: 071-240 7200); check for credit card surcharges. Never buy tickets from scalpers on the street or unofficial agencies. The Leicester Square discount ticket booth opens at 12 noon for matinées and 2:30PM for evening performances.

55

The lights of Leicester Square

James Smith's redoubtable stick and umbrella store

The principal shopping areas Major West End department stores are clustered along **Oxford Street,** with Selfridges the biggest of them. John Lewis (whose "never knowingly undersold" policy guarantees a refund if you find goods on sale cheaper elsewhere) has a fine stock of furnishings, fashions and decorative items, while the ubiquitous Marks and Spencer (nicknamed Marks and Sparks) is known for good-value clothing. Virgin Megastore and H.M.V. have big selections of CDs and cassettes. Around the corner, **Regent Street** comes into its own in the weeks before Christmas when the illuminations are switched on; during this period, Hamleys, the undisputed king of the toyshops, fills to bursting capacity and has spectacular displays. Almost adjacent is Liberty, renowned for Liberty print fabrics and stylish clothes; the mock-Tudor building itself is worth a look.

Stereos and electrical goods are available at discounted prices in the shops along **Tottenham Court Road**; at the corner of Goodge Street and Charlotte Street, Nice Irma's has Indian-inspired candlesticks, cushion covers and more. Further east at 53 New Oxford Street, James Smith, umbrella manufacturers, has an eye-catching Victorian shopfront boasting "Life Preservers, Jagger Canes and Swordsticks."

Charing Cross Road constitutes the heart of London's bookstore territory (another Victorian Smith's is here, this one a tiny snuff shop). Foyles, the largest bookstore, has an impressive stock though the layout can be confusing. There is a particularly fascinating array of specialist second-hand bookshops just off Charing Cross Road in Cecil Court. Just to the west, Soho is densely packed with ethnic food stores, including Chinese supermarkets in Chinatown, and numerous Italian delis. **Covent Garden** has an absorbing variety of stores and boutiques, including the Tea Shop in Neal Street, a cheese shop and bakery in Neal's Yard, and a dolls' house shop in the piazza itself.

St. James's Street off Piccadilly has a clutch of old-fashioned shops: Berry and Rudd wine-merchants, Lock's the hatmakers and Lobb's the shoemakers; close by, in Jermyn Street, Paxton and Whitfield sells hundreds of cheeses.

Kings Road in Chelsea is the place for chic fashions, stylish interior design shops and people-watching; a smart antiques market (Monday to Saturday) extends along one part.

Great for window shopping Harrods, Knightsbridge, is the grandest department store of them all; many visitors go just to collect a carrier bag. Harrods prides itself on its range and quality of stock; the food-halls conjure up Edwardian splendor. **Burlington Arcade** off Piccadilly, a perfectly preserved Regency shopping arcade, retains its early 19th-century air with considerable dignity; a behatted, immaculately attired beadle patrols the alley and notices forbid hurrying or whistling. High-class galleries and boutiques attract the wealthy; others merely window-shop. **Fortnum and Mason**, Piccadilly, is the food store *par excellence*, with high-priced hampers for those who can afford them; quality teas make more affordable souvenirs. The famous exterior clock features moving figurines and musical chimes on the hour.

Street markets always provide good entertainment. Easily the most atmospheric is **Brick Lane** (Sunday mornings only), off Bethnal Green Road in the heart of Cockney London, now the heart of the Bengali community. It is unashamedly shabby and hugely crowded, and the mishmash of wares is bizarre, ranging from suspiciously cheap stereos to bargain CDs to secondhand junk. Don't miss the bagel store! Note this is not the same as the nearby (and overrated) Petticoat Lane market. Weekend-long markets with lots of antiques include **Camden Lock** and **Greenwich**. **Portobello Road**, W11, operates Monday to Saturday (junk stalls on Friday, antiques on Saturday).

57

Speakers' Corner
At the corner of Hyde Park, close to Marble Arch at the western end of Oxford Street, this bastion of free speech provides memorable free entertainment, at lunchtime Monday to Friday but at full throttle on Sunday morning. Anyone can set up a soap-box and speak on anything he or she likes as long as there is no blasphemy, defamation, treason or breach of the peace laws.

Only the best: a selection of Fortnum and Mason's gift baskets

Accommodation

Hotels London is one of the most expensive European capitals for hotel rooms. Those who can afford high prices will appreciate the style and service at such long-established and prestigious establishments as the Ritz, Claridge's, the Savoy and the Connaught; be prepared for lots of formality, however, and do not expect air-conditioning as a matter of course. The top modern hotels are in the same price bracket. Among the best areas to stay are the West End (W1, NW1, SW1, WC2), Bloomsbury (WC1), Kensington (W2, W8, W11), Knightsbridge (SW7) and Chelsea (SW3).

A top hotel for some: others will choose a B & B

Reserving accommodation
London Tourist Board has accommodation lists and operates a reservation service. For help dial 071-824 8844. The Visitor Call, a phone guide to London, offers information on 35 topics (current exhibitions, popular attractions, street markets, etc). The number for General Advice is 0839 123435; calls are charged at 36p/48p per minute.

Bed and Breakfast More modest Bed and Breakfast (B & B) accommodation comes at roughly double the price you would expect to pay outside London; there is a reasonable selection around Victoria (SW1) and Bloomsbury (WC1); the King's Cross area (also WC1) is cheap but has a reputation as a red-light and drugs-peddling district. Out to the west, Hammersmith (W6) has some large hotels and has convenient subway connections to central London; the immediate area is unprepossessing, however. Small hotels and B & Bs exist in many suburbs, and can cut your hotel costs; aim for a location convenient to the Underground, and check the journey time and the timing of the last train back.

Service at its most discreet . . .

Hostels Budget travelers are seved by youth hostels; the central locations are in Noel Street, W1, Bolton Gardens, SW5, Holland Park, W8, and Carter Lane, EC4; three farther-flung hostels are in Highgate West Hill, N6, Wellgarth Road, NW11, and Salter Road, Rotherhithe, SE16. All these get heavily booked in summer especially, and reservations are advised (national YHA tel: 07278 55215). Additionally, numerous colleges offer accommodation in the summer; halls of residence at White Hart Lane, N17, and Wood Green, N22 (both well out into the northern suburbs) are run as summer hostels and there are some cheap options in Earl's Court. The International Students Hostel at 99 Frognal, NW3 (tel: 071-794 6893), is a females-only establishment in Hampstead.

Eating out

Breakfast For a leisurely start to the day, plump for breakfast at one of the big hotels such as the Savoy (the Strand, WC2; tel: 071-836 4343). Devotees of Chinese *dim sum* brunch should look no further than New World (1 Gerrard Place, W1; tel: 071-734 0396).

Lunch For quick lunches, the ubiquitous sandwich bars and no-frills restaurants serving plates of lasagne and risotto are a good and frugal bet; there are several of these in the West End. Many pubs and wine bars offer food, though some get crowded and smoky; the long-established Gordon's Wine Bar (47 Villiers Street, WC2; tel: 071-930 1408) is set in a subterranean vault by the Thames. Look around Soho and Covent Garden for Asian restaurants, which offer good-value lunches; for Japanese food try Ajimura (51 Shelton Street, WC2; tel: 071-240 0178). Big museums and galleries, including the National Gallery, Tate Gallery and Festival Hall, have good self-service cafeterias. There are a number of excellent southern Indian vegetarian restaurants, one of the bargains of London, along Drummond Street, NW1, near Euston and handy for Regent's Park.

Afternoon tea Tea is served with considerable flair at such prestigious hotels as the Ritz (reservation advisable; Piccadilly, W1; tel: 071-493 8181) and Brown's (Dover Street, W1; tel: 071-493 6020), although prices are high and there is a formal dress code.

The evening For a treat, try one of the great French restaurants such as Bibendum (Michelin House, 81 Fulham Road, SW3; tel: 071-581 5817) in the eye-catching Michelin building, or Nico Central (35 Great Portland Street, W1, tel: 071-436 8846). Those who wish to live it up in style without breaking the bank may like Kettner's (29 Romilly Street, W1; no reservations), part of the Pizza Express chain.

Among London's residential districts Hampstead, Camden Town, Islington, Bayswater, Kensington and Chelsea have a good choice of places to eat. See also Hotels and restaurants, pages 281–2.

For a taste of tradition, take tea at the Ritz

Pubs in London
Pubs of special character include the *Cittie of York* (with Britain's longest bar; 22 High Holborn, WC2), the *Lamb and Flag* (in Covent Garden; 33 Rose Street, WC2), the *Museum Tavern* (near the British Museum; Museum Street, WC1), the *Princess Louise* (spectacular Victorian tiled interior; 208 High Holborn, WC1), the *Lamb* (Bloomsbury, with old fittings, Lamb's Conduit Street), *Ye Olde Cheshire Cheese* (ancient tavern, former haunt of writers Dickens and Johnson; Wine Office Court, 145 Fleet Street, EC4) and the *Dove* (riverside pub with terrace, 19 Upper Mall, Chiswick). Fuller's and Young's are two excellent "real ale" London brews.

THE WEST COUNTRY

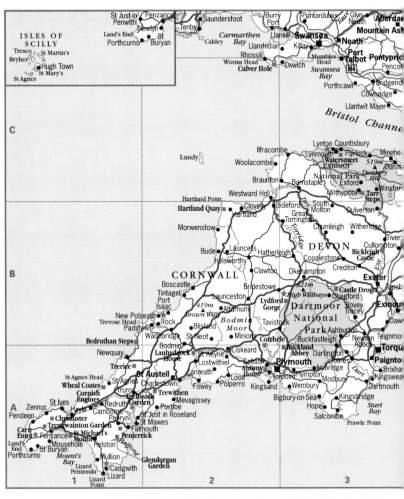

ISLES OF
SCILLY

Tresco • St Martin's
Bryher •
• Hugh Town
St Agnes's
St Mary's
St Agnes

St Just-in
Penwith • Penzance • Saundersfoot
Newlyn • Tenby
Land's End • St Buryan • Caldey
Porthcurno • St Buryan

Carmarthen
Bay Llanelli
Killay Swansea Neath
Llanrhidian Port Mountain As
Rhossili Mumbles Talbot Pontypric
Worms Head • Oxwich Head M4 Penco
Culver Hole Swansea Porthcawl Bridgend
Bay Cowbridge
Porthcawl
Llantwit Major

Bristol Channe

C

Lundy

Ilfracombe Lynton Countisbury Minehe
Woolacombe Lynmouth • Porlock 519m Duns
Watersmeet Dunkery
Braunton Exmoor Hill Winso
Barnstaple National Park Exford Tarr
Westward Ho! Withypool Steps
Hartland Point Clovelly Bideford South Dulverton Witherid
Hartland Quay Hartland Molton
Morwenstow Great Chumleigh Witheridge
Torrington
Bude • Launcells Hatherleigh **DEVON** Tiver
Holsworthy Copplestone Cullompton
CORNWALL Clawton Crediton **Bickleigh**
Boscastle Okehampton **Castle**
Tintagel Bridestowe **Exeter**
Port Launceston 621m **Castle Drogo** Tops
Isaac Altarnun **High Willhays** Chagford **Exmou**
New Polzeath 419m **Lydford** **Dartmoor** Bovey
Trevose Head Rock **Brown Willy** **Gorge** Tracey Daw
Padstow Blisland Bodmin **National** Ashburton Newton Teignmo
Wadebridge Moor Tavistock **Park** Abbot **Torqu**
Bedruthan Steps Bodmin St Neot Minions **Buckland** Dartington **Paignto**
Newquay **Lanhydrock** Liskeard **Abbey** Totnes Brixha
House Lostwithiel Saltash Ivybridge Kingswea
Trerice St Keyne Cotehele **Plymouth** Dartmouth
St Agnes Head Lanreath Antony Torpoint Modbury **Dart**
Wheal Coates **St Austell** Fowey **House** Plympton
Cornish Charlestown Polperro Kingsand Bigbury-on-Sea Kingsbridge
Engines Truro Looe Wembury Start
Zennor St Ives **Trewithen** Hope Salcombe Bay
Pendeen Hayle Camborne **Garden** Mevagissey Prawle Point
Chysauster Penryn St Just in Roseland
Carn **Trengwainton Garden** St Mawes
Euny Penzance **St Michael's** Falmouth
Land's Mousehole **Mount** **Penjerrick**
End St Buryan Helston
Porthcurno **Mount's** Mullion **Glendurgan**
Bay Lizard **Garden**
Peninsula Cadgwith
Lizard Lizard
Point

1   2   3

A

B

60

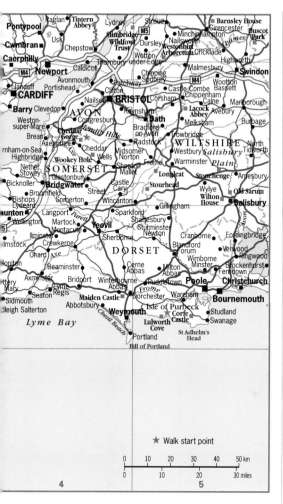

★ Walk start point

| 0 | 10 | 20 | 30 | 40 | 50 km |
| 0 | | 10 | | 20 | 30 miles |

The West Country The tapering southwestern peninsula of England culminates in the rugged clifflands of western Cornwall, where Land's End forms the big toe of Great Britain. Called the West Country, the area offers perhaps a fuller range of activities, landscapes and experiences than any other in Britain, and as a result, you'll find crowds of other visitors here, especially during the summer. People from all over Britain spend their vacations here, in indolent ease or in a whirl of activity. The climate is mild and the sprawling resorts of Torquay and Bournemouth head the sunshine league; this is also a major retirement area. To many, the West Country is synonymous with dairy country; the locals are big cheese-eaters, and you can gorge out on a cream tea or even mail home some clotted cream, a cholesterol-watcher's nightmare. Further temptation is provided by lardy cake, a gooey raisin-topped bakery product largely confined to the West Country.

Land's End, Cornwall

THE WEST COUNTRY

62

BEST PLACES TO GO
Coastal towns and villages
Cornwall Boscastle, Port Isaac, Padstow, St. Ives, Mousehole, Cadgwith, St. Anthony in Roseland, Portloe, Mevagissey, Charlestown, Fowey, Polperro, Kingsand.
Devon Lynmouth, Clovelly, Sidmouth, Dartmouth, Salcombe, Newton Ferrers, Plymouth.
Dorset Lyme Regis, Abbotsbury, Weymouth.
Small towns inland
Cornwall Launceston
Somerset Dulverton, Wells, Dunster, Glastonbury.
Dorset Beaminster, Sherborne, Shaftesbury.
Wiltshire Marlborough, Bradford on Avon, Devizes.
Historic cities Bath, Bristol, Exeter, Salisbury.
Coastal features *Cornwall* Tintagel Castle, Bedruthan Steps, Gurnards Head (near Zennor), Porthcurno open air theatre, Logan Rock (near Treen), St. Michael's Mount, Mullion Cove, Fal Estuary, Dodman Point, Rame Head.
Devon Valley of Rocks, Baggy Point (near Croyde), Hartland Quay, Hobby Drive (near Clovelly), Hooken Cliffs (near Beer), Bolt Head, Bolt Tail (both near Salcombe).
Somerset Porlock Toll Road
(continued on page 63)

Cornwall Until the opening of the Tamar railway bridge in the 19th century, Cornwall was the remotest county in England. That may be hard to believe at the peak of summer, as tourists descend upon the coastal villages and the narrow lanes jam with traffic, but the area still has a distinct sense of locale—partly real, partly manufactured by the heritage industry. The Cornish language has gone, the tin mines are all but defunct, and Tintagel has but a tenuous link with King Arthur's Camelot (a link stoutly reinforced by interested hoteliers and shopkeepers). But plenty is real enough: Cornish place-names live on, and the superlative coastline encompasses awe-inspiring headlands and secret coves that bring to life tales of smugglers and shipwrecks. Cornwall is a summer playground, ideal for water sports and family fun, less good for scenic drives (the roads seldom follow the coast close enough) and more interesting for its archaeology, holy wells and ancient stone crosses than for its architecture. Cornish villages are plain, sturdy-looking affairs of granite walls beneath Delabole slate roofs. There is nothing very ancient-feeling about much of central Cornwall, which largely grew up around the mining and china clay industries. However, no part of the county is further than a half-hour away from the coast (in normal driving conditions!), where you can usually walk along a coast path in comparative solitude, surrounded by unrivaled beauty.

Devon South Devon has the best beaches (such as Blackpool Sands near Stoke Fleming and Bigbury-on-Sea) and some busy seaside resorts—Torquay, Paignton, Teignmouth, Dawlish, Brixham and Exmouth, each pleasant enough at the shore but not worth going out of your way to see. Sidmouth has a conspicuously well-preserved Regency seafront. Much of the action focuses around the estuaries, notably the grand finale of the River Dart at Dartmouth, and the Kingsbridge Estuary. Of central Devon, Dartmoor is by far the best-known part, a world of windswept wastes and wilderness, tors and relics of early settlers; granite is the predominant building material, although on the edges you will see the cob walls and thatched roofs, a Devon vernacular hallmark. Exeter, sadly, was bombed during the last war and you have to search around for its best corners; but the city repays such exploration and makes a good base. The rest of central Devon is less well known, a terrain of hilly farmlands, sandstone walls and swift-flowing rivers. In the far north, moorland meets the sea in Exmoor, which has primeval grandeur, England's highest cliffs and Devon's longest stretch of unspoilt coast—but a damp climate.

Somerset and Avon While the **Somerset** coast has little to speak of outside Exmoor (which straddles the Devon border), there is much to explore inland. The little-visited Quantock Hills have a fine heritage of country churches; the Mendip Hills are dull-looking until you encounter Wells, the Cheddar Gorge and Burrington Combe. Southward lie the Levels, a flat, drained fenland once beneath the sea; Glastonbury Tor and the low-rise Polden Hills protrude above the far side. Taunton, the main town

in the heart of cider-making country, has a bland
streetscape redeemed by an impressive church and an
absorbing museum.

The small county of **Avon** takes its name from the river
that flows through Bath and Bristol. Bath is the obvious
first choice among cities to visit in the West Country,
delightful for wandering, but hellish to drive in, while
Bristol is a large port, with a great maritime heritage and
an elegant suburb, somewhat like Bath, called Clifton.

Dorset The home of Dorset Blue Vinny cheese, the county often has the tag "Hardy's Wessex" applied to it,
though the ancient kingdom of Wessex in fact extended
into Wiltshire, Somerset and Hampshire. There is scarcely a corner of Dorset that does not appear under a
pseudonym in Thomas Hardy's literary output. Although
over three-quarters of the county's heathlands have disappeared since 1945, the inland areas still have an
ancient, primitive look, with sweeping downs, clumps of
beech trees, thatched villages and prehistoric burial sites
(tumuli) and hillforts; the rugged cliffs offer great geological interest and variety.

BEST PLACES TO GO
(continued from page 62) Selworthy Beacon, Brean
Down.
Dorset Lyme Regis under-
cliff, Chesil Beach, Isle of
Portland, Lulworth Cove,
St. Albans Head, Old Harry
Rocks, Poole Harbour.
Walking The 500-mile
South West Coast Path
follows the coast from
Minehead (Somerset) to
Poole (Dorset); Exmoor,
north Cornwall and east
Dorset are the most dra-
matic bits; Dartmoor is best
for inland walking; other-
wise inland Exmoor, the
Dorset downs, the
Mendips, the Quantocks.
Offshore escapism Isles of
Scilly, Lundy Island.
Prehistoric sites Wiltshire
downs, west Cornwall.

Thatched cottages in Lustleigh, Devon

Wiltshire An inland county, Wiltshire has a gentle landscape of prairie-like chalk downlands with its northern
reaches just in the Cotswolds. Most of its interest is man-
made—as in the curious hill "carvings" of horses and regimental badges on the hillsides. More famous is the
legacy of early inhabitants, notably at Stonehenge and
perhaps even more memorably at Avebury. Salisbury
Cathedral is the pinnacle of the Early English style; a bus
service from Salisbury station to Stonehenge makes a
feasible day-trip from London. Wiltshire's largest town,
Swindon, grew up in the railroad era (its railroad museum
is a magnet for train buffs) and witnessed an economic
boom in the 1980s; smaller places, including Devizes,
Marlborough and Bradford on Avon, are much more
attractive.

There is in the Cornish
character, smouldering
beneath the surface, ever
ready to ignite, a fiery
independence, a stubborn
pride.
  Daphne du Maurier,
Vanishing Cornwall (1967)

Walks

Cheddar Gorge, Somerset   61C4

Parking lot adjacent to Butchers Arms near gorge entrance. Walk along the road at the bottom of the gorge; at the far end (1 mile) across from the gate into a nature reserve, take the West Mendip Way on the right, up through woods. Fork right to follow the top edge of the gorge; the views are astonishing. Drop down by steps at Prospect Tower. (2 hours)

Lizard, Cornwall   60A1

Start at Lizard village. For the best of this celebrated coast, take the road east to Church Cove and turn right along the coast path, past Lizard Point, the southernmost point on the mainland, and to idyllic Kynance Cove. Follow the toll road inland, branching right by a National Trust sign onto a path back to Lizard village. (2 hours)

Lulworth Cove, Dorset   61B5

Parking lot at Lulworth Cove. Take the steep path above the inside of the Cove, which gives a good aerial view. Then head west, taking the path from the parking lot, along the coast to Durdle Door, a natural arch eroded away by the waves. The rugged coast east of the Cove, famous for its "fossil forest" (fossilized algae that clung to tree stumps), is army training land, but open most weekends, at Easter and all August. (1 to 2 hours)

Lydford Gorge, Dartmoor National Park, Devon   60B3

Parking lots by gorge; entrance fee. Walk through this densely wooded gorge with the White Lady Waterfall at one end and the Devil's Cauldron, where the River Lyd swirls in a gloomy chasm, at the other. The full trail takes 1½ hours, or you can take short walks from the parking lots.

Valley of Rocks, Exmoor National Park, Devon   60C3

Start at Lynton. Take the small road between the Valley of Rocks Hotel and the church; it becomes the coast path. The Valley of Rocks and its wild goats soon come into view. Climb Castle Rock, the most prominent feature, for the view and return along the road, branching left after 1,300 ft. by a stone shelter to ascend Hollerday Hill and then drop into Lynton. (1½ hours)

Avebury's stones stand silent as daily life goes on around them

Warm-toned Georgian elegance: The Circus, Bath

▶▶ Avebury   61C5

A village unlike any other, Avebury is encompassed by a huge Bronze Age stone circle which, like Stonehenge (see page 84), seems to have been erected for a mystical or ceremonial purpose (see panel). The Alexander Keiller Museum explains Avebury's archaeology; an aisled manorial barn houses a museum of rustic bygones.

▶▶▶ Bath   61C5

A spa center since Roman times, Bath regained its popularity in the 18th century as a place for taking the waters and it remains the finest Georgian townscape in Britain. Parks, classical terraces, squares, an architectural "circus" and a Royal Crescent, much of it the design of John Wood the Elder and Younger (father and son), were laid out in that heyday when Beau Nash, archetypal English dandy, was the master of ceremonies and led fashionable society. The city has an elegant uniformity thanks to the use of the golden-hued Bath stone. Jane Austen stayed here and drew on her company as material for her novels, including *Northanger Abbey*.

Bath is a delightful place for casual wandering. Museums include an outstanding **Museum of Costume▶▶** within the Assembly Rooms, the **Bath Industrial Heritage Centre▶** with its re-creation of a Victorian brass foundry, the **Building of Bath Museum▶** (with the **Museum of Naive Art▶** next door), the **Victoria Art Gallery** and the **Holburne Museum▶** of fine arts; on the edge of town at Claverton Manor is the **American Museum▶**, where 17th- to 19th-century interiors have been re-created.

The **Pump Room▶▶**, the **Roman Baths▶▶▶** and **Bath Abbey▶▶** form the historical core at the heart of the city (see Walk on following page).

Corsham Court▶▶, near Chippenham, has magnificent state rooms. Capability Brown, usually known as a land-scape gardener, worked on the house in the 1740s.

Prehistoric landmarks at Avebury
Avebury's stone circle, which can be walked around in its entirety, connects to the so-called *Stone Avenue*, parallel rows of stones that lead south to the site of another circle, the *Sanctuary*. Across from the parking lot, a path leading south passes close by *Silbury Hill*, the largest prehistoric earthwork in Europe; it is thought to have played an astronomical or religious role. The path continues south of the A4 to *West Kennet Long Barrow*, an ancient burial chamber, which can be entered.

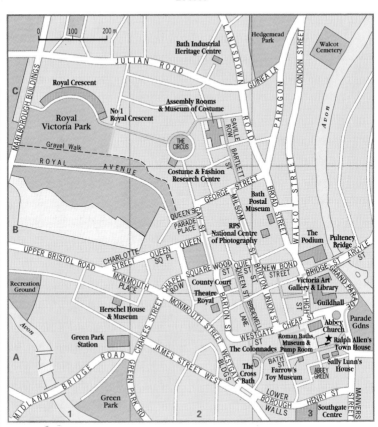

BATH

Walk **Bath city center**

At the **abbey►►**, look at the west front depicting Bishop Oliver's dream of angels that inspired him to rebuild the abbey in 1499. From there, walk past the **Roman Baths►►►**, Britain's finest Roman remains: baths, cold plunges, a hypocaust room and part of a Temple to Sulis, goddess of the springs, can be seen. Adjacent is the **Pump Room►►**, epitome of Bath's timeless spirit; here you can sip afternoon tea to the strains of chamber music by the statue of Beau Nash.

Carry on along Old Lilliput Alley. **Sally Lunn's House**, a bakery producing the original Sally Lunn cakes to a secret recipe, is the oldest house in Bath (1482); a kitchen museum tells the story. Beyond Grand Parade reach **Pulteney Bridge►►** (1774, designed by Robert Adam), with stores along both sides. In Milsom Street pass the **National Centre of Photography**. Walk up Saville Row past the **Assembly Rooms (Museum of Costume)►►**, walk around **The Circus►►►** (John Wood the Elder, begun 1754) and continue into **Royal Crescent►►►** (John Wood the Younger, 1767–74), No. 1 is open to the public. Drop down to Queen's Parade Place. Continue past **Queen Square** (1729–36); novelist Jane Austen stayed at No. 13 in 1799. Return via Bath Street to the abbey.

► **Bodmin Moor** 60B2

The top of Cornwall resembles a smaller version of Dartmoor, its bleak open moors dotted with granite tors, ponies and sheep. Brown Willy (1,375 ft.) is the county's highest point. Tracks onto the moor from the windswept hamlet of **Minions** give excellent views and lead past the **Hurlers Stone Circle►** (Bronze Age). At nearby Darite, **Trethevy Quoit►** is a Bronze Age burial chamber with its capstone still in place. Villages ringing the moor are well off the tourist beaten path. **Altarnun►** is a tranquil haven off the busy A30; its spacious church has magnificent 16th-century bench ends with carvings of jester, piper and dancers. In **Trewint** a tiny cottage is a simple shrine to John Wesley, father of Methodism, while **St. Neot** Church has the finest medieval stained glass in Cornwall. **Launceston►** occupies a hilltop crowned by a mighty Norman castle keep; twisting streets, a town-wall gateway, a restored steam railway and a local museum head its other attractions. Huge **Lanhydrock House►** (NT) epitomizes high living back at the turn of the century.

►► **Bradford on Avon** 61C5

A charming base for the southern Cotswolds, the stone-built town rises steeply, terrace by terrace, with flagged steps connecting its narrow lanes. Former cloth mer-

The medieval Town Bridge, Bradford on Avon

chants' mansions and humble medieval and 18th-century weavers' cottages set the tone; oddly named Top Rank Tory is the street with the best views. In Barton Farm Park stands a splendid 14th-century **tithe barn**.

    Lacock Abbey► (NT), some 9 miles northeast, retains 13th-century cloisters, chapter house and sacristy. A barn (owned, like much of the village, by the National Trust) houses the Fox Talbot Museum, in memory of the pioneer photographer who lived here from 1827 to 1877.

Bodmin Moor: three curious collections
Jamaica Inn, signed from the A30, is the setting for Daphne du Maurier's eponymous novel of lawless days and smugglers. Its upper story is home to Potter's Museum of Curiosities, a collection of oddities that includes tableaus of stuffed animals playing cricket, attending village school and so on. At Lanreath is an ever-growing folk museum of familiar and not-so-familiar objects of everyday and yesterday. Near St. Keyne, the Paul Corrin Musical Collection focuses on old-style mechanical musical instruments—pianolas, fairground organs and the like—demonstrated by the owner.

67

A lost church
Bradford on Avon's Church of St. Laurence, thought to be 7th–8th century, is one of Britain's most complete Saxon churches, yet it lay completely forgotten for many years. Looking over the town from a house above the church, a 19th-century vicar noticed the cruciform shape of the building, parts of which had been incorporated into a school, a house and a factory wall. In 1858, restoration was carried out and its interior can once more be seen.

■ **The harsh Atlantic winds buffet a wild, rocky coast, a graveyard for hundreds of ships. Eerie ruins of tin mines perch on treeless hillsides. The long coast is popular for its scenery, sights, and excellent swimming and surfing beaches. Accordingly, you have to be prepared for crowds at the peak of the season, and also for some unsightly resort development, especially between Padstow and Newquay. But it's still remarkably easy to get away from it all if you are prepared to walk for a mile or two along the coast path.....■**

68

Penwith's rich archaeology
Inland Penwith is peppered with reminders of early peoples. Major sites include two Iron Age villages, Carn Euny and Chysauster (both well signposted), where the wall layout has survived intact. Chûn Castle is an Iron Age fort with visible stone ramparts, while Lanyon Quoit is a good Bronze Age burial chamber and Men-an-Tol is a stone hoop of unknown purpose, used in recent times as a folkremedy for rickets; all three sites lie near the Madron–Morvah road. Close by St. Buryan, near the road, Merry Maidens stone circle is Bronze Age, the maidens supposedly turned to stone for dancing on the Sabbath.

One foot forward ...
Not everyone who sets out on the 1,000-mile walk to John o'Groats, at the other end of Britain, makes it; one unfortunate recently managed to trip over the starting sign he had put up and thus broke his leg with his very first stride.

The Devon border to Padstow The village of Morwenstow bears the indelible stamp of Rev. Robert Hawker, Celtic poet and priest here from 1834 to 1875. He adorned the vicarage with chimneypots in the form of miniature church towers and on the cliffs near by erected a driftwood shack for meditation and opium-smoking (it still stands). His memorial is in the church, which has Norman arches and 16th-century bench ends. **Bude** is an unremarkable resort town and a major surfing base, with a large beach; a small museum on the quay tells the story of the Bude Canal, which ends here. Inland, **Launcells Church▶**, standing all by itself, escaped the fervor of Victorian restorers, and little has changed since the 15th century. **Boscastle▶** occupies a craggy, precipitous creek; craft stores and a museum of witchcraft entertain the crowds, while the best views are from the clifftop just west of the harbor. **Tintagel▶** achieved fame for its legendary connections with King Arthur; the ruined medieval castle postdates Arthur, but the site is nevertheless magnificent, atop an impregnable headland, reached by a steep staircase. The adjacent village is a tourist trap of the tackiest kind, redeemed somewhat by the Old Post Office (NT), a small-scale manor house preserved as an outstanding example of Cornish domestic architecture. **Port Isaac▶▶** may stake a claim as the most authentic-feeling Cornish fishing village, a hodgepodge of cottages and narrow alleyways, with a wholesome whiff of seaweed.

Padstow▶ is a busy resort town of considerable charm. It lacks a beach (try Harlyn Bay, west of town) but has a harbor packed with brightly painted craft; fresh fish are on sale at quay warehouses and served at a number of good seafood restaurants. Prideaux Place, at the top of the town, looks Elizabethan but house tours in the summer months reveal whimsical Strawberry Hill Gothick (see Shobdon, page 122) alterations as well as the original plaster ceilings. The adjacent Camel Estuary offers sailing and gentle walks.

Bedruthan Steps to Land's End West from Padstow the summer crowds thicken rapidly. Many of Cornwall's safest and cleanest beaches are found between Padstow and Newquay. The immediate hinterland is spoiled by modern development, but **Bedruthan Steps▶▶** is an impressive coastal feature, comprising massive rock buttresses, detached from the cliff itself. **Newquay** has a brash bustle: nightspots, loud-music pubs, theme parks and surf stores. It also offers good beaches, a well-stocked zoo and a pretty harbor. Out of town, **Trerice▶** (NT) is a handsome Elizabethan manor house with a minstrels' gallery and intricate plasterwork ceilings.

St. Ives▶▶, a delightful port turned resort, has attracted artists and beachloving vacationers for a century. Although it has been considerably cleaned up since its heyday as a fishing port, its back streets have unmistakably Cornish character. Sculptress Barbara Hepworth was one of many 20th-century artists who settled here; her studio is now a museum with her sculptures gracing its garden. A branch of the Tate Gallery features the St. Ives school of artists in one of the most striking settings of any gallery. Down the coast at **Zennor** a folk museum has an appealing selection of Cornish bygones while the church is home to a legendary mermaid, carved on an ancient bench end.

Cornwall's westernmost knob is known as **Penwith▶▶▶** and has some of the most dramatic coastal scenery in England, with lonely heather moors inland. **Land's End**, Britain's southwesternmost mainland point, is the place to come if you collect geographical extremities. A signpost gives distances to places throughout the world (add your home town and pose for the photo); the crowds and theme park dwindle to nothing within ten minutes' walk along the cliff southwards, where the scenery gets better and better. The outdoor **Minack Theatre▶** clings to a breathtaking cliff site at Porthcurno, while quaintly named **Mousehole** (pronounced "Mouzal") has some pretty corners near its harbor.

St. Ives, a former fishing port with a tradition of art

A shopkeeper holds some Cornish pasties (traditional meat and vegetable pies)

Mining in Cornwall
Up to the last century Cornwall was a world leader in copper and tin production; lead was also produced. The evidence of its active past is everywhere, from the settlements of the Bronze Age people who exploited surface deposits of tin, to the 19th-century mining towns of Camborne, Redruth and St. Just, and the haunting legacy of abandoned mines and engine houses such as Wheal Coates near St. Agnes Head. In medieval times tin was weighed and stamped at stannary towns, which included Penzance and Truro. See also page 20.

Cornish inventions
It was a hard and dangerous life for miners, and mine accidents were numerous. Cornish innovations which made the job easier included Sir Humphry Davy's miner's safety lamp, Richard Trevithick's steam-powered beam engine, and the rock drill.

■ **Eastward from Penzance the coast gets more sheltered; the cliffs are less mighty, the seaboard is lusher and more populated than the north coast. Deep-water harbors are packed with craft: industrial ships, private yachts and ferries—every village and town seems to have a sign advertising fishing and sharking trips by boat. Visitors in spring and early summer will be right in time for Cornwall's justly famous gardens.....■**

Lizard transmitters
The Lizard peninsula is an important past and present telecommunications center. A memorial near Poldhu Cove commemorates the birth of transatlantic transmissions—it was from here that in 1901 Marconi sent three dots (a morse "S") to Newfoundland; his first message which followed was " What hath God wrought." Inland, the Lizard is dominated by the space-age form of the Goonhilly Downs Earth Station, the receiving center for satellite-relayed telephone calls. A tour of the site takes you into an old control tower and you can see the nerve center of the whole operation.

Penzance to Falmouth The town of **Penzance** has been knocked about by the 20th century, but it retains corners of Georgian streetscape, at its best in Chapel Street with its capricious Egyptian House, an early 19th-century precursor to art deco. The National Lighthouse Centre records the essential function of lighthouses on a perilous coast. Surveying the main street is the statue of Sir Humphry Davy, inventor of the miner's safety lamp and the town's foremost son in its tin-mining heyday.

St. Michael's Mount▶▶▶ (NT) shimmers ethereally in the sea, an isle capped by a castle. Those who have seen Mont St. Michel in Brittany can be excused for a sense of *déjà vu*, and in fact it was the Benedictines from Brittany who founded a church on the site, which became a fortress after the Dissolution of the monasteries. The owners today are the same family who snatched possession after the Civil War. At low tide you can walk to it along a causeway across the sands; at other times take the little ferry. It has a tremendous view from the roof terrace and an intriguing warren of rooms inside.

The **Lizard peninsula** juts out to form Britain's southernmost acres. Its inland portion is flat and bleak. **Kynance Cove**▶ epitomizes the best of the tumbledown cliffscape of the western Lizard, with a wonderfully sited beach amid the so-called serpentine rocks. There are several rock

Mevagissey: dependent more on tourism than fishing

St. Michael's Mount, a haunting view

workshops at **Lizard** village, which is itself of little appeal. The eastern Lizard, beyond **Cadgwith▶**, with its thatched cottages sloping down to the sea, has hidden, verdant creeks in the vicinity of the **Helford River**, including around the tiny waterside village of Helford itself.

Falmouth, Cornwall's largest town, is no great beauty but it's the base for boat trips up Carrick Roads, alternatively known as the Fal Estuary▶including excursions upriver to **Truro**, the Cornish capital (not itself of major interest, although it has a 19th-century cathedral). Perfectly preserved Tudor castles, St. Mawes and Pendennis, guard the great estuary. Subtropical plants abound at the delicious churchyard of **St. Just in Roseland▶**, which dips down to the water's edge.

Portloe to the Tamar Portloe▶ is an unspoiled fishing hamlet, hard to get to—and long may it continue to be; it has real character and nothing to attract large-scale commercialization. **Veryan**, inland, is known for its five early 19th-century round houses. **Charlestown▶**, a carefully preserved port, is still used by the china clay industry, whose white refuse heaps dominate the area.

Fowey▶▶ rises terrace by terrace above the deep-anchorage Fowey Harbour, with Polruan across the water. Blockhouses that used to guard the harbor stand silent sentinel. A delightful resort town, Fowey comes to life during the late summer regatta.

Mevagissey has become too popular for some people's tastes, with busloads of visitors cramming into its little harbor, but the place resumes its quiet charm when they have gone; ice cream, fish and chips and a model railroad are the attractions for tourists. **Polperro▶▶** is distinctly prettier and more groomed, though no less popular, with an appealing maze of alleys around its photogenic harbor; you may prefer to park at Talland Bay to the east and walk in along the level coast path rather than struggle with traffic jams.

The **Tamar Estuary** forms the Devon/Cornwall border; the river can be explored by boat trip from Plymouth. The large village of **Kingsand** has pretty corners and a small beach. **Antony▶** (NT) is the earliest and finest classical-style house in Cornwall, with fine woodland gardens. **Cotehele▶▶** (NT) is an extraordinary medieval relic, a completely unmodernized house; its estate buildings (saddler, smithy, wheelwright, etc) are well preserved. By the Tamar is moored the last Tamar barge in existence.

Subtropical gardens
Penjerrick, Glendurgan (NT), and Trebah gardens, close together west of Falmouth, were all the creation of the Foxes, a Quaker family, who aimed to create Paradise on Earth. They came close to succeeding, for each garden displays spectacular subtropical species. For other gardens to visit in south Cornwall, see Gardens, page 16.

71

Looe, a lively resort in a pleasant setting

Lundy Island

A popular day-trip by ferry from Bideford (in summer also from Barnstaple) is to Lundy, a little island some 39 miles north of Hartland Point. Its cliffs are a major site for birdlife; over 400 species are recorded, including puffins (*lunde* being the Norse for puffin). From 1925 to 1954 Lundy's owner Martin Harman tried to make it a separate kingdom; he did not succeed, but the island still issues its own stamps. Lundy's isolation in the Bristol Channel has given it a long history of smuggling. The Marisco Tavern serves beer brewed on the island.

▶▶ **Bristol**   *61C4*

The city center was badly bombed in 1940 and postwar planning was unimaginative. However, careful searching reveals many gems, among them **Christmas Steps**, a 17th-century relic; the **Church of St. Mary Redcliffe▶** with its majestic proportions; the **cathedral▶** (begun 1142), notable for its Norman chapter house and organ case carved by Grinling Gibbons; and the **New Room**, Britain's first Wesleyan (Methodist) chapel. Outside the Exchange in Corn Street are the famous **Bristol Nails**, four small bronze pedestals upon which city merchants completed their financial deals, "paying on the nail." A curious architectural folly, the **Cabot Tower▶** provides an excellent city view.

Docking activity is now concentrated in Avonmouth, but the revamped dockland area still has a boaty atmosphere, with sailing dinghies, a July regatta and boat tours around the harbor. Here too is the absorbing **Industrial Museum**, which acknowledges the life of Isambard Kingdom Brunel, the 19th-century engineer who designed the world's first ocean-going propeller ship, the **SS Great Britain▶**. Launched here in 1843, it is now on public show in the dry dock where she was built.

Clifton▶▶, an elegant Georgian suburb, has honey-stone squares, crescents and terraces, including Royal York Crescent. Brunel's **Clifton Suspension Bridge**, constructed between 1836 and 1864, spans the Avon Gorge in quite spectacular fashion. Nearby an 18th-century **camera obscura** offers views over Bristol.

Brunel's superlative Clifton Suspension Bridge

Don't drop your Ls

The hallmark of Bristol speech is the adding of the letter *L* to the ends of words. Thus *area* becomes *areal*, *Australia* becomes *Australial* and *Bristowe*, the old city name, becomes *Bristol*.

▶ **Clovelly**   *60B2*

A captivating if self-conscious fishing village, Clovelly is so steep that cars have to be left at the top. The Hobby Drive was constructed by a 19th-century owner of Clovelly Court as a scenic road; it's well worth the modest toll). In high season the village is overrun with visitors.

Hartland Quay▶▶, to the east, gives access to some of the most formidable cliffs in the West Country, the strata fantastically contorted into bizarre cross-sections.

▶▶▶ **Dartmoor National Park**   *60B3*

Southern England's largest area of wild country, Dartmoor is a great expanse of blustery moors punctuated by weathered granite outcrops known as tors. Sheep and Dartmoor ponies graze the open grasslands, wandering between Bronze Age hut circles and burial mounds. The moor can be a bleak place—it's England's place south of the Pennines—but there are cosy cob-and-thatch villages to come down to in the lusher valleys (some offering Devon cream teas), and several fine country-house style hotels. Indoor attractions are few: this is a place to be outdoors – picnicking, touring, walking or riding horseback.

On Dartmoor's east side, lush farmland meets the barren moors. **Hay Tor**▶▶ is the most visited viewpoint, easily accessible. **Hound Tor**▶▶, close by, is well marked by signs and lies next to a well-preserved abandoned medieval village, where you can still make out the fireplaces. West of **Buckland**, whose church clock has the letters MY DEAR MOTHER instead of numerals, **Bel Tor** presides over the Webburn Valley. The **Dart Valley**▶ is full of choice corners, including Combestone Tor and the medieval stone "clapper" bridge at Dartsmeet, junction of the West and East Dart rivers.

Widecombe in the Moor▶ draws visitors for its valley setting, its fame from the folksong "Widecombe Fair" and for its church, the "cathedral of the moor." **North Bovey**▶ is much quieter and quite uncommercialized, with a pretty green, thatched cottages, a stone cross and a village pump. **Chagford** is a large but sleepy village; **Moretonhampstead**, a crossroads town, is a shade busier and has a fine row of 17th-century almshouses; to the west, on the B3212, the **Miniature Pony Centre** shows several rare farmyard breeds (not just ponies).

In northeast Dartmoor the River Teign has carved a course through a deep valley with an enchanting deciduous forest. From **Fingle Bridge**▶, an old packhorse bridge, paths lead along the river and up onto moorland viewpoints; the Hunter's Path passes the back entrance to **Castle Drogo**▶▶(NT), architect Edwin Lutyens's early 20th-century masterpiece, an improbable marriage of granite medievalism and Edwardian Arts and Crafts style. The main entrance is near **Drewsteignton**, which has a charming village square.

Two main roads cross the central moor; the B3212 passes through **Postbridge**, with its notable medieval "clapper bridge," and grim **Princetown**, dominated by a high-security prison originally built for Napoleonic prisoners of war. The northwest moor is the highest and most remote landscape of all; it is used for army training but on certain days (including most weekends) you can drive along the potholed **army road**▶ from Okehampton Camp.

Two outstanding features justify a visit to the western fringes: **Brent Tor**▶, a plain church atop a huge rock and looking far into Cornwall, and **Lydford Gorge**▶▶ (see Walks, page 64), a deep and tortuous ravine (admission charged) with a waterfall and whirlpool.

The towns encircling Dartmoor National Park are not of great interest, although **Ashburton** has some attractive streets and **Buckfastleigh** boasts a modern Benedictine

Hound Tor, Dartmoor   73

Dartmoor's mailboxes
Many visitors to Dartmoor in the 19th century liked to try to locate Cranmere Pool, scarcely more than a puddle and remotely situated in the moors above Chagford. Someone had the idea of placing a mailbox here, the idea being that a self-addressed postcard would be left here by one walker and picked up and sent on by the next. The fad caught on and now there are some 400 boxes in various places. Today you can record your visit with the rubber stamp provided.

Prehistoric processional routes
Rows of stones erected in the Bronze Age are believed to have marked processional routes. Above the Erme Valley in south Dartmoor, one of these stretches 2 miles from Stall Moor to Green Hill. A more accessible, but much shorter, row is found just south of the B3357 east of Merrivale.

abbey, a butterfly park and otter sanctuary, and the terminus of the steam-powered South Devon Railway which wends its way 7 miles to Totnes. A museum of Dartmoor life at **Okehampton** tells of country life and ways; a fragment of a medieval castle caps a hillock on the edge of town.

Buckland Abbey▶, a former Cistercian monastery, was once home to Sir Francis Drake, born at nearby Tavistock. The house has some relics from his famous ship, *Golden Hind* (including a drum and banners), but it was more Sir Richard Grenville, an earlier occupant, who stamped his character on the house; he added the intricate plasterwork in the Great Hall.

▶▶ Dartmouth   60A3

An old naval town, attractively set on steep slopes which drop to the River Dart, Dartmouth has real atmosphere, with small craft on the river and in the little harbor and a maze of back streets. The August regatta sees the town at its most exuberant. Beside Duke Street is the arcaded **Butterwalk**, a former dairy market and now a local museum. In the quayside gardens stands the world's first steam pumping-engine, built in 1725 by Thomas Newcomen, a Dartmouth resident. Two Tudor castles guard either side of the harbor entrance; **Dartmouth Castle**▶ has a magnificent view from its roof terrace.

Dartmouth is a good base for excursions, including **Totnes**▶ (best reached by boat) with its Norman castle and steep medieval streets, and **Salcombe**▶, a yachting center with a handsome location on an estuary. Ferries cross the Dart to Kingswear, where steam loco-hauled trips can be taken on the **Dart Valley Railway**.

Early settlers on Dartmoor
The moorland gravels yielded copious quantities of tin, exploited by Bronze Age settlers. Among the most striking of their relics are *Scorhill Stone Circle*, on Shovel Down above Gidleigh (near Chagford), a Bronze Age stone circle of 23 uprights, and *Spinsters' Rock*, off the A382 south of its junction with the A30, a neolithic tomb with its capstone held in place by three uprights.
Grimspound, between Widecombe in the Moor and the B3212, reached by a path up from the road on to Hamel Down, is a large walled enclosure with 24 discernible hut circles.

74

Dartmouth quay: boat trips can be taken up river or out to sea

► **Dorchester** *61B4*

Although not an outstandingly attractive country town in itself, Dorchester is the center of the countryside of Thomas Hardy's novels, in which the town features as Casterbridge; it is often visited for that reason. It has a good local museum celebrating numerous aspects of the county and displaying Hardy's study.

Maiden Castle► is a huge earthwork on the southwestern edge of Dorchester; its massive concentric ramparts date from the 1st century BC.

Dorchester, a typical English country town, little different today from Thomas Hardy's "Casterbridge"

Hardy's Birthplace►, the humble thatched cottage where Thomas Hardy was born in 1840, is reached via a short walk along a track from a parking lot at Higher Bockhampton. To see inside the cottage, you must make an appointment. A marked trail leads to Duddle Heath, a fragment of the "untamed and untamable wild" of the Egdon Heath of Hardy's writings. Although Hardy's body was buried at Westminster Abbey, his heart is buried here in the family plot at **Stinsford Church►**. Close by is the grave of Cecil Day Lewis, a former Poet Laureate.

A prominent tower some 5 miles southwest of Dorchester, confusingly called the **Hardy Monument►**, commemorates Admiral Thomas Hardy, Nelson's flag-captain at the Battle of Trafalgar. From here there's a view over Chesil Beach and the Isle of Portland.

THOMAS HARDY COUNTRY

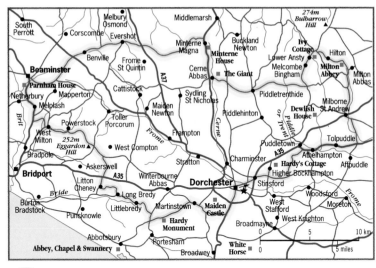

Drive **Thomas Hardy Country**

This tour (approx. 70 miles) explores the heartland of the countryside immortalized in the writings of Thomas Hardy: local life has changed beyond recognition but many elements are still there – thatched villages, rolling downlands, manor houses, ancient monuments.

From **Dorchester** take the A35 east, branching off for **Stinsford▶** and detouring to Hardy's Birthplace at **Higher Bockhampton▶** (see page 75). At **Tolpuddle** the cottage museum pays homage to the Tolpuddle Martyrs who formed a trade union and were transported for their pains. Take minor roads north to **Milton Abbas▶▶**, an 18th-century estate village of rustic thatch and whitewash: the owner of Milton Abbey house nearby (now a school) had the village rebuilt here to improve the view from his house. The abbey church and finely roofed Abbot's Hall are open.

Take lanes west to **Cerne Abbas▶▶** to look at the famous Giant, best seen from an overlook on the A352 road north. Follow the A352 to **Minterne**

Magna, where a turn-of-the-century house harbors a fine collection of trees and shrubs (open in season).

❏ Looming over the demure village of Cerne Abbas is an extraordinary prehistoric hill-carving of a naked club-bearing man (the Cerne Giant) revealing all for the world to see. Its origins and purpose are unclear, but it is thought to be a fertility or cult symbol. ❏

Continue west to **Beaminster▶**, a delightful scene of small-town rural England with an attractive square, and past **Parnham House▶**. Drunken lanes meander southeast through **Powerstock**, attractively placed on a hillside, and past **Eggardon Hill▶**, an impressively bleak Iron Age hillfort site. Continue on through **Littlebredy** and up to the **Hardy Monument▶** (see page 75). Drive east via the B3159 and minor roads to pass **Maiden Castle▶** (parking lot on Dorchester side). The A354 leads northward into Dorchester.

Lulworth Cove, a semi-circular scoop in the coastline

The Fowles connection
At Lyme Regis a sinuous sea-wall known as the Cobb gained fame through the movie of John Fowles's novel *The French Lieutenant's Woman*, where crazed Sarah Woodruff stared out to sea in despair while Charles Smithson explored natural history in the undercliff just west of town. The Cobb is of medieval origin, and the undercliff, still a wild place and riddled with landslips, is designated a National Nature Reserve.

▶▶ **Dorset Coast** *61B4–5*

Dorset's varied seaboard has a refreshing beauty: behind mighty roller-coaster cliffs lie unspoiled hinterlands that seem to have emerged only recently from the primeval past.

Dorset's coast is famous particularly for fossils, no place more than **Lyme Regis**▶, a charming resort beloved of novelist Jane Austen. The narrow lanes and Regency seafront cottages have changed little since her visits at the turn of the 19th century. Huge ammonite fossils can be seen in garden walls and in special fossil stores. The thatched honey-stone village of **Abbotsbury**▶▶ crouches beneath a hillock crowned by a lone chapel; dedicated to St. Catherine, it was once the property of the Benedictine abbey which gave the village its name. A great tithe barn and the swannery (very much alive) are other abbey leftovers. Close by, **Chesil Beach** (or Bank) is one of the most extraordinary features of the British coastline. **Weymouth**▶, an elegant resort with an early 19th-century flavor, made popular by George III, lies behind a curving bay. Further east lies **Lulworth Cove**▶▶, abutted by amazing cliffs that offer ideal cross-sections for the aspiring geologists who flock here along with fishermen, skindivers and walkers heading for **Durdle Door** (see Walks, page 64), a fine natural arch. East of Lulworth, army ranges permit only occasional access to impressively rugged cliffs as far as Kimmeridge. **St. Aldhelm's Head** juts into the sea and has a primitive chapel on its summit. Beyond the seaside resort of **Swanage** lie **Old Harry Rocks**▶, chalk stacks detached from the cliff, and the sands of **Studland**. Seaward, views extend to the Isle of Wight. Inland, the **Purbeck Ridge** offers a panorama of Poole Harbour and the largest of Dorset's heathlands. The ridge is interrupted dramatically at **Corfe Castle**▶▶, where the jagged pinnacle of a Norman castle rises above the gray-stone village.

The Chesil Beach phenomenon
The 18-mile shingle bank was created by the deposit of millions of pebbles through the process of long-shore drift, the lateral shift of material as a result of the waves meeting the shore at an oblique angle. The beach links the Isle of Portland to the mainland and encloses a lagoon known as the Fleet, a peaceful haven for birds. Because of the steeply shelving seaward side of the beach, it attracts anglers (but swimmers must stay clear: this is one of Britain's most dangerous beaches). The pebbles increase in size from west to east.

Tarr Steps, an ancient bridge built of "clapper" stones

▶ **Exeter** 60B3

Prior to destruction in a World War II air raid (one of a series targeted on historic sites), Exeter was one of southern England's most attractive ancient cities. Amazingly the **cathedral▶▶** escaped almost unscathed, and makes it worth the effort to visit the otherwise large-ly rebuilt city center. The twin towers are Norman, its nave displays the longest span of Gothic vaulting in the world. Look too for the astronomical clock in the north transept, the bishop's throne and the intricately carved misericords.

The porticoed **Guildhall** in the High Street is England's oldest municipal building. Within **Princesshay** is the entrance to a 13th-century underground water system, which you can explore by guided tour. The pick of the museums is the **Maritime Museum▶▶** with its collec-tion of over 100 historic vessels brought from the world over; many can be boarded.

▶▶ **Exmoor National Park** 60C3

A small but varied national park, Exmoor encompasses unspoiled coast, moors and quiet farmland straddling the Devon and Somerset borders. The coast is the main focus of interest, but inland there are lonely moors and fine river valleys. Unusually for England, the moors often reach the clifftops, and the Exmoor coast is a fine place for walks, where you can set off on the coast path and return over windswept hillsides.

The Coast Road (A39) In the northwest of the National Park, **Parracombe's Church of St. Petrock▶** is a com-pletely unaltered medieval building, threatened with demolition in the last century but preserved thanks to a campaign led by John Ruskin, influential writer, critic and social reformer. At **Lynton**, a dozy but amiable resort, strangely shaped crags adorn the **Valley of Rocks▶**, where wild goats sniff the sea breezes (see Walks, page 64); **Heddon Valley** is another popular area for walks. A cliff railway connects Lynton with **Lynmouth** below, prettily situated by a small harbor and, in season, it's more animated than its neighbor. Eastward, the River Lyn lines a magnificent wooded valley; you can walk along the river to an idyllically sited café at **Watersmeet▶▶**, at the join-ing of the East Lyn River and Farley Water, or head on to the hills for the best views; close by, the cliffs near

Exeter Arts Festival
Exeter's arts festival lasts for two weeks some time during May, June or July. Classical music, including opera and ballet, predomi-nates but there are also plays, movies, poetry read-ings and children's events.

Countisbury exceed 1,050 ft. and are some of England's highest. **Oare** and **Malmsmead** are at the heart of Doone Country, the setting of R.D. Blackmore's *Lorna Doone*, based on a real family of outlaws who once frequented these parts. **Culbone**, north of the main road, boasts England's smallest church, alone in the woods. **Allerford▶** has a pretty packhorse bridge and a fascinating amateur-run local museum within its old school, while tiny **Selworthy▶** has a group of immaculate thatched cottages and a large church with a fine wagon roof.

Inland Exmoor Sheep and ponies roam the breezy hills, red deer the eastern forests. Over the years the moors have dwindled in extent, encroached upon by farmland and pastures, but recent National Park measures have safeguarded what remains. A road tour from Dunkery Hill to Exford, then to Dulverton and west along the Park boundary to Twitchen gives a good idea of the moor. **Winsford▶**, **Exford** and **Withypool** are three attractive villages in this area; **Dulverton▶** has heaps of small-town charm. South of Withypool, **Tarr Steps▶** is a 1,000-year-old clapper bridge, the finest of its kind in the country, spanning the River Barle. **Dunkery Beacon▶▶** is an easily climbed hill, a 10-minute walk from the road, which on a clear day offers a far-ranging view across Devon and Somerset and over the Bristol Channel into South Wales. **Dunster▶▶** rates as one of the most perfect small towns in England, with its ancient yarn market at the hub of its tapering street of medieval buildings, and the castle towering above. The fashionable 19th-century architect Salvin upgraded the castle interior, but it retains earlier features, including a 17th-century staircase and leather wall-hangings that tell the story of Antony and Cleopatra.

A shopfront in Dunster, an important cloth center in the 16th century

Stag hunting on Exmoor
From Norman times on, Exmoor was a royal hunting forest, and forest laws were enforced by special wardens. The red deer live on, and are the subject of the controversial Exmoor hunts; the Devon and Somerset staghounds are kenneled at Exford, with meets held from August to April. As public opinion increasingly condemns bloodsports, the National Trust, a major landowner hereabouts, recently balloted its members on the subject. The majority vetoed the continuation of the hunts, but the Trust decided against an immediate ban.

79

Sir Francis Drake
English schoolchildren are often told the story of Francis Drake finishing off a game of bowls on Plymouth Hoe before turning his attention to the Spanish Armada. Devon-born, he was the first Englishman to sail around the world and as a darling of Elizabeth I was knighted for his efforts. In 1588 he achieved the great victory over the Armada; the weather played a major role – a third of the Spanish vessels were shipwrecked. This was Drake's last great naval exploit, although he pioneered a leat (channel) bringing fresh water from Dartmoor to Plymouth.

80

▶▶ Glastonbury   61C4

The town huddles around the base of Glastonbury Tor, a green hillock capped by the tower of St. Michael's Chapel. Visible from far around, the Tor was an island in early times, when the sea extended across the Somerset Levels. The **abbey▶** has long been a place of pilgrimage: the Legend of Glastonbury records Joseph of Arimathaea coming and burying the chalice used in the Last Supper. There are links too with Arthurian legend.

▶▶ Longleat   61C5

"We have seen the lions of Longleat" proclaim the bumper stickers; the hugely popular safari park and allied attractions (butterfly park, Dr. Who display and more) have made Longleat a household name. The house, completed in 1580, was ahead of its time: it looks out to its park rather than gazing into a courtyard, with a uniform design on its four sides. Inside are 16th-century tapestries, portraits, and rare manuscripts; 19th-century embellishments— marquetry, fireplaces and gilded ceilings—were added by Italian craftsmen after the 4th Marquess of Bath returned from a Grand Tour. The fascinating kitchen also dates from this period. Capability Brown landscaped the grounds in 1757; they feature the world's largest maze.

The resplendent lower dining room, Longleat House

▶ Plymouth   60A2

A major naval base for many centuries, Plymouth sprawls in a complex natural harbor. After World War II bombing much of the center was rebuilt in a rather solid, monolithic style; head for the old area west of Sutton Harbour, with the **Merchant's House** in St. Andrew's Street and the **Pilgrim Fathers Memorial**. Most famous of all is the waterfront area known as **The Hoe▶**. Here is **Smeaton's Tower**, a re-erected form of the Eddystone lighthouse; close by are the excellent **Aquarium of the Marine Biological Association** and the 17th-century **Royal Citadel**, a vast fortress. West of the center, the two **Tamar Bridges** cross into Cornwall: the graceful 1961 road suspension bridge and Brunel's 1859 railroad bridge.

■ **In Dorset you can walk from Ryme Intrinseca to Beer Hackett; in Kent you can try getting your tongue around Trottiscliffe (pronounced Trozlee); in County Durham you can go to Pity Me; while in Hereford and Worcester there is a village called Upton Snodsbury. England's place-names have amused and bemused visitors and locals alike, inspiring both affectionate parody and rhapsodic poetry.....■**

Historical pointers By the time of the Norman invasion in 1066, the settlement pattern in England was already largely established. Place-names give a host of clues as to how and when England developed. Generally the suffix gives the key element, with the prefix acting as a descriptive defining element—Doncaster, for example, tells us of a Roman camp (*castra*) on the River Don.

Settlers from the East As Saxons began to settle in England, they introduced their own place-names rather than using the existing Celtic ones—the only native place-names to have survived adopted natural features such as hills, rivers and valleys. Early Saxon names included heathen names such as those of gods, for instance Woden (Wednesbury) and Thunor (Thunderfield). The suffix -*ing* survives from that period, particularly in Surrey and East Anglia, while later Saxon names included the commonest suffixes, -*ham* (home) and -*ton* (enclosure, farm or manor).

Scandinavian settlers ensconced themselves in eastern England, where today there are still many names ending with -*by* (Grimsby, Whitby, Wragby, etc): the vast majority are in the eastern counties. Remote areas had names unto themselves: Lympne and Lyminge in east Kent and numerous Cornish names (Trelissick, Marazion, Nanjizal) are unique to those parts. The suffix Chipping (Chipping Campden, Chipping Sodbury, Chippenham, etc) indicates a market place; the word is related to the German *kaufen* (to buy) and appears to be the root of Copenhagen.

Later changes In the 19th century, mining and other industrial settlements created new names—ranging from matter-of-fact New Mills to the intriguing likes of Indian Queens and Booze. The Avon seaside resort of Weston upgraded itself into Latin, and was renamed Weston-super-Mare. The odd euphemism took place—the Devil's Arse cave was tamed to Peak Cavern, and Pigg Hill became Peak Hill. Craven Arms in Shropshire was originally just a pub; a railroad town grew around it and the name stuck.

Place-name quirks
• Some places were merely mapmaker's accidents: Unnear appears on several early 19th-century maps of Mid Wales, but was no more than the corruption of a map-maker's query—Quaere.
• Few 20th-century place-names exist; the new towns of Peterlee (named after a trade union leader) and Telford (after Thomas Telford, the engineer) are exceptions.
• Westward Ho! is Britain's only place-name bearing an exclamation mark.
• Coldharbour (meaning a shelter from bad weather) is the commonest minor place-name.

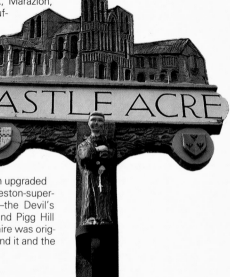

THE WEST COUNTRY

Salisbury Cathedral

▶ **Quantock Hills**　　　　　　　61C4

A forgotten corner of rural England, if there ever was one. The hedges grow high around the sunken, drunkenly crooked lanes, the churchyards hide behind banks of cow parsley, and private manor houses lurk behind estate walls. Villages are sleepy, typically of sandstone and color-washed cottages. Dense woodlands cloak the lower slopes. On the top is a plateau of heather moors crossed by ancient trackways.

Medieval wool-trade prosperity left a legacy of fine churches in the Quantocks: 16th-century carved bench ends are a specialty; the best include those at **Broomfield, Spaxton, Crowcombe** and **Bicknoller.**

William Wordsworth and his sister Dorothy stayed in 1797 at Alfoxton Park at **Holford,** keeping fellow poet Samuel Taylor Coleridge company (see panel). The latter lived for some years at **Nether Stowey▶**, where his cottage has been restored by the National Trust and filled with mementoes of his life and works.

The **West Somerset Railway▶**, the longest private line in Britain, operates steam and diesel trains along the track from Bishop's Lydeard (near Taunton) to Minehead on the coast.

▶▶ **Salisbury**　　　　　　　61C5

Salisbury's **cathedral▶▶▶** is gloriously all of one style, being built mostly between 1220 and 1258 in Early English Gothic. Its noble spire, added 1334–80, soars 404 ft., higher than any other in the country. On clear days, it's worth the effort to climb the tower to the base of the spire. Reached through the cloisters, the octagonal chapter house boasts a superb medieval carved frieze depicting scenes from the books of Genesis and Exodus, and has the best preserved of four manuscripts of the Magna Carta, the first bill of rights foisted by barons on King John in 1215. England's largest cathedral close surrounds the precincts; houses open to the public here are the 13th-century **King's House**, now home to the Salisbury and South Wiltshire Museum (exhibits related to Stonehenge and Old Sarum, ceramics and a pre-National Health Service doctor's office), **Redcoats in the Wardrobe** (regimental museum) and **Mompesson**

Silver sands at Gimble Porth, Tresco, the Scilly Isles

House (NT), a fine Queen Anne house with a walled garden and a rare collection of English drinking glasses. The rest of town, laid out on a spacious grid plan by Bishop Poore in the 13th century, has many attractive corners.

Wilton House►► The 17th-century home of the Earls of Pembroke in nearby Wilton is not on the grandest scale but shows exemplary taste; Inigo Jones designed most of it, including the Double Cube Room, hung with Van Dyck portraits. Here too is the room where some of the D-Day invasion planning took place.

►► Scilly, Isles of 60C1

An idyllic retreat beyond the southwestern tip of the British mainland, the Scillies, as they are often known, comprise five inhabited islands. Each is surprisingly different from the other and there is much to interest the naturalist, particularly birdlife. Daffodils, narcissi, iris and tulips are commercially grown.

Hugh Town is the principal township on **St. Mary's**, the largest island (only 3 miles wide at its maximum girth); Star Castle, built 1593–4 as a fortress against a possible Spanish invasion, is now a hotel. Paths follow the coastline; there is a remarkable concentration of prehistoric burial chambers to explore, while at Peninnis Head are curiously weathered rocks. The island of **Bryher** is windswept, with simple facilities and gorse-clad hillsides that dazzle with yellow in spring. **St. Agnes**, the smallest inhabited island, has an old lighthouse of 1680 (now a private house but still providing flashes). Troy Town Maze, a curious piece of folk art with stones laid out on the turf, may have been created by an 18th-century lighthouse-keeper with time on his hands. **St. Martin's** is treeless, with a prominent day-mark cone (1683) on its highest point, and has splendid beaches; Higher and Lower Towns between them muster a population of around 100. **Tresco**►► is renowned for its sub-tropical gardens of Tresco Abbey, the major attraction of the Scillies, created by Dorrien Smith. The island is fun to explore (no cars, just tractors), with a trio of forts and several white-sand beaches.

Old Sarum
Old Sarum (EH), the original site of Salisbury, was finally abandoned in Norman times because of its exposed hilltop position. Old Sarum Church was founded in 1078, but five days afterwards was struck by lightning and largely destroyed. The town moved to New Sarum (present day Salisbury) soon after, yet up to 1832 it was the classic "rotten borough" represented by two Members of Parliament (including, toward the end, William Pitt) to serve a non-existent electorate. Old Sarum is on the edge of Salisbury.

Scilly practicalities
The archipelago, 28 miles west of Land's End, is reached from Penzance heliport (just out of town on the A330) by a 20-minute helicopter trip, by plane from Land's End aerodrome, or by a 2½-hour boat ride to St. Mary's. There is a good boat service between the other islands. Bicycles can be rented on St. Mary's.

Stonehenge, compellingly immense and silent

Stonehenge – the facts
Stonehenge began as a simple ditch and bank (2800BC); sarsen stones from Wiltshire and stones from the Preseli Hills in Wales were added around 2000BC. In the Bronze Age, around 1600–1500BC, the whole was remodelled with uprights and cross-lintels. The central axis aligns with the sun on Midsummer's Day and other alignments may have enabled the circle to perform a calendar function.

Stonehenge – the enigma
Archaeologists may never know the precise mystical, religious or ceremonial significance of Stonehenge, the reason for its location or why the stones were brought from Wales. More extreme theories have included notions of inspirations from beings from outer space, a creation by King Arthur and his circle of models of male and female sexuality, a bird trap, a model of the solar system, and a cosmic scheme related to the Egyptian pyramids and built by the people of Atlantis.

▶▶ Stonehenge 61C5

Britain's most famous prehistoric stone circle, a World Heritage Site, stands alone on Salisbury Plain, a sparsely populated area of chalk downland that is studded with mementoes of early inhabitants. Its origins and purpose remain a mystery (see panel). Visitors flock here in their thousands; plans are in hand for the rerouting of the main road and for a much-needed upgrading of its facilities.

▶▶ Stourhead 61C5

In 1741, inspired by a Grand Tour of Europe, Henry Hoare II, the son of a wealthy banker, returned home to Stourhead and decided to relandscape his grounds with classical temples, a triangular lake and rare plants. He created one of the highest achievements of English landscape gardening. The Palladian mansion suffered a fire in 1902 but still has good Chippendale furniture, paintings and a library. This and the adjacent village of Stourton are owned by the National Trust.

▶▶▶ Wells 61C4

England's smallest cathedral city is set near the eastern end of the Mendip Hills. The handsome streets of limestone houses are dwarfed by the magnificence of the **cathedral▶▶▶**, significant above all for the richness of its early 13th-century west front (recently restored), adorned with 356 statues. Building started on the choir in about 1180 and finished with the cloisters in 1508, following the designs of Bishop Reginald de Bohun. A problem of subsidence at the crossing was resolved by the remarkable innovation of inverted "scissor" arches, which despite the obvious Gothic provenance look curiously timeless in style. Here too is the world's second oldest clock, with its 14th-century face showing phases of the moon and the position of the sun. The stained glass, chapter house and carving deserve time to be savored in full.

Close by is the moated **Bishop's Palace▶** with its drawbridge and turrets and ruined medieval hall. **Vicar's Close** is the best of Wells' streets. The **Church of St. Cuthbert's** has a fine Perpendicular tower and roof; beasts and angels feature among the roof bosses.

Cheddar Gorge▶▶▶ is the most spectacular feature of

the Mendip Hills, themselves a gently rolling whaleback plateau perforated with limestone caverns, some of which have collapsed to form gorges. A road follows the bottom of Cheddar Gorge beneath the massive gray cliffs; fanciful names have been given to many of the crags. A staircase at the entrance to the gorge, on its south side, leads up to a ramshackle tin prospect tower; views are even better from above. See also Walks, page 64. Also by the gorge entrance are the **Cheddar Caves▶**, of which Gough Cave is recommended for its weird limestone formations. There is nothing much worth stopping for in Cheddar itself, although the medieval market cross is a very fine one.

Axbridge▶ is a pleasing, small town that sees far fewer visitors than Cheddar Gorge or Wells. Its fetching, rather irregular central square is overlooked by the timber-framed King John Hunting Lodge, a 15th-century merchant's house that is now home to a small museum. **Burrington Combe▶** is a lesser version of Cheddar Gorge. During a storm here in 1792, Reverend Augustus Toplady sheltered beneath a rock and composed the hymn "Rock of Ages." **Dolebury Warren▶**, a grassy ridge between Burrington Combe and the A38, has splendid views from its Iron Age hillfort, extending over the Severn Estuary to South Wales and southwards toward Bath. Jutting out into the Severn Estuary just south of Weston-super-Mare, **Brean Down▶▶** gives phenomenal four-way views of hills and estuary; this too has the site of an ancient hillfort on its summit.

Wookey Hole▶ is a colorfully lit cavern, said to have housed the witch of Wookey (her alabaster ball and comb and the bones of her goat are kept in the town museum in Wells). It's a fun place to bring children, with waxworks and vintage penny-in-the-slot machines by the exit.

Cheddar cheese
Cheddar itself is of course best known for Cheddar cheese. The hard cows' milk cheese was first made here in the early 12th century, perhaps even earlier. The traditional method is to "cheddar" or cut the firm curd into small pieces and to drain the whey before packing the residual matter into cylinders some 12–15 inches in diameter; the cheese is then wrapped in cheesecloth and coated with wax. It is left to mature (originally this was done in local caves) for anything from three months to two years according to the strength desired.

85

Fairground rides, in the old Papermill at Wookey Hole

SOUTHERN ENGLAND

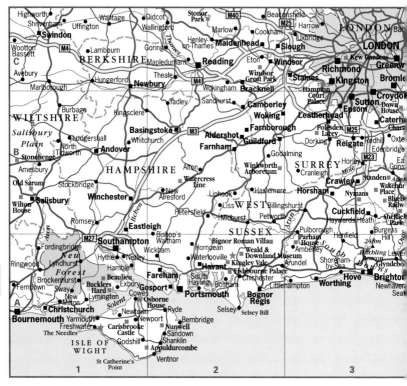

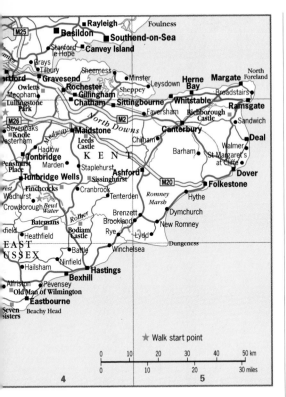

Southern England The southeastern counties make up a comparatively affluent corner of Britain. Proximity to the capital and a green-belt policy restricting growth around London have pushed up property prices in that cherished ring of countryside, so that the villages have become affluent commuter caches; beyond the green belt spreads a sizeable stretch of suburbia. Yet for all the urban pressures, the region has surprisingly deep pockets of rural countryside; west Kent, southern Surrey and much of Sussex represent some of the most varied lowlands in Britain.

The Weald The area between the North and South Downs is known as the Weald, a word related to the German word *Wald*, or "forest," which suggests an area once covered with woodlands; even today the tree cover is appreciable, but pasture fields, enclosed by hedgerows, are the predominant feature. A mirror-image geology makes the Weald easy to comprehend: the two outlying flanks of chalk downs are the remants of a great chalk dome that once covered southern England; it has been breached in the middle and the underlying greensand exposed, appearing as ridges running through Kent and Surrey; Wealden clays cover the low levels in between the hills. Accordingly, the Wealden landscape is complicated and varied, a patchwork of hedge-lined pastures, small woodlands and the odd patch of heathy ground. The North and South Downs rise abruptly from

Wye Down in Kent, part of the North Downs

BEST PLACES TO GO
Historic cities Canterbury, Rochester, Winchester.
Castles and royalty
Berkshire Windsor.
Hampshire Portchester, Solent defenses at Portsmouth, Southsea, etc.
Isle of Wight Carisbrooke, Osborne House.
Kent Deal, Dover, Rochester, Walmer.
Sussex Bodiam, Pevensey.
Roman remains *Kent* Lighthouse and painted house at Dover, Lullingstone Villa (near Eynsford), Richborough Castle (near Sandwich).
Sussex Bignor Villa (near Amberley), Fishbourne Palace (near Chichester).
Small towns Arundel, Chichester, Cranbrook, Faversham, Lewes, Petworth, Rye, Sandwich, Tunbridge Wells.
Seaside towns Brighton, Broadstairs, Eastbourne, Hastings.
Naval heritage Chatham, Portsmouth.
Coastal scenery *Isle of Wight*.
Sussex Seven Sisters and Beachy Head (near Eastbourne), Fairlight Cove (Hastings).
Kent Cliffs between Folkestone and Walmer.

the plain, the steeper escarpments sporting rough grassland, coppiced woods and scrubs. But modern agriculture has removed much of the herb-rich grassland from the South Downs, where the plough has turned downs into flinty fields of earth and crops. Wealden buildings traditionally have timber frames and are often hung with pantiles. Square and circular oast houses, built as kilns for drying hops, are an important feature of the Kentish scene, although they are no longer used for that purpose. Hop-gardens (fields of regimented wooden poles, upon which hops are grown) and orchards are other striking features, though there aren't as many of them as there used to be. The area is particularly rich in grander houses and gardens; the best are listed on pages 16–17 and 102–3.

Kent, Sussex and Surrey Kent is indeed a mixed bag; the north coast is part marshy, part industrial, although the historic dockyard in Chatham and the center of Rochester are attractive. Inland Kent has numerous pretty villages such as Penshurst, Chiddingstone and Shoreham; of its inland towns, Canterbury, Tunbridge Wells and Tenterden stand out, though the county town of Maidstone is undistinguished. On the coast, Dover deserves more than a fleeting glance for its castle, and Broadstairs and (to a lesser extent) Folkestone are pleasant resorts. The **Sussex** shoreline is almost entirely built up, much of it with 20th-century residential development, and the beaches are not remarkable; one interesting place to visit is the De La Warre Pavilion, a Bauhaus-inspired design, in the unlikely setting of Bexhill. The most rewarding coastal towns by far are Hastings and Eastbourne, in contrasting styles but both abutting fine cliffs; and Brighton, a semi-shabby seaside resort, still has tremendous atmosphere, with its Royal Pavilion rating as one of the country's most extravagant follies. Chichester Harbour is the big yacht haven for Sussex. Much of inland Sussex is genteel, with tony villages and lots of historic buildings, teashops and antique shops, as in Arundel,

An old building in Kent is given a new lease of life

There are a number of vineyards in the South, producing highly commendable wines

Amberley and Alfriston. By contrast, the Ashdown Forest in East Sussex is an exhilarating heathland, almost upland in feel; this is the landscape of the Winnie the Pooh stories of A. A. Milne, with idyllic glades and sandy tracks—picnic country *par excellence*. **Surrey**, Britain's most wooded county, has been largely developed into affluent commuter suburbs, but it has some delicious countryside, ideal for walking—notably in the greensand country around Haslemere and the vicinities of Shere and Leith Hill, at 965 ft. the highest point in the Southeast.

Hampshire and Berkshire The county of **Hampshire** rolls gently inland, the best of its country in the far east around Selborne and in the far west by the heaths and woodlands of the New Forest. Winchester has a compact but fascinating medieval center. The coast doesn't have much to offer aesthetically, but Portsmouth has an important naval heritage. Southampton, a large industrial and commercial center that was heavily bombed in World War II, has a few corners of historic interest (medieval town walls, Tudor House and the oldest bowling green in the world) as well as aviation and maritime museums and a fine art gallery. Both these towns, and Lymington, have ferries to the **Isle of Wight**, a pleasant base, with plenty to tempt families and walkers, despite the suburbanization along its eastern coast. The island has an excellent public transportation system (some may prefer to leave the car on the mainland to avoid the expense of taking it on the ferry), and its south coast is one of Britain's sunniest spots.

Berkshire has a split identity, divided north–south by the M4, with downlands merging into Wiltshire and Hampshire to the west, while its eastern edge is Windsor Great Park. At Windsor Castle you can see inside the state apartments of the Queen's favorite residence. Crowds throng the town all year round, and a number of side-attractions have sprung up; you can escape from the bustle by taking a boat trip along the Thames or a walk into Eton or the park. The Thames defines Berkshire's northern border from Windsor to Streatley; the river, which runs down from Buckinghamshire and Oxfordshire, has a placid beauty and a boating scene that can only be in England.

In quitting the great Wen [London] we go through Surrey . . . There are erected within these four years, two entire miles of stock-jobbers' houses on this one road, and the work goes on with accelerated force! . . . What an at once horrible and ridiculous thing this country would become, if this thing could go on only for a few years!
  William Cobbett (1822), *Rural Rides*

We're all having a jolly good time at Ramsgate, At good old Ramsgate by the sea, Plenty of stuff to eat, Plenty of stuff to drink, Plenty of girls upon the "prom" to give you a saucy wink.
  Popular song (1927)

I will go out against the sun Where the rolled scarp retires, And the Long Man of Wilmington Looks naked toward the shires; And east till doubling Rother crawls To find the fickle tide, By dry and sea-forgotten walls, Our ports of stranded pride.
  Rudyard Kipling (1865–1936), on the Sussex landscape.

The Bluebell Line: vintage steam at Horsted Keynes

Brighton's beginnings
In 1754 Dr Richard Russell came to what was then the fishing village of Brighthelmstone and pre-scribed sea water as a cure for a variety of com-plaints; many people took his advice and the village acquired spa status. Georgian and Regency terraces followed as the élite arrived in the foot-steps of the Prince Regent. Once a playground for the rich, Brighton later got a reputation as a rendezvous for naughty weekends; the railroad age added a sleazy element. Graham Greene's novel *Brighton Rock* is based on the seedy world of 1930s gang war-fare.

▶▶   **Bluebell Railway**   86B3

In 1960 the Bluebell was the first standard-gauge steam railroad to be re-opened as a tourist attraction; in many ways it is the pick of the bunch, with some of its carriages dating from the 1890s and the stations evocatively fur-nished with Victorian advertising signs, fire buckets and gas-lamps. Its round trip takes an hour (special restaurant trains and other events at weekends) and currently runs between Sheffield Park and New Coombe Bridge via Horsted Keynes (where there are bus links to East Grinstead, where the line may eventually extend). Sheffield Park Gardens (see page 17), owned by the National Trust, make a pleasant destination.

▶▶▶   **Brighton**   86A3

This is the oldest and perhaps the most interesting British seaside resort, albeit one that may not appeal to every-one. The Prince Regent, later King George IV, came here after his secret marriage to Mrs Fitzherbert and initiated the fashion for seaside vacations and bathing machines. He converted a farmhouse purchased in 1784 into his capricious **Royal Pavilion**▶▶▶, an oriental extravaganza simply bristling with minarets and onion domes; inside, it's just as exotic, one of the most extraordinary interiors in Europe. Chandeliers and gilt glitter, *chinoiserie* trap-pings and rich décor are lavished everywhere.

Despite the obvious decay (itself a Brighton hallmark) of the **seafront**, you can still see traces of its elegant hey-day. **West Pier**, Britain's finest such structure, is sadly derelict and in need of rescue but **Central Pier** is very much alive, with fish-and-chips shops, tacky souvenir booths and fortune-tellers. Summer weekends still draw the crowds to the amusements, aquarium and privately run seafront train, one of the oldest electric railroads in the world. The nude beach, Britain's first, lies discreetly out of sight from the pier; the main beach is shingle. Cream- and sky-blue period streetlamps and white stucco terraces proliferate. The best streets lie to the east at **Kemp Town▶**, an outstanding example of early 19th-century town planning, with a crescent at its hub. To the west, **Hove** has similarly good blocks.

   The Lanes▶ survive from the once humble fishing village of Brighthelmstone; ironically this is now the most chic area of Brighton, with expensive antique shops, sidewalk cafés and galleries in its warren of narrow alleys. Brighton's main **museum▶** has some eye-catching turn-of-the-century furniture and an 18th-century Cabinet of Curiosities.

   A conspicuously attractive town by the South Downs, to the northeast of Brighton, **Lewes▶** is genteel and graced with some very pleasing streets. Many of the timber-framed houses were given a fake brick veneer, fashionable in the 18th century, with the widespread use of "mathematical tiles," thin fascia tiles resembling bricks; these can be spotted at the corners of buildings, where the tiles have come away slightly from the main structure.

91

▶ **Broadstairs**   87C5

The prettiest of the seaside resorts in Thanet in East Kent is Broadstairs; all its charm is concentrated on the seafront, with seven miniature sandy coves beneath low cliffs. It's a combination of sedate resort and fishing port; you can still watch fish unloaded and eat shellfish on the harbor wall. The town has a pleasantly old-fashioned air—right down to the chrome-fitted ice cream parlor preserved on its seafront. Charles Dickens knew and loved Broadstairs well; he spent several summers at what has since been named "Bleak House," where you can see the desk at which he wrote *David Copperfield*.

   Almost joined to Broadstairs, **Ramsgate▶** is more run down: the 20th century has not been kind to it, but it's worth a stroll around for some Regency streets and an outstanding early 19th-century church by A. W. N. Pugin, perhaps the greatest church architect of his day. The coastal walk from Broadstairs to Ramsgate takes about 30 minutes.

Room with a view: Dickens's desk in Broadstairs

Bloomsbury connections
Three places associated with the Bloomsbury Group are found in the South Downs, north of Brighton. *Monk's House* at Rodmell (south of Lewes) was the home of Leonard and Virginia Woolf. *Charleston Farmhouse*, near Alciston, was the home of Duncan Grant and Clive and Vanessa Bell (the latter being Virginia's sister), and its walls and furniture are still decorated with their paintings; the garden is reminiscent of the Bloomsbury days. The Group added further decorations in the form of murals in *Berwick Church*.

Walks

Tennyson Down, Isle of Wight   86A1

Start from Freshwater Bay. The coast path leads west along a grassy ridge, with views of the sea on three sides. Pass the Tennyson monument and continue to the island's western tip; an old fort, Needles Old Battery, gives views of The Needles, a set of rock pinnacles battered by the waves. Return the same way. (2½ hours)

Ditchling Beacon, West Sussex   86A3

Start from parking lot adjacent to Ditchling Beacon. Here the South Downs rise to their third highest point and are capped by the site of an Iron Age hillfort. Follow the South Downs Way west along the escarpment edge. In 2 miles you reach the famous Jack and Jill windmills. Return the same way. (2½ hours)

Bewl Water, Kent/East Sussex border   87B4

Start from visitor center parking lot. An attractive reservoir, Bewl Water is the largest lake in the Southeast and is circled by a well-marked and scenically varied path. It is too long for a day's walk, but pleasant for strolls.

Lullingstone Park, Kent   87C4

Start from parking lot at visitor center off the A225. This is a popular outing for Londoners; trails from the center take in river, woodland and grassland landscapes (about 1½ hours). Longer walks in the vicinity can incorporate the pretty villages of Shoreham, Otford and Eynsford.

Ashdown Forest, East Sussex   87B4

Start at the Poohsticks Bridge parking lot in Ashdown Forest (take the B2026 south of Hartfield 1¼ miles, turning west at junction with minor road; the parking lot is 220 yds. on north side of road). This is the heartland of A. A. Milne's *Winnie the Pooh* stories. A path leads to the bridge where the game of Poohsticks was played; return to the car park, turn right on the road, then left after 100 yds. on a path that rises out of the trees onto heathland (where Piglet supposedly lived). Walk up to the monument to Milne on Gill's Lap: this is the Enchanted Place of the stories, an ideal picnic spot with a view encapsulating the splendor of the 'forest'. Return the same way. (1½ hours)

Poohsticks Bridge, Ashdown Forest

▶▶▶ Canterbury 87B5

Canterbury has witnessed two very dark hours. One was the murder of Thomas à Becket in the cathedral in 1170, the other a World War II "Baedeker raid" in 1942 (so called because targets were historic rather than military). The medieval city center was destroyed but miraculously the cathedral, seat of the Archbishop of Canterbury and the premier church of England, was unscathed.

Yet today the city's sense of history is as compelling as ever. You can walk through the **West Gate** (museum inside), as countless pilgrims have done for eight centuries, and pass a number of charitable hospitals founded in medieval times as places to accommodate pilgrims (St. Thomas's Hospital and the **Poor Priests' Hospital▶** are open to the public, the latter housing the high-tech city heritage museum). The old city center is largely contained within the **city wall**, but just outside lie **St. Augustine's Abbey**, founded by St. Augustine in 597, its church and cloister foundations still apparent, and **St. Martin's Church**, England's oldest church in continuous use and once the headquarters of St Augustine.

The Buttermarket and Christ Church Gate, Canterbury

The **cathedral▶▶▶** precincts are entered by Christ Church Gate, much ornamented with heraldic motifs. The cathedral, built in Caen limestone, boasts several outstanding features, among them Bell Harry, the 230-ft. high central tower, an outstanding collection of 12th- and 13th-century stained glass, a Norman crypt and the Black Prince's tomb. Adjacent is the 15th-century Great Cloister, where you can find a stone marking the deathplace of Thomas à Becket. Just behind the cathedral, Green Court is fronted by the Norman Staircase, the ruins of the monks' dormitory and the graceful buildings of the **King's School**, a prestigious private establishment that counts Christopher Marlowe and W. Somerset Maugham among its former pupils.

The village of **Chilham▶▶** has a handsome half-timbered square, with a church at one end and a castle entrance at the other. The castle (17th-century with a Norman keep) hosts falconry displays and a Battle of Britain museum, and has rose, herb and vegetable gardens.

93

■ **The seaside holiday is one of the great British inventions, which like other good things has spread down the class ladder. In the 18th century the only people who could afford a vacation of more than one day were the aristocracy and the rich. Later, resorts like Bournemouth and Eastbourne were planned to attract middle-class business. The coming of the railroads and the invention of the nation-wide "bank holidays" in Victorian times spurred the development of cheerful resorts for the working class—Blackpool, Margate, Skegness and their like.....■**

Beach belles
When the fashion for sea bathing began in the 18th century, men and women customarily swam naked, but as it spread, so did modesty. The bathing machine carried people, shielded from view, right out among the waves but, even so, women took to wearing all-enveloping flannel gowns tied with a drawstring at the neck. Elaborate Victorian and Edwardian costumes made of flannel, worsted or serge looked much like day dresses, with frilly caps, stockings and shoes. The one-piece swimsuit for ladies came in before World War I, with sleeves and reaching to the knees.

Before the 18th century people occasionally swam in rivers and lakes, but eyed the sea askance. It was dangerous and it tasted nasty. Even in the Royal Navy, a seaman who could swim was a rarity. When seabathing began, it was for health rather than pleasure. A drawing of 1735 shows men and women in the sea at Scarborough, a health spa with a mineral spring on the Yorkshire coast. The spring enriched the local doctors and it seems to have occurred to them that perhaps the rolling ocean so plentifully at hand, the salt-laden water and brisk North Sea breezes, might be profitably exploited as well.

'So bracing' Certainly this was what happened on the Sussex coast, where the obscure fishing hamlet of Brighthelmstone was transformed into glamorous **Brighton**, queen of the briny. A doctor named Richard Russell, who moved there in 1753, proclaimed the virtues of crabs' eyes, cuttlefish bones and woodlice washed down with a hearty pint of seawater. His successor, an Irishman named Anthony Relham, opportunely discovered the salubrious qualities of fresh sea air, heightened, he said, by Brighton's fortunate lack of noxiously perspiring trees.

The effect of all this nonsense was to draw well-to-do invalids and hypochondriacs to the Sussex shore. When the Prince Regent took to visiting and built for himself the glamorous Royal Pavilion, the new resort's success was assured.

Some fishing villages and minor ports grew gradually into resorts, while others were planned for profit by shrewd local landowners and developers. **Llandudno** on the North Wales coast

"For me and my gal" at Brighton.

Carlisle Parade. Hastings

Above: ice cream and beach huts, Walton on the Naze
Below right: just sitting, Brighton Palace Pier

was laid out by the local Mostyn family and remains a charming Victorian resort, lording it over brash **Rhyl** and **Prestatyn**, which were developed later for Lancashire mill-hands. At **Skegness** on the Lincolnshire coast in the 1870s, the Earl of Scarborough built a resort to lure the middle classes, but the Great Northern Railway brought hordes of tourists from the Midlands industrial towns and Skegness became a leading working-class resort. The first in a chain of Butlin's holiday camps opened there in 1937.

Places with a sandy beach naturally cashed in, as did towns with a mild climate and plenty of summer sunshine. The Thames Estuary resorts of **Margate** and **Southend** enjoy Britain's highest July/August temperatures, followed by those along the south coast from Torquay to Folkestone. The highest sunshine figures are held by **Sandown** and **Shanklin** on the Isle of Wight.

"Beside the seaside" Health remained a factor— "Skegness is *So* Bracing," the posters proclaimed—but sheer fun took precedence as resorts sprouted piers and promenades, amusement parks, cliff railways, zoos, excessively flowery gardens, bandstands, dance halls, freak shows, tattoo parlors, tacky postcards, fortune tellers' booths, ice-cream and rock-candy stands to spice up the simpler pleasures of swimming, sunbathing, sand castles and donkey rides. The seaside landlady became a comic cliché, with her iron-bound notions of gentility, strictly regulated mealtimes and green plants in a fussy parlor. On August Bank Holiday Monday in 1937 more than half a million people swarmed into Blackpool in 50,000 motor vehicles and 700 trains, the earliest of which arrived at 3:55AM.

Since World War II, with growing affluence, more cars and much longer vacations, patterns have changed. Some people still go faithfully to the same resort every year. Blackpool and Brighton are both going strong, but most British seaside resorts have not been able to compete with the package tour abroad. Bad publicity about polluted beaches has not helped. The traditional seaside holiday seems increasingly a pleasure of the past.

Piers of the realm
The pier, that familiar feature of the seaside, is descended from the much earlier quay, built to land cargo and passengers on an open shore. In 1823 Brighton constructed its famous Chain Pier, like a suspension bridge tiptoeing gracefully into the English Channel (which destroyed it in a storm in 1896). Though built for boat-passengers to and from Dieppe, it was a pleasure pier as well. It had souvenir booths and a camera obscura and was appreciated as a way of enjoying the sea without being seasick. Sadly, piers are an endangered species now, desperately expensive to repair and maintain.

All the way through
One of the traditional seaside delights is rock, a stick of hard candy that is usually white in color with the resort's name in pink or red letters, mysteriously running through the stick's whole length. Blackpool and Morecambe both claim to have invented the delicacy, but there is also a tradition that it originated in the inland mining town of Dewsbury in the 1860s. As late as the 1970s Blackpool was manufacturing two tons of rock a day in the summer.

The Medway towns

The three Medway towns of Rochester, Chatham and Gillingham together form a large industrial sprawl in the north of Kent. The most historic of these is Rochester. Pre-industrial Rochester is compact but impressive, with a medieval cathedral, an absorbing museum within the Guildhall, and the ruins of a Norman castle giving mighty panoramas over the River Medway below.

Kingley Vale

Europe's largest yew forest spreads over a shoulder of the South Downs, a wonderful ancient-feeling place, dark and eerie, where trees have collapsed and then continued to grow from their horizontal positions, making a bizarre collection of shapes and forms. A nature trail circles the site. The forest's origins are a mystery; could it have been a plantation? Yews were once valued for making bows and arrows. The view from the Bronze Age bell barrows (burial mounds) on the summit extends over Chichester Harbour .

▶▶ **Chatham Dockyard** *87C4*

The historic dockyard here was once a naval center of ship-building and -fitting; today it incorporates Britain's largest concentration of landmarked buildings. Warehouses, ship-building sheds, a dockyard church, and a rope-works and flagloft (the longest brick structure in the world when it was built) have been opened up together with a visitor center.

▶ **Chichester** *86A2*

The cathedral city for Sussex, Chichester, is based on a simple criss-cross layout centered on a fine 16th-century Butter Cross and, with ancient city walls and handsome Georgian streets, it is an enjoyable place to explore. Its medieval **cathedral**▶ (early Norman with Early English additions) is unusual—it's not tucked away in its own close, and it has a detached belfry. The interior has some distinguished modern features: a tapestry by John Piper, a painting by Graham Sutherland and glass by Chagall. The Mechanical Music and Doll Collection is the most off-beat of the city's museums, while Pallant House specializes in modern British art, displayed within an elegant early 18th-century house.

On the edge of Chichester, **Fishbourne Roman Palace**▶▶ is thought to have been built for one Cogidubnus, a Briton who supported the Romans and was made senator. Now much has been recreated, with a dining room, mosaics in full view, and the garden laid out as it probably was. The palace, built in four wings around a courtyard, was begun in AD75, and burned down in 280. The partition walls, heating system, bath and hypocaust have been excavated.

To the southwest of the town, **Chichester Harbour**▶ is a big yachting center. Extending over a huge area, its east side is mostly unspoiled mudflats and complex, marshy inlets. **Bosham** is one of the best places to appreciate the setting: the much-painted village has a picturesque church steeple, waterfront cottages and boating scenes. East Head juts into the southeast corner of the harbor: here sand dunes and saltmarshes make a good setting for an exhilarating stroll. Daily boat tours from Itchenor take 1½hrs (for a recorded timetable tel: 0243 786418).

Due north of Chichester is the **Weald and Downland Open Air Museum, Singleton**▶▶, an excellent rural

The Weald & Downland Open Air Museum, Singleton

Boat-building at Amberley Chalk Pits Museum

museum with reconstructed buildings rescued from all over Kent and Sussex—including a farmhouse, toll cottage, smithy, school and watermill.

A sleepy, unblemished village, much of it thatched, **Amberley▶▶** is beautifully set beneath the South Downs, some 13 miles northeast of Chichester. Glimpse through the churchyard gate to the 16th-century manor within a massive medieval wall; the former residence of bishops of Chichester, the old castle was dismantled by Cromwell's men. It perches on the edge of Amberley Wild Brooks, an area of watermeadows known for its rich birdlife and marshland plants. Near the station at the south end of village, the Amberley Chalk Pits Museum has displays of small-scale Sussex industries and crafts, located in a former chalk pit; here are a blacksmith, potter, boat-builder, printer, narrow-gauge railway, vintage buses, wheelwright and even a collection of antique wireless radios. Nearby is the Elizabethan manor house **Parham House▶**, begun in 1577 by Sir Thomas Parham, who later sailed with Sir Francis Drake to Cadiz; its deer park has lakes and a walled garden.

Arundel▶▶ is a handsome, compact town. The main street climbs from the canalized River Arun up to the sprawling medieval-Victorian castle (home of the Dukes of Norfolk and their ancestors for over 700 years) and the nearby Roman Catholic cathedral. The castle and adjoining park are open to the public. The Wildfowl Reserve just north of town is a great place to observe the birdlife at close quarters from specially constructed blinds. The English cricket season traditionally sees the touring team playing its first match against Lavinia, Duchess of Norfolk's XI at Arundel.

A little to the north, **Bignor Roman Villa▶**, one of Britain's largest Roman houses, has splendid mosaic floors (depicting gladiators, Ganymede and the eagle etc). The villa was occupied during the 2nd to 4th centuries and was discovered during ploughing in 1811. Stane Street, a Roman road now turned into a path, cuts straight across the beautiful downland close by.

Chichester: flint walls in St. Richard's Walk

The Channel tunnel

The project to build a link from England to France has germinated for a long time; diggings were made way back in Napoleonic times. The Anglo-French venture that has finally come to fruition, a railroad tunnel from Folkestone in Kent to Sangatte near Calais, has created a mountain of complications. Naturalists were aghast at the construction waste, dumped beneath the cliffs near Dover. British Rail made errors over a high-speed rail link to London: houses were bought up for demolition, the route was changed and houses remained empty. The recession came, and time and financial estimates went awry. The Eurotunnel exhibition center in Folkestone gives you an overview.

▶ Dover   87B5

The major cross-Channel port since Roman times (when it was known as Dubris), Dover has for long assumed a military role. It was badly bombed in World War II and redevelopment has been lackluster—a wasted opportunity, given its cliff and valley setting. But the famous white cliffs of Dover (a symbol of homecoming for Britons) still beckon across the Channel. The **castle▶▶**, high above the town, stands proud as one of Britain's finest examples of an intact Norman keep; an "All the Queen's Men" exhibition and a model of the Battle of Waterloo enliven its musty interior. The shell of the **Pharos**, a Roman lighthouse, is close by, and Kent's major **Saxon church** (adorned by Victorian encaustic tiles that would look well in a bathroom but ruin the effect here) completes the trio of Dover's finest buildings. Nineteenth-century ramparts and ugly barracks surround the castle, a reminder of its recent military use, and an extensive **tunnel system** under the castle is open to the public. The French coast looks surprisingly near on a clear day: Cap Gris Nez, a chalk headland in Picardie, is the most prominent feature. In the town center, a few Georgian and Regency terraces remain unscathed; the major sight is the **Roman Painted House▶**, with its complex central heating system and its modestly painted walls on display. The **White Cliffs Experience▶** gives an interactive view of Dover's history: you can row a Roman galley and walk through a Blitz-damaged street.

Eastbourne pier, a Victorian confection

The first cross-Channel flight

The cliff walk northeast from Dover passes Blériot's monument, commemorating the first powered flight across the Channel. Louis Blériot (1872–1936), whose early flying experiments included towing gliders along the River Seine, made the historic flight from Calais to Dover on July 25, 1909.

Deal and Walmer▶ are both on the coast to the north of Dover, and both have castles built by Henry VIII in the plan of a Tudor rose. Walmer is all villas and rocky beach; Deal has a pretty ex-fishermen's quarter of narrow streets.

▶ Eastbourne   87A4

A well-heeled town of chintzy hotels, genteel stucco, and brass bands on the promenade, Eastbourne is a neatly preserved example of a middle-class 19th-century English seaside resort. The beach is rocky.

The South Downs end in style just west of Eastbourne at **Beachy Head and the Seven Sisters▶▶**. There's a sheer drop of 525 ft. at Beachy Head, the chalk cliffs towering above a lighthouse. Further west, the Seven Sisters are a series of dry valleys chopped off by the sea to form a roller-coaster cliff. Beware of the unfenced edge.

Alfriston►► is a village with a strong medieval atmosphere, with old-world houses, cafés and antique shops. The 14th-century Clergy House, a pre-Reformation vicarage, was the first building acquired by the National Trust and is a carefully restored half-timbered house with its original clay floor. Adjacent, the church, dubbed Cathedral of the Downs, has good 14th-century features. In the street are two fine inns, the Star and the George, and the stump of a market cross as a memento of busier days. Nearby and best seen from south of Wilmington village is the **Long Man of Wilmington►►**, an enigmatic chalk carving on the downs of a man bearing a staff in either hand. "He" is probably Anglo-Saxon, although no written record before the 18th century has been found. The Norman-Tudor priory in **Wilmington** now houses a worthwhile agricultural museum.

Eastward along the coast from Eastbourne is **Pevensey Castle►**. Its 4th-century Roman fort walls enclose a medieval castle and keep. Nearby William landed in 1066, to launch his invasion of Britain (see panel).

► ▬▬▬ **Hastings**   *87A4*

Hastings itself is an endearingly seedy seaside resort, recommended if you like places of decaying grandeur. St. Leonards on Sea, into which it merges, has some particularly fine and well-cared-for Regency terraces. The picturesque and distinctly spruced-up **old town** lies east of the commercial center; the former fishermen's quarter lies close by a group of curious tall wooden sheds, called deezes, built for storing fishing nets. Several attempts to build a harbor have failed and the fishing boats are still hauled up onto the rocky beach, nowadays by motor. Pleasant walks onto the sandstone cliffs extend eastward to **Fairlight Cove** along a surprisingly wild coastline.

Bodiam Castle►► (NT), 12 miles inland from Hastings, dates from the 14th century. Surrounded by a wide moat filled with water lilies and with walls at their original height, the ruins are substantial enough for one to picture the building at its prime.

The stark, white bluff of the Seven Sisters

The Battle of Hastings
Every British schoolboy and schoolgirl knows the date 1066, when the Battle of Hastings between William of Normandy and King Harold took place at Battle (as it is now called). Oddly, the great turning point in English history was a surprisingly haphazard affair: the English (Saxons) should have trounced the French, who were vastly outnumbered and fighting uphill. However, the Saxons made a strategic blunder in storming downhill when they thought some of the Normans were retreating; this left a hole in the Saxon defenses on the top of the slope, which the Normans promptly filled.

Battle Abbey
William I, "the Conqueror," vowed that if he was victorious he would found an abbey here, on the battlefield where he defeated Harold's English forces; the high altar marks the spot where Harold is said to have fallen, pierced in the eye with a Frenchman's arrow. Today a battlefield trail and an audiovisual display detail the story of the battle. Of the abbey, the gatehouse of 1338 and the east range are still intact.

Some island houses to visit
Osborne House was built as a retreat for Queen Victoria in 1845 and she died here in 1901. The State Apartments provide a rewarding insight into Victoria's lifestyle. Dating from the 18th century, *Appuldurcombe House* is gutted and stands as a spooky skeleton, with a triumphal gateway to nowhere in its Capability Brown landscaped grounds. *Arreton Manor* is a graceful stone house built around 1600, with furnishings and paneling of the period. Among several museums it incorporates is the National Wireless Museum, acknowledging the work of Marconi, who made his pioneering experiments nearby.

100

The Tennyson connection
Alfred Lord Tennyson stayed at Farringford Park House (now a hotel) near Freshwater Bay; his Victorian fan club (autograph hunters and all) tracked him down here and he is still remembered by the monument on Tennyson Down.

Cowes High Street

Sailing past the Royal Yacht Squadron, Cowes

►► Isle of Wight 86A1

The diamond-shaped island is reached by ferry or catamaran from Portsmouth (landing in Ryde), Southampton (landing in Cowes) and Lymington (landing in Yarmouth). Although much built up and geared towards tourism, the isle has plenty of scenic variety, with chalk downs inland and some splendid coastal cliffs. There are enough sights and family attractions to justify a hop over from the mainland.

On the south coast, grassy whaleback hills provide outstanding views for walkers; at the western end of **Tennyson Down►►** (see Walks, page 92) is a set of fragile chalk pinnacles known as **The Needles**. Close by, the multi-colored sands of Alum Bay are sold in souvenir glass bottles of every shape and size. The island's southernmost point, **St. Catherine's Point►**, has a lighthouse open to visitors; St Catherine's Hill is capped by an oratory in the tower of a 14th-century chapel, once used as a beacon. Further north, **Yarmouth►** is the most appealing town on the island, a pretty port with whitewashed cottages and one of the numerous Solent forts built by Henry VIII. The coast and rivers have some attractive marshy landscapes, as found along the **River Yar** and **Newtown Estuary.** The east coast is mostly developed: **Ryde, Shanklin, Sandown** and **Bembridge** are suburban-looking resorts, good spots for low-key vacations though not particularly striking, although Shanklin has preserved its old village near Shanklin Chine, a gorge leading to the sea. **Cowes** has a sailboat atmosphere; in late June the Round the Island Yacht Race features over a thousand competitors and in August Cowes hosts a regatta. **Ventnor** snuggles beneath an undercliff.

The only inland town, **Newport** is the island's capital. Nearby are the impressive remains of **Carisbrooke Castle►►**, one of the best-preserved Norman shells in the kingdom, with inner rooms dating from 1470; Charles I spent time here pending his execution. The castle has Britain's only surviving donkey wheel, once used to haul water from a deep well. Tour buses stop off at **Godshill►**, a pretty village of stone and thatch; it boasts a model village, a toy museum and a natural history center.

► **New Forest** 86A1

The New Forest, in western Hampshire, has survived into the 20th century surprisingly intact. Established in 1079 as a hunting forest for Norman royalty, it still feels incredibly remote. Essentially it is a tract of lowland heath and mixed forest, much in "inclosures" (plantations); it is splendid territory for walking, camping and picnics. There are no major hills, but there is enough variety to spice interest; it tends to be more open on the west side. Wild ponies and red deer are commonly seen; the former graze on heathlands and are owned by Commoners who hold historic grazing rights.

Bolderwood► features an ornamental forest drive and a deer sanctuary, while Lord Montagu's **National Motor Museum**►► at Beaulieu, the finest collection of its kind, celebrates the golden age of automobiles; adjacent are **Beaulieu Abbey**► and **Palace House**►, Montagu's stately home (complete with monorail and vintage bus rides). Just downriver, **Bucklers Hard**► is a picturesque hamlet with a nautical flavor; the story of this former boat-building center is told in its Maritime Museum. **Exbury Gardens** includes a celebrated collection of azaleas, rhododendrons, magnolias and camellias. More offbeat is **Peterson's Tower**, Sway, built in the 1870s to show off the virtues of concrete and now a hotel. The **New Forest Museum** at Lyndhurst sets the scene.

A woodland glade in Rhinefield, in the New Forest

► **Petworth** 86B2

The attractive town features clusters of timber houses and enticing back streets and stands adjacent to the park of **Petworth House**►►. This grand mansion was built by the Duke of Somerset in the late 17th century and has been Percy family property ever since Norman times. Today the National Trust maintains its interior, which includes virtuoso wood-carving by Grinling Gibbons and a superb collection of paintings by J. M. W. Turner (who was a regular visitor), Rembrandt and others.

Squatters' rights
A few scattered thatched hamlets are found in New Forest clearings. Typically such settlements owe their origins to squatters' rights, whereby common land could be occupied by anyone building a house within one day, provided smoke was seen to be rising from the chimney by dusk.

Houses of the Weald

■ **The counties of Kent, West Sussex, East Sussex and Surrey boast a remarkably varied range of houses that are open to the public. Many of those described below make pleasant day-trips from London. Several are included in the Drive on pages 106–7. Some houses may be closed during winter months and it is always worth checking on opening times with local Tourist Information Centres......■**

The National Trust (NT)
The National Trust is a major landowner; it was formed in 1895 to safeguard Britain's places of historic interest and natural beauty. Property it acquires is held in trust for the nation. Many of the NT's hundreds of country houses, gardens and other places of interest are open to the public. Cards giving free admission to any property are available, on payment of a membership fee, from these and from NT information centers, or by mail from PO Box 39, Bromley, Kent BR1 1NH.

Polesden Lacey► (NT), near Dorking, Surrey was built by Thomas Cubitt in 1824 and remodelled in Edwardian times for Mrs Greville, a society hostess. The house has a lovely rural outlook from its North Downs perch, and fine gardens. Collections include photographs from Mrs Greville's collection.

Standen► (NT), near East Grinstead, West Sussex, is a delightful Arts and Crafts house, designed in the 1890s by Philip Webb, a friend of leading artist-craftsman William Morris. It still has its original electric light fittings and has a collection of ceramics by William de Morgan. Towards Tonbridge, **Penshurst Place►►**, Penshurst, Kent, lies amid charming lowland countryside, an outstanding example of domestic 14th-century architecture, owned by the Sidney family, Earls of Leicester, whose forebears include Sir Philip Sidney, the Elizabethan poet. It has a splendid hall with a chestnut ceiling, and a fine long gallery. Nearby **Hever Castle►►**, Hever, Kent, was the birthplace of Anne Boleyn, second wife of Henry VIII. The moated Tudor house owes much of its present appearance to the 20th-century renovation by William Waldorf Astor, a wealthy American. He added mock-medieval features and laid out delightful grounds with great avenues of chestnuts and limes, a yew maze, yew topiary in the form of chessmen, and an Italian garden filled with sculpture. Some 5 miles north, **Chartwell►►** (NT), near Westerham, Kent, was Sir Winston Churchill's home from 1924 until his death in 1965. It is no grand mansion, but a plain, comfortable house filled with mementoes of one of the great men of the century. Be prepared for great

The Italian Garden, Hever Castle

lines on weekends. General Wolfe, general of the British army at the capture of Quebec from the French, was born in 1726 at **Quebec House►** (NT), Westerham, Kent, close by; an exhibition illustrates his role in the campaign that led to British supremacy in Canada.

Penshurst Place, famous for its medieval Baron's Hall

Charles Darwin lived for the last 40 years of his life at **Down House►** near Downe, Kent. Here he wrote his seminal work *On the Origin of Species* (1859), the book that changed mainstream thinking on evolution.

Immediately southeast of Sevenoaks, Kent, **Knole ►►** (NT) is England's largest house, with 365 rooms, 7 court-yards and 52 corridors; little has been altered since the early 17th century. A former archbishop's palace which later fell into the hands of Henry VIII, Knole has been in the hands of the Sackvilles from the time of Elizabeth I. Its sheer size requires mental stamina. The huge deer park is always open to the public. **Ightham Mote►►** (NT), near Shipbourne, Kent, is one of the finest houses of its period in this region, a 14th-century moated building of immense character, with a Tudor chapel with painted ceiling, a splendid Great Hall, and a 14th-century chapel and crypt.

Close by the North Downs in northern Kent, **Owletts►** (NT), near Cobham, is a restrained redbrick Carolean house, which boasts a plasterwork ceiling and a staircase of the same period. Do not miss the collection of memorial brasses in nearby Cobham Church.

Leeds Castle►►, to the east of Maidstone, Kent, was once a residence of Henry VIII but is not as genuine a stately home as some: the furniture and contents were later brought in with the aim of re-creating a country house; but the grounds and building themselves are real enough, and the place has warmth and an idyllic lake setting. About 13 miles south near Goudhurst, Kent (not far from **Sissinghurst**, see Gardens, page 17), is **Finchcocks►**, an early Georgian house noted for its collection of keyboard instruments, while 12 miles south again at Burwash, East Sussex, is **Bateman's►** (NT), the 17th-century house where author Rudyard Kipling lived from 1902 to 1936 and completed *Puck of Pook's Hill* and *Rewards and Fairies*. The mill next door houses one of the oldest water-driven turbines, still grinding flour for sale. Kipling's 1928 Rolls Royce is on display.

The Wealden forests
The Weald has not always been the countryside of fine mansions, charming villages, rich farms and hop-fields that we see today. In centuries gone by, it was deeply forested, its oaks supplying the timber that built the British Navy. The trees were also felled by charcoal burners to smelt the Sussex iron. Patches of this ancient forest remain, in the forests of St Leonards and Ashdown.

103

SOUTHERN ENGLAND

104

Portsmouth's historic ships
HMS *Victory* was Lord Nelson's flagship at Trafalgar; see the appalling living conditions of the crew and the spot where Nelson fell in battle on October 21, 1805. Henry VIII's favorite battleship, the *Mary Rose*, keeled over in 1545 in the harbor, in sight of the king. In 1982 the wreck was brought to the surface and is now kept under special conditions, an intriguing time capsule of Tudor life. HMS *Warrior* was the world's first iron-hulled warship, now restored to its former glory; visitors are free to walk around the four decks.

Naval defenses at Portsmouth
The naval base has been attacked many times and the Solent defenses, developed during Henry VIII's reign and again in the 19th century, are very much part of the landscape. Among those which can be visited are Southsea Castle, built in 1544, which still has tunnels (exhibits include fish-bone ship models made by Napoleonic prisoners of war); Spitbank Fort, out to sea and reached by a short boat trip, with a labyrinth of passages; Fort Nelson at Fareham; and Fort Brockhurst at Gosport.

Nelson's flagship, HMS Victory

▶▶ **Portsmouth**   86A2

A sprawling port and industrial city, heavily bombarded in World War II, Portsmouth is unique among British towns in being built on its own island. This has been a major naval base since the 12th century, and in 1495 was host to the world's first dry dock; at its peak, some 25,000 were employed in building and serving the fleet. In 1982 the South Atlantic Task Force was prepared here for the Falklands War. For the visitor, Portsmouth rates alongside Greenwich (see page 46) as the center for finding out about Britain's maritime history.

The **Historic Dockyard▶▶▶**, close by Portsmouth Harbour Station, is the chief attraction, where a trio of famous warships are berthed (see panel). The **Royal Naval Museum** (entry fee separate, or combined with ticket for HMS *Victory*), charts naval history from 1485 to the Falklands War, and features the stories of the Trafalgar campaign and the Siege of Malta. **Port cruises** operate between April and October, weather permitting.

Eastward lies **Southsea**, an Edwardian seaside resort, where the **D-Day Museum▶** commemorates the allied invasion of Normandy on June 6, 1944 with the sights and sounds of Britain at war and the 260 ft. Overlord Embroidery (a latter-day Bayeux Tapestry). The **Royal Marines Museum** traces the 300-year history of the Marines and has an Arctic display, junior commando assault course and Falklands multimedia theater. Also in Southsea, the **Portsmouth Sea Life Centre** is an innovative aquarium with a ceiling-high "window onto the ocean."

Elsewhere in town are **Charles Dickens' birthplace** (Commercial Road), a three-room museum, **Portchester Castle▶**, from which the Romans co-ordinated the defense of southeast England, the **City Museum** (Museum Road; old shopfronts and more) and **Eastney Industrial Museum**, with two Watt engines, in steam at weekends.

▶▶ **Rye**   87B4

A small, sweet town of cobblestones and timber-framed houses, Rye is perched on a slight rise above Romney Marsh. Mermaid Street is one of the prettiest thoroughfares in southeast England. Originally a Cinque Port (see panel, page 105), Rye now lies inland by some 2 miles. In

Church Square, Rye

medieval times the town was frequently attacked by the French, who set fire to it in 1377; the Ypres Tower is a rare pre-fire survivor and now houses the local museum. The Gun Garden below looks down the River Rother towards Rye Harbour. Novelist Henry James lived at Lamb House (NT) from 1898 to 1916.

To the northeast lies **Romney Marsh▶**. The sea has receded, leaving the marsh, now drained and fertile farmland grazed by chunky Romney sheep. A long way inland, the old Saxon shore is visible as an abrupt escarpment edge; at its foot runs the Royal Military Canal, built in Napoleonic times as a defense. Romney Marsh is sparsely populated but has some good medieval churches, the most memorable, perhaps, being the drunkenly askew church at Brookland, with its detached belfry. Camber Sands offers one of the cleanest and most pleasant beaches in the Southeast.

Winchelsea▶ is a quiet hilltop town just southeast of Rye, still ranged around its medieval grid plan, with many handsome old houses. Some have vaulted cellars once used for storing wine imported from France. Three town gates survive.

Beyond Romney Marsh, the **Romney, Hythe and Dymchurch Railway**, a mere 15-inch gauge, runs between the picturesque hillside town of Hythe (there's a bizarre collection of human skulls in the church crypt) and Dungeness, perhaps Britain's most surreal place, where fishermen's shacks crouch on a vast rocky bank beneath the shadow of Dungeness B Nuclear Power Station (free guided tours).

▶   Sandwich   *87B5*

Though it's of modest size, Sandwich has a remarkably intact medieval center, all the better for being off the tourist beat. Take a walk along the river on the earth ramparts, visiting the Barbican, a toll bridge-cum-gateway. Notable among public buildings are a Tudor guildhall and three medieval churches.

Northwest of town and on the bank of the Stour, is **Richborough Castle▶**, a Roman fort for legions crossing the English Channel and on their way along Watling Street to London and beyond.

Fishing boats on the beach at Dungeness

The Cinque Ports
During the reign of Edward the Confessor (1042–66) a confederation of Channel ports was formed for the defense of the coast and for 300 years these Cinque Ports (French for "five ports") had the monopoly on supplying ships and men for the royal fleet, enjoying certain privileges in return. The original five ports – Sandwich, Hastings, Hythe, New Romney and Dover – were later joined by Winchelsea and Rye, and several other towns were also attached. After the 14th century, as harbors silted up and the coastline shifted, the Cinque Ports declined in importance. Today, only Dover is an active port.

Martello Towers
A feature of the Kent and Sussex coasts is the string of 74 Martello Towers, built 1805–12 to resist a possible French invasion; some are derelict, others are converted to private houses; English Heritage maintains one at Dymchurch, in Romney Marsh (Kent) and opens it to the public in summer.

THE WEALD

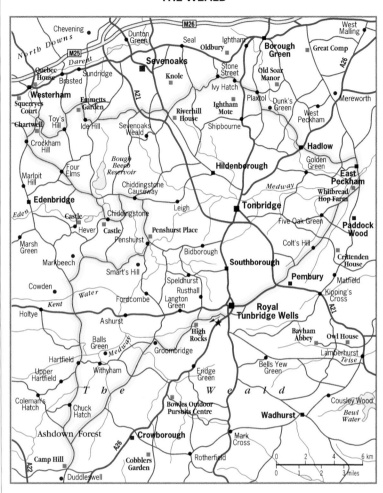

The Pantiles, Tunbridge Wells

Drive The Weald

Starting at Royal Tunbridge Wells, this is a circular tour of approximately 70 miles. You'll see the weather-boarded and pantile-hung cottages, the undulating woodlands and unspoiled farmland of the Weald and you can visit a host of country houses and attractive gardens. Allow plenty of extra time if you plan to stop at all the places mentioned.

Start at **Tunbridge Wells►**, a pleasant old spa town with echoes of its 18th-century heyday, including the delightful Pantiles, a Regency arcade. Leave by the A26, but soon fork right and then left to pass **High Rocks►**, a popular place for climbers.

At **Groombridge** take the B2188 which rises onto the sandy heathlands of **Ashdown Forest►**, the landscape of A.A. Milne's *Winnie the Pooh* stories. Detour south along the B2026 – just before the next junction, Camp Hill on the right is a fine viewpoint. Return north along the B2026 through **Hartfield** and turn off past Cowden railroad station to follow back lanes to **Penshurst►►** known for its great house (see page 102) and picturebook cottages.

Continue on the B2176 and then a minor road to **Chiddingstone►**, where a splendid half-timbered group of buildings owned by the National Trust includes the Castle Inn, close by an eye-catching Gothic castle.

Weave around minor lanes past **Chartwell►►**, Churchill's house (see page 102), through pretty **Ide Hill** village, with its spacious green, around the south side of **Knole Park►►** and close to **Ightham Mote►►** (see page 103). Return via **Plaxtol**, **Hadlow** with its huge 19th-century folly tower and **East Peckham,** where oast houses mark the site of Whitbread Brewery's demonstration hop farm (open).

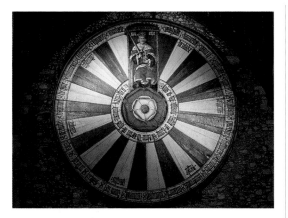

"The Round Table" in Winchester names King Arthur's knights—but was made about 700 years after his death

►► Winchester 86B1

The capital of Saxon England, Winchester became a major religious and commercial center in medieval times. Its importance has drastically ebbed, but its substantial medieval core is well preserved and its long-established College remains one of Britain's great public schools.

Winchester College
Students of Winchester College, one of the country's leading public schools (see panel on Eton College, page 109), are known as Wykehamists, harkening to its 14th-century foundation by the Bishop of Winchester, William of Wykeham. Seventy scholars were here taught classics and other disciplines before studying at New College, Oxford (another Wykeham foundation). The school probably was used as a model for Eton College, founded by Henry VI. Both have quadrangles, a chapel and a hall.

The Watercress Line
Also known as the Mid-Hants Railway, the privately owned 10-mile railroad runs through the Hampshire countryside from New Alresford to Alton (where it connects with British Rail), giving a good feel for train travel in the age of steam. The carriages are old BR ones, the staff dress in period costume and the stations look and feel right. The watercress beds which gave the line its nickname can still to seen around New Alresford and watercress soup is served on the line's evening diner train.

Visitors will spend most of their time in the vicinity of the **cathedral**▶▶▶, the longest medieval cathedral in Europe. It has an outstanding Norman crypt, much Perpendicular work and monuments to Jane Austen and to Isaak Walton, of *Compleat Angler* fame; Walton resided in No. 7 in the **cathedral close**, a charming precinct abutted by the flying buttresses of the cathedral and by the rambling half-timbered Cheyney Court (dating from 1148). Close by is the **City Museum**▶, with a strong Roman section.

The **High Street** and **Broadway** have been the main axis of the city since Roman times. At the top end, West Gate, one of two surviving city gates, occupies a Roman site; a small museum upstairs has a drawing of Wren's scheme for a royal palace (which never got off the ground). Nearby is the Great Hall, where hangs "King Arthur's Round Table," a resplendent medieval fake. Down along Broadway is a 1901 statue of King Alfred, King of Wessex, who is buried nearby, and the Abbey Gardens, a quiet haven close to the Gothic revival guildhall (1871) housing the Tourist Information Centre. The half-timbered **City Mill** straddles the River Itchen near by. In **College Street**, a plaque records the house in which Jane Austen died in 1817, aged 42. **Winchester College**▶ can be visited by guided tour between April and September: it has a "quad" like those found at Oxford and Cambridge university colleges. **Wolvesey Castle**▶ ,a gaunt shell of a bishop's palace built in 1130 and dismantled by Parliamentarians in the Civil War, stands next to elegant **Wolvesey Palace** (1684), which superseded it.

A 15–20 minute walk along the watermeadows to the south brings you to **St Cross Hospital**▶▶, founded in 1136 as a charitable institution, an extraordinary time-warp place with cloistered seclusion, a fine Norman chapel and an antiquated kitchen. By an ancient rule of the charitable trust, Wayfarer's Dole — bread and ale — is still given to anyone who asks for it specifically.

On the banks of the River Test, 10 miles southwest of Winchester, is the pleasant, small town of **Romsey**, well worth a visit for its wonderful Norman **abbey**▶▶ built mainly in the 12th century by Henry de Blois, Bishop of Winchester, and full of little treasures.

Winchester Cathedral, low and exceptionally long

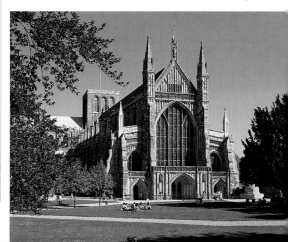

Windsor Castle as seen from Eton College boatyard

►►► Windsor and Eton 86C2

109

The two towns are a short walk apart, separated only by the Thames. It is an easy trip by train from London but it needs a very full day to get around the sights. Visitors to Windsor and Eton often tie in a trip to the gardens at Wisley (see page 16). Open-top buses run between the main sights in Windsor and Eton every 15 minutes.

The pleasant town of **Windsor** is dominated by the presence of the **Castle►►►**, Europe's largest, a Royal Family residence which opens its doors to visitors. Times of the daily Changing of the Guard are posted near by (generally 11AM). St George's Chapel, the hugely popular State Apartments and the extraordinarily detailed Queen Mary's Dolls' House are high points: fortunately these escaped a major fire in 1992.

Other sights in town include Madame Tussaud's waxworks at the **Royalty and Empire Exhibition►** in Windsor railroad station (you can have your photograph taken in old-style sepia, dressed in Victorian gear), an exhibition of the **Queen's Presents and Royal Carriages►** in the Royal Mews Stables, **Frogmore House** (the late 17th-century house of Queen Charlotte and Queen Victoria's mother), a **toy museum** and a display of all the major **crown jewels of Europe** (in replica). **Windsor Great Park** is lovely for **walking**.

Over the river lies **Eton**, its appealing main street in front of **Eton College►►**. The chapel is a very fine example of the 15th-century Perpendicular style, reminiscent of King's College Chapel, Cambridge. The quad also looks like Oxford or Cambridge University colleges. The Museum of Eton Life celebrates the life and times of Eton College.

From **Windsor**, boat trips run to **Bray Lock** in the heart of the **Thames Valley►►**. The river has a classic quality of Edwardian summer days. At **Maidenhead**, fanciful villas and spacious gardens back on to the river; Sunday afternoon walkers stroll along the towpath to **Boulter's Lock**. The village of **Cookham►** has been immortalized by the works of artist Stanley Spencer; a gallery here has a number of his works. **Henley-on-Thames►** is famed as the focus of the Royal Regatta, first rowed in 1839.

The Heart of England This is a region that reflects, as deeply as any other, that elusively diverse nature of the English landscape: for it includes both the Cotswolds, the epitome of rural England, and the more workaday face of the industrial "Black Country," the economic hub of the Midlands.

The Black Country The area known as the Black Country falls within the county of **West Midlands**, which is dominated by the urban sprawl of West Bromwich, Wolverhampton and others; adjacent is Birmingham, Britain's largest city after London. There are tangible signs that Birmingham, nicknamed "Brum," has turned the corner and is witnessing a cultural awakening. Visually it has little to offer apart from a few survivals of Victorian splendor and an extensive canal network (larger than that of Venice) —the city is mostly a jungle of highway overpasses and

BEST PLACES TO GO
**Historic cities and country
towns** *Gloucestershire*
Cheltenham, Chipping
Campden, Cirencester,
Gloucester, Painswick,
Tewkesbury, Winchcombe.
Hereford & Worcester
Bewdley, Hereford,
Ledbury, Leominster,
Stourport, Worcester.
Oxfordshire Abingdon,
Burford, Dorchester,
Henley, Oxford.
Shropshire Bishop's
Castle, Cleobury Mortimer,
Clun, Bridgnorth, Ludlow,
Much Wenlock,
Shrewsbury.
Staffordshire Lichfield.
Warwickshire Stratford-
upon-Avon, Warwick.
Industrial heritage
Birmingham, Didcot
Railway Centre, Ironbridge,
Severn Valley Railway.
Walks Abberley Hills,
Cannock Chase, Chiltern
Hills (see panels on page
115), Cotswold Hills (partic-
ularly the Cotswold Way
and the western escarp-
ment), Clent Hills, Forest of
Dean, Ironbridge Gorge,
Lickey Hills, Malvern Hills,
South Shropshire, Lower
Wye Valley (page 171), the
Wrekin, Wyre Forest.
Village-to-village drives
Chiltern Hills, Cotswold
Hills, Herefordshire,
Shropshire.

19th- and 20th-century suburbs. One spearhead of the revival has been the City of Birmingham Symphony Orchestra, based at the Symphony Hall, which has emerged as one of the world's great orchestras; the D'Oyly Carte Opera Company, which specializes in the satirical Victorian operettas of Gilbert and Sullivan, has also recently made the Alexandra Theatre its home. The National Exhibition Centre and International Convention Centre bring in many business travelers. The excellent Black Country Museum at Dudley evokes life in an indus-trial village in the 1900s, and Cadbury World (the Chocolate Experience) gives a look inside the candy facto-ry established at Bournville by the Cadburys, a Victorian Quaker family. The City Museum and Art Gallery has the world's finest collection of Pre-Raphaelite paintings. Other indoor attractions include Jacobean Aston Hall, the Barber Institute (art collection), the Museum of Science and Industry, Blakesley Hall (a 16th-century farmhouse), the Jewellery Quarter Discovery Centre, Birmingham Railway Museum, Selly Manor Museum and Sarehole Mill (an 18th-century watermill, said to be the inspiration for J.R.R. Tolkien's fantasy novel *The Hobbit*). East of Birmingham, the ancient city of Coventry had its heart knocked out by bombing in 1940, and the ruins of its medieval cathedral stand beside Basil Spence's innovative postwar replace-ment.

The English Marches Shropshire and the old county of Herefordshire encompass a lot of unspoiled countryside, of black-and-white and red-brick villages and of the assertive south Shropshire Hills; it is ideal for those who like to make their own discoveries. To the west it adjoins the even lesser-known, and much less populated Welsh Marches or border-lands. Only the pleasant market town of Ludlow and Ironbridge Gorge, birthplace of the Industrial Revolution, are firmly on the tourist trail; Shrewsbury, Hereford and numer-ous smaller towns and villages such as Much Wenlock and Ledbury are well-kept secrets. Walkers may like to head for the hills around Church Stretton and for the Malvern Hills. The russet-earthed territory of rural Herefordshire, its

The Post Office, Eastnor, below the Malvern Hills

Old musical instruments at Snowshill Manor

113

pastures grazed by docile Hereford cattle, is amiably sleepy and has several outstanding churches, some tucked well away. The former county of **Worcestershire** has the cathedral city of Worcester for its centerpiece.

The Cotswolds and their fringes East of the fruit and vegetable heartlands of the Vale of Evesham, the buildings change color dramatically as one climbs up into the **Cotswolds** (mostly belonging to **Gloucestershire** and **Oxfordshire**). Its honey-yellow stone villages and towns have enchanted generations of visitors; the area is rich in both places to visit and accommodation of all types.

Non-Cotswold Gloucestershire includes Gloucester, Cheltenham and the lowlands abutting the Severn Estuary, the final stages of Britain's longest river. On a waterside site, the naturalist Peter Scott set up the celebrated wildfowl reserve at Slimbridge. In the Forest of Dean, once a coal and charcoal producing area, the villages are not particularly attractive, but there are verdant walks, including the Sculpture Trail (west of Cinderford). The Lower Wye Valley (see under Wales) is close at hand.

The fringes of the Cotswolds harbor some of the greatest visitor attractions of central England, including Oxford, Blenheim Palace and Shakespeare's Stratford-upon-Avon. These are close enough to London for day-trips. Notable arrays of stately homes and manor houses open to the public are found in **Warwickshire** (Baddesley Clinton, Charlecote Park, Coughton Court, Farnborough Hall, Kenilworth Castle, Packwood House, Upton House, Warwick Castle) and **Buckinghamshire** (Chenies Manor, Chicheley Hall, Claydon House, Nancy Astor's Cliveden, Dorney Court, Disraeli's Hughenden Manor, Wycombe Park and above all the trio of Rothschilds' properties— Ascott House, Mentmore Towers and Waddesdon). Closer to the capital lie the **Chiltern Hills**, whose rural enclaves have been carefully preserved by Green Belt legislation and whose villages look distinctly prosperous.

Only the wanderer
Knows England's graces,
Or can anew see clear
Familiar faces.

And who loves joy as he
That dwells in shadows?
Do not forget me quite
O Severn meadows.

Ivor Gurney, "Song" (on Gloucestershire), written in the World War I trenches

▶▶ **Blenheim Palace** *111A3*

This is more of a gilded palace than a charming English country house, impersonal in scale but undeniably impressive, with its sumptuous state rooms, furnishings, tapestries and door-cases carved by Grinling Gibbons. It is reckoned to be the finest true baroque house in Britain.

Blenheim Palace, a vast and sumptuous edifice

Blenheim was built to the design of John Vanbrugh for the 1st Duke of Marlborough, one John Churchill. It was a reward from Queen Anne in recognition of his crushing victory over the French at Blenheim in Bavaria in 1704. More recently, in 1874, it was the birthplace of Winston Churchill, and the contents include some fascinating Churchilliana.

The palace stands in a great park laid out by Henry Wise, gardener to Queen Anne, and later modified by Capability Brown. Leave an hour or two for exploring the numerous walks, beechwoods and formal features that include the Triumphal Way, Italian Garden, ornamental bridge, lake and Column of Victory.

▶ **Bridgnorth** *110C2*

Bridgnorth's site is quite remarkable, astride a sandstone cliff above the River Severn; steep paths and winding lanes connect the high and low towns, together with a cliff railway. Much of the center is a pleasing amalgam of half-timbering and plum-red brick, centered around the town hall (1652). Guided tours leave from the Tourist

Bridgnorth's caves
Ethelward (died 924), grandson of Alfred the Great, is traditionally said to have lived in a cave in Bridgnorth, leading the life of a recluse, surrounded by his beloved books. The four rock chambers he made his home can still be seen near the top of Hermitage Hill (close to the A454); a footpath leads to them. Some former cave dwellings, inhabited up to 1856, can be found near the cliff railway.

Office, Listley Street. Be sure to stroll along Castle Walk, which forms a clifftop esplanade, passing the alarmingly slanting bulk of a Norman castle ruin.

At Stanmore Hall, 2 miles east of Bridgnorth is the **Midland Motor Museum►**, a collection of some 100 vintage vehicles, including 1920s and 1930s classic models.

The **Severn Valley Railway►►**, running between Bridgnorth and Kidderminster, successfully recaptures the style and flavor of long-distance travel of yesteryear. Steam locomotives haul old-fashioned carriages through the lovely countryside of the Severn Valley, giving a 16-mile ride of just over an hour. The stations are particularly well preserved. The railroad runs through **Bewdley►** and has helped put the town on the map. Bewdley's compact center has a legacy of Georgian brick and older half-timbered buildings, similar to Bridgnorth. The highlight is Load Street, which tapers outward by its 18th-century church, sandstone guildhall and Old Shambles (which now contains Bewdley Museum). At its far end, Thomas Telford's bridge (1798) spans the Severn. West of the town lies **Wyre Forest►**, an extensive area of broadleaved woodland, designated a National Nature Reserve. A Forestry Commission visitor center gives information on marked trails. **Harvington Hall►**, near Kidderminster, is a moated Elizabethan manor house with an exceptional number of priest holes, or hiding places, including false chimneys and a false step in a staircase.

Stourport-on-Severn► is an industrial town, but it's given considerable character by its heritage of 18th-century canalside architecture, including a fine warehouse with pristine wooden clocktower. The town stands at the confluence of the rivers Stour and Severn; waterway engineer James Brindley created the canal.

►   **Chiltern Hills**   *111A4*

Stretching some 50 miles from the Thames Valley west of Reading to the vicinity of Luton at their northern edge, the Chilterns are a modest rising of chalk downs to the northwest of London. Although the area is very much part of the City stockbroker belt, once you are clear of the large suburban developments you find yourself in deep countryside, with pretty brick-and-flint cottages, some fine manor houses and pleasant country pubs. The beech-woods that made the area an important furniture-making center at one time are still a distinctive feature of the landscape.

In the grounds of West Wycombe Park

The Ridgeway
The eastern half of the long-distance Ridgeway Path follows the western escarpment of the Chilterns. Near Wendover it climbs over Coombe Hill, where a Boer War memorial marks the highest point in the Chilterns; close by you can glimpse Chequers, the country retreat of British prime ministers since 1921. Ivinghoe Beacon looks over the seemingly endless south Midlands plain. Walks here extend into the woodlands of the Ashridge Estate, past the monument to the 3rd Duke of Bridgewater, the 18th-century canal developer, and to the pretty village green at Aldbury.

More walks in the Chilterns
Between Luton and Whipsnade, the Dunstable Downs is a fine escarpment popular with walkers and kite-fliers; gliders and superb sunsets add to the pleasures. Near Tring, off the Chilterns proper, the Tring Reservoir National Nature Reserve provides plenty of interest in the way of birdlife and canal scenes. Burnham Beeches is a glorious place for fall colors (it is surprisingly easily to lose the way; look out for the helpful maps). The Chess Valley has very attractive walks, with the pretty villages of Chenies, Latimer and Sarratt as focal points.

West Wycombe and the Dashwoods
The most notorious member of the Dashwood family was undoubtedly Sir Francis Dashwood, who set up the Hell Fire Club, a black-magic brotherhood more interested in drinking and whoring than satanic rites. Its meeting places included the West Wycombe Caves (open to the public, just north of the village street), and the hollow gold ball on top of the Church of St. Lawrence. The Dashwood memorials are within the curious roofless, hexagonal mausoleum (1764) next to the church.

As one who long in
    populous city pent,
Where houses thick and
    sewers annoy the air,
Forth issuing on a
    summer's morn to
    breathe
Among the pleasant
    villages and farms
Adjoin'd, from each thing
    met conceives delight.
    John Milton (1608–74),
    Paradise Lost

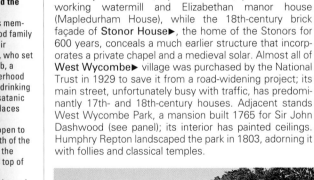

At **Mapledurham►**, by the Thames, you can visit a working watermill and Elizabethan manor house (Mapledurham House), while the 18th-century brick façade of **Stonor House►**, the home of the Stonors for 600 years, conceals a much earlier structure that incorporates a private chapel and a medieval solar. Almost all of **West Wycombe►** village was purchased by the National Trust in 1929 to save it from a road-widening project; its main street, unfortunately busy with traffic, has predominantly 17th- and 18th-century houses. Adjacent stands West Wycombe Park, a mansion built 1765 for Sir John Dashwood (see panel); its interior has painted ceilings. Humphry Repton landscaped the park in 1803, adorning it with follies and classical temples.

The last working mill on the Thames, at Mapledurham

Benjamin Disraeli, the 19th-century Conservative prime minister, lived at **Hughenden Manor►** (NT) just north of High Wycombe; his library and study have been carefully preserved and his character is firmly imprinted on the Victorian house. **Beaconsfield, Princes Risborough, Berkhamsted** and **Wendover** are basically commuter towns today, but each has an old and attractive center.
In 1665 John Milton came to **Chalfont St Giles** as an old and blind man, escaping plague-ridden London to spend a year in a cottage (now a **museum►**) where he completed *Paradise Lost* and began *Paradise Regained.* Close by, traditional Chiltern buildings can be seen at the Chiltern Open Air Museum. In the Chess Valley, **Chenies** is a tiny 19th-century village built for estate workers of the medieval step-gabled brick **manor►** (open to the public) of the Russell family, the Earls and Dukes of Bedford.
Whipsnade Wild Animal Park►►, planned by the Zoological Society of London, is one of Europe's foremost animal collections, located in a spacious park; close by, **Whipsnade Tree Cathedral** was created by Edmund Kell Blyth in 1931 as a war memorial, with trees laid out in aisles, transepts and cloisters.

"Baker's bells," in Southgate Street, Gloucester

► **Gloucester** 110A2

Gloucester's down-to-earth redbrick textures contrast rudely with the dreamy golden hues of the nearby Cotswolds, but the city offers some rewards in its small but absorbing medieval center and its revived 19th-century docks.

Just off the main historic axis of Westgate Street, with its **Folk Museum**, lie the dignified precincts of the **cathedral**►►. From the outside it is a pleasing medieval mishmash; within, its glory is the glass of its east window, one of England's largest, and the 14th-century fan-vaulting in the cloisters, England's earliest. Close by is the **Beatrix Potter Museum**, in the house featured in the Beatrix Potter children's story, *The Tailor of Gloucester.*

Meanwhile, in the **docks** the towering redbrick warehouses have been partly converted to offices, shops and cafés; you can take 40-minute trips around the site on an old Thames craft. Here the **National Waterways Museum**► charts the development of Britain's canals, the entertaining **Robert Opie Collection of Advertising and Packaging**► wallows in nostalgia for vintage ephemera, and the **Regiments of Gloucester Museum** details 300 years of regimental history.

Gloucester's neighbor, **Cheltenham**► is an elegant Regency spa, with its pump room designed in the best 19th-century Greek Revival tradition. A mineral spring was discovered here in 1715, allegedly by observing the comings and goings of a healthy-looking pigeon population; pigeons feature on the town's crest today. Cheltenham later received the royal approval of George III and it acquired its handsome terraces, wrought-iron balconies and leafy thoroughfares. Other attractions are the art gallery and museum, Holst's Birthplace Museum where the composer of *The Planets* was born in 1874, the annual festivals of music (July) and of literature (October), and the racecourse.

To the northwest, **Tewkesbury**►, where the Avon and Severn meet, is a handsome town of high-medieval and later façades. The **abbey church**► is one of England's finest examples of Norman ecclesiastical architecture.

117

Three Choirs Festival
This major music festival takes place in the last week of August and rotates in a three-year cycle between Gloucester, Worcester and Hereford cathedrals. Its origins go back to the early 18th century; from the 1890s three organist-conductors (one from each cathedral) were appointed and a distinguished list of works by some of the country's greatest composers were given their first performance, including *Fantasia on a Theme of Thomas Tallis* (1910) by Vaughan Williams, the *Colour Symphony* (1922) by Bliss, and the *Choral Fantasia* (1931) of Holst. Elgar directed his own music until his death in 1934.

■ **Touring country par excellence, the Cotswold Hills is an area of beautiful honey-colored limestone villages, tucked away manor houses, cottage gardens, russet-earth fields enclosed by drystone walls, and lonely country roads leading to nowhere in particular.....**■

118

South Cotswolds houses
Buscot Park (NT), near Faringdon, is an 18th-century house renowned for its paintings and porcelain. Also near Faringdon is *Great Coxwell Tithe Barn* (NT), built by the monks of Beaulieu and reckoned to be one of England's finest. An oddity is *Woodchester Mansion* (near Stroud), an unfinished Victorian country house.

The Cotswolds present timeless tableaus of rural England. The scenery is pleasant rather than dramatic, with the best of the views from the western edges. There are plenty of hotels, some very high class indeed, and the area is strong on sights (with plenty for children). Wool was the key to the area's medieval prosperity, and the wealth it created is commemorated in a striking legacy of grand churches. Almost every town and village seems to have a Sheep Street.

The area is described in two parts, the one lying south of the A40, the other north.

The south The undoubted capital of the south Cotswolds, Cirencester▶▶ is a handsome town with more bustle than most of its neighbors, and plenty of specialty shops for browsing. In Roman times, only London was bigger than Cirencester (Corinium) and these and later days are celebrated in the excellent Corinium Museum. Dominating the market square is the cathedral-like parish church, with its fan-vaulted porch and grand interior. One of the finest streets is Cecily Hill, the far end of which leads into Cirencester Park (pedestrians only), the grounds of Lord Bathurst's stately home.

Stone-mullioned windows grace the tiniest of houses

South Cotswolds gardens
Among many outstanding gardens are the *Rococo Garden* outside Painswick, *Westonbirt Arboretum* (a Forestry Commission collection of over 17,000 trees), *Barnsley House Garden* (Georgian summer-houses, laburnum walk, herbaceous borders), *Batsford Park Arboretum* (rare trees) and *Miserden Park* (topiary, shrubs, borders and more, in a woodland setting).

The Cotswolds

The Cotswold stone of Calcot

At **Bibury**►► a triple-arched footbridge over the Coln leads to Arlington Row, a group of former weavers' cottages. The former Arlington Mill houses the Cotswold Museum, while the rest of the village is full of unspoiled corners and pretty cottage gardens. The Victorian artist-craftsman William Morris, who with his pre-Raphaelite friends "discovered" the Cotswolds and in 1871 came to live at nearby Kelmscott, declared Bibury to be the most beautiful village in England. More low-key, cozy charm is found in abundance in the **Colns** (Coln St. Aldwyn, Coln Rogers and Coln St. Dennis) and the **Duntisbournes** (Duntisbourne Abbots, Duntisbourne Leer and Duntisbourne Rouse, the latter having a little Saxon church). **Fairford**► prides itself on its splendid "wool church," famed for its late 15th-century stained glass.

Painswick►► has an appealing, sloping knot of central lanes and gray-stone walls; grand houses jostle cheek by jowl with minute cottages. Best of all is the churchyard, dominated by 99 yews; an explanatory leaflet describes the fine 16th–19th-century tombstones. The surrounding area is lush and deep-set, the numerous viewpoints including **Painswick Beacon** and **Haresfield Beacon**. **Slad** is the village of writer Laurie Lee who captured the pre-automobile age so evocatively in *Cider with Rosie*. **Stroud** is not particularly attractive, but just south are some finely sited towns and villages, including **Wotton-under-Edge** and **Dursley**, snug beneath the escarpment, and **Minchinhampton**, on a breezy hilltop site.

Chedworth Roman Villa► (NT), excavated 1864–6, stands alone in the woods near Chedworth and gives an excellent insight into high living of the Roman period; mosaic floors and hypocaust and bath systems have been unearthed. Uley Bury, known as **Hetty Pegler's Tump**, after the wife of its 17th-century owner, is a neolithic burial mound with its stone slabs still in place. You can enter: get a key from the neighboring house.

Family attractions (south)
South of Burford, the *Cotswold Wildlife Park* features white rhinos, tigers and more. At *Prinknash Abbey*, a living community of Benedictine monks, there is a bird sanctuary and pottery. At Northleach are two absorbing attractions, *Keith Harding's World of Mechanical Music* (antique mechanical instruments) and the *Cotswold Countryside Collection* (exhibits from yesteryear housed in a former prison). Further afield, the *Wildfowl and Wetlands Trust* at Slimbridge on the Severn Estuary has a huge collection of wildfowl and *Berkeley Castle* is famous for the dungeon in which Edward II was gruesomely murdered in 1327.

The Cotswolds

Family attractions (north)
The *Gloucestershire Warwickshire Railway* operates steam trains between Toddington and Winchcombe, while the *Cotswold Farm Park* (west of Stow-on-the-Wold) is home to rare animal breeds. Just outside Witney, the *Cogges Manor Farm Museum* offers a look at rural Edwardian life in Oxfordshire, with craft and farming demonstrations.

North Cotswolds houses
Stanway House is a good example of Jacobean architecture, while *Broughton Castle* near Banbury is a moated medieval manor, and *Snowshill* (NT) contains an eclectic collection of bicycles, dummies of Samurai warriors and much, much more. By contrast *Sezincote* was remodelled in the 1800s as an Indian fantasy; the Prince Regent paid a visit in 1807 and found in it inspiration for his Brighton Pavilion. *Sudeley Castle*, an imposing part-ruined stately home outside Winchcombe, was the burial place of Henry VIII's sixth wife, Catherine Parr.

North Cotswolds gardens
The magically hidden-away gardens of *Hidcote Manor*, north of Chipping Campden, are pure joy: a 20th-century creation of a series of "rooms" bounded by hedges and walls. Close by, *Kiftsgate Court Gardens* have rare shrubs and a fine rose collection.

The north In the far north, Chipping Campden►► should not be missed for its showpiece main street, primitive open-sided market hall, the 11-room Woolstaplers Hall Museum and a fine church with Gloucestershire's largest memorial brass. The great manor house of Campden has gone but its Jacobean lodges and gateway remain. Chipping Campden is just large enough to be a town, but its pace is unhurried and its charms preserved without being commercialized. By contrast, **Broadway** is a tourist magnet its elegant (but traffic-ridden) main street well lined with gift boutiques and tearooms. The village lies beneath the Cotswold escarpment on the brink of the Vale of Evesham, a major fruit-growing area with roadside stalls selling produce in season; the abrupt transition from Cotswold stone to Midland red brick is quite striking.

Other quieter sub-escarpment villages nearby have charm in plenty, including **Buckland** and **Stanton**. Within the town center of **Winchcombe►** you can find a gar-

A Cotswold house, perfect foil for a summer garden

goyle-covered church (look for the splendid weathercock) and an old-fashioned ambience; attractions include a folk museum and a railroad museum. Just out of town by the A46, **Cleeve Hill►** is a blustery highland (only 1,040 ft., but it feels higher), a place for strolls, kite-flying and enjoying the view westward to the Malvern Hills (see page 125). **Hailes Abbey►** is a ruin of a 13th-century Cistercian foundation; there is a small museum.

Stow-on-the-Wold and **Chipping Norton** are conveniently placed market towns, the latter with a superb 19th-century tweed mill. **Bourton-on-the-Water** is almost too pretty to be believed; it is the most commercialized village in the Cotswolds, drawing crowds to its model village, perfumery exhibition, model railroad, Birdland aviary, Motor Museum and Village Life Exhibition. By contrast, neighboring **Lower Slaughter►** is an unspoiled delight, with cottages and an old mill overlooking a brook. **Burford** has an impressive church and a distinguished main street lined with stores and inns, sloping down to an ancient stone bridge. Close to Witney is **Minster Lovell►** with its spooky, ruined 15th-century hall.

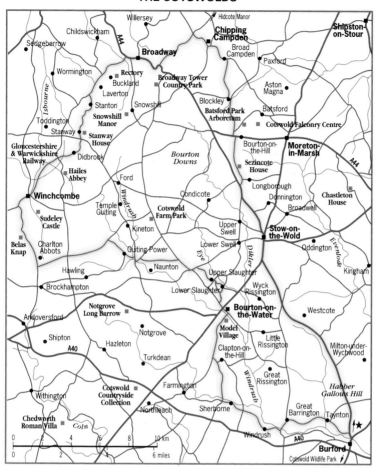

THE COTSWOLDS

121

Drive **The Cotswolds**

This tour promises golden stone-built villages, dignified manor houses and fine views (approx. 55 miles).

Start from **Burford►**, descending the main street, and carry on past **Stow on the Wold** to branch off, past **Sezincote House►►** and **Blockley**, which still has a few of its old silk-throwing mills. Continue to **Chipping Campden►►**; head southwest to the A44 where you turn right (Broadway Tower, a famous scenic overlook is soon off left) to **Broadway**. Take the

B4632 to skirt peaceful **Buckland**; branch off left through **Stanton** and **Stanway** and rejoin the B4632 close to the turning to **Hailes Abbey►**.

Continue into **Winchcombe►**, stopping off for **Sudeley Castle►**. Pass **Belas Knap** prehistoric burial mound and **Guiting Power**. The villages of **Upper Slaughter** and **Lower Slaughter►** lead up to busy **Bourton-on-the-Water**. Finish by exploring the quiet countryside around **Great Barrington**.

THE HEART OF ENGLAND

Cider in Herefordshire
The alcoholic apple drink has a venerable tradition in the county; in former days, many farms produced cider specially for farm laborers. True farmhouse "scrumpy" cider is now a rarity, but the drink has enjoyed a revival in recent years. Bulmer's Cider, one of the largest operations, produces in Hereford (there is a factory shop). A Cider Museum (not part of Bulmer's) displays cider-making methods ancient and modern. Near Pembridge, a village on the Black and White Villages Trail, Dunkerton's Cider is an engagingly rustic outfit, operating from a barn, and Weston's, a much larger company, produces at Much Marcle.

► **Hereford** *110B1*

The capital of the old county of Herefordshire, renowned for its eponymous cattle breed and for cider making, stands pleasantly by the River Wye. An unfortunate inner ring road cuts in too close to the center, but there are nevertheless some good medieval (and later) streets. The highlight is the sandstone **cathedral**►► (begun in 1107) with its library of over 1,400 chained books and its priceless Mappa Mundi, a 13th-century map of the world.

Southwest of the town is **Abbey Dore**►. Only a portion of what was a huge Cistercian abbey church remains, but it gives you an idea of what it was like in its heyday; the Early English work, immense stone altar and 17th-century glass linger in the memory. Nearby **Kilpeck Church**►► is a perfect Norman building, breathtakingly embellished inside and out with virtuoso carvings of birds, mythical beasts and angels. Prudish Victorians removed many of the more salacious, but look for the ones they missed.

Exquisite Herefordshire School carving at Kilpeck

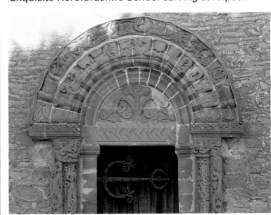

The **Black and White Villages Trail**►► is a well-marked car tour west of Hereford through some beautiful, unspoiled half-timbered villages, including **Weobley, Pembridge, Eardisland** and **Lyonshall**.

At **Shobdon**► the stonework of the old church, which may well have been by the same person who sculpted Kilpeck, was turned into a garden ornament in the mid-18th century for a nearby house; the "new" church built in its place has an interior of wedding-cake "Strawberry Hill Gothick," a style of architecture named after that used in writer Horace Walpole's 1747 house at Strawberry Hill in Twickenham, near London. Further north, **Croft Castle**► (NT) is a fascinating mixture of medievalism and Georgian Gothic.

► **Lichfield** *111C3*

The trio of sandstone spires of the **cathedral**► dominates a gracious close of 17th-19th century buildings. There is much Early English and Decorated work. The west front has 113 statues, including 24 English kings. The city's most famous son was man of letters Dr Johnson (1709–84), subject of Boswell's biography.

Ironbridge Gorge

■ **The wooded gorge of the River Severn gave birth to the Industrial Revolution. What happened at Ironbridge signaled the emergence of Britain as the first industrial nation in the world, and was the catalyst for a dramatic change in the face of the country, as the Midlands and northern England became a great industrial heartland.....■**

Here in 1709 Abraham Darby first smelted iron ore with coke instead of charcoal, making mass-production of iron possible for the first time. The gorge soon filled with industrial activity. Today it is a picturesque, semi-rural area and you have to imagine the racket and smoke of the great ironworks and other industries—but the first-rate **Ironbridge Gorge Museum**, spread over six sites, skilfully brings it all alive. Ironbridge is just south of Telford.

What to see The **Iron Bridge** itself was the world's earliest iron structure of its kind (built in 1779). **Blists Hill Open Air Museum**►►►, the largest site, is a working Victorian town re-created in 42 acres of woodland. There are iron furnaces, a toll-house, period shops, a colliery, a saw-mill and an inclined railroad once used for linking two canals. **Jackfield Tile Museum**►► is housed in a huge Victorian tile factory that had lain abandoned; today it has been re-opened and tiles are put on display. The **Coalport China Museum**►► marks the original site of the Coalport china works, based here from the 1790s until the 1920s; today there is a stunning display of china as well as some early brick beehive kilns. You have to wear a hard hat to enter the gloomy **Tar Tunnel**►, where bitumen was once extracted. At **Coalbrookdale Furnace and Museum of Iron**►►► you are indeed in historic territory, the very spot where Darby sparked the industrialization of Britain.

History today: the daily round at Blists Hill

Ironbridge town rises steeply above the Iron Bridge

Don't miss
There is too much to see in a day in the gorge; if you have only a short time, concentrate on Blists Hill, the Iron Bridge and Coalbrookdale. You can buy separate tickets for each site, or a "passport" that allows return visits on different occasions. Buses run between the sites.

English Heritage
Stokesay Castle is just one of hundreds of historic properties that are in the guardianship of the government organization English Heritage. Its sister organizations are Cadw: Welsh Historic Monuments (for Wales), Historic Scotland (for Scotland) and Manx National Heritage (for the Isle of Man). Properties include prehistoric and Roman remains, medieval castles and abbeys and working industrial monuments as well as some stately homes. Membership in any one of these groups provides free admission to the historic sites protected by all four organizations.

The Feathers, one of the finest examples of 17th-century half-timbering in Britain

Ludlow Castle: the keep, seen from the Tudor stables

▶▶ **Ludlow** 110C1

This is often acclaimed as England's most perfect country town—and it is easy to see why. On its hilltop site its streets spread elegantly out from the ancient butter cross; close by is a local history **museum**, and just behind stands the cathedral-like **Church of St. Laurence**▶▶. Within its soaring interior, the patron saint's life and miracles are celebrated in the great east window, and there is a renowned set of 15th-century carved misericords. Poet A. E. Housman (see page 130) is buried in the churchyard.

Broad Street is Ludlow's most celebrated thoroughfare, with its timber-framed Tudor buildings and 17th- to 19th-century brick façades combining happily along the gentle slope to a gateway at the bottom end. The **Feathers Hotel**, a riot of half-timbering, is the outstanding house of its period. **Ludlow Castle**▶▶, founded by Roger Montgomery, Earl of Shrewsbury, in 1085, was built to withstand both Welsh and Norman incursions; its long list of distinguished visitors includes Sir Philip Sidney, Edward IV and Catherine of Aragon. A Norman chapel within the castle has an unusual circular nave. During the Ludlow Festival in June and July, outdoor performances of Shakespeare plays are held in the inner bailey, attracting large audiences.

Ludlow is splendidly situated for exploring the Welsh Marches, and the South Shropshire Hills (see page 130) are within close reach. **Stokesay Castle**▶▶, near Craven Arms, is an outstandingly well-preserved example of a 13th-century fortified manor house; it was designed with windows unusually large for those lawless times. The adjacent church dates mostly from the 17th century but has a Norman doorway.

▶▶ Malvern Hills 110B2

The jagged Malvern ridge rises between the low plains of Herefordshire and the Vale of Evesham. From a distance it looks like a mountain range; close up it reveals itself as a friendly upland stripe offering superb views from the easily accessible paths along its spine.

Its advantages as a defensive site were exploited by Iron Age man: Worcestershire Beacon (the highest point, 425m) and Herefordshire Beacon are both well-preserved hillforts. To the west there are views of Eastnor Castle, a 19th-century mock-medieval extravaganza designed by Robert Smirke and A. W. N. Pugin in the Gothic Revival style. In the further distance are the hills of the Welsh Marches; to the east is the Cotswold escarpment.

Worcester▶ is famous as the home of Royal Worcester porcelain and Worcestershire Sauce. It was an important center in the Civil War, as you can learn from the exhibition in the Commandery in Sidbury Road, Charles II's headquarters during the Battle of Worcester. The city is a mix of the sublime and the mundane: a fine cathedral (look in for the monuments, crypt, cloister garden and marble pulpit), but insensitive post-war development that mars the center. The county cricket ground, stationed by the Severn with a magnificent view of the cathedral, is a classic place for watching the English summer game.

Just west of Worcester, **Lower Broadheath**▶ was the birthplace on June 2, 1857 of composer Edward Elgar (see panel). The modest cottage commemorates his life with scores, photographs and concert programs.

Malvern Wells and **Great Malvern**▶ lie right under the Malvern Hills. Malvern Water put the area on the map as a spa after a Dr. Wall wrote in 1756 of the medicinal value of the waters. The priory church, the glory of Great Malvern, has magnificent 15th-century stained glass.

Southwest is **Ledbury**▶. The town's broad high street focuses on John Abel's 16th-century half-timbered market house. Pretty Church Lane leads to the church, with its "gold vane surveying half the shire," in the words of locally born John Masefield, former Poet Laureate.

A Royal Worcester vase

125

Sir Edward Elgar (1857–1934)

Elgar's musical education was derived mainly from his experience as a violin player, as a singer at the church where his father was organist, and from browsing the scores in his father's music shop in Worcester. For a long time he felt the musical world was set against him, yet the fact that he was mainly self-taught probably gave him a freshness of vision and made him perhaps the greatest English composer since Henry Purcell. Elgar's early works were recognized only locally but his international reputation was assured when Richard Strauss acclaimed the ever-popular *Enigma Variations* (1899). *The Dream of Gerontius* (1900) enjoyed success in the Three Choirs Festival (see panel, page 117) in 1902. The *First Symphony* (1908) and the *Pomp and Circumstance Marches* (1901–30) won widespread popularity. His music epitomizes Edwardian England in its nostalgic qualities.

Worcester's spectacular Guildhall, dated 1722

MALVERN

Christ Church College

Tom Quad, the main quadrangle, is so called because of Tom Tower, designed by Sir Christopher Wren and named after the bell, Great Tom, which strikes the hour. Ever since 1682, at 9:05PM it has rung 101 times, commemorating the original number of students; this signaled the time for students to be back in college. The 16th-century college hall has portraits of some of the college's distinguished former members, including William Gladstone, Lewis Carroll, John Ruskin and W. H. Auden.

Oxford versus Cambridge

The two universities maintain an ancient rivalry, most obviously displayed in the University Boat Race, rowed on the Thames in west London every spring, and in the Varsity rugby match, played at Twickenham in the fall.

"Oxbridge" subtleties

Oxford and Cambridge universities are referred to jointly as "Oxbridge."
•When steering a "punt," a shallow boat, on the river in Oxford you stand inside the boat; in Cambridge you stand on its platform.
•Only at Oxford does formal academic dress feature a mortar board as well as a gown.
•In Cambridge, colleges have courtyards, in Oxford they are known as quadrangles (or quads).
•At Cambridge, students' academic work is charted by directors of studies; at Oxford the terminology is tutors.
•There are more colleges at Oxford, and they mostly have fewer students than their Cambridge counterparts.

▶▶▶ **Oxford**   *111A3*

What you'll first notice about this, the home of one of the great universities of the world, is its stunning heritage of historic buildings, the number of students swarming around, and the co-existence of a bustling city with large swaths of greenery along the Cherwell and Thames (or Isis) of Christ Church Meadow. As with Cambridge, there is no single campus in Oxford: the colleges are set in cloistered seclusion behind high walls; most are open to visitors in the afternoon.

Most notable among the university buildings are the **Sheldonian Theatre**, built in 1664 as a ceremonial assembly hall, and the **Radcliffe Camera**, a great domed building, now a reading room for the **Bodleian Library**, which contains well over 5½ million volumes. The Bodleian is one of five "copyright" libraries in the United Kingdom, entitled to receive a copy of every book published in the country. The view from the tower of **St. Mary the Virgin**, the university church, extends over the city centre. **Christ Church▶▶**, founded as Cardinal College by Cardinal Wolsey in 1525, is the largest college, has the biggest quadrangle, and its chapel (which predates the college) is England's smallest cathedral; the college picture gallery contains works by Dürer and Michelangelo. **Magdalen College▶▶** (pronounced "Mawdlin") has its own deer park. **All Souls College** has a highly scholarly reputation and admits only graduate students, while **St. John's College** is the wealthiest of all, and has luscious gardens. **New College▶** (founded 1379) has a splendid chapel with a statue of Lazarus by Jacob Epstein. Also seek out **Oriel▶**, **Merton▶**, **Queen's▶** and **Keble▶** colleges, the latter a relative newcomer whose ornamental red-brick buildings are Victorian masterpieces.

Of Oxford's museums, the outstanding attraction is the **Ashmolean▶▶**, a treasure-house of art and antiquities whose exhibits include a 9th-century brooch made for King Alfred. The city's history, both town and gown, is illustrated in the **Museum of Oxford**, while a more gimmicky but populist approach is provided by the **Oxford Story**, where you sit at moving desks on a voyage through the city's past.

Sightseeing **buses** tour the center at frequent intervals; they can be joined at the railroad station and other points.

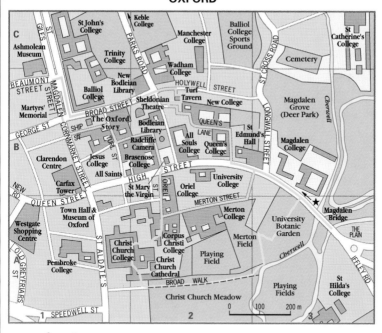

OXFORD

(map labels:)
ST GILES, St John's College, Keble College, Manchester College, Balliol College Sports Ground, St Cross Road, St Catherine's College, Ashmolean Museum, Trinity College, Cemetery, PARKS ROAD, Wadham College, BEAUMONT STREET, New Bodleian Library, HOLYWELL STREET, Balliol College, Sheldonian Theatre, Turf Tavern, New College, Martyrs' Memorial, BROAD STREET, The Oxford Story, Bodleian Library, QUEEN'S, St Edmund's Hall, Magdalen Grove (Deer Park), Cherwell, LONGWALL STREET, GEORGE ST, CORNMARKET STREET, MAGDALEN STREET, SHIP ST, TURL ST, Radcliffe Camera, ALL LANE, All Souls College, Queen's College, Magdalen College, Clarendon Centre, Jesus College, Brasenose College, STREET, University College, Carfax Tower, All Saints, St Mary the Virgin, HIGH, ORIEL, Oriel College, MERTON STREET, NEW RD, QUEEN STREET, Town Hall & Museum of Oxford, Merton College, University Botanic Garden, Magdalen Bridge, Westgate Shopping Centre, ST ALDATE'S, Corpus Christi College, Merton Field, THE PLAIN, OLD GREYFRIARS ST, Pembroke College, Christ Church College, Christ Church Cathedral, Playing Field, Cherwell, JEFFERY RD, BROAD WALK, Christ Church Meadow, Playing Fields, St Hilda's College, SPEEDWELL ST, 0 100 200 m, 1, 2, 3

Walk Magdalen Bridge to the Botanic Garden

Start from Magdalen Bridge, pass **Magdalen College►►** and turn right into Queen's Lane, which weaves past **St Edmund's Hall►** (founded 1220) and **New College►** (1379). Just before the Bridge of Sighs

Oxford's University Museum, on Parks Road near Keble College

(which spans the street), take an alley on the right, passing the Turf Tavern, an old pub with an appealing court-yard. Turn left along Holywell Street and continue past the **Sheldonian Theatre**, with its array of sculpted heads of Roman emperors, and along Broad Street to the **Martyrs' Memorial**, where three bishops were burned for their Protestant beliefs in the 1550s. Diagonally opposite is the **Ashmolean Museum►►**. Double back along The Broad and turn right down Turl Street to the **Radcliffe Camera** and **Bodleian Library**. Cross the High Street, taking Oriel Street, on its south side, to enter **Christ Church►►** by the gate near the col-lege's picture gallery (if closed, con-tinue along Merton Street to the start of the walk), crossing Tom Quad and leaving by the turnstile at the south side of college to follow Broad Walk along **Christ Church Meadow**. The **University Botanic Garden►** is the oldest of its kind in the country.

The canal system

■ **There are few pleasanter ways to explore Britain's scenery, wildlife and history than an easygoing voyage along the inland waterways. The slow, unhurried pace of a narrowboat gives a chance to take a long look at things for once. Canals run through towns as well as the countryside, and supply unexpected perspectives. Spectacular flights of locks, aqueducts, tunnels and bridges, warehouses and workshops, pleasant pubs and inns are the legacy of a time when the canal system seemed to hold the future of Britain's transportation system.....■**

Waterways vacations
Britain's canals are now used primarily for leisure—boating trips, horse-drawn barge trips, fishing, towpath walks. For information about waterways vacations, contact: Customer Services, British Waterways Board, Willow Grange, Church Road, Watford, Hertfordshire WD1 3QA (tel. 0923 226422).

Canal art
During the 19th century a rich tradition of canal art developed. Boat owners covered the boats and their interiors and utensils with a riot of roses and castles, daisies and marigolds in simple patterns and vivid primary colors—a popular art form similar to the one which developed in the same period in traveling fairs.

Some (2,000 miles) of navigable inland waterways have been described as the British tourist industry's best-kept secret. From prehistoric times down to the 18th century, travel by river was generally faster, safer and more comfortable than travel by road. Rivers like the Severn, the Thames and the Trent bustled with boats carrying goods and people, and towns along their banks prospered as inland ports.

The Canal Age dawns The trouble with rivers is that they do not always go where you want them to, they silt up, water levels vary and shallows block navigation, as do periodic floods. Attempts to control and improve rivers were made from early times, and artificial cuts were made to shorten routes, straighten bends and evade shallows. The Canal Age in the 18th and 19th centuries brought much more radical action. A network of artificial rivers was constructed to mesh with the natural waterways and create an efficient system covering much of the country. The canals were the principal arteries of the first stage of the Industrial Revolution.

The first canal of this period was begun in Lancashire in the 1750s to link St. Helens with the Mersey, but much more excitement arose in the 1760s when the **Duke of Bridgewater** ordered the construction of a canal to be built to carry coal mined on his estates at Worsley a distance of (7½ miles) into Manchester. The duke's engineer was an illiterate genius from Derbyshire named **James Brindley**. The Bridgewater Canal was soon extended to the Mersey, linking Manchester with Liverpool. (The Manchester end is now part of the Castlefield urban heritage area.)

Not only did the duke's canal halve the price of coal in Manchester, but the spectacle of canal boats crossing the River Irwell at Barton on an aqueduct, above the barges on the river, fired the public imagination. A bold plan was swiftly hatched to build a canal joining the Trent and the Mersey—Josiah Wedgwood, the great chinamaker, was one of its most eager promoters—from which other canals would run to the Thames and the Severn. This would link Britain's four most important rivers together and provide an inland waterway connection between London, Birmingham, Hull, Liverpool and Bristol. Brindley was the engineer for the Trent and Mersey, which was completed in 1777, five years after his death, and the other components of the plan soon followed.

The heyday The success of the early ventures set off "canal mania," a frenzy that had subscribers flocking to meetings all over the country to invest their money in new waterways. It reached its peak in 1793, when Parliament passed 24 canal construction acts in that single year. One politician of the time said he hoped his grandchildren would be born with webbed feet, since no dry land would be left in England for them to walk on.

A total of 170 miles of canal in 1770 grew to 1,600 miles by the end of the century and 4,250 miles in the 1850s as armies of "navvies" (navigators)—tough, brawling, hard-drinking laborers, the terror of peaceful folk—drove the new waterways across country on giant embankments and through cuttings and tunnels. The earliest tunnels had no towpaths and the boats had to be "legged" through by the crew, lying on their backs or sides, walking along the brickwork.

The canals' brief heyday was ended by the railroads from the 1830s on, and the development of car travel almost finished them off. Even so, some 4 million tons of goods are still carried on the waterways every year, though they are used far more today for recreation.

Narrowboats in the sky
Among the most spectacular engineering feats of the canal engineers were flights of locks and aqueducts. The most famous staircase of locks is probably the Bingley Five Rise on the Leeds and Liverpool Canal, which climbs 60 ft. The most sensational of aqueducts is the superb Pontcysyllte near Llangollen in North Wales, designed by the great Scots engineer Thomas Telford in the 1790s. The canal is carried across the aqueduct for 335 yds in an iron trough almost 12 ft. wide, with an iron towpath set above it. Boats still go across and visitors can also walk across on the towpath.

The Rochdale Canal at Hebden Bridge: boats were once pulled by horses plodding along the towpath

Shrewsbury Castle: its origins are Norman

▶ **Shrewsbury** *110C1*

The town has a natural defensive site, within a tight loop of the meandering River Severn, with a castle to guard the land-linked neck of land. Shrewsbury's charms are less well-known than those of nearby Ludlow, but its collection of Tudor half-timbering and red-brick Georgian, reminders of prosperity brought by the wool trade, is remarkable. Look for example at **Owen's Mansion** and **Ireland's Mansion** (both near the arcaded old market hall), and **Council House Court**: the timber-framing includes decorative cable-molding and quatrefoils.

Finds from the Roman city of Wroxeter (Uriconium), a short way out of town, are displayed in Shrewsbury's **Rowley House Museum**. Robert, Lord Clive (of India) was the local M.P. in the 1760s; you can visit his house (**Clive House**). **Bear Steps**, a tiny alley, looks medieval, with a hall founded in 1389 as a guild for wool merchants.

As you walk around town the odd street names may intrigue you. Butcher Row is self-explanatory (although the butchers are not in evidence), Grope Lane suggests a variety of possibilities but Wyle Cop, where Henry VII had a house, may baffle you—it means "hill top." The meaning of Dog Pole is uncertain: it may have had to do with a low gate or "ducken poll" where one had to stoop to get through.

The **South Shropshire Hills**▶▶ are south of Shrewsbury, the heartland of the territory immortalized in A. E. Housman's 1896 poem *A Shropshire Lad*. **Church Stretton** is the jumping-off point for the **Long Mynd** area, a massif of bracken- and bilberry-clad hills deeply cut by valleys such as Ashes Hollow and Carding Mill Valley (parking available in the latter); these and nearby Caer Caradoc, itself best reached by walking from Hope Bowdler, offer magnificent walking. The **Stiperstones** are a series of quartzite rocks atop a breezy ridge close to **Snailbeach**, where a weird moonscape of white slag heaps is a reminder of a defunct lead industry.

Timber carving in the Square, Shrewsbury

▶▶ **Stratford-upon-Avon** *111B3*

Long since celebrated as the birthplace and deathplace of William Shakespeare, Stratford-upon-Avon is swamped with visitors. The Shakespeare connection looms large at every turn; the souvenir shops are stocked with miniature ceramic models of Anne Hathaway's cottage, there is a shopping mall christened Bard's Walk. For devotees of the Bard the town is a must; but be warned, some find it a disappointment. The attractions can be divided into three categories: the historic Shakespeare sites, the town itself and the ancillary attractions tacked on for visitors who wonder why they have come here. The town is agreeable enough, with plenty of half-timbered buildings and a pleasant boating scene on the Avon; look in Holy Trinity Church for a famous memorial to Shakespeare, quill pen in hand.

An open-topped bus tours the sites at 15-minute intervals (board at any point on its route). The places in town can be easily reached on foot, but the bus is handy if you want to take in Anne Hathaway's Cottage and Mary Arden's House; a ticket (valid for one day only) allows its holder cut-price entry to Shakespeare properties. You can get round them all in one full day if you start early.

Shakespeare's Birthplace

Foremost among the sites maintained by the Shakespeare Birthplace Trust is obviously **Shakespeare's Birthplace**▶▶ itself. Entrance is through a visitor center and the cottage's garden. Inside, an auction notice describes the property ("a truly heart-stirring relic") when it came up for sale in 1847 and was purchased, for £3,000, as a national memorial. A miscellany of Shakespearean bits and pieces makes up the exhibits. Shakespeare's daughter Susanna and her husband Dr. John Hall lived at **Hall's Croft**▶, a rather grander house, now furnished with Tudor trappings and home to an exhibition about medicine in Shakespeare's day and the career of Dr. Hall.

Shakespeare died in New Place, a house adjacent to **Nash's House**▶; New Place is no longer, but an Elizabethan-style knot garden marks the site, and Nash's House itself houses Tudor furniture and exhibits relating to Stratford's past.

A national treasure
Before the auction in 1847, Shakespeare's Birthplace had been in the keeping of two widowed ladies, who had made a good thing out of showing such relics as "the identical lantern with which Friar Laurence discovered Romeo and Juliet at the tomb." The house was a ruinous mess but, spurred by the approaching tricentenary of Shakespeare's birth in 1864 and a rumor that a wealthy American planned to ship the house across the Atlantic, the people of Stratford determined to buy the property. The place was cleaned up, judicious restoration was done and a shilling (5p) was charged for admission. The town can never have regretted its investment.

I know a bank whereon the
  wild thyme blows.
Where oxlips and the nod-
  ding violet grows
Quite over-canopied with
  luscious woodbine,
With sweet musk-roses,
  and with eglantine:
There sleeps Titania some
  time of the night,
Lull'd in these flowers with
  dances and delight;
And there the snake
  throws her enamell'd
  skin,
Weed wide enough to
  wrap a fairy in.
  William Shakespeare, *A Midsummer Night's Dream*

THE HEART OF ENGLAND

Shall I compare thee to a
summer's day?
Thou art more lovely and
more temperate:
Rough winds do shake the
darling buds of May,
And summer's lease hath
all too short a date: . . .

But thy eternal summer
shall not fade,
Nor lose possession of
that fair thou ow'st
Nor shall death brag thou
wander'st in his shade,
When in eternal lines to
time thou grow'st; . . .

William Shakespeare,
Sonnet XVIII

Out of town at the village of Shottery, **Anne Hathaway's Cottage▶** was the home of Shakespeare's wife Anne before her marriage; it is a picturesque thatched timber building that gets full to bursting point at peak times (you may have to line up to get in). Nevertheless the old-world atmosphere has been kept intact, thanks to the Trust's foresight in purchasing the cottage back in 1892. Less hectic, but equally good an example of domestic Tudor architecture (minus the thatch) is **Mary Arden's House▶**, the farmhouse childhood home of Shakespeare's mother, at the village of Wilmcote. This has been set up as a farm and countryside museum, with falconry flying demonstrations, rare farm breeds and exhibits evoking rural life in the last century.

Shakespeare productions are performed at the **Memorial Theatre** by the Royal Shakespeare Company, one of the country's most distinguished theater companies, with a worldwide reputation (for details tel: 0789 269191); the **RSC Collection▶** exhibits over 1,000 props and costumes used for past performances. The company has a London base at the Barbican (see page 46).

Also in town, the **World of Shakespeare** gives a fizzed-up history show of the sights and sounds of Shakespearian England in a 25-minute presentation, while the **Butterfly Farm** re-creates a jungle environment as a setting for some 1,000 exotic butterfly species. Stratford is home to the **National Teddy Bear Museum**.

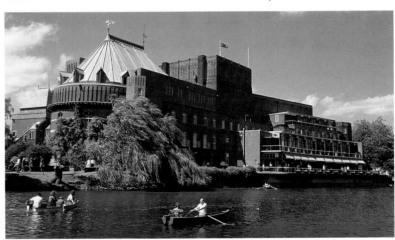

The Memorial Theatre, the Stratford home of the Royal Shakespeare Company

▶▶ **Waddesdon Manor** *111A4*

Ferdinand de Rothschild had this French renaissance-style château built in the Buckinghamshire countryside in the 1870s and 1880s, with no expense spared. It is breathtaking in its opulence—the contents as much as the house itself. Harkening back to the golden days of collecting, the treasures include clocks, Sèvres porcelain, lace and paintings. Within the grounds, designed by a French landscape gardener, are two grand fountains and an aviary. Waddesdon, in the care of the National Trust, is the grandest of a trio of local Rothschild mansions (all open to the public): the others are **Mentmore Towers▶** and **Ascott▶** (NT).

Warwick Castle, seen rising sheer from the river

▶▶ **Warwick** *111B3*

Warwick is a pleasant country town with a magnificent castle that has become one of Britain's most visited stately homes. Indeed, on weekends and at vacation periods your visit may be spoiled by the crowds of sightseers.

The center of the town was rebuilt after a fire in 1694; a walk around **High Street** and **Northgate Street** takes you past some of the finest buildings, including Court House and Landor House. The **County Museum** (admission free) in the market square is a good place to bring children, with displays including natural history, a model of old Warwick and the historic Sheldon tapestry map of Warwickshire; its **Doll museum**, on a separate site, displays antique toys and games. Two of Warwick's medieval town **gateways** survive, complete with chapels. Of these, Westgate Chapel forms part of **Leycester's Hospital▶**, a spectacularly tottering half-timbered range enclosing a pretty courtyard; inside, the main interest is provided by the Queen's Own Hussars regimental museum. Pre-fire features of the collegiate **Church of St. Mary▶** include the fan-vaulted Beauchamp Chapel, with an outstanding collection of Warwick tombs, and a Norman crypt (complete with a tumbrel, part of a medieval ducking stool).

Warwick Castle▶▶ looks at its very best from Castle Bridge, where the 14th-century walls are reflected in the waters of the Avon. There is a walk along the ramparts and, inside, a tour of the palatial mansion takes you from the grim austerity of the original dungeons to the gloomy but sumptuous opulence of rooms later adapted for comfortable living. There are waxworks of a royal weekend party and there is much to explore within the grounds, including a recreated Victorian rose garden, the formal Peacock Gardens and an expanse of open parkland.

Kenilworth Castle
On the western edge of Kenilworth, the huge sandstone castle is the site for events featuring medieval pageantry, drama and music. The castle was built as a fortress in Norman times but was much adapted by the Earl of Leicester, Queen Elizabeth's favorite, whose neglected wife Amy Robsart died nearby in mysterious circumstances (it was never ascertained whether her fall down stairs was murder, accident or suicide). The Virgin Queen was compelled by the resulting controversy to distance herself from Leicester, whom she eventually had executed for treason.

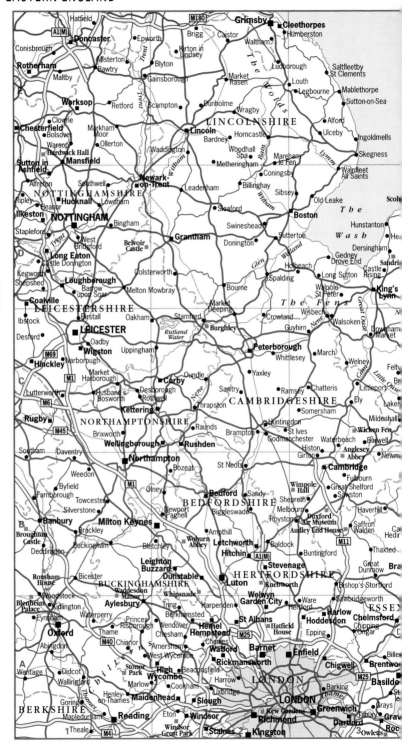

0   10   20   30   40   50 km
0   10   20   30 miles

Burnham Overy Staithe
Wells-next-the-Sea
Cley-next-the-Sea
Blakeney
Holkham
Holkham Hall
nham Hall
arket
Binham
Little Walsingham
Fakenham
oughton all
Houghton Hall
Holt
Sheringham
Cromer
Felbrigg Hall
Mundesley
Blickling Hall
Aylsham
Bure
North Walsham
Bawdeswell
Hoveton
Wroxham
Stalham
Horsey
Potter Heigham
Hemsby
Wensum
NORFOLK
astle
Acre
Castle
Acre
East Dereham
Taverham
Horning
Caister-on-Sea
Swaffham
Yare
Hathersett
Norwich
Acle
Brundall
The Broads
Great Yarmouth
Belton
Reedham
Watton
Wymondham
Loddon
Yare
undford
rime's Graves
Grime's Graves
Attleborough
Long Stratton
Lowestoft
Thetford
Diss
Bungay
Beccles
Kessingland
Waveney
Halesworth
Stradbroke
Blythburgh
Southwold
Walberswick
Dunwich
xworth
Eye
Bury St Edmunds
ckworth
ixworth
Framlingham
Saxmundham
Leiston
Snape
Thorpeness
Stowmarket
Needham Market
Deben
The Maltings
Aldeburgh
SUFFOLK
Gipping
Lavenham
Woodbridge
Orford
Orford Ness
Long Melford
Sudbury
Hadleigh
Ipswich
stead
Dedham
Earls Colne
Stour
East Bergholt
Manningtree
Orwell
Felixstowe
Harwich
The Naze
Colchester
Kelvedon
Tiptree
Wivenhoe
Brightlingsea
Walton on the Naze
Frinton-on-Sea
Vitham
Witham
West Mersea
Clacton-on-Sea
don
Blackwater
Bradwell-on-Sea
uch
Burnham-on-Crouch
ayleigh
Rayleigh
Foulness
Southend-on-Sea
anvey Island
Canvey Island
eerness
Sheerness
Sheppey
Minster
Leysdown   4
Margate
North Foreland   5

The Norfolk Broads: the River Ant near How Hill

Eastern England This region extends from the northern edge of London to the brink of Humberside. There are no uplands: the rural landscape is flat or gently undulating agricultural country, with only the Lincolnshire Wolds, Bedfordshire's Dunstable Downs and Leicestershire's Charnwood Forest rising to any appreciable height. Fields are often prairie-like in scale. It pays to choose carefully where you travel.

East Anglia The most consistently picturesque area of eastern England is East Anglia, the collective term for **Norfolk**, **Suffolk**, northern **Essex** and eastern **Cambridgeshire**: here, above all, the prosperity brought about by the medieval wool trade left a noble legacy of church architecture and villages and towns of handsome timber-framed and plaster-fronted cottages. A specialty of the countryside immortalized by the paintings of Constable on the Essex/Suffolk border is pastel-colored plasterwork ornately decorated with relief patterns known as "pargetting." In Norfolk, flint walls and Dutch gable ends, reflecting former trading links with the Low Countries, are a common sight. Windmills are ubiquitous, the skies are vast and the light effects subtle.

Scenically, the coast is the most appealing part: south Essex is drably built-up around the Thames Estuary, but east of Ipswich the Suffolk seaboard has lots of interest for the walker and naturalist, although the presence of Sizewell nuclear power station is unfortunate. The Norfolk Broads National Park is an excellent place to rent a sail-it-yourself boat. More solitary beauty is abundant along the unspoiled north Norfolk coast. North of Cambridge lie the **Fens**, a vast expanse of fertile, flat, black-soil farmland, formerly beneath water but drained by cuts and sluices; Wicken Fen near Ely gives an idea of what the Fens were like before this great agricultural upgrading.

On a still day, the light can have the delicate outlines of a Japanese picture. On a stormy day, even in summer, the grey sea batters itself against the shelf [of pebbles], dragging the shingle down with a scrunching, grating, slithering sound. To anyone born on the Suffolk coast, this sound has always meant home.
Imogen Holst, *Britten*, in the "Great Composers" series (1966)

The inland shires There are various pockets of interest inland. Hertfordshire has some fine country houses and oases of rural charm such as Ayot St Lawrence and Benington, but Hertford, Hemel Hempstead and others are commuter satellites. **Bedfordshire** has grand houses such as Luton Hoo and Woburn Abbey, but the former hat-making center of Luton and Bedford itself are uninteresting. Northampton is famed for shoe-making, but not for the quality of the countryside in **Northamptonshire**; however, the ironstone villages of Badby and Everdon, and around Rockingham Forest, make for pleasant walking and touring country, and there is an appealing canal scene and canal museum at Stoke Bruerne. Milton Keynes is the newest of Britain's new towns, loosely based on Frank Lloyd Wright's scheme for Broadacre City in the U.S.A., with a low population density and with much thought given to landscaping and separating pedestrians and traffic. **Leicestershire** is endowed with some large country estates and rolling countryside on its eastern side, but further west many of its towns belong to the industrial east Midlands; Leicester, the county town, is an industrial center, though it does have an excavated Roman site within the Jewry Wall Museum and a good Museum of Technology. Belvoir Castle, home of the Duke of Rutland, is one of the grandest of 19th-century statements of wealth and social prominence. **Nottinghamshire** is the county of Robin Hood, although what is left of Sherwood Forest is inevitably smaller and tamer than in the famous outlaw's day; the great country estates known collectively as the Dukeries include Newstead Abbey and others, while Clumber Park is a popular strolling-ground. The writer D. H. Lawrence lived at Eastwood, in the Nottinghamshire coalfield, and his house is open as a museum. Nottingham itself is no great beauty but has an attractive lace market and an excellent crop of museums.

Cambridge and the cathedral cities Visitors come above all to the university city of **Cambridge**, whose colleges and river combine in perfect composition. Former alumni include Oliver Cromwell, John Milton, Isaac Newton, Lord Byron and Charles Darwin. **Ely**, **Norwich**, **Peterborough**, **St Albans**, **Southwell** and **Lincoln** each have splendid cathedrals, abbeys or minsters; of these places, Norwich and Lincoln deserve a longer look.

St. Albans Abbey: much of its brick and flint is Roman

BEST PLACES TO GO
Historic cities Cambridge, Lincoln, Norwich.
Small towns: Bury St. Edmunds, Ely, Lavenham, Little Walsingham, Louth, Newark-on-Trent, Saffron Walden, St. Albans, Southwell, Stamford, Thaxted, Woodbridge, Wymondham.
Coastal towns and villages Aldeburgh, Burnham Overy Staithe, Cley, Dunwich, Southwold, Wells-next-the-sea.
Walks *Bedfordshire* Dunstable Downs, Ampthill Park.
Cambridgeshire Wicken Fen, Cambridge to Grantchester via the river, Grafham Water, Hemingford Grey and St. Ives.
Essex Sea wall at Tollesbury, Epping Forest, Hatfield Forest.
Hertfordshire King's Walden and St. Paul's Walden, Ivinghoe Beacon, Tring Reservoirs, Essendon.
Leicestershire Bradgate Park, Beacon Hill, Burrough Hill, Rutland Water, Grand Union Canal.
Lincolnshire Lincolnshire Wolds.
Norfolk Holkham Gap, Cley, Horsey Mere, Yare Estuary, Sandringham country park.
Northamptonshire Canal towpath at Stoke Bruerne, Knightley Way from Preston Capes to Fawsley Hall.
Nottinghamshire Clumber Park, Cresswell Crags.
Suffolk Southwold, Minsmere, Flatford Mill.

137

The collegiate system

Colleges are the life and soul of the university of Cambridge, just as they are at Oxford (see page 126). The colleges are where most students live, eat and have their supervisions (in which small groups of students discuss their work with teachers). Lectures, examinations and societies are organized on a university basis, but there are comparatively few "university" buildings as such.

Excursions from Cambridge

Wimpole Hall (NT) is Cambridgeshire's grandest house, a formal Georgian composition. It has restored Victorian stables and a large park. Rare breeds of domestic animals and a barn display of two centuries of farm machinery may be seen at adjacent Home Farm. *Anglesey Abbey* (NT), built in about 1600, has impressive grounds laid out this century. *Duxford Air Museum*, part of the London-based Imperial War Museum, claims to hold Europe's largest collection of historic military aircraft.

▶▶▶   **Cambridge**   *134B3*

The home of one of the world's oldest and greatest universities is a city ideal for casual wandering. It is a place of cloistered tranquillity, students on bicycles and riverside beauty, as well as a bustling market town. Many of the best bits are not obvious at first sight; look for obscure entrances into secretive courts and gardens. Respect "Private" notices, but otherwise wander at will. Some colleges close to visitors April through June. The Tourist Information Centre, Wheeler Street, offers guided tours.

The university comprises about 30 colleges scattered around the city, of which 16 have medieval origins. **King's College** has the most famous building; its **chapel**▶▶▶, a symphony of fan-vaulting and magnificent stained glass, is regarded as the finest example of the Perpendicular (15th-century Gothic) style. Nearby, **Clare College**▶ is a formal composition, like a Renaissance palace. The grand Palladian **Senate House** is used for formal functions, including graduation ceremonies. **Trinity College**▶▶ has the largest courtyard in Oxford or Cambridge, and Christopher Wren's famous library (open to the public) in Nevile Court. More modest in scale is **Queens' College**▶, with its half-timbered courtyard and striking painted hall. The Mathematical Bridge here is a wooden structure, constructed without using any bolts—until curious engineers dismantled it and were unable to reassemble it as it was!

The river Behind Trinity and King's, the River Cam slices through a delectable swath of greenery, fringed by neat gardens and lawns; this area is known as The Backs. Punts (boats originally designed for gathering reeds for thatching) can be hired near Silver Street Bridge. Walk south through watermeadows for 2 miles to Grantchester, or head north from Magdalene Street Bridge to watch college rowing crews training.

The **Fitzwilliam Museum**▶▶ (admission free) is a major collection of art, medieval manuscripts, armor and more. The **Cambridge and County Folk Museum**▶ is packed with local memorabilia and **Kettle's Yard**▶ is an idiosyncratic private house and modern art gallery.

The Fitzwilliam: in itself a most imposing building

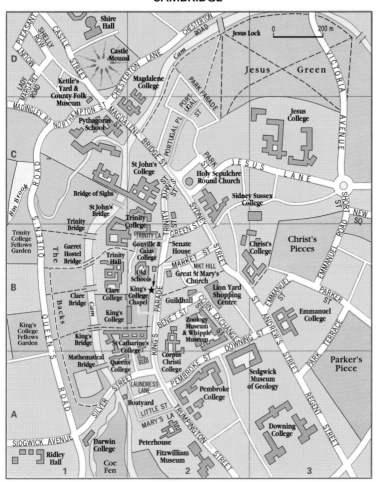

CAMBRIDGE

Walk **The best of the colleges, the river and the streets**

With the **Church of Great St. Mary's** (fine view from **tower▶**) on your left, follow King's Parade (which becomes Trumpington Street). On the right is **King's College** with its superb **chapel▶▶▶**. Pass **Corpus Christi** (its Old Court is hidden at the back) and **Pembroke** (chapel by Wren); farther on are **Peterhouse** (founded 1284, the oldest college) and **Fitzwilliam Museum▶▶**. Enter Little St Mary's Lane, turn right by river (where you can rent a punt). Pass Mill Inn, cross Silver

Street Bridge to pass **Queens' College▶**. Take a path on right across grass for classic views from **the Backs**. Garret Hostel Lane leads over river to Trinity Lane. Turn left past **Trinity Hall▶**. Enter **Trinity▶▶** and St. **John's▶** colleges from Trinity Street; at river, take walkway on right to a footbridge by **Jesus Lock** and turn sharp right across Jesus Green to enter Portugal Street. Return to the start past Norman **Round Church▶** and **Sidney Sussex College** in Sidney Street.

Grime's Graves
A major center of England's neolithic flint industry occupies a site in Thetford Warren, the conifer forest on the low-lying sandy tracts of the Breckland (east of Ely). Over 400 shafts have been discovered; neolithic men climbed down these shafts to work in cramped tunnels, chipping away the flint for use in tools and weapons. One shaft is open to the public.

Wicken Fen
Britain's oldest nature reserve, located south of Ely and now owned by the National Trust, gives an idea of what the fens were like before they were drained. Villagers left the fen undrained to preserve its supply of reeds for thatching; it is in parts wooded, wetland and meadow, with waterways enclosing the site. A nature trail takes you past a re-erected pumping mill, some bog oaks (logs submerged for thousands of years under the fen and recently unearthed) and the birdwatchers' blind, from the top of which Ely Cathedral can just be seen.

▶▶ **Ely** 134C3

The little town is dwarfed by its great cathedral, occupying a slightly elevated site that lets it dominate the pancake-flat Fenland plain for far around. The region is still called the Isle of Ely—a reminder of the days when the town was more or less an island in the undrained marsh. There is surprisingly little to see in town, but the cathedral▶▶▶ ranks among the greats.

Part of the building shows Norman work, including the west front and tower, but restoration was soon needed: in 1250 the east end was rebuilt in Purbeck marble. In 1321 Alan of Walsingham supervised the building of the Lady Chapel; when the central tower collapsed the next year he created the wonderful octagonal lantern, lodged on eight oak pillars, that graces the building today (divine intervention must have prevented a further collapse: the structure has alarmingly little to support it). Attached to the cathedral are a stained-glass museum and a brass-rubbing center. Around the precincts are the houses of the King's School, an eminent "public" school founded by Henry VIII.

The River Ouse at Ely

▶ **King's Lynn** 134D3

Once a member of the Hanseatic League, a powerful commercial association of towns in northern Germany formed in the 14th century, King's Lynn still has a slightly Continental look in its darkened red-brick buildings. It traded with northern Europe for many centuries and its docks and industrial area are still very much functional. St. George's Guildhall (1420) is the oldest guildhall in England, and has a splendid beamed roof; this and twin-towered St. Margaret's Church (Norman, with fine memorial brasses) make a visit to the town worthwhile.

The villages of **Castle Rising** and **Castle Acre**▶, respectively 4 miles north and 13 miles east of King's Lynn, both have an impressive Norman castle. West of Castle Acre, the priory church of a Cluniac foundation survives almost intact.

Fenland churches▶▶ Among the finest of these are **Walpole St. Peter**, with superb benches, font and pulpit, and **Walsoken**, a Norman church with a magnificent roof and a 16th-century wall-painting of the Judgment of Solomon.

Lincoln's Steep Hill, in the most ancient part of the city

Museums in Lincoln
Lincoln's indoor attractions include the *City and County Museum*, local history within a medieval friary; the *Museum of Lincolnshire Life*, with a sizeable collection of horse-drawn vehicles, and domestic and agricultural bygones; the *National Cycle Museum*, with over 140 machines dating from the 1820s; and the *Usher Hall Gallery*, which exhibits applied arts, including a noted collection of watches, memorabilia relating to poet Alfred, Lord Tennyson (born at Somersby in the Lincolnshire Wolds) and paintings by Lincolnshire watercolorist Peter de Wint.

▶▶▶ Lincoln   134E2

The massive towers of Lincoln's superb cathedral soar high from a hilltop site. The cathedral, castle, museums and historic streets provide plenty of attractions for a full-day visit. However, outside the small historic core much of the city is quite undistinguished.

The cathedral▶▶▶, one of England's finest, was largely rebuilt in the 13th and 14th centuries after an earthquake in 1185 destroyed an earlier structure. Highlights are the elaborate west façade, the carved choir stalls and the stained-glass rose windows, the Dean's Eye and the Bishop's Eye. High up, the Lincolnshire Imp steals the show; the story goes that he got too close to the angels and was turned to stone for his sins. Steps lead up the central tower to a viewing spot.

Minster Yard, the cathedral close, has Georgian and medieval houses. **Steep Hill** lives up to its name, climbing from the River Witham, past the Jew's House, inhabited from Norman times, and continuing beyond the cathedral as **Bailgate**. The street is spanned by Newport Arch, a Roman gateway into the city. Opposite the cathedral's west façade, **Exchequergate** leads to **Lincoln Castle▶** which dates from Norman times and has thick walls, gateways, towers and a 19th-century prisoners' chapel.

Spalding
A major bulb-growing center in the Fens, Spalding hosts the Flower Parade every May. It's one of the great free shows of eastern England, where often as many as three million tulips are used to decorate the floats in a procession accompanied by bands and general bonhomie. Springfield Gardens, a tulip and rose grower, hosts the parade and has fine shows of hyacinths, tulips and narcissi.

▶ Norfolk Broads National Park   135C5

Ever popular with boat enthusiasts and birdwatchers, the National Park is an area of reedy lakes (called "broads"), waterways and fertile fens formed from flooded peat-diggings; windmills, erected to pump water to drain the farmland and now mostly defunct, proliferate. The broads themselves are difficult to see except from a boat; one of the best waterside walks is in the vicinity of Horsey, where the pumping mill is open to the public. The National Trust owns the broad of Horsey Mere; marsh harriers, bitterns and otters make up part of the local population. Other strolling grounds include the banks of the rivers Bure, Thurne and Yare.

Numerous boatyards accommodate visiting boats; boat rentals are available at Wroxham and Hoveton.

■ **The virtue and the joy of this little-explored corner of English coast is its isolation. The area also has a tremendous sense of place and history, and lots to interest the naturalist. Dutch gables, flints, huge medieval "wool" churches, and weather-beaten coastal villages supply the manmade elements—saltmarshes (Europe's largest expanse), vast sandy beaches, prolific birdlife and dramatic skyscapes are among the natural attractions.....■**

Great Norfolk houses
Blickling Hall (NT) is a lovely red-brick 17th-century house, famed for the Jacobean plasterwork in its Long Gallery. *Holkham Hall* is a neat Palladian mansion built for Thomas Coke, 18th-century agricultural pioneer. *Felbrigg* (NT), a tall-chimneyed, 17th-century pile in a wooded park, has Georgian furnishings and a fine 18th-century library. *Houghton Hall* exudes Palladian elegance and was the seat of Sir Robert Walpole, the first English prime minister. *Sandringham* was built in the 19th century as a country home for the Prince of Wales, the future Edward VII (house open only when the Royals are not in residence, park and drives always open).

142

A shrimping boat at Wells-next-the-sea

The villages Cromer, famed for its crabs, and Sheringham are demure Edwardian resorts atop crumbly cliffs; from the latter a private steam railroad heads towards Holt. Inland lies Norfolk's highest land (heathy upswellings rather than fully fledged hills). Cley▶ has an often-photographed windmill (periodically open). While Blakeney is a yachting center, where mast-stays flap in the wind and a gravelly bank leads to Blakeney Point (still building up westwards). Inland, Binham▶ has a superb 13th-century priory church, with the remains of an 11th-century Benedictine priory alongside.

Wells-next-the-sea produces 80 percent of English whelks; the attractive port looks out over wide saltmarshes. A walk westward brings you to Holkham Gap, where Corsican pines stabilize the dunes, flanking an immense beach. Another privately operated steam railroad connects Wells with Little Walsingham▶, a pilgrimage centre for 900 years with both Roman Catholic and (very high-church, incense-filled) Anglican shrines to Our Lady of Walsingham. It's fascintaing even to non-pilgrims.

The "seven Burnhams" are a scattering of hamlets and villages all named with the prefix Burnham. Burnham Overy Staithe▶ broods over saltmarshes with a fetching harbor scene—close by are a tower windmill and pretty watermill. Burnham Thorpe is famed as Admiral Lord Nelson's birthplace—every other pub hereabouts seems to be called the Nelson or the Hero. The nation's greatest sailor died on board HMS *Victory* (see page 104) after defeating the French and Spanish at Trafalgar in 1805; he was buried in St. Paul's Cathedral in London but there are memorials in Burnham Thorpe Church. Burnham Market is an attractive village set around a spacious green. Hunstanton is an uneventful resort with chalk cliffs, the setting for L. P. Hartley's trilogy *Eustace and Hilda*.

The wildlife Among the best places for observing Norfolk's wildlife are the reserves at Holme-next-the-sea, at Cley, a site with reedbeds and shallow lagoons, and Blakeney Point, reached by boat from Morston or by a long coastal walk over sand and rocky beach from Blakeney. The coast supports a huge population of waders, with wood and curlew sandpipers in summer; great tern colonies exist at Scolt Head island, common and gray seals breed here, and there are sizeable numbers of fall migrants and wintering birds.

►►► Norwich 135C4

Tucked well away from the tourist mainstream in the northeast corner of East Anglia, Norwich (it rhymes with porridge) is considerably less overrun by the tourist industry than most other great cathedral cities in England. It is the major commercial center for the region and a university city, too, which gives it a workaday bustle. For the visitor there is enough to fill a weekend, and you can escape to the Norfolk Broads for peace and space (see page 141). The market place (one of England's grandest), antique showrooms and specialty shops (including the Colman's Mustard shop) make for fascinating browsing, and there is a fair range of theaters. The medieval center has a mishmash of good streets, the finest being **Elm Hill**, **Bridewell Alley** and **Colegate**, a number of eye-catching ancient buildings (head for the **Guildhall** and **Pull's Ferry**) and a multitude of outstanding medieval churches, notably **St. Peter Mancroft** (Perpendicular) and **St. Peter Hungate** (fine hammerbeam roof).

Top of the sights is the **cathedral►►►** (founded 1096), surrounded by a lovely close of houses and boasting some remarkable detailing in the roof-bosses, misericord carvings, glass and stone vaulting; the Norman cloister is the largest in the country. More prominent is the **castle►**, sited on a commanding mound; guided tours take you around the Norman keep, battlements and dungeons.

Museums in Norwich
Bridewell Museum, Bridewell Alley, shows the trades and industries of Norwich over two centuries, in a former prison. *Castle Museum,* Castle Meadow, displays a celebrated collection of paintings by the Norwich school; ceramics (including hundreds of tea-pots), archaeology and natural history (Norfolk's last pair of great bustards are here, in stuffed form). *Sainsbury Centre for Visual Art,* University of East Anglia campus (western edge of the city), has an outstanding art collection, admirably and innovatively displayed. *Strangers Hall,* Charing Cross, is a medieval merchant's house displaying costumes, textiles, toys and period furnishings.

Norwich: Pull's Ferry, with 15th-century watergate

► Saffron Walden 134B3

From medieval times until the 18th century this was a center for the saffron crocus industry. The legacy of its wealth is a knot of historic streets around the largest parish church in Essex. The former Sun Inn in Church Street is outstanding among many examples of the East Anglian craft of pargetting (decorative external plasterwork). On the Common is an enigmatic turf maze; Bridge End Gardens has a more conventional hedge maze.

Just west of the town is **Audley End House►►**. Although only a fraction of its original size, it represents Jacobean architecture on its grandest scale. Vanbrugh and Robert Adam were responsible for early 18th-century alterations; Capability Brown landscaped the park.

143

■ That fragile national asset, the British countryside, is adored for its infinite variety. Yet the landscapes of Thomas Hardy and John Constable have already been transformed in the name of progress. In recent years public attitudes have greened, but is it too late?.....■

A conservation Who's Who
English Nature, the Countryside Council for Wales and Scottish Natural Heritage are the official bodies responsible for conserving flora, fauna, and geological and physiographical features; they manage National Nature Reserves. Local Nature Reserves are managed by local authorities in consultation with the above-named national bodies. In addition, numerous conservation trusts and wildlife trusts own reserves.
The Countryside Commission is the official adviser to the government on matters concerning the rural environment; it is responsible for the establishment of National Trails ("official" long-distance footpaths).

144

The protection of birdlife
The Wildfowl and Wetlands Trust at Slimbridge in Gloucestershire is dedicated to the protection of wetland sites and has wildfowl collections at eight centers in the U.K. The Royal Society for the Protection of Birds (R.S.P.B) is the principal body concerned with wild birds and their environment and has 120 reserves in the U.K.

The shaping of the landscape The countryside is made by a combination of human and natural activity; patches of the primeval tree-cover that once cloaked much of the country exist here and there; but slash and burn led to a legacy of barren moorland, while farming produced a patchwork of hedge-lined fields, and wealthy landowners created great estates and hunting grounds. Yet so embedded in Britain's national culture is the landscape that this unique blend of elements has become "nature" in the public imagination. No value can be placed on landscape beauty, but the populace tends to expect it to be available for them to enjoy.

Agricultural revolutions Pressures for change have intensified. There are many contentious issues: agricultural improvements creating larger and more "efficient" fields, the use of chemical fertilizers and pesticides that adversely affect the water table, the construction of factory-like barns and farms, the removal of small woodlands and the introduction of alien evergreen plantations (environmentalists argue they can be deserts for wildlife), to name a few. The statistics make sobering reading: since 1945 the British countryside has lost 40 percent of

Britain's footpaths and hedgerows: precious things

its traditional woodlands, 60 percent of its heathlands, 80 percent of its chalk downland pastures and 95 percent of its herb-rich hay meadows. Many hedgerows are extremely ancient and harbour diverse wildlife; an estimated 125,000 miles of hedgerows have been ploughed out.

Whose countryside is it anyway? Farmers, estate owners and institutions such as company retirement funds legally own much of the country's farmland and forests, and no value can be put on the public's enjoyment of the great outdoors. Access to the countryside has increased greatly in the past 30 years, and with it an awareness of the threats that loom large. As a proportion of the total population, the number of people employed in farming and forestry is not large but the agri-business lobby is strong.

Pressures on land Road-building, housing and industrial development, cable-bearing pylons and mineral extraction have marred many corners of Britain. In a small island, pressure to exploit the countryside is inevitably strong, and it would take courage for a government to resist growth. However, the balance between environmental and economic interests is getting increasingly tricky to achieve.

Helping hands? The National Trust, a charitable body (see panel page 102), holds much of Britain's finest land for public enjoyment in perpetuity: it has been responsible for safeguarding large areas of coast, downland, upland and forest. Hundreds of important wildlife sites have been acquired by local and national nature trusts as nature reserves; many others are designated Sites of Special Scientific Interest (S.S.S.I.s)—but that status by no means guarantees a safe haven in the planning jungle. National Parks and Areas of Outstanding Natural Beauty may have stricter planning guidelines but often they face another problem—how to manage the sheer number of visitors.

Tax concessions on planting forests have recently disappeared, but many areas of upland Britain (particularly the Scottish Highlands) are already blanketed with evergreen plantations. The presence of the Army on training land has preserved the wildness of some areas, notably the Brecklands in Norfolk and parts of Dorset, but there is a strong feeling that the Ministry of Defence should move out to allow more public access.

Investing in the environment The planning system restricted urban growth in the post-war years, and public hearings have amended road-building and other construction projects; "green belts" around major cities have halted the creeping suburbanization of some beloved tracts, including the Weald and Chilterns. But agricultural changes (including construction of farm buildings) have until recently been outside the scope of the system. The creation of Environmentally Sensitive Areas (E.S.A.s) means that farmers within them are entitled to grants if they maintain traditional farming practices, and subsidies are given to hill farmers. Sensibly targeted government and E.C.-initiated schemes could save the day.

The campaigners
The Council for the Preservation of Rural England (C.P.R.E.), the Council for National Parks and the Friends of the Earth are among the leading conservation campaigners. The National Trust (NT) is Britain's largest owner of scenic countryside; the catalyst for its formation was the unsuccessful battle to save Thirlmere, in the Lake District, from conversion into a reservoir in the 1870s. The Ramblers' Association and the Open Spaces Society are pace-setters for the campaigns for public access to the countryside.

145

Voluntary work
The British Trust for Conservation Volunteers (36 St Mary's Street, Wallingford, Oxfordshire OX10 0EU, tel: 0491 839766) runs some 600 conservation volunteer vacations (footpath maintenance, drystone walling and so on); participants pay a small amount towards food and accommodation.

Nature on the Suffolk coast
Walberswick, a scattered hamlet, abuts reedbeds, mudflats and heath, a habitat for bearded tits, reed warblers, bitterns, water rails and marshland plants. Much of the former port of Dunwich has disappeared beneath the sea; Dunwich and Westleton heaths are nearby, and Minsmere is a freshwater lake owned by the Royal Society for the Protection of Birds (over 280 bird species have been recorded locally, including bearded tits, nightjars, woodpeckers and nightingales). Access to Minsmere reserve is tightly controlled but birdwatchers' blinds are open to the public.

Southwold: choose from today's catch at the harbor

▶ **St. Albans** 134A2

Less than 20 miles from London, St. Albans has preserved its provincial character surprisingly well. Its **abbey church▶** is a medieval foundation built on the site where Alban, the first British martyr, was executed in the 4th century. Its brick-and-flint architecture dates from the 11th century and has been added to in every century since. The Roman city of **Verulamium▶** lies in a nearby park; excavations include a semi-circular amphitheatre, part of the city walls, foundations of houses and a temple. Site finds are well displayed in the Verulamium Museum.

The **Gardens of the Rose▶**, the Royal National Rose Society's home at Chiswell Green, on the southwest edge of St. Albans, have some 30,000 bushes, at their heady best in July. Some 5 miles east of St. Albans, Jacobean **Hatfield House▶▶** has been in the same family since it was bult for Robert Cecil in 1611. It has sumptuous state rooms and formal knot and scented gardens.

▶ **Southwell** 134D1

The medieval minster in this small Nottinghamshire town is not England's best-known, but the chapter house (begun in 1292) boasts some of the country's most breathtakingly intricate carving: a celebration of Sherwood Forest's foliage in stone, featuring oak, maple, vine and ivy leaves. Two of the three Norman towers were rebuilt after a fire in 1711, but the nave, crossing and transept display characteristic Norman simplicity.

▶▶ **Southwold** 135C5

A bewitching seaside town, Southwold is a center for exploring the best of Suffolk's coast. The former home town of essayist and novelist George Orwell (Eric Blair), it was largely replanned after a fire in 1659 around a charming series of greens edged by flint, brick and color-washed cottages. The great Perpendicular church has a superb interior, a white lighthouse gleams behind the Sole Bay Inn, and the town museum and Sailors' Reading Room have displays on local maritime life. Just south of town, the River Blyth has an attractive boating scene. Around Southwold lie numerous marshlands, some unspoiled low-lying coast and much heathy grassland—the traditional sandlings, or sheepwalks, on which Suffolk's economy depended in the wool-prosperous Middle Ages—making an area of exceptional interest for naturalists.

Southward 16 miles, **Aldeburgh▶** is a small coastal town, the birthplace of George Crabbe, an 18th-century poet. His poem "The Borough" was adapted by Benjamin Britten for his opera *Peter Grimes,* a brilliant evocation of life on this coast, which premièred in 1945. Britten (1913–76) is buried in the churchyard of St. Peter and St. Paul; a memorial window was designed by John Piper. Britten co-founded Aldeburgh's esteemed June music festival, which is centered on the old maltings at Snape.

Just north of Aldeburgh is **Thorpeness▶, a** seaside resort village planned in the early 20th century as a weatherboarded and half-timbered "olde-English" haven. Beside the Meare, the village's artificial lake, stands a former corn windmill, moved here to pump water to the adjacent extraordinarily tall former water tower, known as the House in the Clouds.

▶▶ **Stamford** *134C2*

An eye-opening oasis of mellow, Cotswold-like limestone buildings, Stamford was the first landmarked area designated in England. Its clutch of medieval churches includes **St. Martin's**, a complete Perpendicular church with a notable 16th-century alabaster monument to Lord Burghley, while **St. Mary's** has a gold-star-embellished 15th-century chapel of the "golden choir." Of Stamford's inns **The George** is the most conspicuous, with its "gallows" inn-sign spanning the street, and its grandiose interior. Look for two good examples of almshouses, 15th-century **Browne's Hospital** and Elizabethan **Lord Burghley's Hospital**.

Capability Brown's landscaped park at **Burghley House**▶ laps the brink of Stamford. The palatial mansion was built by one William Cecil, chief minister to Elizabeth I. The Elizabethan exterior belies an interior refurbished 100 years later, full of baroque flourishes, including a dazzling array of Italian plasterwork and painted ceilings in the "Heaven" and "Hell" rooms. **Rutland Water**, to the west, is a huge reservoir and major recreation area. Further afield, 14 miles southeast of Stamford, **Peterborough** is sprawling and industrial but worth a visit for its medieval cathedral, pleasant market place and Georgian streets.

▶ **Woburn Abbey** *134B2*

Britain's largest animal safari park forms part of the grounds of this stately home, the seat of the Russells, the Dukes of Bedford, since 1550. Despite its abbey origins— a Cistercian foundation prior to the Reformation—the house is an 18th-century Palladian composition set in a deer park landscaped by Humphry Repton. Within it is the finest set of Canaletto paintings to be found anywhere. You can really feel the long family connection with the house (which claims to be the birthplace of afternoon tea), with portraits and accumulated possessions spanning many centuries.

George Bernard Shaw
The great Anglo-Irish dramatist George Bernard Shaw lived at Shaw's Corner (NT), in the village of Ayot St Lawrence near Welwyn, from 1906 until his death in 1950. Numbered among his most famous plays are *Arms and the Man*, *Saint Joan* and *Heartbreak House*. Shaw's Corner epitomizes his plain living and high thinking; his hats, glasses, pen, desk and exercise machine are there, as if he has just stepped outside the door. He died in the dining room and his ashes were scattered in the garden.

147

The Blyth Estuary, near Southwold

CONSTABLE COUNTRY

Map of Constable Country showing towns including Glemsford, Kentwell Hall, Lavenham, Somersham, Nether Hall, Cavendish, Melford Hall, Monks Eleigh, Kedington, Clare, Foxearth, Long Melford, St James's Chapel, Hintlesham, Haverhill, Stoke-by-Clare, Great Waldingfield, Kersey, Hadleigh, Steeple Bumpstead, Ridgewell, Sudbury, Boxford, Layham, Hempstead, Toppesfield, Great Yeldham, Gestingthorpe, Raydon, Great Sampford, Hedingham Castle, Bulmer Tye, Stoke-by-Nayland, Higham, East Bergholt, Sible Hedingham, Castle Hedingham, Bures, Nayland, Stratford St Mary, Finchingfield, Dedham, Flatford Mill & Lock, Thaxted, Halstead, Boxted, Manningtree, Gosfield, Wakes Colne, West Bergholt, Ardleigh, Great Bardfield, Earls Colne

Drive Constable Country

As pretty as a picture: the candy colors of local plasterwork, the village greens and the great medieval churches, paid for by the prosperous wool trade, have changed little since Constable's day. The countryside is mild and agreeable if unspectacular: it is the towns and villages—well endowed with tearooms, craft and antique shops—that have most appeal (approx. 90 miles).

Start at **Sudbury**, where Thomas Gainsborough's birthplace is now a museum. The route follows the River Stour, along the B1508 to **Bures**, then eastward through **Stoke-by-Nayland►**, where the church tower (a familiar feature in Constable's paintings) presides over the Maltings and Guildhall. **Dedham►** has an

Gainsborough's House, Sudbury

attractively broad main street and the building of Constable's school survives; the artist Alfred Munnings lived here and his works are displayed in his former house. Near **East Bergholt**, Constable's birthplace, is **Flatford Mill►** (also reached by a pretty 1¼ mile river path or by boats rented in Dedham); Willy Lott's Cottage by the millpond is still recognizable as the setting for Constable's *The Haywain.*

Turn northwest along the B1070 through **Hadleigh►**, a handsome town by the River Brett with a fine church and half-timbered Guildhall. Detour through **Kersey►**, a charming village of one street, and join the A1141 to **Lavenham►►**, with its resplendent half-timbering, a huddle of inns and an outstanding church. Westward, **Long Melford►** has antique shops, a magnificent church, and two fine stately homes adjacent.

The A1092 heads past **Cavendish**, a confection of pink rendering and thatch around the green, and **Clare**, with its market place and flint-built church noted for its woodcarving. Seek out the church, windmill and Recorders' House at **Thaxted►►**. Eastwards lies **Finchingfield►** with a delightful green and windmill. **Castle Hedingham►►** has a mighty Norman keep.

■ The landscape of East Anglia has always held a special fascination for painters. Gainsborough and Constable both came from Suffolk, and Gainsborough's birthplace in Sudbury is now a museum. Constable was born at East Bergholt and pictures like "The Haywain" and "Flatford Mill" made the winding valley of the Stour "Constable country" even in the painter's own lifetime.....■

Philip Wilson Steer painted the Suffolk coast in the 1880s. **Sir Alfred Munnings**, who painted all over his native East Anglia, settled at Dedham after World War I and his house is now a museum. **John Nash**, one of this century's major landscape artists, lived and worked in Essex for years before his death in 1977.

"Fishing boats off Yarmouth" by John Sell Cotman

The Norwich School Norwich's Castle Museum has a splendid collection of paintings by the Norwich School of painters, which began in 1803. Its chief figures were **John Crome** and **John Sell Cotman**. Crome, shrewd, boozy and born in a pub, was much the more successful, to the anguished jealousy of Cotman, who is now regarded as the greater painter, admired for his ability to impose simple and satisfying patterns on the natural scene. The work of the Norwich School echoes the Dutch school of landscape painting. They responded to a similar setting— a flat landscape studded by windmills and grazed by cattle beneath an immense sky of towering cloudscapes.

The wealth and the comparatively isolated position of Norwich in the early 19th century meant that most of its painters were known only locally. The local gentry wanted representations of the scenes they knew—the tranquil Norfolk landscape, picturesquely dilapidated cottages, ruined towers and crumbling abbeys, cattle and sheep, river and coastal views. The Norwich School painted the rural scene as it was in the last days before the Industrial Revolution changed the face of Britain.

Above: from "Wood scene" by John Crome, 1810

If you paint a pigsty, dignify it.
    John Crome (1768–1821), to his son

How much real delight have I had with the study of Landscape this summer. Either I am myself much improved in "the Art of seeing Nature" (which Sir Joshua Reynolds calls painting) or Nature has unveiled her beauties to me with a less fastidious hand—perhaps there may be something of both so we will divide these fine compliments between us . . .
    John Constable, to his future wife (1812)

WALES

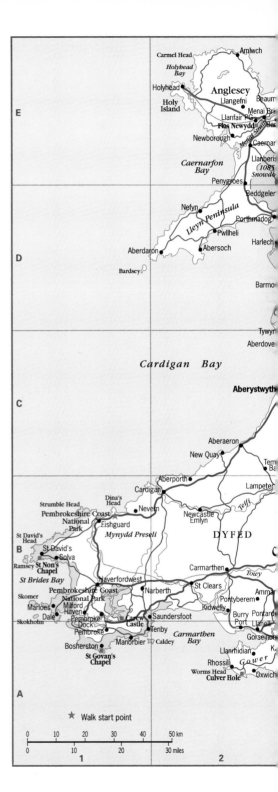

Carmel Head
Amlwch
Holyhead Bay
Holyhead
Anglesey
Llangefni
Beaum
Holy Island
Menai Br
Llanfair P.G
Bar
Plas Newydd
Newborough
Caernar
Penygroes
Llanberis
Caernarfon Bay
(1085
Snowd
Beddgeler
Nefyn
Lleyn Peninsula
Porthmadog
Pwllheli
Harlech
Aberdaron
Abersoch
Bardsey
Barmo
Tywyr
Aberdove

Cardigan Bay

Aberystwyth

Aberaeron
New Quay
Tem
Ba
Aberporth
Lampeter
Cardigan
Dina's Head
Strumble Head
Neven
Newcastle Emlyn
Teifi
Pembrokeshire Coast
National Park
Fishguard
DYFED
St David's Head
Mynydd Preseli
St David's
Solva
Ramsey
St Non's Chapel
Haverfordwest
Carmarthen
Towy
St Brides Bay
Pembrokeshire Coast
Narberth
St Clears
Amma
Skomer
National Park
Milford Haven
Pontyberem
Marloes
Kidwelly
Burry Pontard
Dale
Carew Castle
Saundersfoot
Port
Llanelli
Skokholm
Pembroke Dock
Tenby
Gorseino
Pembroke
Manorbier
Caldey
Carmarthen Bay
K
Bosherston
Llanrhidian
St Govan's Chapel
Rhossili
Gower
Worms Head
Culver Hole
Oxwich

★ Walk start point

0 10 20 30 40   50 km
0   10   20   30 miles
1   2

WALES

151

Great Ormes Head
Llandudno
Colwyn Bay
Conwy
Llanfairfechan
Abergele
Rhyl
Prestatyn
Rhuddlan
St Asaph
Bodnant
Denbigh
Hint
Connah's Quay
Chester
Helsby
Neston
Ellesmere Port
M56
Runcorn
Widnes
Port Sunlight
Bebington
Birkenhead
MERSEYSIDE
LIVERPOOL
St Helens
Bootle
Wallasey

CHESHIRE
Mold
Moel Famman 555m
Ruthin
Gresford
Wrexham
Erddig
Malpas
Whitchurch
Ellesmere
Wem
Shawbury
Nesscliffe
Shrewsbury
Minsterley
Stiperstones
SHROPSHIRE
Long Mynd
Church Stretton
Munslow
Craven Arms
Clun Forest
Stokesay Castle
Ludlow
Knighton
Croft Castle
HEREFORD
Shobdon
Eardisland
Pembridge &
Lyonshall
Leominster
Old Radnor
Kington
Weobley
Willersley
WORCESTER
Clyro
Hay-on-Wye
Wye
Hereford
Kilpeck
Abbey Dore
Llanthony
Goodrich Castle
Symonds Yat
Monmouth
Coleford
Raglan
Tintern Abbey
Usk
Chepstow
Caldicot
Avonmouth
M5
Clifton
Portishead
Nailsea
Clevedon
Congresbury
AVON
Weston-super-Mare
Cheddar Gorge

CLWYD
Llyn Brenig
Betws-y-coed
Cerrigydrudion
Horseshoe Pass
Llangollen
Ruabon
Dee
Chirk
Oswestry
Llanymynech
Llanfyllin
Plas Newydd
Pistyll Rhacadr
Corwen
Bala
Llyn Tegid
Llyn Vyrnwy
Vyrnwy
Welshpool
Powis Castle
Llanfair Caereinion
Montgomery
Newtown
Severn
Carno
Caersws
Llanidloes
Llangurig
Rhayader
Radnor Forest
POWYS
Llandrindod Wells
Newbridge on Wye
Beulah
Builth Wells
Llangammarch Wells
Erwood
Talgarth
Brecon
Usk
Sennybridge
Brecon Beacons
Pen-y-Fan 886m
Black Mountains
Crickhowell
Abergavenny
National Park
Brynmawr
Ebbw Vale
Blaenavon
Abertillery
GWENT
Cwmbran
Pontypool
Bargoed
Risca
Cumbran
Newport

WYNEDD
Blaenau Ffestiniog
Snowdonia
National Park
wsfynydd
Dolgellau
892m
der Idris
astell y Bere
Mallwyd
Centre for Alternative Technology
Machynlleth
Dylife
Llyn Clywedog
752m
Plynlimon
Ponterwyd
Devil's Bridge
Claerwen Reservoir
Tregaron
Abergwesyn
brian Mountains
Wye
Flan Village
Llanwrtyd Wells
Llandovery
ndeilo
Carreg Cennen Castle
Carmarthen Van 802m
Dan-yr-Ogof Caves
Pont-Nedd Fechan
WEST GLAMORGAN
Glyn Neath
Hirwaun
Aberdare
Mountain Ash
MID GLAMORGAN
vansea
Port Talbot
M4
Neath
Maesteg
Pencoed
Pontypridd
Llantrisant
Bridgend
Cowbridge
SOUTH GLAMORGAN
Llantwit Major
Porthcawl
St Fagan
Tredegar
Merthyr Tydfil
Caerphilly
M4
St Fagans
Llandaff
CARDIFF
Barry
mbles
ead
ansea Bay
Tawe
Neath
Taf

Bristol Channel
3
4

Snowdonia Centre for Alternative Technology

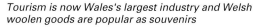

Tourism is now Wales's largest industry and Welsh woolen goods are popular as souvenirs

The fishing industry has seen decline—but there is always activity in a harbor

Wales Constitutionally Wales is closer to England than Scotland is; there is no separate legal system, and the two principalities have been unified since 1535. Yet the Welsh are proudly independent in culture and outlook; the Welsh language, impenetrable to an outsider, is very much alive (much more so than Gaelic in Scotland) and is taught in schools. Welsh is the first language of many, particularly in North and West Wales; signs ("dim parcio/no parking," "croeso i Gymru/welcome to Wales") are predominantly bilingual; roughly one in five of its inhabitants is a Welsh speaker. Plaid Cymru, the Welsh Nationalist Party, has sent Members to Parliament since 1966 and devolution—restoration of some powers to the local Welsh government—is a current talking point. There are strong traditions of choral singing and of Nonconformism, virtually every village having at least one chapel. The Welsh love of music, literature and art manifests itself in the numerous eisteddfods, in which music, poetry, drama and fine arts feature. Welsh domestic architecture on the other hand is humble—typically sturdy stone-built farmsteads and houses beneath slate roofs; the railroad age added red and yellow brick façades. Grand houses are a rarity, but there are plenty of medieval castles to visit. Wales also prides itself on its educational system; it has the highest teacher/pupil ratios in the UK and a higher proportion of 16-year-olds continue their higher education than in England.

Wales is compact and scenically diverse, with a wet climate, friendly people and a living culture: it constantly surprises visitors.

South Wales For all its proximity to central and north-west England, Wales is strikingly remote. Cross into South or Mid Wales from the English border and the hills rise immediately. The southern borderland (the border country often being termed as the Marches) is defined

precisely by the gorge of the **lower Wye**, whose scenic reaches are punctuated by features such as Tintern Abbey, Chepstow Castle and Symonds Yat rock. Farther into South Wales lie the coalfields and the dying industrial heartlands of the **mining valleys**, which though hardly picturesque have their own fascination. **Cardiff**, the Welsh capital, is the administrative and cultural capital. The coast becomes increasingly seductive as you proceed westward; Nash Point near Llantwit Major on the Glamorgan coast displays extraordinary candy-striped rocks, while the **Gower**, on the back doorstep of the industrial city of Swansea, has magnificent bays and cliffs. **Pembrokeshire**, too distant for mere day-trips, is a favorite destination for seaside vacations without the host of commercialized trappings found in so many English resorts.

Mid Wales This nebulous term is applied to a relatively unknown region, sparsely populated except by sheep, which are encountered everywhere (one-quarter of the E.C.'s sheep population are here). The **Brecon Beacons National Park** offers the grandest scenery, with its best-known tracts on its eastern side—the Black Mountains, the Brecon Beacons and the secondhand bookshop town of Hay-on-Wye. Further west, the **Cambrian Mountains** are scarcely inhabited and largely impenetrable by car, except for a handful of spectacularly lonely mountain roads laid along routes used by drovers taking sheep to market in the pre-automobile era. Aberystwyth is the principal seaside town of Mid Wales, whose coast, though not as scenic as Pembrokeshire, does have a few pleasant places, such as Llangranog.

North Wales Along the north coast stretches a line of resorts, largely undistinguished with the notable exception of Llandudno. But more significantly, North Wales contains the **Snowdonia National Park**; here are the highest mountains in England and Wales, and a good range of attractions, including castles, mines and steam-hauled railroads. Nevertheless, this can be a frustrating area to visit: roads are often sunk down in the valleys and the scenery slips by quickly; but there are outstanding walks at varying levels of difficulty, from easy forest strolls to tough scrambles up challenging scree-covered mountain slopes.

Rounding up the sheep

BEST PLACES TO GO
Small towns *Dyfed* Llandeilo, St. David's. *Gwent* Chepstow, Monmouth. *Gwynedd* Conwy. *Powys* Llandrindod Wells, Llanidloes, Montgomery, Presteigne.
Castles Caernarfon, Caerphilly, Conwy, Harlech.
Coastal towns Llandudno, Tenby.
Walking areas Brecon Beacons National Park, Gower, Offa's Dyke Path, Pembrokeshire Coast National Park, Snowdonia National Park, Lower Wye Valley. See Walks, page 158.
Industrial interest Snowdonia National Park, the South Wales mining valleys
Scenic drives *Mid Wales* Elan Valley, Beulah to Tregaron, Llanidloes via Dylife to Machynlleth, Rhayader to Aberystwyth. *Brecon Beacons National Park* Gospel Pass (Hay-on-Wye to Llanthony). *Snowdonia National Park* see Drive, page 170.

153

WALES

*Anglesey Sea Zoo:
all-weather fun*

► **Anglesey** *150E2*

Wales's largest island is flat and fertile, and it is its shores that provide most of its attractions to visitors. Good beaches include **Newborough Warren**, which offers distant views of Snowdonia, and **Amlwch Bay**.

Pioneering neolithic man built an amazing number of chamber tombs on Anglesey, the most notable being Bryn celli ddu and Barcloddiad y Gawres. The island's geographical position en route to Ireland and its gold and copper inevitably attracted the Celts too; a great hoard of Iron Age chariot fittings and weapons was found at Llyn Cerrig Bach. In medieval times, when the island's productive farmland provided valuable supplies for granaries in England, Anglesey was held by the English. Edward I built a stronghold in the 1290s at **Beaumaris►►**; the castle was never attacked and the moated shell survives to this day. The town's former prison houses a museum where you can find ghoulish delights such as the treadmill, the condemned cell and the route to the scaffold.

Between Anglesey and the mainland is the Menai Strait, spanned by Thomas Telford's suspension bridge, the longest such structure in the world when it was constructed (1826) and one of the Scottish engineer's greatest achievements. Overlooking the strait is **Plas Newydd►** (NT), the Pagets' 18th- and 19th-century family home; it has a remarkable *trompe l'oeil* mural in the dining room, painted by Rex Whistler in the 1930s. **Holy Island**, attached to the rest of Anglesey by a ½-mile causeway, is good for birdwatching and, although the industrial port of Holyhead is disappointing, there are exhilarating walks on Holyhead Mountain. Ferries leave from Holyhead for Dublin in Ireland.

Porth Dafarch Beach, Holy Island

The druids of Anglesey
The religious leaders of the Celts were the Druids and Anglesey was famed far and wide as a druidic center. Tacitus, the Roman historian writing in the 1st century AD, speaks of Anglesey as the place where youths aspiring to the priesthood were sent to be schooled in philosophy, religion and poetry; in more sinister mode, he also speaks of human blood being smeared on the Druids' altars and human entrails being used for prophesies.

►► Brecon Beacons National Park 151B3

The Park is an east–west upland of four distinct areas, the Black Mountains, Fforest Fawr, the Brecon Beacons themselves and (confusingly) the Black Mountain. It is less rugged than Snowdonia but has some fine views and excellent walking; it also attracts fewer visitors.

The eastern flanks comprise the **Black Mountains**, a series of ridges enclosing deep sheep-grazed valleys. Drive up from **Hay-on-Wye►**, a small town crowded around its castle and a mecca for secondhand bookshop browsers. Above Hay the **Gospel Pass►►** is perhaps the most scenic drive in the Park, with easy access to the summit of Hay Bluff. The road dips into a valley, past the ruins of 13th-century **Llanthony Abbey►**. Up an obscure side valley **Patrishow Church►** boasts a rare musicians' gallery and an eerie mural of a skeleton bearing a shovel, scythe and hour-glass. Farther west, the A479 skirts the massif between the attractive towns of **Crickhowell** and **Talgarth** before passing through **Tretower►**, with its fortified medieval manor by the ruin of an earlier castle.

The **Brecon Beacons** are really a sandstone ridge culminating in Pen y Fan 2,907 ft., the highest point in Wales outside Snowdonia. The graceful M shape of the twin summits is seen from far around. To the south is the little **Brecon Mountain Railway**. Brecon itself is an amiable market town with a small cathedral and a military museum. Out of town, the **Brecon Beacons Mountain Centre** is the main National Park information outlet.

Predominantly grassy upland, **Fforest Fawr** includes, near Pont Nedd Fechan, the superlative "**waterfall country**"►► of the wooded Nedd, Hepste and Mellte gorges (see Walks page 158). **Dan-yr-ogof Caves►** nearby are part of Britain's largest known cave system; one has a re-creation of a Bronze Age dwelling, another presents a history of caving in a sound-and-light show.

To the west, the **Black Mountain** is an expanse of moors and forests dominated by the craggy ridge of **Carmarthen Fan**. Much of it is for the serious walker only, but **Carreg Cennen Castle►►**, a majestically placed ruin in a valley close to Llandeilo, merits a detour.

The National Park includes the highest land in South Wales

Love-spoons
Throughout rural Wales during the 17th, 18th and 19th centuries, young men would spend many long, dark evenings carving ornamental wooden "love-spoons." These would be presented as tokens to the girls or women they courted; if accepted it was a sign that courtship would lead to marriage. They are still produced as souvenirs; the Brecknock Museum in Brecon and the Welsh Folk Museum at St Fagans (see page 157) have fine collections of this genre of folk art.

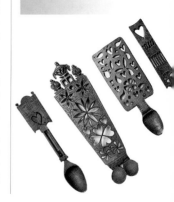

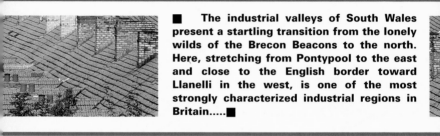

■ The industrial valleys of South Wales present a startling transition from the lonely wilds of the Brecon Beacons to the north. Here, stretching from Pontypool to the east and close to the English border toward Llanelli in the west, is one of the most strongly characterized industrial regions in Britain.....■

"Nye" and the NHS
Aneurin Bevan, or Nye as he was fondly called, was born the son of a miner in 1897. As a boy he was himself a miner and had early trade union experience in the South Wales Miners Federation. In 1929 he was elected M.P. for Ebbw Vale and held the seat until he died in 1960. One of Parliament's greatest orators, he has gone down in history as the minister who in 1948 introduced the National Health Service providing the people of Britain with a comprehensive medical, dental and welfare service funded largely by general taxation.

An old pit head

How green was my valley Between narrow fingers of abruptly rising ridges runs a series of deep dales grooved with long rows of houses built in the heyday of the Valleys' industrial prosperity.

Toward the end of the 18th century, the Industrial Revolution heralded a new dawn; peasants from rural areas migrated *en masse* into the Valleys as ironmasters established works at Aberdare, Dowlais, Hirwaun and Merthyr Tydfil. In 1804 Richard Trevithick gave birth to the railway age with his steam railroad from Merthyr to Abercynon. The Merthyr ironworks supplied cannon for the British forces in the Napoleonic wars and rails for railroads across the globe.

Coal, choirs and rugby Later, iron production ceased and the Valleys specialized in coal extraction; the coalfield witnessed a great influx of new population. Work was hard, and often dangerous, but community life brought its rewards—passions for rugby and choral singing; the Valleys choirs still carry away the honors at the International Eisteddfod (see panels, pages 160, 163). Numerous leading socialists were born and bred here, including Aneurin Bevan, son of a miner who was to be the instigator of the National Health Service (see panel), and Neil Kinnock, former leader of the Labour Party.

Facing the future Now most of the collieries have gone, the coal seams having been nearly exhausted. The smoke has cleared from the air, and greenery has returned; evergreen plantations cloak the upper slopes. Today only Tower Colliery at Hirwaun seems to have a future among the nationally owned pits; but open-cast mining continues and some 90 private mines are operated, providing employment for around 850 people. Unemployment overall, however, is running high and many houses stand empty.

Service industries are alive, and the area has awakened to its tourist potential. At Pontypool there is the Valleys Inheritance Centre, while the Crawshays' castle, Cyfarthfa Park, Merthyr Tydfil, now houses a museum. At the Big Pit Museum in Blaenavon former miners, well-stocked with anecdotes, show visitors the pit-head showers, winding machine and the depths of the mine. There are guided tours, too, round the casting sheds of the nearby Blaenavon Ironworks, whose blast furnaces date from the 18th century.

There is a limit, however, to the number of such attractions that can be opened up for visitors.

► **Cardiff** *151A4*

Although it is located in the industrial heartland of Wales, Cardiff is a surprisingly clean and liveable place. Despite its status as Welsh capital and as home of Welsh rugby union and of the (much-acclaimed) Welsh National Opera, Cardiff is not a particularly Welsh city. Bute Park cuts a swath by the banks of the Taff, close to the civic center, a gleaming group in Portland stone begun in the 1890s. **Cardiff Castle**►► dates from Norman times but had money poured into it in the 1860s and onward by the fabulously wealthy 2nd Marquess of Bute (who built the city's docks and made Cardiff the world's prime coal port); the result was a mock-medieval fantasy of Ludwig II proportions, designed by William Burges.

Cardiff has a fine array of **museums**►►. At the wide-ranging **National Museum of Wales**, collections include a group of paintings by French impressionists as well as silver, ceramics, fossils, dinosaur skeletons and shells. Cardiff Bay now has numerous attractions: engines, early locomotives and boats are on show at the **Welsh Industrial and Maritime Museum**; a three-dimensional model of the bay can be seen in the **Cardiff Bay Visitor Centre**; and **Techniquest** is one of the largest hands-on science centers in the country, a "wonderland of science and technology" for all age and experience levels.

Castell Coch
Another fairy-tale concoction of William Burges was Castell Coch, on the edge of Cardiff, designed for the 3rd Marquess of Bute. It was never completed, but there are hints at what might have been in the breathtaking splendo r of the giltwork, painting, tiles, statues and carvings. Murals of Aesop's fables decorate the drawing room, while the ceiling of Lady Bute's bedroom is painted with the story of Sleeping Beauty.

157

On show at the Welsh Industrial & Maritime Museum

The medieval **Llandaff Cathedral**► is dominated by the figure of "Christ in Majesty" by Jacob Epstein, an impressive if not totally likeable creation in concrete. The **Welsh Folk Museum**►► at nearby **St. Fagans** has a collection of rural dwellings from all over Wales, including a farmhouse, a terrace from the mining valleys, a Unitarian chapel and domestic and farming relics.

A little north of Cardiff, double-moated **Caerphilly Castle**►, dating from the 13th and 14th centuries, is the largest castle in England and Wales after Windsor. South of Abergavenny, **Big Pit Mining Museum, Blaenavon**►► is the best attraction in the industrial Valleys, successfully capturing the atmosphere of a working mine (see opposite page).

Walks

Dinas Island, Pembrokeshire *150B1*
Coast National Park, Dyfed
Off the A487 east of Fishguard; parking lot near Sailors' Safety Inn. The "island" is in fact a peninsula, ideal for an exhilarating circular walk of 1 to 1½ hours along the clifftop path, passing Dinas Head, the highest point, and Needle Rock, with its large bird-life population. A well-trodden public footpath cuts across the narrow neck of land to complete the circuit.

Llyn Idwal, Snowdonia *150E2*
National Park, Gwynned
Parking lot by Idwal Cottage Youth Hostel on the A5. The nature trail around Llyn (lake) Idwal gives straightforward access to supremely dramatic scenery, passing the crags of the Devil's Kitchen beneath Glyder Fawr (1½ hours). The slopes support a rare flora, including alpine species, and the area is a designated National Nature Reserve. Trail leaflet available on site.

Moel Fammau, Clwyd *151E4*
Parking lot and picnic site on the B5429 between Llanbedr-Dyffryn-Clwyd and Llandyrnog. The walk up from the road to the partly collapsed Jubilee Tower gives views westward to Snowdonia and eastward to the Peak District. Start from the picnic site and walk through the forest

(following blue or red markers); return along the open ridge to drop down to the road, then turn left to the starting point. (1½ hours)

The Nedd, Hepste and *151B3*
Mellte Waterfalls, Brecon
Beacons National Park, Powys
Parking lot at Pontneddfechan, east of Glyn Neath. These mighty waterfalls crash their way along wooded gorges in the southern fringes of the National Park. The Hepste and Mellte Falls can be reached by a woodland path from Craig y Ddinas parking lot at the east end of Pontneddfechan or from Porth yr Ogof to the north; the highlight is Sgwd yr Ira, where you can walk behind the curtain of the fall. (1 to 2 hours)

Symonds Yat, Lower *151B4*
Wye Valley, Hereford and
Worcester/Gwent border
Parking lot at end of the B4432, north of Coleford. This renowned scenic overlook over the Wye gives access to one of the prettiest parts of the gorge. Descend to the west, past a refreshment stand and on a marked path to the riverside Saracen's Head Inn, where a chain ferry takes you across. Turn left on the far bank to the wire suspension bridge (it will bounce as you cross); return on the old railroad track on the east bank. (1½ hours)

Pennygarreg Reservoir Dam, Elan

►► Elan Valley and the Cambrian Mountains
151C3

Sometimes dubbed the Welsh Lake District, the **Elan Valley** is a chain of reservoirs gracing the great unpopulated wilds of the Cambrian Mountains. The lakes supply water to Birmingham, and both the dams and Elan village, built for the reservoir workers, are in characteristically solid Edwardian style. The Elan Valley Visitor Centre in Elan village has details of walks; the trackbed of an old railroad used in construction of the reservoirs is a good route for enjoyable lakeside strolls. An exciting **mountain road►►** climbs the Cambrian range, leaving Rhayader for the Elan Valley and continuing past abandoned lead and zinc mines to **Devil's Bridge►**, where three bridges, stacked one upon the other, span a gorge. A narrow-gauge **steam railroad►** with quaint cars runs from here to **Aberystwyth**, the main seaside resort for Cardigan Bay. The bay-windowed Victorian guesthouses on the seafront overlook a rocky beach, hemmed in by the bulky bluff of Constitution Hill from where you can see Snowdonia and the Preseli Hills. A cliff railway makes an effortless ascent to the top and a camera obscura enhances the panorama on sunny days.

►► Erddig
151D4

Although not a particularly distinguished house architecturally, Erddig (NT), 2 miles south of Wrexham, is an excellent introduction to life below stairs in a country mansion. The National Trust rescued the house when mining subsidence threatened the structure; all the service buildings and most of the contents survived intact and it is now preserved as a fascinating picture of the workings of a country estate in the 18th and 19th centuries. The Yorke family, who lived here from 1733 to 1973, treated its servants kindly and as a visitor you see the house somewhat through a servant's eyes, entering not by the main door but through the servants' quarters, where portraits and photographs of generations of domestic staff hang on the walls.

Devil's Bridge
The oldest of the three bridges here dates back at least as far as the 12th century and was used by Cistercian monks from nearby Strata Florida. Legend has it that the Devil built it to assist a woman whose cow was stranded on the far side of the river; the Devil in return was to have the first living creature to go across. However, the woman threw a piece of meat over and a mangy dog crossed the bridge to get it. The other bridges were built in 1753 and 1901.

159

Far left: the family bicycle collection at Erddig

Welsh culture and politics

■ **Look at any vacation brochure or tourist poster for Wales and you are likely to come across the same well-worn images: male voice choirs; young girls in chimneypot Welsh hats, playing the harp; mist-shrouded mountains and lakes, and rugged mining valleys. Like all clichés, they convey only a superficial picture. The reality is far more vital: a combination of sentimental reverence for the past and passionate concern for the future. One element links all the many strands of politics and culture in Wales: a fervent sense of Welsh identity.....■**

The National Eisteddfod
Welsh-language culture is seen at its most robust at an eisteddfod. All over the country, local eisteddfodau (literally "sittings") are set up in schools and chapels, where singers, dancers, musicians, actors, artists and writers of all ages compete to reach the next level in the categories of Awdl (a complex, ancient form of Welsh poetry) and Pryddest (free verse). The nationwide contest culminates, in the first week of August, in the National Eisteddfod, presided over by the Gorsedd of Bards in their druidic robes.

Lloyd George (1863–1945), Wales's finest statesman

Dylan Thomas summed up the eccentricity and claustrophobia of small-town Welsh life in his play *Under Milk Wood*. The action is set in Llareggub, a mythical fishing community whose name read backwards is the rude phrase "Bugger all." One of its residents, the Reverend Eli Jenkins, captures the emotional exuberance of Welsh culture with his cry "Praise the Lord! We are a musical nation!" Music and poetry have an influence which is recognized and nurtured in Wales. The famous male voice choirs, some of which now perform and record all over the world, are still rooted in the close-knit mining communities of South Wales and the farming and slate-mining areas of the north; and the Eisteddfod (presided over by Bards chosen for their contributions to Welsh life), a well-known celebration of Welsh culture, is an important focus for the 500,000 or so Welsh-speakers in Wales (see panel).

The Welsh language The survival of this ancient Celtic language—one of Europe's oldest—does much to explain the defensive pride of the Welsh. Banned from use in official channels by Henry VIII, one of the Welsh Tudor dynasty, the language lived on in the home and in the arts. Fluency in English became essential for anyone wishing to get ahead in life, and many parents with ambitions for their children favored and encouraged its use. But Welsh continued to be the language of worship, and as Nonconformist chapels sprang up in the wake of religious revival, it survived as the linchpin of many communities.

Political issues With new generations came new attitudes, and the 20th century saw a battle to re-establish Welsh education. Plaid Cymru, the Welsh Nationalist Party (which now has four M.P.s in Westminster), began in the 1920s calling for a return to the agrarian, Welsh-speaking way of life—a call not welcomed by the struggling industrial communities of South Wales, where socialism still has a firm hold.

In the 1960s and '70s nationalism took a more radical turn, as young members of Cymdeithas yr Iaith Gymraeg (the Welsh Language Society) kept the "language issue" in the headlines with acts such as painting out Anglicized place-names on road signs. In recent years the language

*As part of the eisteddfod druid ceremony, a
handmaiden makes her offering to the crown bard*

has enjoyed a revival—it's now included in the statutory
school curriculum, a Welsh TV channel has been established and a lively pop culture has developed, willing to
absorb the dreaded Anglo-American influence.

The current "hot" political issue in Wales is immigration
and the decline of Welsh communities. A small minority
of activists have attracted publicity and hostility by setting
fire to a series of empty second homes. Meanwhile
English "incomers" living on the northern Lleyn peninsula have been issued with threats and deadlines for leaving
the country. Most Welsh people are quick to condemn
these acts, which veil the very real fears of communities
whose younger generations are leaving in search of work,
while cottages are sold at unaffordable prices to absent
landlords and stand empty for half the year, turning once
vibrant areas into sad and ghostly places.

Conflict in the field For a glimpse of the whole Welsh
nation at its sentimental and raucous best, try and get
hold of a ticket for one of the international rugby matches
at Cardiff Arms Park—preferably Wales vs England, when
rivalry is strong and emotions are high. Hearing a stadium
full of fans singing the Welsh anthem before watching
what they regard as their national game is enough to bring
a lump to the throat—whatever the final score might be.

The 'Welsh Not'
In 1847 education com-
missioners preparing a
report for the government
in Westminster visited
schools in Wales. There
they heard children using
their native Welsh
language, which they
attacked as immoral and
backward. From then on a
campaign to stamp out the
use of Welsh was rigorous-
ly pursued—often by the
Welsh themselves. Pupils
overheard slipping into the
language were forced to
wear wooden boards
around their necks bearing
the words "Welsh Not."
The commission's report,
bound between blue
covers, was never really
forgiven and has passed
into Welsh history as the
Treason of the Blue Books.

A Norman stronghold
Like southern Pembrokeshire, the Gower has been a "little England beyond Wales," with a long history of English-speaking. In the 12th century the Normans held the Gower and built a chain of castles, of which remains exist at Oxwich, Oystermouth, Pennard, Penrice and Weobley.

Taking the waters
Llandrindod Wells, Builth Wells, Llangammarch Wells and Llanwrtyd Wells are the spa towns of Mid Wales. Back in 1732, Rev. Theophilus Evans tried the highly sulphurous waters and thus found a cure for his skin ailment. Chalybeate and saline springs were discovered close by and the area became known as a place for taking the waters. A Mrs. Jenkins found a sulphur source in 1736 at Llandrindod, and by the 1830s Llangammarch was offering barium chloride as a remedy for heart conditions.

▶▶ **Gower** *150A2*

The Gower peninsula stretches out west of Swansea. The residential and industrial outskirts of that city abruptly give way to green countryside, rolling commons and a coast that, on its southern seaboard, is the rival in miniature of Pembrokeshire (see pages 165–6). It has great limestone cliffs and superb sandy beaches, followed for their length by a coast path, while the north seaboard is low-lying and marshy. There is some resort development, but generally the Gower is rural and unspoiled.

The western tip is the best part of all: here **Rhossili Down**, a moorland ridge with views of the entire peninsula, dips to a sublime and seemingly endless beach; westwards stretches **Worms Head**, a high-tide island accessible on foot by those courageous enough. Nearby, **Mewslade Bay** shows rock strata tilted and folded, just like a geography textbook. Farther east are more good beaches at **Oxwich Bay** and at tiny **Brandy Cove**. Gower oddities include **Llanrhidian village**, with a mysteriously carved leper stone in the church and a village green dominated by a pair of gigantic stones.

▶ **Llandrindod Wells** *151C3*

A rare instance of a spa town whose traditions are still alive. A few years ago Llandrindod's Victorian pump-room was semi-derelict; today it stands proudly in restored state and offers its waters for all to try. Grand red-brick terraces and spa hotels, ornate wrought-iron arcades and balconies and spacious tree-lined streets suggest something larger than a town of under 5,000 in the heart of Mid Wales sheep country. Somehow it has kept its period character, and it deserves the success of its Victorian Festival in September when barrel-organs and civic pomp return to the streets.

Cefnllys▶ is an Iron Age hillfort strikingly situated above the River Ithon beside a lone church and the (now robust) Shaky Bridge. There is a nature trail along the river.

The **Beulah to Abergwesyn road▶▶**, an old drovers' road to the southwest of the town, takes a spectacular course over the wilderness of the Cambrian Mountains.

Toward New Radnor, the quaintly named waterfall **Water-break-its-neck▶** is to be found north of the A44.

Llandrindod Wells: its hotels recall its heyday as a spa

The view from Castell Dinas Bran, near Llangollen

Old Radnor Church► is possibly the finest parish church in Wales, with a lovely medieval screen, Britain's oldest organ case and a font hewn from a prehistoric monolith.

►► Llangollen, Vale of 150D4

This deep valley, hemmed in by natural terraces of limestone crags, is a landmark on the A5. From it the A542 rises up the hairpin turns of the **Horseshoe Pass**, engineered by Thomas Telford. **Llangollen** itself, site of the world-famous international musical eisteddfod (see panel), is of little intrinsic interest but is a busy tourist center, convenient base for a number of attractions. On the valley floor stand the picturesque ruins of **Valle Crucis Abbey►**, a Cistercian foundation of 1201; notable features are the Early English west façade and the vaulted 14th-century chapter house. An outstanding timber roof installed in St. Gollen's in Llangollen is said to have been taken from here. On the edge of Llangollen, horse-drawn barge trips operate along the **Llangollen Canal**; the canal's proudest moment occurs farther east as it crosses the valley on the Pontcysyllte Aqueduct, built by Telford in 1805. Steam railroad lovers should visit the **Llangollen Railway Society**. Above town is the so-called **Panorama Walk**, really a small road but quite panoramic; even better views are from the 8th-century ruin, **Castell Dinas Bran►**, but it is a steep climb.

Wind turbine at the Centre for Alternative Technology

164

The Centre for Alternative Technology
The center was established in 1974 as a place for promoting environmentally friendly technologies. A water-powered cliff railway whisks you up to the site entrance and a trail takes you around an informative exhibition that includes an energy-efficient house, ecologically oriented gardens and displays of solar heating and other alternative energy sources. Although obviously an idealized set-up, the Centre is a great place for talking to people (several workers live on site), and learning how to cut your energy bills, improve your garden and give a greener tinge to your lifestyle. Plenty of appeal for children.

Just south of town, **Plas Newydd**►► is a remarkable mock-Tudor inspiration, home for half a century starting in 1780 to eccentric recluses, Lady Eleanor Butler and Miss Sarah Ponsonby, the "Ladies of Llangollen." They transformed a cottage into this remarkable half-timbered house, where they entertained a distinguished number of guests, including Sir Walter Scott and the Duke of Wellington. The house is whimsical in the extreme and full of personal touches.

Pistyll Rhayader► Wales's tallest waterfall is at the head of a remote valley south of Llangollen. The fall has been engineered to give the water a twist as it tumbles, but the effect is pleasing. There is easy access by road.

Pistyll Rhayader, Wales's most spectacular waterfall

Machynlleth
151C3

A market town centered on a clocktower (of a design that seems to be mandatory for Welsh towns), Machynlleth is comfortably set in the peaceful hills south of the Snowdonia National Park. It is an uneventful place in a pleasant kind of way. The town's hinterland is partly inhabited by a significant hippie population. Topping the bill of local attractions is the excellent **Centre for Alternative Technology**► (see panel).

The road to **Dylife**► is a scenic drive that runs over the shoulder of Plynlimon, a boggy upland from which rise the Wye and the Severn, the two great rivers of Wales. At Dylife a stream plummets into a gorge via Ffrwd Fawr, a splendid waterfall. A scenic overlook at a curve in the road takes in Cader Idris, the major summit in southern Snowdonia.

A boat trip leaves Martin's Haven for Skomer Island

▶▶▶ **Pembrokeshire Coast National Park**   *150B1*

As its name implies, the National Park is largely confined to a coastal strip. Here are magnificent cliffs, sandy coves (many excellent for swimming if you can bear the chilly water), complex natural harbors and a diversity of wildlife which ranks on a par with the best of Cornwall. The south and north parts of the Park are strikingly different: a wave-cut platform, now raised high above sea level, leaves the southern cliffs mostly level-topped, while farther north the scene is more exciting, with assertive bluffs, soaring headlands and dramatic variations in height. Southern Pembrokeshire was for a long time a "little England beyond Wales," owned by the English, who left a legacy of English place-names and Norman castles for keeping watch over the unruly Welsh. Regrettably, the Army's foothold on the south coast in the vicinity of Castlemartin means restricted access. Walking is the main draw of the north, which is less populated and consequently less busy in season. Scenic drives are very few—the roads generally keep too far inland; a much better bet is to take in some of the coastal path, which snakes around the intricate seaboard for some 180 miles.

Towns and villages Most famous is undoubtedly **St. David's**▶▶. Scarcely more than a large village of craft shops, galleries and cafés, it keeps its great Norman cathedral half-hidden in a valley, alongside the considerable ruins of a 14th-century bishop's palace. Allegedly, relics of St. David, patron saint of Wales, lie beneath the altar. Of the coastal towns, **Tenby**▶▶ is perhaps the most appealing, with its maze of narrow streets, a harbor surrounded by tiers of color-washed Georgian and Tudor merchants' houses, a castle up the hill and a five-arched gate in the town wall. It is very pretty—and it suffers for that in summer, with bumper-to-bumper traffic. **Pembroke**▶ is less important than one would expect, a one-street market town completely dominated by an exceptional Norman castle, occasionally the setting for public medieval banquets. **Fishguard** is split in two by the lie of the land, with the lower town crowded around the

Island hops
Skokholm and Skomer are major bird sanctuaries, supporting the largest concentration of Manx shearwaters in Britain. Puffins abound on Skomer, and Skokholm has a population of storm petrels. Boat trips start from Martin's Haven. Ramsey Island has lots of gray seals, which can be seen off the mainland too, and cliff-nesting birds including choughs; boat trips begin from Whitesands Bay and St. Justinian. Caldey Island, reached by boat from Tenby, is home to a community of Cistercian monks.

St. David's Cathedral: 39 steps (or "Articles") lead down to its door

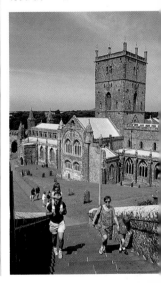

The inland hills
The National Park also encompasses the Preseli Hills, a tract of remote upland near Fishguard that is scattered with the burial mounds and hillforts of early settlers. It was from here that the bluestone rocks were transported to Wiltshire for the construction of Stonehenge (see page 84), a feat that has baffled archaeologists. The rocks may have been moved by raft: this is technically feasible but more plausible perhaps is the theory that they were naturally moved closer to Stonehenge by glaciers during the last ice age, possibly to the Somerset Mendips.

harbor, where ferries leave for Rosslare in Ireland, and the upper town pleasantly grouped around sloping streets. Much smaller, Solva▶ is a boating center and one-time port prettily set at the end of a narrow and steep-sided bay.

The best of the coast In the south, the indented headlands and traceried bays around **Dale** and **Milford Haven** (itself an industrial port adjacent to oil refineries, but worth seeing for its natural harbor site) have constantly changing views, while **Wooltack Point▶▶** near Marloes looks out to Skomer and Skokholm islands. At Bosherston a series of **lily ponds▶** makes a popular walk which can be tacked onto a visit to a fine beach. On the margins of some luscious estuary landscape east of Milford Haven is **Carew Castle**, adjacent to a tide mill and an 11th-century Celtic cross. Perched among Pembrokeshire's cliffs are three primitive hermitage chapels, **St. Govan's**, just west of St. Govan's Head, **St. Justinian's** and **St. Non's** (both near St. David's). **St. David's Head▶▶** and **Strumble Head▶** have rugged grandeur; it is sometimes possible to see the Wicklow Mountains in Ireland from these. Among the most popular swimming beaches are **St. Bride's Bay, Tenby, Saundersfoot** and **Whitesands Bay**, but there are numerous smaller ones offering greater privacy.

▶▶ Powis Castle 151D4

A great border stronghold, owned by the Herbert family from 1587 to 1952, Powis is memorable for its lavish state apartments and superb terraced gardens.

Montgomery▶ More English than Welsh in character, the tiny town center focuses around a gracious square with an 18th-century town hall and a pleasing assemblage of plum-red-brick façades that date from Elizabethan times. The castle mound above town was the stronghold of Roger de Montgomery, who in the 13th century launched assaults on the Welsh.

Tiny St. Govan's Chapel, tucked in the cliffs

The Welshpool and Llanfair Railway
The privately operated steam railroad operates along 8 miles of track between Welshpool and Llanfair Caereinion. Its chief distinguishing features are the narrow 30-inch gauge and the antique wooden cars from the Zillertal in Austria.

▶▶▶ Snowdonia National Park   *151D3*

Snowdonia is unsurpassed among the national parks of England and Wales for the wild drama of its scenery. Ideal for walking, rock-climbing and horse-riding, it has a fair offering of scenic drives, although these tend to be confined to valley routes and are limited in scope.

The main mountain group is quite compact, centered on Snowdon, the highest point in England and Wales. Perhaps the hallmark of Snowdonia is the individuality of each of the main summits: each has its distinctive shape and visitors soon find their personal favorites. Snowdonia's coast is disappointing, ribboned as it is by main roads and with no cliffs to speak of. Sightseeing interest on the other hand is particularly rich, with a host of nostalgic railroads, old mines, and medieval castles.

The main centers In northern Snowdonia **Betws-y-coed** (pronounced Bettus-ee coe-ed) is a touristy village of Victorian hotels and craft shops. It has grand scenery on its doorstep and walks along the Llugwy River and the Swallow Falls, and a series of attractive reservoirs close by to the west; the big mountains keep hidden, however. Also central and with a touch more charm, the Victorian mountain resort village of **Beddgelert▶** lies close to the Aberglaslyn Gorge, Moel Hebog and Snowdon. A much-publicized but probably bogus attraction here is Gelert's Grave, Gelert being the noble 13th-century Prince Llywelyn's dog (see panel). An absorbing tour can be taken round **Sygun Copper Mine▶▶** (but be prepared for crouching, climbing 100 steps and smoky explosions). **Bala** too gets busy in high season; Wales's largest lake adjoins it, but the scenery is not quite so stupendous.

Of the north coast seaside resorts **Llandudno▶** is by far the most attractive. It's one of Britain's best-preserved Victorian seaside towns, with its elegant curving bay, its pier, Punch and Judy shows on the sands and a miniature tram up to Great Ormes Head. **Conwy▶▶**, also on the coast but a historic walled town, is the most rewarding town for casual wandering, with a splendid castle and what is reputed to be Britain's smallest house. **Caernarfon▶▶**, too, boasts a great castle and is a place everyone should try to visit (although for some travelers it may be too far out to serve as a base). **Harlech** straddles a slope above marshland, one of the few portions of this coast not to be followed by a main road; good beaches lie to south. The castle is the spectacular attraction.

Mountains of slate-scraps surround **Blaenau Ffestiniog**, at the heart of the Snowdonia slate industry. A town of slate roofs upon sturdy terraced houses, it is not pretty but has some appeal and is right in the center; it is establishing itself as a tourist town now that the old **Llechwedd Slate Caverns▶▶** have been opened to the public. At Llanberis is the **Welsh Slate Museum▶** and a branch of the National Museum of Wales, **Power of Wales▶**, which offers trips to Dinorwig underground hydro-electric pumped storage station.

Dolgellau▶, the only town in the park boundary, is a place of gray-stone houses and narrow streets; life revolves around its market place. It makes a good base for touring southern Snowdonia and it has some excellent easier walks on its doorstep, including Cregennan Lakes

167

Great little trains of Snowdonia
The *Snowdon Mountain Railway* climbs 3,280 ft. from Llanberis to the summit. Many people walk back down. *Ffestiniog Railway*, built for the slate industry and now one of the most scenic of all Britain's private railroads, runs from Porthmadog to Blaenau Ffestiniog. *Bala Lake* and *Llanberis Lake* railroads run alongside the lakes from which they take their names. The shorter *Welsh Highland Railway* starts from Porthmadog.

Gelert's grave
The story goes that Prince Llywelyn left his dog Gelert guarding his infant son; when he returned to find the child covered in blood he assumed Gelert had killed his son and immediately slew him. Only too late did he realize the dog had in fact saved his son from the jaws of a wolf. The "grave" is probably the invention of an 18th-century pub-owner trying to increase business.

WALES

Mountain safety
Beware! The Snowdon Mountains may not compete in height with the Alps or Rockies but they are full of dangers and have claimed many lives. Be sure to be properly dressed, shod and equipped; check the weather forecast, take a good map, compass and provisions, and tackle only those walks well within your abilities. Leave a note with your hotel of where you are going and when you intend to return.

at the foot of Cader Idris, the old railroad track along the magnificent Mawddach Estuary, and the Precipice Walk (hair-raising for those with tiny children) above the Mawddach Gorge. Further west, **Barmouth** is an unremarkable seaside resort.

The major peaks The king of them all, **Snowdon** (Yr Wddfa in Welsh) rises high and majestic to 3,560 ft., five ridges (known collectively as Eryri, "abode of eagles") radiating from its central pyramid. Not surprisingly, it is the most popular mountain ascent, not just because it is the highest but also because of the views both on the way up and from the top. Paths approach from all directions, or you can cheat and use the Snowdon Mountain Railway (see panel, page 167); the route from Llanberis, parallel to the railroad, is the easiest but least interesting path, while the Horseshoe Route (along knife-edge ridges) is the most enthralling and demanding. The first half of the Miners' Track from Pen y Pass (see Drive, page 170) takes you into the wilds, rising past lakes and abandoned copper mines to a splendid corrie beneath the summit and main ascent—this initial stage provides an unchallenging way of sampling the start of what is a great mountain route.

Almost as high as Snowdon and just as spectacular are

Y Garn, seen from Llyn Ogwen

Caernarfon Castle, Edward I's most magnificent

Glyder Fawr (3,277 ft.) and **Glyder Fach** (3,261 ft.), two peaks on a great ridge with rock pinnacles and precipitous drops, the **Carneddau group** and (lower but with good views) **Moel Siabod** (2,861 ft.). The southern giant is **Cader Idris** (2,930 ft.), a complex sprawling mass with some reassuringly gentle slopes but huge panoramas.

Houses, castles and gardens Penrhyn Castle▶▶ is an imposing mock-Norman pile built by slate magnate Lord Penrhyn in the mid-19th century; architect Thomas Hopper gave it battlements and turrets, and a grandiose interior which epitomizes high living of the period. Genuine castles abound in Snowdonia. Most famous of all is **Caernarfon Castle▶▶**, begun in 1283 after Edward I's conquest of Wales. It was the setting in 1969 for the investiture of the Prince of Wales; his investiture robes are on show here, together with a display of the dynasty of the Welsh princes. **Harlech Castle▶▶**, also founded in 1283, has a fine site above the coast; although seemingly impregnable it was taken by Owain Glyndwr in 1404. **Conwy Castle▶▶**, another of Edward I's foundations, is sited in the town wall (which you can walk around); it has 21 semi-circular towers and overlooks a castellated suspension bridge, one of some 1,200 bridges designed by Thomas Telford between 1792 and his death in 1834. Much less substantial, but beautifully set among the hills, are the castles of **Dolwyddelan▶** (near Blaenau Ffestiniog) and **Castell y Bere▶** (near Abergynolwyn).

Bodnant Gardens▶▶, near Llanrwst, rate among Britain's finest horticultural creations. Try to visit **Portmeirion▶▶**, an Italianate *trompe l'oeil* fantasy village created by Clough Williams Ellis in this century to awaken popular interest in architecture. It has often been used as a film set; the T.V. series *The Prisoner* was made here, and it was here Noel Coward wrote *Blithe Spirit*.

The Canal Terrace, Bodnant Gardens

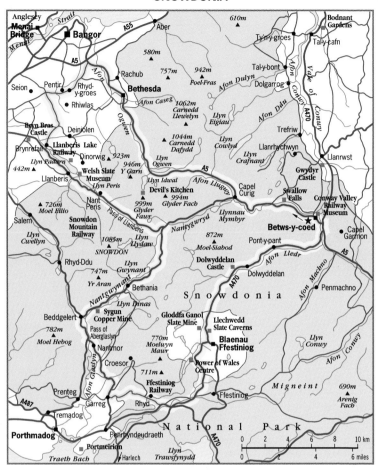

SNOWDONIA

Drive Snowdonia

A circuit of the grandest uplands in Wales (approx. 65 miles).

Start at **Betws-y-coed** and take the A5 past the entrance to the spectacular **Swallow Falls►** to Capel Curig. Continue past Llyn (lake) Ogwen; from the parking lot at its far end, a short path leads to **Llyn Idwal►►**, beneath the vast crags of the Devil's Kitchen (see Walks, page 158). Beyond the mining town of **Bethesda** take the B4409, then the A4086 past **Llanberis** base station for the

Snowdon Mountain Railway►. At the top of the **Llanberis Pass**, the Miners' Track and Pyg Track leave for an exciting ascent of **Snowdon**. Continue on the A498 past **Beddgelert►** and along the **Pass of Aberglaslyn**. Take the B4410 and A496 to **Blaenau Ffestiniog**, passing **Ffestiniog Hydro-electric Station►**, **Gloddfa Ganol Slate Mine►** and **Llechwedd Slate Caverns►►**. **Dolwyddelan Castle►**, farther up the valley (A470), is supposedly the birthplace of Prince Llywelyn the Great.

Looking north from Symonds Yat

▶▶ **Wye Valley** *151B4*

The River Wye defines the English/Welsh border for its glorious finale, as it enters a sandstone gorge whose slopes are cloaked with woodlands that display breathtaking colors in the fall. Once the gorge was a hive of industrial activity, the trees supplying charcoal for ironsmelting; brass was invented here in 1568. The valley established a name for itself during the late 18th-century Romantic movement, whose poets sought a deeper appreciation of the beauties of nature. **Ross-on-Wye**, though not in the gorge proper, has a mock-Gothic town wall built in the 1830s at the time of this "picturesque discovery." Its much-photographed arcaded market house is two centuries older. **Symonds Yat▶**, a rock reached by a stairway, overlooks a bend of the Wye. **Goodrich Castle▶** is an impressive 12th-century sandstone bulk, intact until a Parliamentary siege in the Civil War.

The Monnow flows into the Wye at **Monmouth▶**, the Monnow spanned by a medieval bridge with a fortified gateway incorporated into it. Above the town, a rustic folly commemorating admirals of the Napoleonic wars caps **Kymin Hill▶**, a good place for views. Turner painted and Wordsworth revered the ruins of **Tintern Abbey▶▶**, an ancient Cistercian foundation set on the valley floor. This is one of the great medieval abbey ruins, roofless but standing to its original height. Its exquisite tracery includes a 66 ft. east window.

Chepstow has a formidable Norman **castle▶▶** with keep and mighty outer wall. The main street rises up to a gateway in the Port Walls, the town wall. Above the east bank, **Wintour's Leap** is a quarried cliff-face by the road with a dizzy drop to the river, while the **Wynd Cliff▶**, on the west bank, offers a wider view.

Sons of Monmouth
Henry V was born in Monmouth Castle, of which nothing now remains, in 1387. Before the Battle of Agincourt he gained the nickname Harry of Monmouth. The central plaza is named Agincourt Square in his honor. Charles Rolls was a pioneer of early aviation, engineering and motoring who was a partner in Rolls-Royce. In 1910 he became the first Briton to die in a flying accident. His statue outside the town hall holds aloft a model aeroplane, and the town museum has a section devoted to his life.

One of the world's first iron bridges— the Regency bridge over the Wye, at Chepstow

NORTHWEST ENGLAND

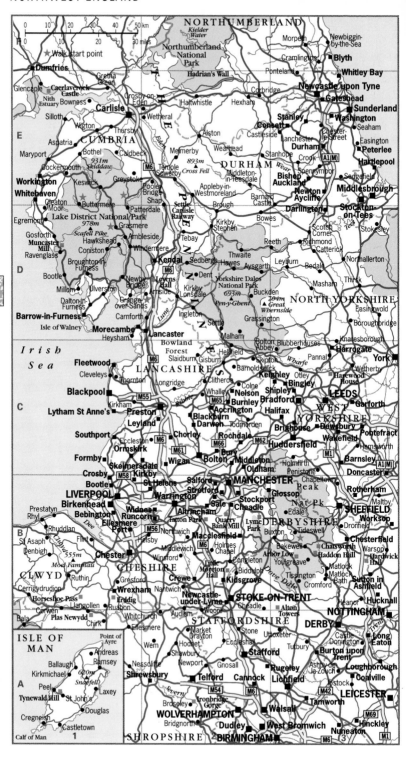

Northwest England This strip covers the region from the industrial northern Midlands to the Scottish border. The most hallowed feature is doubtless the **Lake District**, within the northerly county of Cumbria.

Lake District delights Here the lakes, high fells, pastures and woodlands offer constantly changing vistas of peerless scenic beauty. It is all at a perfect scale for exploration on foot, as equally suited for those wanting a gentle saunter with the mountains as a backdrop as for aspiring rock-climbers; boat trips on the lakes add a further option. Roads and parking lots get annoyingly busy in peak periods, but out of season driving is a delight. Public transport is a feasible option (Ambleside and Keswick would make good bases), though it restricts what can be visited. The Lake District scores highly for quantity and quality of accommodation, for the range of sights suitable for those all-too-frequent rainy days and for the scope of other outdoor activities, which include sailing, mountain biking, horse-riding and angling (swimming in the lakes is discouraged because of undercurrents). As a general rule, the western Lake District has the most spectacle and wildness; the east is milder, more crowded and has more indoor sights.

The rest of Cumbria Outside the Lake District, the rest of Cumbria offers a long and not especially beautiful coastline, but an interesting one: along it are the early industrial town of Whitehaven, well worth a visit; St Bees Head (ideal for birdwatching); and the free visitor center at Sellafield nuclear reprocessing plant, set up to woo support for the nuclear industry. Northern Cumbria is fairly flat, but it has nice views across the Solway Firth to southern Scotland and the bits-and-pieces historic city of Carlisle. Southern Cumbria is fringed by the great expanse of Morecambe Bay, an important site for wading birds and the setting for Britain's fastest incoming tides; tourist offices have details of guided walks over the bay (follow routes precisely to avoid the quicksands).

Lancashire, Merseyside and Greater Manchester The more built-up parts of Morecambe Bay lie within Lancashire—Blackpool, Morecambe and Southport were

Dove Dale: its beauty is best appreciated on foot

173

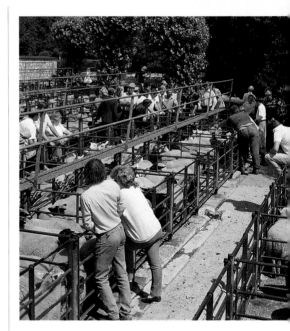

The sheep market at Bakewell

developed as resorts to serve the cotton-mill towns that sprang up in the 19th century. Those mill-towns changed the face of the county and heralded a major phase in the industrialization of Great Britain. The mills have closed or changed to other uses but these urban landscapes, immortalized by the paintings of L. S. Lowry (see panel, page 183), still exist, the straight lines of millworkers' row houses being their dominant feature: Burnley and Accrington are examples. Manchester and Liverpool were the great cities created by this expansion; today Manchester is more prosperous, but Liverpool wins on museums and atmosphere. The Forest of Bowland in northern Lancashire is, despite its name, a tract of high, open country; access is limited but there are exhilarating views.

Cheshire, Derbyshire and Staffordshire Cheshire extends from the Welsh border to the brink of the Peak National Park; between lies a fertile plain, pockmarked by tiny lakes and ponds called meres. Black and white half-timbering and red brick are predominant building materials, seen to best advantage in Chester, remarkable for its intact city walls. Cheshire, Staffordshire, Derbyshire and South Yorkshire share the **Peak District**, a very accessible and much-visited national park; although it cannot compete with the Lake District for scenic quality, it has lovely limestone dales, austere gritstone moors, caverns and some fine country houses (notably Chatsworth and Haddon Hall). Other houses in **Derbyshire** include Calke Abbey and Hardwick Hall. Derby has a number of good museums; Derby porcelain is on display at the Derby Museum and at Royal Crown Derby. Stoke-on-Trent (**Staffordshire**) is the china-making capital.

Walks

Arnside Knott, Cumbria   172D2
Parking lot by seafront at Arnside.
The wooded limestone hill is laced
with paths to its summit, where a
view opens out over the southern
Lake District and Morecambe Bay,
one of Europe's most important sites
for waterbirds of the wader family.
The quickest way up is southward
through the village, on residential
roads that give way to paths. (1 hour)

Buttermere, Lake District   172E1
National Park, Cumbria
Parking lot at Buttermere village. A
well-trodden path leads to
Buttermere. The path around the lake
is straightforward and level, but is
graced with a fine mountain
backdrop; the path weaves out of forest, through a section of tunnel and
along the water's edge (1½ hours).
Optional add-ons include the ascent
of Haystacks, the jagged, dark-topped
fell to the south.

Grasmere and Rydal Water,   172D1
Lake District National Park,
Cumbria
Parking lots at Grasmere village. Seek
out the path along the south side of
these two lakes: walk past Grasmere
Church on your right, take the left fork
of roads to reach the lakeside path,
which leaves the road near a
boathouse. After a short wooded section, climb up to the level path along
Loughrigg Terrace on your right for
grandstand views of Wordsworth's
valley. Continue on around Rydal
Water or head back by dropping
through woods, over a bridge and the
A591 to take a minor road to
Wordsworth's Dove Cottage at the
edge of Grasmere village. (1½ hours)

Monsal Dale and Chee Dale,   172B3
Peak National Park, Derbyshire
*Parking lots at Miller's Dale (old sta-
tion).* Turn left along the railroad track
(Monsal Trail) to enter Miller's Dale;
the trail swings away from the
railroad as it passes through a tunnel.
You pass the Wye's old textile mills,

rejoin the railroad and cross Monsal
viaduct (2½ hours). In the other direction from the parking lot, the trail
soon leaves the railroad track for an
exciting stepping-stone route along
the Wye as it enters a gorge beneath
Chee Tor, a popular haunt of rock-
climbers. (2 hours)

Ullswater, Lake District   172D1
National Park, Cumbria
Parking lot at Glenridding. Begin by
taking the lake steamer from
Glenridding to Howtown, and follow
the well-trodden lakeside path back
(allow 4 hours); it undulates delightful-
ly and ducks in and out of woods with
sudden vistas. An optional add-on is to
climb Hallin Fell, close by Howtown,
by a path up its southern side.

*A Lake District scene between
Rydal Water and Grasmere*

Blackpool Tower and the Promenade

■   **Blackpool**   172C1

In Victorian times Blackpool was the traditional day-out treat for millworkers in the Lancashire cotton towns; it is still the liveliest and brashest seaside resort in the North: it offers unsophisticated fairground fun, nightlife, pleasure gardens and views of Morecambe Bay and the Lakeland fells from Blackpool Tower. Trams travel up the seafront to Fleetwood, giving the best view of the Illuminations (August to November). The beach has had a bad record in recent years for pollution.

▶   **Carlisle**   172E1

Cumbria's largest town has recently spruced itself up as a regional shopping center. This does not rank among the great cathedral cities, but there is enough here for an absorbing half-day in the compact historic center.

For centuries, Carlisle was plagued by border skirmishes and the **castle▶▶**, dating from 1092, was much attacked and repeatedly rebuilt (the view from its walls is a real stomach-churner). The keep is 12th-century; inside, the story of the Border Regiment is told with spectacular uniforms and weapons. Don't miss the haunting graffiti carved by captives in the prison.

The castle is today rather ignominiously chopped off from the rest of the old city by a busy road. Over the way are some good Georgian and earlier streets, the medieval **cathedral▶**, one of Britain's smallest, notable above all for its east window with its 14th-century glass, and an outstandingly lively city museum in **Tullie House▶**.

Settle–Carlisle line▶▶ Part of the national railroad network, this most scenic line was saved in recent years by a volunteer-led campaign. From Settle, in the Yorkshire

The Citadel, a prominent landmark at the center of Carlisle

Dales, the route crosses the high Pennines in spectacular fashion, over the Ribblehead Viaduct in the shadow of Whernside and along the Eden Valley. Special steam trains sometimes run on the route.

▶▶   Chester   172B1

Founded as the Roman city of Deva, Chester was a major port until the River Dee silted up in medieval times. Its fortunes then slumped until a revival in the 18th century. Today, it has plenty to show for these three periods.

Foremost is the **city wall▶▶**, one of the finest in the country, which provides a fascinating 2-mile walk, raised above street level for much of the way. A number of its gateways are still in place and Roman masonry can be seen here and there within it, although much of its fabric is medieval. Roman finds are exhibited at the **Grosvenor Museum▶** (free). By **Newgate**, on the east side, part of the **Roman amphitheatre** (Britain's largest) can be seen near a park that also has remains of a Roman central heating system and some re-erected columns. The staggered crossroads of the city center, where often a picturesquely attired town crier bellows out public announcements, have Roman origins.

Of medieval Chester, the most famous feature is **The Rows**, which has an upper tier of shops with its own walkway above street level. Nobody quite knows why it developed this way, but its success lives on as a thriving shopping area. The central streets harbor a pleasing mix of half-timbered Tudor, red-brick Georgian, and exuberantly elaborate 19th-century fake black-and-white buildings. Chester's Victoriana also includes a Gothic-style **town hall**, where the Council Chamber and Assembly Rooms are open to the public, in Northgate Street. The red sandstone **cathedral▶** was restored in the 19th century, but its superbly carved 14th-century choir stalls are unaltered.

An 18th-century visitor was Daniel Defoe, who enjoyed the local Cheshire cheese.

Chester Zoo▶ is 3 miles north up the A41. Animals roam in enclosures that simulate natural environments.

The Cross, at Chester's historic heart

177

■ **The Lake District National Park—Lakeland, the English Lakes or just the Lakes, call it whatever you will—is a microcosm of breathtaking variety and scenic perfection. Its character wavers between windswept mountainous upland and drystone-walled, sheep-nibbled lowland pastures. It is outstanding for outdoor pursuits, particularly walking, climbing and sailing, but the climate is fickle: benign-looking summer days have a habit of clouding over suddenly. Fortunately the area has plenty of indoor attractions, especially for literary pilgrims.....■**

178

William Wordsworth

Wordsworth was born in Cockermouth in 1770 and a happy childhood there was to influence his poetry in later life. His favorite home was Dove Cottage, in Grasmere, where he lived from 1799 to 1808, following a lifestyle of plain living and high thinking, with his wife, Mary, and sister, Dorothy. He loved the place deeply and walked over, mused upon and wrote about every corner of the vicinity; aptly, he is buried in Grasmere churchyard. Wordsworth spent the last years of his life, less happily, at Rydal Mount, dying in 1850.

Literary Lakeland

The Wordsworths were the center of a group of friends, among them poets Samuel Taylor Coleridge and Robert Southey. Tennyson reputedly wrote *Idylls of the King* at Mirehouse, near Keswick and, later, poet Matthew Arnold and critic John Ruskin both made their homes here. In this century, Beatrix Potter wrote and illustrated her enchanting children's stories at Hill Top in Near Sawrey, while Arthur Ransome set his *Swallows and Amazons* in the Lakes.

The north and west Keswick►, the major center for the northern lakes, is a gray-slate Victorian town, full of walkers, tourists, bed-and-breakfast signs and outdoor sports shops. Here are the Fitzpark Museum (with its "piano" of Cumberland slates) and a unique pencil museum. Just east is the prehistoric **Castlerigg Stone Circle►**. **Derwent Water►►►** is breathtakingly beautiful; a boat service circuits the lake. **Lingholm Gardens►** on its western shores look their best when the rhododendrons and azaleas are at their prime in early summer.

Borrowdale appealed to early discoverers of the "picturesque;" Castle Crag is a good vantage point. The main road heading over **Honister Pass** skirts **Buttermere►►►**, magnificently located and looking like a miniature Scottish loch. **Cockermouth►**, outside the Park, is a likeable market town of colorwashed terraces and odd corners.

North of Keswick, the fells flatten and the crowds disappear, but the moors have a quiet beauty of their own. **Hesket Newmarket**, with its green and its old market cross, is the prettiest village hereabouts. Southeast of Keswick, **Thirlmere►**, a lake enlarged into a reservoir, is the most popular starting point for walks up Helvellyn (3,117 ft.). The lake of **Ullswater►►►** twists its way south from Pooley Bridge, the scenery getting better all the while; a steamer plies the length of the lake. By the A592, **Aira Force►►** is a popular waterfall, tumbling into a shady chasm at the side of Gowbarrow Park, the hill where Wordsworth saw that host of golden daffodils. East of Ullswater, **Askham►** is a trim village of stone cottages.

The Lake District's western tracts are less accessible and are a great place to get away from it all. **Wast Water►►►** is one of the great sights, looking to the heights of Great Gable, and Scafell Pike is the highest peak in England at 3,207 ft. **Ennerdale** is quieter but overshadowed by evergreen plantations. **Eskdale►** is mellow and broad; the narrow-gauge Ravenglass and Eskdale Railway runs along the valley to the tiny village of Boot with its restored corn mill. At the dale's east end, the **Hardknott Pass►►►** is the great scenic drive of Lakeland, rather like taking your car for a fell walk; the Isle of Man may be visible from the remains of a Roman fort at the top. Motorists can continue along **Wrynose Pass** or into the **Duddon Valley (Dunnerdale)**.

The south and east Windermere, England's longest lake, has wooded shores sprinkled with villas built by 19th-century industrialists; steamers ply the length of the lake and from Lakeside, at the southern end, a steam railroad runs to Haverthwaite. **Bowness** is a tourist trap, clogged with traffic in summer; **Windermere town**, away from the lake, is mere railroad-age suburbia. **Ambleside**, at the lake's northern end, is more attractive, particularly up the hill. On Windermere's shores are a number of gardens (Holehird▶, Stagshaw▶ and Graythwaite▶), the **Brockhole National Park Visitor Centre▶** and the absorbing **Windermere Steamboat Museum▶**. For good views, it is an easy walk up **Orrest Head** from Windermere, or farther south, **Gummer's How** .

West of Windermere, the landscape rolls gently, thickly cloaked in trees; in **Grizedale Forest** woodland paths are enhanced by modern sculptures. **Stott Park Bobbin Mill▶** demonstrates the process of bobbin making. Visit the pretty village of **Hawkshead▶▶** out of season—or wait in line for the parking lot and join the crowds in its quaint little streets; it has craft shops, tearooms, a Beatrix Potter gallery and Wordsworth's former school. Just out of the village, **Tarn Hows▶** is a pretty, if over-visited, pair of tarns artificially merged into one as a landscape feature. Above the village of **Coniston,** beneath the Old Man of Coniston, are spectacular relics of its bygone copper-mining industry. Glide silently over **Coniston Water** on the National Trust's antique steam yacht, *Gondola***▶▶**.

North of Ambleside, the A591 enters more mountainous terrain; **Grasmere▶▶** and its surroundings are immortalized by the works of Wordsworth (see panel, page 178). Today the village is a busy resort with several good shops. Westward looms **Langdale Pikes**.

Farther south, **Cartmel▶▶** is a handsome village, less overrun than Hawkshead, with a fine priory church and a pretty square. For views over Morecambe Bay, walk up **Hampsfield Fell** from Grange over Sands. **Kendal▶** (just outside the National Park) deserves special mention for its Art Gallery and Museum of Lakeland Life and Industry.

Far left: the Windermere Steamboat Museum

Know your Lakeland terms
Small lakes are called *tarns*, mountains are always *fells* (from the Nordic fjaell), streams are known as *becks*, spotted black-faced sheep are *Herdwicks*, white-faced ones are *Swaledales*, loose stones created by freeze-thaw weathering are termed *scree*. *Force* means waterfall. Bassenthwaite Lake is the only lake in Lakeland termed as such: all the others are *meres* or *waters*. "Lake Windermere" is a useful term to avoid confusion with Windermere, the town, but Lake District purists will shudder if they hear you say it!

179

Grasmere, beloved of William Wordsworth

Drive **The Lakes**

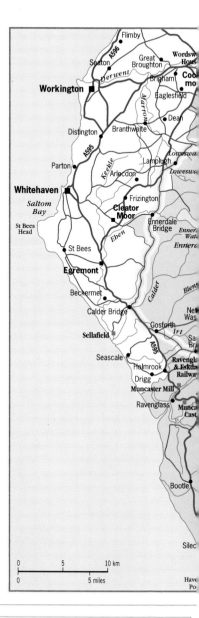

A succinct cross-section of the best of the Lakes (approx. 80 miles), taking in Wordsworth's Grasmere, spectacular high passes and the less-visited western areas.

From **Keswick** the route heads south along the A591 past **Thirlmere▶**, beneath the shadow of Helvellyn, and past the Wordsworths' former houses, Dove Cottage at **Grasmere▶▶** and Rydal Mount, **Rydal**. Turning west at the resort town of **Ambleside**, you soon enter **Langdale**, passing beneath the impressive forms of Langdale Pikes, whose slopes were once home to a neolithic axe factory. A minor road loops around the end of the dale, above Blea Tarn, to turn right onto the **Wrynose Pass**. This leads into the magnificent **Hardknott Pass▶▶▶**, passing the substantial remains of a Roman fort on the right after the summit; drop into **Eskdale**, with glimpses of its narrow-gauge railroad. Fork right to **Santon Bridge** (from where you can detour to majestic **Wast Water▶▶▶**) and continue to **Gosforth**, with its renowned **Celtic cross ▶** in the churchyard. Take the A595 to **Calder Bridge**, then fork right to **Ennerdale Bridge** via a high-level road with views of the coast and **Sellafield nuclear reprocessing plant** (its visitor center is now a major draw). Beyond **Lamplugh** bear right and right again on minor roads to **Loweswater** and the B5289, where you turn right for a superb finale past **Buttermere▶▶▶**, up the **Honister Pass**, along **Borrowdale** and beside **Derwent Water▶▶▶**.

180

❏ Houses open
Brantwood, east side of Coniston Water: home of critic, artist John Ruskin.
Dalemain, near Penrith: Norman pele tower, Elizabethan rooms, priest's hole.
Dove Cottage, Grasmere: Wordsworth's home for his most productive period.
Hill Top (NT), Near Sawrey: Beatrix Potter's farmhouse.
Holker Hall, near Cartmel: flamboyant Victorian house in Elizabethan style.
Levens Hall, near Levens: Elizabethan manor, gardens. Steam attractions. ❏

THE LAKE DISTRICT

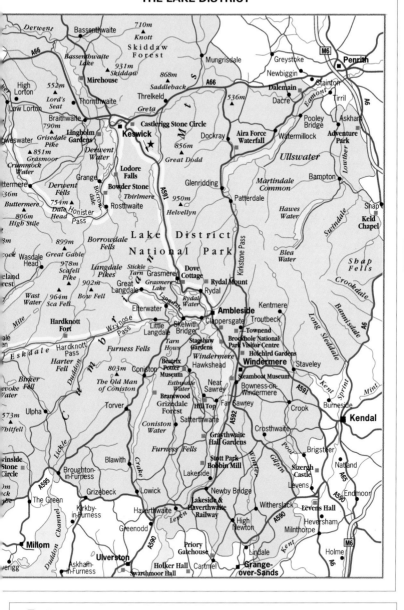

181

❏ Houses open (continued from page 180)
Mirehouse, near Keswick: manuscripts of Tennyson, Wordsworth, etc.
Muncaster Castle, Eskdale: built around pele tower; bear menagerie, owls, etc.
Rydal Mount, Rydal: Wordsworth's last house; grander than Dove Cottage.
Sizergh Castle (NT), near Levens: Elizabethan panelling, carvings; gardens.
Townend (NT), Troutbeck: traditional Cumbrian farmhouse.
Wordsworth House (NT), Cockermouth: birthplace of William Wordsworth ❏

Museums and galleries in Albert Dock

Animation World A "hands-on" display of animation models and cartoons, with workshops, studios and sets.

Beatles Story The Fab Four, who immortalized Penny Lane and the Cavern Club, are the focus for this sight-and-sound experience of the music of the 1960s.

Merseyside Maritime Museum An ambitious museum tracing the history of the port in a restored complex surrounding the Canning Half-Tide Basin: piermaster's house, pilotage building, boat hall, ship-building and an excellent display on European emigrants.

Tate Gallery A branch of the great London establishment, concentrating on modern art. Free.

Other museums and galleries in Liverpool

Liverpool Football Club Visitors Centre, Anfield Road: trophies, memorabilia, video moments and a look into the playing fields.

Liverpool Museum and Planetarium, William Brown Street: science and natural history. Museum free.

Museum of Liverpool Life, William Brown Street: social history of the city: housing, education, work and industry.

Sudley, Mossley Hill Road: former house owned by shipping magnates, the Holts, with a distinguished art collection (Turner, Gainsborough, Reynolds) and fine furniture by George Bullock.

Walker Art Gallery, William Brown Street: among Britain's finest provincial art galleries: Italian, Dutch and pre-Raphaelite paintings, modern art and sculpture. Free.

In the rejuvenated docklands

►► **Liverpool** 172B1

Industrial activity on Merseyside has declined and the city has lost population in this century; out of the center, run-down streetscapes are testimony to some of the worst urban problem areas in Britain. Yet despite tangible signs of a long economic slump, Liverpool has an exhilarating sense of place, recalling its 19th-century heyday as England's second greatest port. After the silting up of Chester's port, Liverpool took over; it flourished in the late 18th century in its trade with the West Indies.

The ocean-going liners of the 19th and early 20th centuries have gone—to get a hint of what it was like to arrive from sea you should take the humbler **ferry** to Birkenhead and back. The **Royal Liver Building** (1911) and **Cunard Building** (1917) stand sentinel by the Mersey waterfront. Architecture in the city center displays a legacy of wealth and civic pride, seen at its best around **Dale Street**, **Water Street** and **William Brown Street**, and around classical **St. George's Hall** (1854). Recently revamped, **Albert Dock►►** (1846) has shops, cafés and a branch of the Tate Gallery installed in the rejuvenated warehouses.

At either end of the plum-brick Georgian townhouses of **Hope Street** stand the city's cathedrals. The **Anglican cathedral►**, the largest of its denomination in the world, is a mightily proportioned Gothic edifice, built between 1906 and 1980 to the design of 21-year-old Giles Gilbert Scott. To make the most of its hillside setting, the conventional east–west orientation was not used. By contrast, the **Metropolitan Roman Catholic Cathedral of Christ the King►** is a squat, tent-like affair set beneath a pinnacled lantern. This design by Frederick Gibberd was adopted after it became apparent that the original plan of Sir Edwin Lutyens was far too costly. Of Lutyens's vast building the foundation stone (1933) and the crypt exist.

► **Manchester** *172B2*

Manchester was the great commercial center for the Lancashire cotton industry. It has suffered some dreary post-war development, but there are several glimpses of impressive 19th-century grandeur and some enjoyable museums. The **town hall**► is a cavernous Gothic creation designed by Alfred Waterhouse that fills one side of Albert Square. Guided tours at 10AM and 2:30PM on weekdays show you the astonishing marble interior. Just north of this are the classical **Royal Exchange**, with its excellent lunar-module-style theater; **Barton Square**, a splendid Victorian shopping arcade of iron and glass; and at the city's heart the **cathedral** (originally a medieval church).

Farther south around **Peter Street** imposing buildings include the Athenaeum (1837), the Theatre Royal (1845) and the Free Trade Hall (1856); just behind, in the former Central Station, is the modern G-Mex exhibition center. In Deansgate is the Gothic Revival **Rylands Library**, with its richly ornamental façade, while just off **St. John Street** is the finest Georgian street in the city.

The recently revived area of Castlefield includes a reconstruction of a Roman fort that once stood here. The canal basin, where the Bridgewater and Rochdale canals meet, has atmosphere; the walk along the Rochdale Canal passes huge Victorian warehouses. The outstanding **Museum**

183

Trams approaching Piccadilly

of Science and Industry►► occupies the world's oldest railroad station; displays include stationary steam engines and a "hands-on" science center. A major draw to the city is the **Granada Studios tour**►, with exhibitions on T.V. and movies, including the set used in the T.V. soap opera "Coronation Street." The **Gallery of English Costume** in Platt Hall exhibits 400 years of fashion.

Manchester boasts a successful new light rail "tram" system that runs right across the city, the MetroLink.

L. S. Lowry (1887–1976)
Manchester-born Laurence Stephen Lowry studied art in Manchester and Salford, and around 1916 developed an interest in painting the bleak landscapes of industrial Lancashire mill-towns. The naive style of the matchstick men figures has been much copied but at the time his choice of subject was quite apart from the mainstream; many of his works had touches of darkness and satire, and an element of the grotesque. Lowry's studio has been recreated in the City Art Gallery in Deansgate, complete with all his clutter and his 78rpm gramophone records. A larger selection of his work is on display at the Salford Museum and Art Gallery.

■ **The centers of such cities as Liverpool, Manchester, Glasgow, Bristol and Newcastle-upon-Tyne are packed with historic interest and cultural attractions. The back streets may not be particularly fascinating and, like every large city in the world, some districts are better avoided, but in most areas you are as safe as in your own home, if not safer.....■**

For many centuries, a town was virtually all center. With its houses and churches, shops and inns huddled as tightly together as sheep in a pen, the town was set apart and snugly protected from the outside world by its surrounding wall. The Industrial Revolution changed all that. Towns swelled and ballooned out over the nearby countryside. Even so, the different areas around a city's historic core still enjoyed a strong sense of identity and neighborhood.

God the first garden made, and the first city Cain.
Adam Cowley, *The Garden* (17th century)

The price of unemployment With the decline of heavy industry since World War II and the steady reduction in the number of unskilled jobs, some of these areas have become cut off from the rest of the city as deprived pockets of heavy unemployment, isolated from working life and the country's general trend of increasing affluence. They are portrayed by the media as "no go areas"—dilapidated and dangerous districts, the home territory of vandals and criminals, with a culture of violence and mindless destructiveness. The majority of perfectly law-abiding inhabitants struggle on as best they can, though constantly in fear. The Moss Side district of Manchester is a notorious example.

A mistaken vision Typically these are areas of high-rise housing, whose towers were put up by the local Council, with all the best intentions, in the 1950s and 1960s. The modern movement in architecture, which unfortunately dominated in 1945, believed in austerely functional high-rise buildings to provide decent, modern housing on a minimum of land. Experience has shown all too clearly,

There are some appalling scenes of dereliction . . .

however, that these towers can destroy any sense of community and create a desolate, urban jungle.

Racial tension Problems arising from racial tensions add fuel to the fire, as do police attempts to arrest drug dealers and other criminals. In the 1980s Britain saw a spate of rioting, notably in the run-down St. Paul's area of Bristol, the Brixton district of South London with its large black population, "Broadwater Farm" in Tottenham in North London (anything less like a farm it would be hard to conceive) and Toxteth in Liverpool. By the early 1990s the new fad of "joy-riding" afflicted inner city areas— stolen cars were raced recklessly, sometimes killing the participants or innocent bystanders.

Putting a brighter face on things What has been described is the face of inner-city Britain that reaches the headlines. But behind these scenes of destitution, steps are being taken to try to give people a sense of pride in their community once more. New housing management plans all over London are brightening up high-rises with fresh coats of paint, creating (in conjunction with better policies on community care) an environment that is not only more pleasant but safer too. All over the country local housing associations are renovating street after street of derelict houses, often former welfare properties.

A new lease of life While these initiatives have been taken on at a community level, substantial investments have also been put into the infrastructure of Britain's major cities. Urban Development Corporations have been responsible for huge rebuilding projects in some of the country's most derelict areas, notably in Wigan, Sheffield and Bradford in the North of England. Empty dockland warehouses and railroad properties have been developed into sleek business and industrial premises. There has been sensitive development of Bristol's commercial center, close to the St. Paul's district, for example; Birmingham, Manchester, Glasgow and Cardiff have all seen large-scale rebuilding. It is in these burgeoning new city centers, with their spanking-new concert halls and arts centers, shopping malls and open spaces, that the visitor to Great Britain at the end of the 20th century will feel a reviving sense of civic pride.

. . . but initiatives are being taken to improve things

Demonstrating a new spirit of enterprise: Manchester's MetroLink trams

The second Blitz
Prince Charles once remarked that far more damage had been inflicted on London by planners and developers after World War II than the entire might of Hitler's Luftwaffe had achieved during it. The same point, unfortunately, is true of too many other British cities and towns, devastated by a postwar alliance of urban planners, property developers and architects. These experts all too often seemed to favor cars and concrete. Whole areas were torn down, often against the wishes of their inhabitants, rebuilt in concrete and pierced by high-speed roads. The only mercy is that the destruction was eventually halted by public resentment and professional misgivings.

185

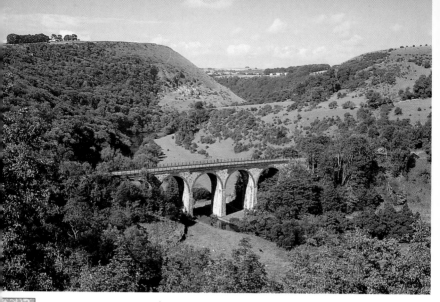

Monsal Dale: the old viaduct now carries a footpath

▶▶   Peak National Park   *172B3*

Britain's first National Park, created in 1951, is encircled by large industrial cities. Though there are no major peaks as such – the district is essentially one of rolling hillscapes – the feeling of escape is exhilarating.

The White Peak Most of the southern park comprises the limestone landscapes of the White Peak, where rivers groove deep-cut gorges, or "dales," beneath a plateau of stone-walled farmland. Most spectacular of all are **Dove Dale▶▶** and its continuation, **Beresford Dale** (despite the crowds), **Monsal Dale▶▶** (with its famous viaduct), the **Manifold Valley▶** just below Wetton, and wooded **Lathkill Dale▶** near Youlgreave. Rewarding villages include **Winster, Alstonefield, Tideswell, Ilam, Ashford in the Water** and **Eyam▶**, whose villagers were ravaged by the plague in 1665 when, following their vicar's lead, they gallantly confined themselves to their village after an infected box of cloth arrived from London. **Tissington▶** has perhaps the loveliest of all Peak village streets, with wide grass road borders and a Jacobean hall. Equally absorbing is **Cromford▶**, an early industrial village where Richard Arkwright set up the world's first water-powered cotton mill in 1771 (now a museum). The Peak's finest prehistoric monument is **Arbor Low▶**, south of Monyash, a 2,000-year-old stone circle. **Castleton▶▶** is the nub of the Peak's caving district (see panel): north of the village, a ridge ends at Mam Tor, known as "Shivering Mountain" because of frequent landslips; Cave Dale looks up to the Norman keep of Peveril Castle, holding its head high above the village.

The National Park boundary excludes all the local towns except for **Bakewell**, home of Bakewell Puddings (way superior to the mass-produced Bakewell tarts). The center is ruined by traffic, but it is more pleasant up the hill around the church and the delightful Old House Museum of relics of the past. Out of town are the Peak's two great houses:

Above: Richard Arkwright
Below: on the High Peak Trail

Haddon Hall►► is a wonderfully preserved medieval house with a panelled gallery, a chapel and walled garden; palatial Chatsworth House►►►, home of the Dukes of Devonshire, has a breathtaking collection of art and furniture. Its grounds were landscaped by Capability Brown and Joseph Paxton (see page 17); Paxton also designed the quaint estate workers' village, Edensor.

Buxton►►, an elegant former spa, is the *de facto* Peak capital. Its classically inspired 18th-century Crescent, an Opera House, pavilion gardens and town hall help to give the town a distinguished air. An excellent town museum features a Wonders of the Peak exhibition, while the Micrarium offers views of the microscopic natural world. Matlock Bath, a former spa, occupies an extraordinary site in the Derwent Gorge. Cable cars make it easy to explore the Heights of Abraham, a park with woodland walks, views and caves. Nearby at Crich is the wonderful National Tramway Museum►.

The Dark Peak Millstone grit is the underlying rock in the northern Peak. The moors and grassland really are dark; the scenery is bleaker and more rugged. Millstones, for grinding grain, were once a major industry—workings litter abandoned quarries and the stone disks now stand on plinths to mark the National Park boundary. The one-street village of Edale lies below the massive peat-bog plateau of Kinder Scout, the highest terrain in the Peak (636m). The A57 heads over the Snake Pass, giving a good picture of the austerity of the northern moors, while

Bakewell: the proof of the pudding is in the eating . . .

the Derwent Reservoirs► near Hope are the most attractive of many manmade lakes. Old cotton-mill towns have a 19th-century workaday character: New Mills is one of the most rewarding, with a gorge cutting through its center. Lyme Hall► has a fine Palladian hall with Grinling Gibbons woodcarving; its park has gentle walks. The gritstone edges such as Stanage Edge provide dramatic level tops, with easy paths and challenging rock climbs.

187

Caves
Of the five limestone caverns near Castleton that are open to the public, Treak Cliff has some fine stalactites and displays of Blue John (a crystalline fluorspar, worked into jewelry and souvenirs, and sold locally), Speedwell Cavern features an underground boat-trip along a tunnel that forms part of an old lead mine, and Bagshawe Cavern near Bradwell may appeal to those wanting to try adventure caving. Peak Cavern on the edge of Castleton has a magnificent entrance and is the largest cave in England. Blue John Cavern has Blue John but no stalactites. On the edge of Buxton, Poole's Cavern has the finest formations.

Lead mining
Lead mining was big in the White Peak until the last century—the Manifold Valley and Lathkill Dale have traces of past mining activity, Magpie Mine near Sheldon being the most conspicuous relic. Many villages expanded for the purpose; today these stone-built settlements are surprising rural and merge into the scenery along with their agricultural neighbors. At Matlock Bath an excellent mining museum lies close to the re-opened Temple Mine, which non-claustrophobics may like to walk around.

■ **This most famous of factory-workers' villages looked forward to a new age of cities: of greenery, clean air and sanitation. It was conceived as a place in which, in the words of its founder, the inhabitants "will be able to know more about the science of life than they can in a back slum, and in which they will learn that there is more in life than the mere going to and returning from work, and looking forward to Saturday night to draw their wages".....■**

Village trail
The Port Sunlight Heritage Centre tells the story of Port Sunlight and a village trail leads visitors round the garden village, taking in the Lady Lever Art Gallery. Set up by Lever after the death of his wife, the gallery contains a surprising wealth of art, including pre-Raphaelite paintings and Wedgwood ceramics.

Fair deals for the workers Port Sunlight was in fact one of several 19th-century innovations in the Wirral. In 1842 Joseph Paxton's Birkenhead Park had been Britain's first public park and in 1853 Prices Patent Candle Company had created Bromborough Pool Village for its workers.

The soap king The industrialist William Hesketh Lever, the first Viscount Leverhulme, was a Liberal Member of Parliament and philanthropist, with an interest in the arts and landscape design. He co-owned a soap factory in Warrington; the success of Sunlight Soap spiralled and in 1887 he came to the Wirral, the peninsula that juts out between the Mersey and Liverpool on one side and the Dee and Wales on the other, to set up a new factory. He acquired Thornton Manor and transformed Thornton Hough into a mock-Tudor village for his estate workers.

A vision of the future The factory village of Port Sunlight was to be a haven of peace and cleanliness. Cottages were built to a high standard in half-timbered Tudor and bricky Queen Anne and Elizabethan styles (no two groups of cottages are the same); gardens and parks were liberally provided. The village's visionary design was a predecessor of the garden cities of Ebenezer Howard, which in turn influenced the growth of the garden suburb and of the first New Towns.

▶▶ Quarry Bank Mill 172B2

The centerpiece of Styal Country Park—a swath of green on the fringes of Manchester—is this water-powered cotton mill, built in the 18th century and now maintained by the National Trust. It gives an excellent idea of the working of a weaving mill, complete with the authentically deafening clatter of the looms. Exhibits explain cotton processing and the working conditions of the time, and weaving demonstrations take place.

▶ Stoke-on-Trent (The Potteries) 172B2

Stoke is a conurbation of six towns—Burslem, Fenton, Hanley, Longton, Stoke and Tunstall—but only locals can tell where one ends and the next begins. At first glance the industrial and residential sprawl is unappetizing, but this is the heart of pottery country and anyone interested in the potter's craft should certainly make a visit. A "China Service" bus from Stoke station provides a convenient way of getting between the sites.

The **Gladstone Pottery Museum▶▶▶** is a preserved 19th-century pottery with bottle-shaped brick kilns (once a common feature of Stoke-on-Trent, but now all but vanished). It has pottery demonstrations and a fine display of ceramics ranging from high-class ornaments to Victorian lavatories. The **Etruria Industrial Museum▶** features the last steam-powered potter's mill in Britain, while the **City Museum and Art Gallery▶** has a huge collection of Staffordshire pottery. Also open to the public are the **Minton Museum▶**, the **Sir Henry Doulton Gallery▶** and the **Wedgwood Visitor Centre▶** at Barlaston, 6 miles south of Stoke.

At Tunstall, the **Chatterley Whitfield Mining Museum▶** has plenty to see on the surface (including a steam-powered winding-engine and colliery buildings) and an informative guided tour down the coal-mine.

Huddled around a courtyard and built in the 15th and 16th centuries, **Little Moreton Hall▶▶** (NT), 9 miles north of Stoke-on-Trent, is the best example of the Cheshire half-timbered "vernacular," with a wainscoted gallery, great hall, chapel and knot garden.

About 15 miles east of Stoke-on-Trent is **Alton Towers**, where the parkland surrounding the ruined home of the 15th Earl of Shrewsbury today is full of the sounds of Britain's most famous theme park.

Staffordshire figurines
Simple figure models in earthenware or salt-glazed stoneware were first made in Staffordshire in the mid-18th century. These included the so-called "pew'" groups of figures seated on a high-backed settle, and the famous soldiers on horseback associated with John Astbury. At the end of the century the range of production greatly expanded and potters such as the Wood family produced classically inspired figures along with busts of contemporary celebrities such as Napoleon. The early Victorian period saw the emergence of the flat-back portrait figure, simply molded representations of royalty, politicians, preachers, actors, literary and sporting characters. Also from this period are the perenially popular, and much reproduced, Staffordshire dogs.

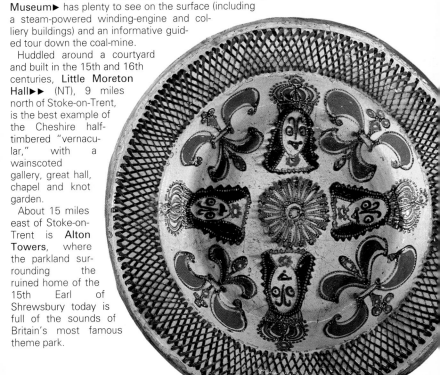

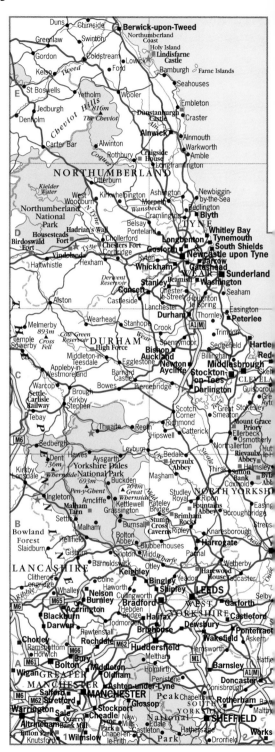

Duns
Chirnside
Berwick-upon-Tweed
Northumberland
Coast
Greenlaw
Swinton
Holy Island
Gordon
Coldstream
Lowick
Lindisfarne Castle
Kelso
Tweed
Ford
Bamburgh
Farne Islands
St Boswells
Yetholm
Wooler
Seahouses
Jedburgh
Denholm
Cheviot Hills 816m
The Cheviot
Dunstanburgh Castle
Embleton
Craster
Carter Bar
Alwinton
Coquet
Alnwick
Alnmouth
Rothbury
Craigside House
Warkworth
Amble
Longframlington
Otterburn
NORTHUMBERLAND
Kielder Water
West Woodburn
Kirkwhelpington
Ashington
Newbiggin-by-the-Sea
Northumberland National Park
N. Tyne
Belsay
Morpeth
Wansbeck
Bedlington
Blyth
Hadrian's Wall
Ponteland
Cramlington
TYNE
Whitley Bay
Housesteads Fort
Chollerford
Chesters Fort
Longbenton
Tynemouth
Birdoswald Fort
Corbridge
Gosforth
South Shields
Vindolanda
Tyne
Ryton
Newcastle upon Tyne
Haltwhistle
Hexham
Whickham
Jarrow
Gateshead
Derwent Reservoir
Beamish
WEAR
Sunderland
Alston
Consett
Stanley
Chester-le-Street
Washington
Castleside
Houghton-le-Spring
Seaham
Wearhead
Lanchester
Durham
Thornley
Easington
Melmerby 893m
Stanhope
Crook
A1(M)
Peterlee
Temple Sowerby
Cow Green Reservoir
Cross Fell
DURHAM
Wear
Spennymoor
Trimdon
Sedgefield
Hartle
High Force
Bishop Auckland
Red
Middleton-in-Teesdale
Eggleston
Newton Aycliffe
Billingham
Middlesbrough
Appleby-in-Westmoreland
Barnard Castle
Stockton-on-Tees
CLEVELA
Warcop
Brough
Bowes
Piercebridge
Darlington
Guisborou
Great Stokesley
Gt Ayt
Settle-Carlisle Railway
Kirkby Stephen
Tees
Scotch Corner
Smeaton
Tebay
Thwaite
Reeth
Richmond
Catterick
Mount Grace Priory
Ellerbeck
Osmotherly
Hut
Sedbergh
Hawes
Aysgarth
Leyburn
Swale
Bedale
Northallerton
Rievaulx Abbey
Dent 736m
Whernside
Yorkshire Dales National Park 693m
Buckden
Jervaulx Abbey
Thirsk
Helmsley
Kirkby Lonsdale
Pen-y-Ghent
703m
Great Whernside
Masham
Sutton Bank
Coxwold
Byla
Abb
Ingleton
Arncliffe
Kettlewell
Studley Royal
Ripon
NORTH YORKSH
Malham Tarn
Grassington
Pateley Bridge
Fountains Abbey
Boroughbridge
Settle
Malham
Burnsall
Stump Cross Caverns
Brimham Rocks
Ripley
Knaresborough
Strens
Bowland Forest
Hellifield
Bolton Abbey
Blubberhouses
Harrogate
Ouse
Slaidburn
Gisburn
Skipton
Middl
Wharfe
Pannal
Wetherby
LANCASHIRE
Barnoldswick
Otley
Harewood House
Tadcaster
Clitheroe
Longridge
Colne
Haworth
Yeadon
Keighley
Bingley
Yeadon
Selby
Ribble
Whalley
Nelson
Cullingworth
Shipley
LEEDS
Garforth
M6
M65
Burnley
Hebden Bridge
Bradford
WEST YORKSHIRE
Castleford
Blackburn
Accrington
Todmorden
Halifax
Dewsbury
Pontefract
Darwen
Rawtenstall
Brighouse
Wakefield
Askern
Chorley
Rochdale
M62
Huddersfield
Hemsworth
M1
Ramsbottom
M66
Meltham
Hatfie
Horwich
Bury
Middleton
Holmfirth
Barnsley
Wigan
Bolton
Oldham
Holmfirth
Penistone
Doncaster
A1(M)
GREATER MANCHESTER
Ashton-under-Lyne
Salford
Chapeltown
Conisbrough
Warrington
M6
M62
MANCHESTER
Peak
Rotherham
Baw
Stretford
Glossop
SOUTH YORKSHIRE
Maltby
Sale
Stockport
New Mills
National
SHEFFIELD
Altrincham
Cheadle
Hyde
Edale
Castleton
Hathersage
Works
Tatton Park
Bank Mill
Chapel-en-le-Frith
Park
Dronfield
Knutsford
Wilmslow

Northeast England This region includes most of the **Pennines**, the chain of hills that forms the backbone of upland England, from the Peak District in the south to the Scottish borders in the north. It also encompasses **Yorkshire**, the largest county in Britain, divided into North, West and South for administrative purposes. It has a reputation for friendliness, with the finest of Britain's medieval cities in York itself and a magnificent heritage of abbey ruins and ecclesiastical architecture.

Industrial Yorkshire The industrial parts of **West Yorkshire** should not be overlooked. The moorland and the scenically sited, 19th-century stone-built mill towns around Calderdale have a strong and unique personality; you can explore canals and hills and the adjacent Brontë country at Haworth. Industrial heritage is the big theme here. Leeds recalls its mill days in the Armley Mills

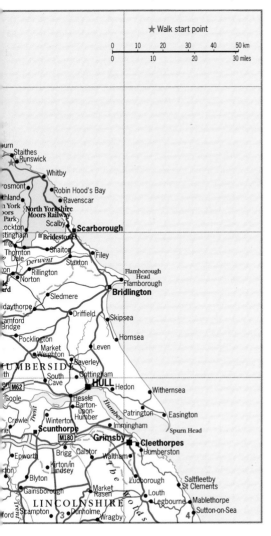

NORTHEAST ENGLAND

A sheep show at Langthwaite in the Yorkshire Dales

192

Museum and at Thwaite Mills; and it has some handsome Victorian and Edwardian shopping arcades. Bradford is still fairly impressive both for its legacy of the past and for its vibrant museums. Sheffield, in **South Yorkshire**, has cultural attractions. Abbeydale Industrial Hamlet is a fitting memento to the city's steel manufacturing days.

The Dales, the Moors and the Vale of York The Yorkshire Dales are for lovers of the great outdoors—an excellent area for car-touring, walking and caving.

East of the Pennines, in the **Vale of York** are York itself, the elegant spa town of Harrogate and the enchanting ruins of Fountains Abbey. Southeast Yorkshire is less visited: the flat agricultural scenery may be humdrum but Selby and Beverley (the latter in **Humberside**) each have splendid churches; Hull has a range of sights, including the Town Docks Museum, which celebrates its nautical past; a huge suspension bridge spans the Humber.

The **North York Moors** are detached from the Pennine chain and have a quite different character. The coast, with its high cliffs and fishing villages, is a joy.

County Durham, Tyne and Wear, Northumberland The **Pennine** landscape becomes bleaker and more lonesome as one proceeds, towards Scotland, through Teesdale, in County Durham, and the Cheviots, in Northumberland. Elsewhere much of **County Durham** has an industrial face, and, like Middlesbrough (in Cleveland) is economically depressed. The open air museum at Beamish is a splendid re-creation of an early 20th-century industrial village, while Durham has a great Norman cathedral. **Tyne and Wear** incorporates a conurbation centered on Newcastle-upon-Tyne; locals here are nicknamed Geordies and are known for their quickfire humor and guttural accent. It is not a prosperous region economically, but the place has considerable verve. On its back doorstep, **Northumberland**, in total contrast, has wide open spaces, the great Roman structure of Hadrian's Wall, and a long and quiet coastline.

BEST PLACES TO GO
Historic towns and cities
County Durham Barnard Castle, Durham.
Humberside Beverley.
North Yorkshire Harrogate, Helmsley, Knaresborough, Middleham, Richmond, Ripon, Scarborough, York.
Northumberland Alnwick, Hexham.
Tyne and Wear Newcastle-upon-Tyne.
Industrial heritage
Abbeydale Industrial Hamlet, Beamish, Bradford, Halifax, Hebden Bridge, Hull, Saltaire.
Scenery North York Moors, Northumberland, South Pennines (Calderdale and Haworth areas), Yorkshire Dales.
Coastal towns and villages
North Yorkshire Robin Hood's Bay, Runswick Bay, Staithes, Whitby.
Northumberland Bamburgh, Berwick-upon-Tweed.
Historic sites and remains
Fountains Abbey, Hadrian's Wall, Holy Island, Rievaulx Abbey.

Walks

Hadrian's Wall, 190D1
Northumberland National Park

Nearly all the interest is along the Wall itself, with its host of Roman features. There is not much reason to go far afield. Simply walking along the Wall is a great experience, with views from the ridge of the Great Whin Sill across lonely Northumberland. For a sample, start at Housesteads fort and walk west, past Craig Lough to Twice Brewed youth hostel and back (2½ hours). In summer you can use a bus service along the B6318 to take you back.

Holy Island, 190E2
Northumberland

Use main parking lot in village (note tide times). The island's best circular walk is three-quarters coastal, all of it level. Follow Sandham Lane north (turn left and left again out of the car park), turn right beyond the dunes and follow the coast around, past Emanuel Head, where an obelisk looks along the coast into Scotland. Pass Lindisfarne Castle to finish by Lindisfarne Priory in the village. (1½ hours)

Ingleton Waterfalls, 190B1
Yorkshire Dales National Park

Parking lot by main entrance to falls. Also known as Ingleton Glen, this splendid gorge is well worth the entrance fee. A circular trail takes in a series of falls of considerable indi-

Lindisfarne Castle, Holy Island

viduality; the most dramatic are the first two, Pecka Fall and Thornton Force. Beyond lies a handily placed refreshment stand, then the path leads into more open country with views of surrounding hills before a finale along the Doe Gorge (2 hours). A booklet available locally explains the geology.

Runswick Bay and Staithes, 191C3
North York Moors National Park

Park just above Runswick Bay village. This walk along the clifftops (part of the Cleveland Way) links two captivating coastal villages. From Runswick Bay village, walk up the road; at the top follow the Cleveland Way as it branches off on the right, soon reaching the clifftop for an easy walk past Port Mulgrave and reaching Staithes harbour. Return the same way. (2½ hours)

Upper Swaledale, Yorkshire 190C1
Dales National Park

Roadside parking, Muker village. This walk from Muker enjoys a magnificent steep-sided section of the dale. Walk into the village, and find a path out of its north end that leads to a bridge over the Swale; continue north up the dale for 1¾ miles to the next bridge (close by Keld). Cross and turn left on the Pennine Way (fork left soon for a short detour to Kisdon Force waterfall). The Way rises slightly, offering fine views. Finally leave it for a farmtrack that drops to Muker. (2½ hours)

Misericords

The folding seats in the choirstalls of many cathedrals and major churches have a carved under-bracket known as a misericord (from the opening words of the 51st Psalm *Miserere mei, Deus*: Have mercy on me, O Lord). When the seats were turned up, the misericords made ledges for the monks to rest on during the long periods of standing in their services. Frequently carved in fanciful designs, the misericords were deliberately made so narrow that there was no chance of dozing off.

Saltaire

This famous example of a "factory village" dates from the 1850s, when Titus Salt, an enlightened industrialist of liberal views and temperance ideals, decided to house his workforce in this garden village of parks and spacious streets, free from Bradford's smog. The place has scarcely changed, though the houses are now mostly privately owned. The mill itself is used for a variety of purposes. Paintings by native son artist David Hockney are on display in a gallery and there is a museum of harmoniums and reed organs. Other sections are leased for commercial use.

►► **Beamish: North of England Open Air Museum** *190D2*

A northern industrial village of the early 1900s is evocatively re-created, complete with colliers' cottages, a pub, trams and steam engines. It is full of fetching cameo details, such as the items on display in the village store.

Take a ride on the open-top omnibus at Beamish

►► **Beverley** *191B3*

Beverley is a delightful town. It has pleasing Georgian brickwork, the North Bar (the only survivor of five town gates), an animated Saturday market and, above all, two gems of church architecture. Begun in Norman times, the **Minster►►** is famed for the quality of its Gothic stone-carving, its 68 misericords (see panel) made by the Ripon school of woodcarvers, and its fine-towered west front. **St Mary's Church►** has a 15th-century west façade and a panelled chancel ceiling depicting early kings, all cloaked and crowned against a gold background.

► **Bradford** *190A2*

A patchily impressive Victorian city (knocked about by postwar planning), Bradford is the fruit of the textile-mill age; the Gothic Revival **town hall** and the spectacular tombs of **Undercliffe Cemetery►** are monuments of past achievement. In recent days, the hugely entertaining **National Museum of Photography, Film and Television►►►** has put Bradford on the map: here you can see yourself read the news, watch a Victorian magic lantern show or 1950s T.V. advertisements; admission is free, and the place is usually full of children. The museum is annexed to a cinema with Britain's only "IMAX" screen, as high as a five-story building; movie shows feature balloon flights or hair-raising journeys into the Grand Canyon.

The **Colour Museum**▶, explores the use of color-chemistry, and the **Bradford Industrial Museum**▶, with rebuilt back-to-back houses, has a tour through the world of textile production.

▶▶   Calderdale   190A1

A former textile valley in the heart of the Pennines, Calderdale is rich with local color. Sturdy rows of stone cottages and the geometry of stone-walled fields stripe the sides of the valley. The largest settlement, **Halifax** ▶ is unjustifiably ignored by many visitors; in fact it is the best preserved of West Yorkshire's industrial towns, with the splendid galleried Piece Hall, the former cloth market built around a great courtyard, and some handsome stone civic buildings. The town hall was designed by Charles Barry (one of the architects of the Houses of Parliament, London). Calderdale Industrial Museum covers the story of mining, local textiles, the Halifax Building Society, and toffee.

Hebden Bridge▶, near the site of the last clog mill in England, is magnificently set at the meeting of two valleys, its gray houses rising row by row up the hillside. From the original Hepton Bridge a cobbled path rises steeply to the hilltop village of **Heptonstall**▶, a fascinating place with cobbled streets, a ruined church and the oldest Methodist chapel in the world in continuous use (since 1764). The village was a busy hand-looming center until eclipsed by the mills in Hebden Bridge.

▶▶   Castle Howard   191B3

In the gentle Howardian Hills, this enchanting early 18th-century house stands surrounded by a vast park adorned with ornamental lakes, a colonnaded mausoleum and a "temple" designed by Vanbrugh. He is commonly attributed with the design of the house itself, yet he was then a man of no architectural experience; it seems likely that his clerk of works, the great architect Nicholas Hawksmoor, had more than a helping hand. The house has portraits by Holbein and others, statues, tapestries, porcelain, furniture and a costume collection. It will be familiar to many as a setting for the T.V. dramatization of *Brideshead Revisited*.

Walks in Calderdale
Calderdale is an excellent base for walking, with the Pennine Way and Calderdale Way striding over open moors and a dense network of public footpaths. From Hebden Bridge, walk along the Rochdale Canal towpath in either direction for glimpses of typical Pennine features such as back-to-back cottages and old mills. This can be combined with a walk up to Heptonstall, which abuts the top of a dramatic gorge (Colden Clough). The area north of Hebden Bridge is a popular beauty spot with strolls through woods, along the river or up to Hardcastle Crags themselves.

195

The mill at Saltaire, pre-eminent in its day

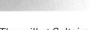

►►► Durham 190C2

Few places in Britain can rival the drama of Durham's setting, its majestic cathedral soaring high over sandstone cliffs and woodlands ribboning the tight curve of the River Wear. The historic center is compact and largely traffic-free, and walking around it is pleasant.

The nave, chancel and transepts of the **cathedral►►►** were built over a single period (1070–1140). The sense of balanced might and soaring space are enthralling—it's Britain's finest Norman church architecture. In the cathedral precincts is College Green, the most complete example of a Benedictine monastery in England. Durham was until 1836 a "palatinate," enjoying royal rights and ruled by prince bishops, who were thus lay and religious leaders.

The main entrance to the cathedral is via **Palace Green**, where the other buildings belong to the **university**, England's third oldest. The **castle►►**, erected to protect the cathedral against Scottish incursions, dates from the 1070s. The university rebuilt the octagonal keep in 1840 but several earlier features survive, including the Great Hall (1284) and the Black Staircase (1662) (guided tours).

For the best views, follow the **riverside path►►**, cross over **Prebends Bridge**, beside weirs and old mills (one houses an **archaeological museum**), and go up to **South Street**. **North Bailey** and **South Bailey** are especially attractive streets, leading past **Durham Heritage Centre**.

The **Oriental Museum►** in Elvet Hall (part of the university) has jade and ancient Egyptian collections.

Durham sits high on a peninsula in a curve of the Wear

Cathedral firsts
Durham Cathedral represents the highest achievement of the Norman style. In addition to the characteristic use of rounded arches, the building has what are thought to be the earliest transverse Gothic-style pointed arches in English architecture: since the cathedral was built largely at a single period, this really shows a transition between the two building techniques. The sense of scale is created by the hitherto unprecedented use of rib-vaulting, which creates greater space between load-bearing columns.

St Cuthbert
The Chapel of the Nine Altars in the cathedral contains the relics of St Cuthbert, brought here by Lindisfarne monks who escaped from Holy Island (see page 199) when Danish raiders arrived in 875. Cuthbert was a shepherd boy from the Lammermuir Hills who decided to dedicate his life to God, living on Holy Island and later the Farne Islands. He remained a lover of all animals.

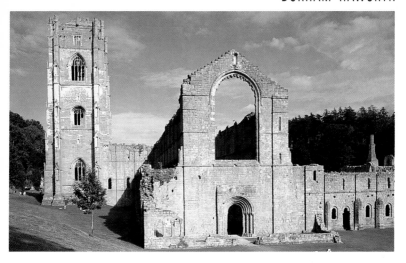

Fountains Abbey: once one of the richest in England

▶▶ Fountains Abbey and Studley Royal   190B2

In medieval times, **Fountains Abbey** (NT) had grange farms and lands across much of northern England and was a major wool producer. Its former prosperity is evident in what are widely regarded as the greatest of Britain's abbey ruins. Founded for 12 Benedictine monks who later changed to Cistercian rule, the abbey still has a 12th-century nave and transepts, a tower completed shortly before the Dissolution, and buildings where the monks lived and worked. Adjacent lies the **Studley Royal** estate; its 18th-century park has follies, a water garden, deer park and delicious vistas of the abbey. St. Mary's Church is a remarkable mock-medieval creation with a painted roof and walls of Egyptian alabaster, built 1871–8 by William Burges.

Ripon▶ is an appealing town with a fine cathedral notable for its west front, misericords and Saxon crypt. Since 886 the nightwatch horn has been blown in the market square at 9pm to guard the town in darkness.

▶▶ Harewood House   190B2

The seat of the Earls of Harewood is a supremely stately composition, completed in 1771, with an impressive list of credits: interiors and furniture by Robert Adam, exterior by John Carr, murals by Angelica Kauffman, formal gardens by Charles Barry, and parkland landscaped by Capability Brown. Painted ceilings, Sèvres and Chinese porcelain, and intricate plasterwork further grace the building, and there is an aviary of exotic birds.

▶ Haworth   190B1

The Brontë Parsonage Museum (see page 198) and a walk taking in the Brontë Waterfalls and Top Withins justify a literary pilgrimage to this popular Pennine village.

The village is a stop on the private **Worth Valley Railway**▶, which steams from Keighley to Oxenhope.

Ripon's saint
St. Wilfred was the abbot of the monastery of Ripon in the 7th century and later became Bishop of York. On the Saturday before the first Monday in August, a procession with floats is headed by a man dressed as St. Wilfred, complete with miter and crook, riding a horse; the dean greets him at the west door and a service of thanksgiving follows.

■ **Charlotte (1816–55), Emily (1818–48) and Anne (1820–49) Brontë were the daughters of an Irish clergyman. The Brontës' lives were constantly beset by ill health and circumstance. Charlotte had an unhappy love affair in Brussels, Emily had no close friends and Anne had a tendency toward religious melancholy. Meanwhile, their brother Bramwell, disillusioned with his attempts to be a writer and artist, took to drink and opium.....■**

My sister Emily loved the moors. Flowers brighter than the rose bloomed in the blackest heath for her; out of a sullen hollow in a livid hillside her mind would make an Eden. She found in the bleak solitude many and dear delights; and not the least and best loved was—liberty.
Charlotte Brontë
(1816–1855)

Haworth's cobbled main street is today lined with gift shops

The Brontë name
The family name was originally Brunty or Prunty but the form Brontë was adopted after Lord Nelson was given the title Duke of Brontë by the King of Naples after the Battle of the Nile in 1798.

The Brontës lived in the bleak parsonage in Haworth, overlooking a graveyard that polluted the water supply, severely reducing villagers' life expectancy. The girls consequently escaped into fantasy worlds. It was Charlotte's determination that got the Brontës into print, after she had chanced upon some secret poetry of Emily's and had been convinced of its worth; the three contributed works to a volume published in 1846 under the pen-names of Acton (Anne), Currer (Charlotte) and Ellis (Emily) Bell; the sales were dismal (two books in the first month), but with Charlotte's drive, the sisters each submitted novels. Emily's *Wuthering Heights*, probably set in the now-ruined farmhouse of Top Withins, and Anne's *Agnes Grey* were published in 1847. Charlotte failed to get *The Professor* published, but the constructive comments of one publisher gave her encouragement: she completed *Jane Eyre* soon after and it won immediate acclaim—Thackeray read it in a single sitting.

Hard times But the sisters had to spend much time nursing their brother Bramwell, and the money from the books went to paying off his debts; after his death in September 1848, Emily contracted consumption and went to her grave three months later. Anne too fell ill and died the next year at Scarborough, after writing *The Tenant of Wildfell Hall*.

Charlotte was brought to London as a literary celebrity; here she made friends with the successful novelist Mrs Gaskell, who later wrote a biography of Charlotte. Meanwhile, Charlotte worked on *Villette*, based on her time in Brussels, and married Arthur Bell Nicholls, their curate, after two years of opposition by her father. She died nine months later in pregnancy.

IN MEMORY OF
EMILY JANE BRONTË
WHO DIED DEC.19TH 1848.
AGED 30 YEARS.
AND OF
CHARLOTTE BRONTË

198

▶▶ **Northumberland Coast** 190E2

England's northeasternmost seaboard is low-lying and virtually unspoiled, characterized by expansive beaches,
profuse birdlife, quiet resorts with golf courses and
sands, and wind-haunted castle ruins. The immediate hinterland is flat, uneventful farmland.

Berwick-upon-Tweed▶▶ changed hands 13 times
between England and Scotland during the period
1100–1510; the Tweed, a famous salmon river which
runs just south beneath a trio of bridges (including 17th-
century Berwick Bridge with its 15 arches) seems the natural border but the town has been English since 1482.
You can take an excellent walk following the 16th-century
walls, the best-preserved fortification of its date in Britain,
which encircle the town; you'll pass the restored quay,
Berwick Barracks (1717, the first purpose-built barracks in
the country, now housing a regimental museum and a
branch of the Burrell art collection) and a rare church built
at the time of the Commonwealth (1652).

Berwick bits and pieces
Although the town of
Berwick is English, the old
county of Berwickshire was
in Scotland and Berwick
Rangers play as a Scottish
football club. With the coming of the railroad,
Berwick's castle was
pulled down to make way
for the station and much of
its stone was used in
Stephenson's railroad
bridge. There is a local
story that the town is still at
war with Germany. Berwick
cockles are not fishes but
an old-fashioned pepper-
mint.

The Farne Islands: a birdlife experience like no other

Holy Island▶▶, accessible by car at low tide (the times
are posted) via a causeway, is excellent for walks (see
page 193) and has great historic interest as the cradle of
Christianity in England (see panel). Lindisfarne Castle,
lone by the shore, was converted in the 1900s by architect Sir Edwin Lutyens and is open to the public.
Bamburgh▶ close by has a Norman castle, revamped in
the 18th and 19th centuries, with porcelain and armor collections. Close to the fishing port of **Craster**, which has a
workaday harbor and kipper smokeries, **Dunstanburgh
Castle**▶ is an eerie ruin, the largest of the Northumbrian
coastal strongholds, begun in 1313 and in decline by
1500. Inland lies **Alnwick**▶, a dignified stone-built market
town and a pleasant base for exploring the area. **Alnwick
Castle**▶ dates from Norman times but has a surprisingly
sumptuous Renaissance-style interior, fine Meissen

Holy Island
In 635, at the request of the
king of Northumbria, Aidan,
a missionary from the
Scottish island of Iona,
landed and founded the
now ruined Lindisfarne
Priory on what is today
known as Holy Island. This
became a Benedictine
monastery in 1082.
Christianity spread from
here across northern
England; a museum tells
the story. The Lindisfarne
Gospels, a famous illumi-
nated manuscript of *c*700,
is now kept in the British
Museum in London.

Lindisfarne nature reserve
Home to wildfowl and waders; a major site for wigeon and the only British wintering ground for pale-bellied Brent geese, the nature reserve includes mudflats and dunes around Holy Island, and the farther-flung Farne Islands. The latter are an important habitat for seals and seabirds; from Easter to October cruises depart from Seahouses—it is an exciting boat ride that offers really close-up encounters with the surprisingly tame wild birds.

china and paintings by Reynolds and Titian; the Victorian architect Salvin was responsible for much of the building, and a century earlier Capability Brown landscaped the parkland. Adjacent Hulne Park is open for walks at the weekends; there is a Carmelite Priory and an 18th-century folly tower. At the mouth of the River Coquet, Warkworth▶ has the dual attraction of a medieval castle and a 14th-century hermitage chapel gouged out of the cliffs, with the hermit's living quarters still intact (walk along the river and take a ferry across).

In complete contrast, Newcastle-upon-Tyne▶ is a sprawling industrial conurbation, definitely not pretty at first sight, but with plenty of atmosphere. Its six great river bridges include Robert Stephenson's double-decker road and rail bridge of the 1840s. A cluster of medieval quayside buildings, the 17th-century guildhall and the castle are pre-industrial survivals, while Grey Street and Eldon Square are fine examples of early 19th-century townscaping. Among Newcastle's many museums are the Art Gallery (paintings by the extraordinary religious visionary John Martin), the "interactive" Museum of Science and Engineering, the John George Joicey Museum (period rooms, audio-visual presentations) and the Hancock Museum (natural history). The local beer, Newcastle Brown, is just as famous as the local "Geordie" accent.

▶▶ **Northumberland National Park**   190D1

Because of its remote location and lack of facilities, this is one of the least visited national parks. Villages are modest and scattered, the grassy hills are quiet and strikingly empty—even at the height of summer you often have only Cheviot sheep for company. It's a great place for solitary walks, although the variety is not immense. Vast Kielder Forest spreads its seemingly endless evergreen

Kielder Water, a man-made lake in a setting of beauty

Housesteads Fort on Hadrian's Wall

plantations, home to red squirrels and deer, over western Northumberland. Kielder Water and the forest trails offer a retreat from the elements, and there is a 12-mile forest drive; boats and canoes rental, are available.

The **Cheviot Hills** reach to the Scottish border; the best of the walks involve treks along solitary sheep-drovers' roads, now quiet grassy tracks, to the ridge which forms the border, taking in the summits of Windy Gyle (2,031 ft.) and The Cheviot (2,677 ft.). Scenic drives tend to be of the there-and-back variety; notable among these is the road along **Coquetdale** from Rothbury, past the craggy Simonside Hills, to Alwinton and beyond. **Rothbury** itself is an attractive sandstone town with a sloping green and a spacious main street; **Cragside►** (NT) on the edge of town was built by the 19th-century architect Norman Shaw and was the first house in the world to be lit by hydro-electric means. The wooded grounds are laced with trails and have lakes, a formal garden and a fine show of rhododendrons. **Ford** is a model estate village for Ford Castle and has craft workshops.

The southern part of the national park holds the finest surviving stretch of **Hadrian's Wall►►►**, the largest Roman monument in Britain (see panel). Of its 74-mile length, remains can be seen along 10 miles, the best sections being between points north of Haltwhistle and Hexham. Walkers may like to make use of a summer bus service which runs along the main road parallel to the Wall. Housesteads Fort, which still has a hospital and latrines, and Chesters, a cavalry fort, are particularly well preserved. At Vindolanda Fort a section of wall is reconstructed as it would have been at the time of the Roman occupation, while at Corbridge are the remains of the garrison town of Corstopitum and a museum of finds. Also try to take in Birdoswald Fort, over the border in Cumbria, and the National Park information center at Once Brewed. **Hexham►** makes an attractive base. It has a superb priory church; both its crypt and bishop's throne are Saxon—before destruction by Danish marauders in 875 it was the largest church in northern Europe. Local history features at the Border History Museum.

Hadrian's Wall
This great fortification at the northernmost point of the Roman empire was planned in AD122 by Emperor Hadrian from Newcastle to the Solway Firth on the Cumbrian coast. The natural feature of the Great Whin Sill, a ridge of hard rock, made an ideal base to the construction for much of its length. To the north lay wilderness and the Picts, and it still feels primevally wild on the wall today. Milecastles were placed at intervals of Roman miles; the Vallum, or southern rampart, was below the wall and is visible in places. Seventeen forts, housing 13,000 infantrymen and 5,500 cavalrymen, were connected by a military road. The best preserved is Housesteads (NT).

▶▶ **North York Moors National Park** *191C3*

This distinctive massif, tucked into Yorkshire's northeast corner, is England's largest tract of heather moor, a plateau dotted with ancient stone crosses, and interrupted by sharply contrasting green dales scattered with red-roofed, yellow-stone farms and hamlets. The most dramatic scenic moments are at the point where the high terrain dips abruptly to the plain, as well as the sublime stretch of coast, which is well supplied with sights, absorbing villages, beaches and walks along the east coast's highest cliffs. This variety of moods is perhaps the key to the area's enduring appeal.

Rievaulx Abbey (pronounced "Reevo") stands desolate, still and beautiful, sheltered from the moors above the Rye Valley

The moors and dales Farndale, celebrated for its wild daffodils, and **Rosedale**, once an ironstone-mining center, typify the contrasts of moorland plateau and lush vales. **Helmsley▶** is a cheery, small market town with craftshops and bookstores, and a handsome market square; close by are the huge east tower of the Norman castle and Duncombe Park, a revamped Palladian mansion memorable for its fine classical entrance hall and panelled saloon, and for its grass terrace complete with temples.

The village street of **Coxwold▶** is without blemish, all trim grass-edged lanes and stone cottages; Laurence Sterne lived and wrote *The Life and Times of Tristram Shandy* at what is now known as Shandy Hall (house open). **Hutton-le-Hole▶▶**, with its sloping, sheep-nibbled green, is home to the Ryedale Folk Museum, where rural buildings have been rebuilt to give an insight into life of yesteryear. **Lastingham Church▶** is built over a remarkable Norman crypt, and the touristy village of **Thornton Dale▶** has some pretty corners by its brook.

The North Yorkshire Moors Railway

The area's major tourist attraction, the **North Yorkshire Moors Railway**►► (operating steam and diesel services), runs from Pickering to Grosmont along unspoiled dale scenery. **Pickering**► itself is a bustling market town with a good local museum and remains of a Norman castle; look in the church for the set of 15th-century murals, one of the most complete in England. **Goathland** has a long green and sheep everywhere; from the Mallyan Spout Hotel a path drops down to **Mallyan Spout**, a waterfall, while south of the village you can walk along a section of Roman road, **Wade's Causeway**►. At **Grosmont** you can peer into the locomotive shed or take a British Rail train into **Eskdale**.

Much of the eastern moors is dominated by commercial forestry, including **Dalby Forest**, laid out with trails, picnic sites and a drive; it abuts **Bridestones Nature Reserve**, where strange mushroom-shaped rocks are clustered on the moor. The western and northern escarpments, followed by the long distance **Cleveland Way** footpath, offer grandstand views towards the Pennines and over industrial Teesside respectively; **Sutton Bank**►, by the A170, is a renowned spot for views.

Along the coast A footpath (the finale of the Cleveland Way) follows the coast continuously; roads reach the coast in only a few places. **Staithes**►► is an authentic-looking fishing village, not too prettified; **Runswick Bay**► is smaller and neater, picturesquely huddled beneath the cliff. **Whitby**►► was once a famous whaling center, hence the whalebone arch above town from which you can look across to the ruined abbey and St. Mary's Church. The town has expanded as a resort but has kept its character in a maze of old streets around the harbor; a few shops still specialize in Whitby jet ornaments. The densely stocked Whitby Museum displays some astonishing local fossils. A beach extends north to Sandsend.

Red-roofed **Robin Hood's Bay**►►, one of the most famous of all English fishing villages, clings to steep slopes that drop to the shore, where low tide reveals rock-pools and fossils; tales of smuggling haunt the quaint hodge-podge of lanes. **Scarborough**►, just outside the Park, is both a Regency spa and a Victorian resort with sandy bays, in some parts genteel and in others given over to arcades and amusements such as Kinderland, a well-conceived adventure playground.

Captain James Cook
The great explorer was born in 1728 at Marton (now part of Middlesbrough, Cleveland), where a museum charts his life and travels. The site of the Cooks' house at Great Ayton is marked by an obelisk and the school James attended is a modest museum. After being a shop apprentice in Staithes, he was apprenticed to a Quaker ship-owner in Whitby (the house where he lived with his master is a museum of Cook's life). From 1768 onward he undertook his voyages of discovery to New Zealand, the east coast of Australia and the Pacific Isles. He was murdered by natives in Hawaii in 1799.

The Laurel Inn, Robin Hood's Bay

York Minster, seen from the north corner of city wall

▶▶▶ York
190B2

York is England's unrivalled showpiece cathedral city: nowhere else has quite such a concentration of medieval and other historic treasures. There are far more museums than can be visited in a single day (see page 206): the Castle Museum, the National Railway Museum and the Jorvik Viking Centre are the top three. Around every corner are outstanding examples of buildings of every period. Shoppers, sightseers and street performers throng the city center, but much of it is pedestrianized and a pleasure to explore on foot. The York Mystery Plays, a 14th-century cycle of 48 plays covering man's fall and redemption, are performed every four years (next performance 1996).

The city wall▶▶▶ The Romans built the original defensive wall around the settlement of Eboracum, at the confluence of the rivers Ouse and Foss; in Viking times the city was known as Jorvik, later corrupted to "York." Today the fabric of the wall is largely medieval. It can be followed along its top for much of its 2¾-mile) length and provides a splendid city overview (see Walk, page 206); west of the river, the wall skirts a largely railroad-age residential area. The wall's gateways are known as bars; on Micklegate Bar during the Wars of the Roses, the heads of enemies would be exhibited on spikes.

The Minster▶▶▶ Built 1220–1475, this is the largest medieval cathedral in Great Britain and the city's crowning glory. Its magnificent glass dates from 1150—look for the depictions of "Genesis" and "Revelation" in the east window, as well as the "five sisters" windows within a quintet of lancets. Look too for the rich interior of the chapter house, the painted roof of the nave, the carved rood screen, the undercroft display and the Treasury.

Threats from below and above

In the 1960s York Minster's lantern tower was threatened with imminent collapse. Only a major project, with supports erected between 1967 and 1972, saved the day; the undercroft exhibition gives a view of this repair operation. In 1984 the Minster was struck by lightning and was badly damaged by the fire that ensued. Some people interpreted this as an act of God after the Bishop of Durham, one of the Church of England's less reactionary bishops, had made outspoken remarks that cast doubt on the literal truth of the Virgin Birth.

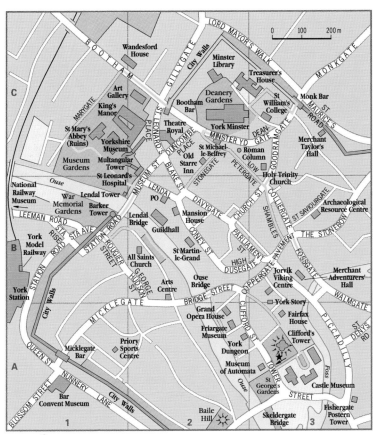

YORK

Walk City highlights

Outside **Castle Museum►►►**, face **Clifford's Tower►**, turn left to take a path to the near side of the tower; beyond Ouse Bridge view the city from the north river bank; recross by Lendal Bridge. Enter the **Museum Gardens**, pass fragments of medieval **St. Leonard's Hospital**; **Multangular Tower**, a Roman relic beside a section of Roman wall; and the ruins of **St. Mary's Abbey**. The **Yorkshire Museum►** is also in this park. Find a gate into Marygate and go to **Bootham Bar**; join the walkway along the top of the wall, with superb views of the Minster. Leave the wall at Monk Bar; **Treasurer's**

House► (NT) is filled with period décor, while **St. William's College** has an exhibition on the Minster. Skirt the **Minster►►►** to its main entrance. Pass **St. Michael-le-Belfrey Church** (fine 15th- and 16th-century glass), detour into Stonegate for its shopfronts; go on along Low Petergate, detour left into Goodramgate for unspoilt **Holy Trinity Church►**. Find **The Shambles►►** York's most famous street. From Fossgate you can visit **Merchant Adventurers' Hall►**; beyond Coppergate are **Jorvik Centre►►**, **Fairfax House** and the **York Story**.

The Shambles, originally a street of butcher's shops

York's museums

Arc St. Saviourgate: "hands-on" archaeology for all: learn how to solve the enigmas of the past.

Bar Convent Blossom Street: still a convent, but housing a museum on early Christianity in northern England

Castle Museum▶▶▶ Eye of York: this alone justifies a visit to York. Collections include a full-scale cobbled street of shops, re-creations of domestic interiors over the centuries and a working watermill by the river.

City Art Gallery Exhibition Square: includes nudes by local artist William Etty.

Clifford's Tower▶ Tower Street: a neat 14th-century quatrefoil castle on a Norman site, with a good view from the top. Scene in 1190 of the mass suicide of 1250 Jews to escape slaughter by their Christian debtors.

Fairfax House Castlegate: a Georgian town house offering an insight into life in the mid-18th century: furniture, clocks and paintings, mostly from Joseph Terry, the Quaker candy magnate and one of the most influential people in York's history.

Guildhall St. Helen's Square: a painstaking re-creation of the original 15th-century building, destroyed in an air raid.

Jorvik Viking Centre▶▶ Coppergate: award-winning time-travel journey into 10th-century Viking York, with recreated sounds and smells: informative, entertaining and lifelike. Go early or late when the lines are shorter.

Merchant Adventurers' Hall▶ Fossgate: the most impressive timber-framed building in the city; the 14th-century hall of a city merchants' guild, still in use.

Museum of Automata▶ Tower Street: entertaining exhibition of gadgetry past and present, including a history of robots and a host of objects to try out.

National Railway Museum▶▶ Leeman Road: Britain's finest selection of historic locomotives and cars (including the royal car used by Queen Victoria). Timetabled working demonstrations.

York Dungeon Clifford Street: a chilling glimpse into a world of punishment and death.

The York Story Castlegate: a model of the city illustrates York's long history.

Yorkshire Museum▶ Museum Gardens: Roman, Saxon and Viking artifacts; statuary and part of a Viking ship.

Walk about Victorian York in the Castle Museum

Drive The Yorkshire Dales

This tour (approx. 55 miles) captures the essence of the Dales, taking in waterfalls, Castle Bolton, unspoiled dales and lonely moors.

From the busy little town of **Hawes** at the heart of Wensleydale, take the

THE YORKSHIRE DALES

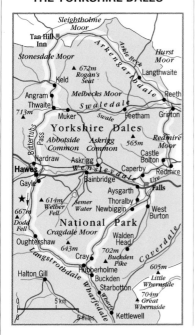

A684 Sedbergh road, turning off very soon for an unclassifed road signposted to Kettlewell. You'll enter the northern end of **Wharfedale** at **Hubberholme** (with its charming church). The B6160 leads over into Bishopdale and **West Burton►**, with its long village green. Proceed past the **Aysgarth Falls**, taking the road rising up to the formidable fortress of **Castle Bolton►►**.

Beyond this, the road rises onto Redmire Moor; pause for views at the top and drop down into **Swaledale** at **Grinton**. The odd castellated structure on the right as you descend is a former shooting lodge and now a youth hostel. Grinton Church, grandiosely dubbed "cathedral of the dales," is worth a short pause, while **Reeth►**, with its inns and folk museum, makes a good halfway stopping-point. The route goes along bleak **Arkengarthdale**, rising to the astonishingly remote **Tan Hill Inn**, England's highest pub, near the meeting of Cumbria, North Yorkshire and County Durham. Re-enter **Swaledale** at **Keld**; beyond **Thwaite** the road to Hawes is known as the **Buttertubs Pass**, so-called because of the stone "sinks," natural limestone features used for cooling butter that was being transported from one dale to another.

Grassington, a good base

208

Nidderdale and Teesdale
Although outside the National Park, Nidderdale's scenery matches the best of the Dales; but access is limited by grouse shooting and reservoirs. How Stean Gorge has small cliffs; near Pateley Bridge (fine folk museum) are Brimham Rocks, a weird, naturally sculpted landscape of tors. Stump Cross Caverns are a tour-it-yourself showcave. North of the Park, within County Durham, lies Teesdale, in the midst of the wildest and emptiest tracts of the Pennines. High Force is the mightiest waterfall in England. With its harsh climate and unusual soils, the designated nature reserve harbors arctic and alpine species, including the rare Teesdale Violet.

▶▶▶   **Yorkshire Dales National Park**   *190B1*

The great Pennine mass that forms the backbone of England has its proudest moments here, in the limestone dales and gritstone moors of the Yorkshire Dales National Park, where villages and field walls are almost universally gray stone. Spend a few days in the area and you will see the subtle differences between one dale and another.

Wharfedale This is a long dale, with several moods. Around **Bolton Abbey**▶, all is pastel-shaded and gentle, graced by the ruined Augustinian priory and the functioning priory church; upriver the Wharfe swirls through a chasm in Strid Wood. **Burnsall**, with its old bridge and green, and **Arncliffe** are two idyllic villages; **Grassington** is larger and busier, with a range of shops and places to eat around its central square. Like many Dales places, **Buckden** and **Kettlewell** grew up around the lead-mining industry; relics litter the moors. Tiny **Hubberholme** has a gem of a church, with a rare musicians' gallery of 1558.

Airedale England's most famous limestone scenery is concentrated in the area **around Malham**▶▶▶, where the subterranean River Aire reappears at the base of Malham Cove, a great inland cliff topped by limestone pavements. A short walk away, formidable Gordale Scar waterfall impressed the early Romantics. Downstream lies **Skipton**, a market town with a rewarding castle restored by the indefatigable Lady Anne Clifford after Civil War damage; a steam railroad heads into Wharfedale.

Swaledale Stone barns, abandoned lead mines (notably in Gunnerside Gill) and Swaledale sheep are features of the landscape along with the fast-flowing Swale itself. **Reeth**▶, ranged around a spacious green, is a charming town of humble proportions. Enchanting **Richmond**▶▶ crowns a hilltop site, its mighty Norman castle staring down to the Swale and over the large market place. There are two absorbing museums (the Richmondshire Museum and the Green Howards regimental museum) and the streets are full of interest, but there is nothing

Looking over barns and stone walls towards Muker

By Buttertubs Pass: one of the deep limestone shafts

self-conscious about the town. Even its theater (1788), the oldest in its original form in England, is concealed by a barn-like exterior. Walk by the Swale, through Hudswell Woods or to the ruins of Easby Abbey.

Wensleydale The dale's cheese-making heritage is illustrated by the rural relics in the folk museum in **Hawes** and shops sell the flaky Wensleydale cheese. This town is conveniently located, but villages such as **Askrigg**, **Bainbridge** and **West Burton▶** have more appeal; **Middleham▶** has a sweet central square and main street, around which stable hands parade horses from nearby racing stables. Of the dale's many waterfalls, **Aysgarth Falls** are the best known and attract more crowds than perhaps they deserve; close at hand are a museum of antique carriages and Aysgarth Church, with its superb screen brought from **Jervaulx Abbey▶**, whose lichen-encrusted ruins can be seen farther east. **Hardraw Force▶**, the tallest waterfall in England, is reached through the pub at Hardraw. **Castle Bolton▶▶** is an impregnable-looking bulk, little altered since the 14th century; here Mary, Queen of Scots was kept prisoner, in some comfort, between 1568 and 1569. **Masham▶** has plenty of local color around its large cobbled market place.

Ribblesdale and Dentdale Settle is a likeable market town, if a bit noisy with quarry traffic; the train journey to Carlisle gives great views (see page 176). The "Three Peaks"—**Whernside** (2,418 ft.), **Ingleborough** (2,372 ft.) and **Pen-y-ghent** (2,274 ft.) are nearby; a popular challenge walk, often started from Horton-in-Ribblesdale, takes in all three. Ingleborough is dotted with pot-holes and caves, including **Ingleborough▶** and **White Scar▶** caverns (both are open to the public), and Gaping Gill, big enough to hold London's St. Paul's. **Ingleton** is the base for walks into **Ingleton Glen▶▶** (see, page 193). Dentdale, in Cumbria, lies below Whernside; don't miss **Dent▶▶** with its cobbled streets, the epitome of the rural Pennines.

Barnard Castle
Just beyond the Park's northeastern boundary, in County Durham, is the town of Barnard Castle, whose namesake castle perches above the Tees. The Bowes Museum here, built in opulent French château style, houses a splendid collection of fine arts. Try to time your visit to catch the "performance" by the automaton silver swan in the entrance hall (12:30 and 4:00PM).

209

Malham Cove

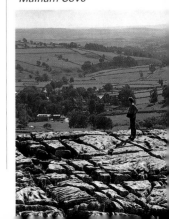

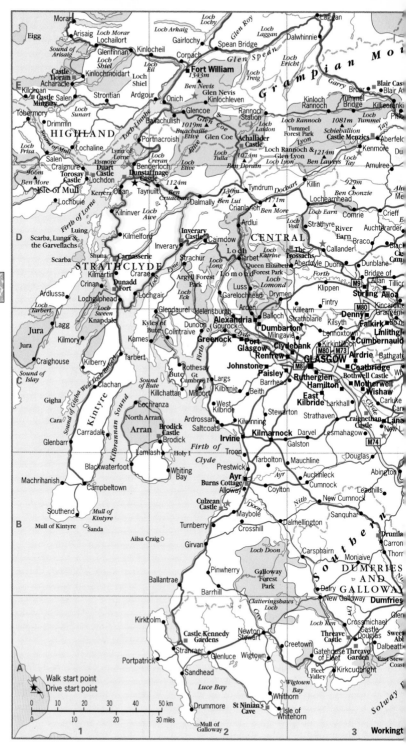

PRODUCT OF SCOTLAND

Glenfarclas

15 YEARS OL

ESTABLISHED

SINGLE MA
SCOTCH WHF

Distilled and Bottle
J. & G. GRANT
Glenfarclas Disti
Speyside, Scot

75 cl

Loch Arklet, in the Trossachs

BEST PLACES TO GO
Cities Edinburgh, Glasgow.
Inland towns and villages
Borders Peebles.
Central Stirling.
Coastal towns and villages
Fife Anstruther, Crail,
Culross, St. Andrews.
Tayside Arbroath,
Montrose.
Great houses *Borders*
Abbotsford, Bowhill,
Mellerstain, Traquair.
Dumfries & Galloway
Culzean, Drumlanrig.
Lothian Hopetoun.
Tayside Glamis, Scone.
Castles *Lothian* Edinburgh.
Central Doune, Stirling.
Dumfries & Galloway
Caerlaverock.
Fife Falkland, Kellie, St.
Andrews.
Lothian Linlithgow.
Strathclyde Bothwell,
Craignethan, Rothesay
(Bute).
**Ruined abbeys and cathe-
drals** *Borders* Dryburgh,
Jedburgh, Melrose.
Dumfries & Galloway
Sweetheart.
Fife St. Andrews.
Tayside Arbroath.
Churches St. Giles High
Kirk, Edinburgh, *Fife*
Leuchars
Royal palaces *Central*
Stirling.
Fife Falkland.
Lothian Linlithgow.
Gardens *Dumfries &
Galloway* Castle Kennedy,
Threave.
Lothian Edinburgh Royal
Botanic Garden.

Southern Scotland Scotland is a nation but no longer an independent state. After having fought long, hard and heroically to maintain its sovereignty, Scotland surrendered its independence in a controversial act of Parliamentary Union with England and Wales in 1707. But the church, the legal and educational systems, and local government were deliberately excluded from the provisions of the treaty and remain to this day proudly Scottish. The Union is naturally dominated by the richer, more populous southern neighbor, who was also the historic enemy, so among Scots has never been outstandingly popular—but it has worked. Those who know southern Scotland through its books already know the country well; Robert Burns and Sir Walter Scott have familiarized the whole world with its language, people, rivers and hills and in this century novelist John Buchan has depicted the local character: strength, self-reliance and doughty self-confidence.

The lie of the land Southern Scotland is composed of the Central Lowlands and the Southern Uplands, a wide band of hills that stretches from coast to coast. In the west this latter, wild area is known as **Dumfries and Galloway** while the eastern part is known as the **Borders**, though in fact both parts have acted since time immemorial as a war-torn border country, a self-governing shield between England and Scotland. The Lowlands occupy a rift valley, comprising the westward flowing River Clyde and the long eastern intrusion of the Firth of Forth. This is the heart of Scotland, studded with ancient Christian sanctuaries, sturdy medieval burghs, royal palaces, baronial seats, thickly populated manufacturing towns and its great rival cities of Glasgow and Edinburgh. The Central Lowlands, encompassing **Strathclyde**, **Lothian**, **Central**, **Fife** and part of **Tayside** regions, are by no means uniformly low-lying. **Edinburgh** is perched

TAMDHU
SINGLE MALT SCOTCH WHISKY
YEARS **10** OLD
PRODUCT OF SCOTLAND 100% SCOTCH WHISKY
DISTILLED AT
TAMDHU DISTILLERY

amongst volcanic hills, **Glasgow** is overlooked by the Campsie Fells, Dundee is fringed by the Sidlaw Hills and the Kingdom of Fife is given a backbone by the Ochil hills. The northern frontier of the Lowlands is the Highland Boundary Fault, which divides the island of Arran in half, continues northeast through Helensburgh to Loch Lomond, skirts through old market towns such as Crieff and Dunkeld to reach Stonehaven on the east coast.

The heritage Most of the great prehistoric monuments of Scotland are found in the north. There are, however, good collections of Pictish and early Christian carved stones to be seen in Angus and St. Andrews. Viking invasions in the 9th century destroyed much of the evidence of Celtic Christianity except for the distinctive round towers at Brechin and Abernethy in Tayside. Dunfermline Abbey and the famous Norman church in Leuchars, near St. Andrews in Fife, are good examples of the Romanesque influence, which came to Scotland in the late 11th century.

This was followed by the Gothic period, well represented by the ruined Border abbeys as well as the surviving cathedrals of Dunblane and Glasgow. The 15th century is the most distinctively Scottish period: the simpler collegiate church developed then, with battlemented towers and stone-slabbed roofs and spires. This period also saw the birth of the tower house with its thick, vertical stone walls, a concept gradually enriched by combining towers into L, T and Z plans; the roofs budded a playful array of corner turrets, crow-stepped gable ends and balconies. The neat burghs, or market towns, are dominated by a broad high street, typically with a mercat cross and the Tolbooth, which served as both jail and town hall.

The 16th-century royal palaces at Linlithgow, Falkirk and Stirling reveal the influence of the Renaissance but it was not before the more peaceful politics of the late 17th century that Scotland produced a truly classical style. Sir William Bruce ushered in this period, but it was dominated by William and Robert Adam, who gave the term Adamesque to their palladian vision of 18th-century Britain. Mellerstain, Culzean and the New Town of Edinburgh are their great works in southern Scotland. In the early 19th century the Romantic movement encouraged a return to a native Scottish spirit, leading to the Gothic-Baronial style of the high Victorian era, which still dominates the land. The crudity of some of this work stands in contrast to the imagination and careful scholarship of turn-of-the-century architects such as Sir Robert Lorimer and Charles Rennie Mackintosh, whose work is epitomized in the Glasgow School of Art.

O Caledonia! stern and wild,
Meet nurse for a poetic child!
Land of brown heath and shaggy wood,
Land of the mountain and the flood,
Land of my sires! what mortal hand
Can e'er untie the filial band
That knits me to thy rugged strand?
Sir Walter Scott, *The Lay of the Last Minstrel* (1805)

Auld Lang Syne
Should auld acquaintance be forgot,
And never brought to mind?
Should auld acquaintance be forgot,
And auld lang syne!

For auld lang syne, my jo,
For auld lang syne,
We'll tak a cup o' kindness yet
For auld lang syne

From "Auld Lang Syne" by **Robert Burns**, sung all over Britain on the stroke of midnight on New Year's Eve. Hogmanay, as the New Year holiday is called, is a time of great celebration in Scotland.

213

Walks

214

Callander Crags, Central   *210D3*
Parking lot on west side of Callander.
A marked path from Tulipan Crescent, by the tennis courts, leads into woods. After a steep climb you'll find splendid views of the Trossachs from the top of the Crags, which form the edge of an abrupt escarpment. (1½ hours)

Culzean Country Park, Strathclyde   *210B2*
Parking lot by Culzean Castle. The country park is laced with trails and has great variety; a detailed map is available on site. Aim to visit the castle, Happy Valley (with its exotic trees), the walled garden and Swan Pond. Maidens village to the south is an alternative starting point, where you can walk along the shore to the estate gates. (1 to 2 hours)

Grey Mare's Tail, Borders   *211B4*
Parking lot by A708 between Selkirk and Moffat. A fine waterfall, visible from the road, but worth taking either of the marked trails for close-up views. The longer trail climbs to the top of the fall and heads for lonely Loch Skeen. (1 to 2½ hours)

St. Abb's Head: the view of the cliffs at White Heugh, where guillemot and kittiwake may be seen

New Lanark, Strathclyde   *210C3*
Parking lot in New Lanark. This remarkable industrial "model" village provides the starting point for walks along the Clyde Gorge, with its dramatic waterfalls. Walk south, parallel with the river, through the village, later forking right onto a track and right again onto a path above the river. Cross the river at a sluice bridge and turn right for further views to reach ruined Corra Castle. Return the same way. (2 hours)

St. Abb's Head, Borders   *211C5*
Parking lot by nature reserve visitor center just west of St. Abb's village. A short path leads toward the village, then turns north parallel with the coast for bracing cliff views. You'll reach the lighthouse at St. Abb's Head, where rock stacks and ledges are nesting sites for 50,000 birds, including puffins. Either return along the cliffs or take the easier lighthouse access road, which also has spectacular views of the coast. (1 hour)

► Angus   211E5

The old county of Angus, now part of Tayside Region, extended westward from the North Sea across prosperous farmland (renowned for its black cattle) to the Grampians. The best scenery is in the "Braes of Angus"—beautiful glens such as Glen Isla, Glen Prosen, Glen Clova and Glen Esk—and on the wild rocky coast between **Montrose►** and **Arbroath►**. Montrose is a delightful summer resort whose Flemish-style architecture reflects centuries of prosperous trading with the Low Countries. The fishing and market town of Arbroath, too, has something of a resort air in the summer. Its most famous monument is the great 12th-century, red stone abbey, a picturesque ruin surrounded by tombstones. Immediately north is the hamlet of **St. Vigeans**, where a museum houses over 40 locally carved stones from the Pictish period (5th–9th centuries) on.

Inland, and north of Arbroath by 14 miles is **Brechin**, a red stone market town on the banks of the South Esk River. Standing proud beside the small cathedral is Scotland's finest **round tower►**. Only three such tall, slender towers are known outside Ireland; they date from the 10th century and were used as the refuge and watchtower of the independent monasteries of the Celtic Church. At **Aberlemno**, 5 miles southwest along the back road to Forfar, are some fine carved Pictish stones.

Due north of Brechin is **Edzell►►**. The ruins of its castle are handsome enough but it is the walled garden, the Pleasance, laid out by the scholar Sir David Lindsay in 1604, that makes the place exceptional. Sculptural reliefs decorate the walls.

In the fertile Vale of Strathmore, a little southwest of Forfar, is **Glamis Castle►►** (as in Shakespeare's *Macbeth*), its brooding bulk standing quiet and solemn in the spacious acres of its deer park. Near the castle, a row of stone-roofed cottages houses the Angus Folk Museum (NTS) of reconstructed interiors and domestic bygones.

►► Arran   210C2

The largest of the Clyde Islands, Arran is a traditional vacation island, easily and quickly reached from Glasgow. Sheltered by the Kintyre peninsula, it enjoys unusually warm weather and has dramatic mountains (Goat Fell rises to 2,867 ft.), deep valleys, and sandy and rocky bays. As you approach the island on the ferry from Ardrossan, **Brodick Castle►** (NTS), an ancient stronghold of the Hamilton family, dominates the shoreline. Its spectacular gardens include one of the finest rhododendron collections in Scotland. Arran is studded with prehistoric stones and is a paradise both for hill-walkers and birdwatchers, and for geologists, who come by the busload because virtually every rock type is represented on the island.

North lies the flatter, fertile island of **Bute**. Another important Clyde resort, the capital town of Rothesay is reached by ferry from Wemyss Bay. Ruined Rothesay Castle, like Arran's, was once the personal property of the Stuart kings. Cromwell destroyed it in the 17th century. By following a minor road to the southern end of the island and then a footpath across a field, you can enjoy the interesting ruins of St. Blane's monastery; it is a lovely spot, with good views of the Firth of Clyde.

Angus titbits
The Angus market towns proudly boast more fish and French fries shops per head of population than anywhere else in the world.
Arbroath has its own, separate culinary status as the home of "Arbroath Smokies," split smoked haddock on the skin.
In 1885 Arbroath entered a team in the Scottish Cup that recorded the highest score in British football. They beat Bon Accord 36:0. The Arbroath goalkeeper was said to have smoked a pipe throughout the match.

215

Brodick Castle and Garden, Isle of Arran

SOUTHERN SCOTLAND

Robert Burns
Often described as Scotland's ploughman poet, Robert Burns (1759–96) was quite well educated for his time. Though his amorous exploits have gained notoriety, his contribution to literature was through poetry which, at best, shrewdly observes the foibles of his fellow men. He also wrote numerous sentimental, lyrical and narrative pieces and was an avid collector and "improver" of Scottish traditional songs. A major theme running through his work was a belief in the universal brotherhood of man.

► **Ayr** 210B2

Admirers of Scotland's national poet, Robert Burns, will need no encouragement to visit his birthplace at Alloway► on the southern outskirts of the seaside resort of Ayr. Burns was one of the few European poets to rival Shakespeare for wit and vigor. The Burns Museum houses many artifacts and manuscripts and the popular **Land o' Burns Centre** uses audiovisual displays to explain the poetry's immediate and enduring popularity.

High on a clifftop 12 miles down the coast road from Ayr, **Culzean Castle►►►** (NTS), built 1772–90 and ancient seat of the Kennedys, hides behind its battlemented exterior a supremely elegant classical interior by Scottish architect Robert Adam, arguably his finest. The celebrated oval staircase rises through three tiers of columns to an exceptional second floor salon. Culzean Country Park, with its walled summer garden, woodland walks, lake and camellia greenhouses, is the most popular of the National Trust for Scotland's properties.

Laid out on the dunes a little south of Culzean is the famous **Turnberry Golf Course**.

Culzean Castle, Robert Adam's supreme creation

THE BORDERS

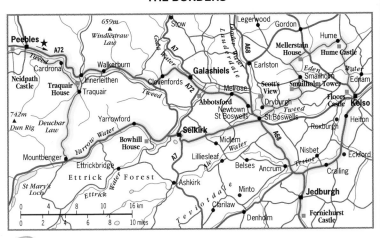

Drive The Borders towns, abbeys and houses to visit

A 100-mile exploration of the best of the Borders towns, abbeys and uplands.

Start from **Peebles** and take the A72 east, following the Tweed, to **Traquair House**►► outside Innerleithen. Continue along the A72 (passing the Scottish Museum of Woollen Textiles in Walkerburn) to reach Galashiels. Here look out for the turning to Walter Scott's house, **Abbotsford**►. From Abbotsford join the A68 but turn off into **Melrose** to look at the ruined **abbey**►►. Head back on to the A68 for St. Boswells and **Dryburgh Abbey**►►. Detour north on the B6356 to Scott's View. Take the B6064 for a look at **Smailholm Tower** on your way north to **Mellerstain House**►►. From here cross to **Hume Castle** and join the B6364 to Kelso to see its ruined abbey and, to the west of town, **Floors Castle**►►.

Follow the A689 south along the Teviot Valley to **Jedburgh** with its ruined **abbey**►►, Jail Museum and Mary, Queen of Scots House. You can detour south of the town to Ferniehurst Castle Centre and the Capon Tree. From Jedburgh take the A68 north to St. Boswells and turn

west onto the A699 to **Bowhill House**, west of Selkirk. Follow Yarrow Water upstream, along the A708, turning north at Mountbenger onto the B709 for the lonely crossing of Deuchar Law to Traquair House. From here a small road on the south bank of the Tweed passes **Kailzie Gardens,** near Cardrona, on the return to Peebles.

Dryburgh Abbey, founded in 1150

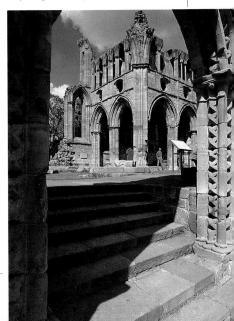

Young Walter Scott, in Smailholm Tower

The Eildon Hills and Walter Scott

Legend has it that these pink hills that rise prominently out of the valley near Melrose were cleft in three one night by the 13th-century wizard Michael Scott (Michele Scot in Dante's *Inferno*), to settle a dispute with the devil (the wizard's spell-book is said to be buried in Melrose Abbey). Geologists insist they are the relics of old volcanoes. Either way, they make excellent walking territory for those staying in Melrose and were a favorite of Sir Walter Scott. Visit Scott's View, beside the B6356 north of St. Boswells, for the view of them he so enjoyed.

▶▶▶ The Borders   211B4

As famous for its salmon as for its tweed, the Borders is a land scarred by centuries of turbulence. Fought over since the days of the Romans, it has many sites that bear silent testimony to this past— tower houses built to ward off border raiders, skeletons of abbeys vengefully destroyed by England's Henry VIII. It is also Sir Walter Scott country, the countryside that inspired Scotland's most celebrated novelist. There is nowhere else quite like it in Scotland—no big mountains but lonely, rounded hills, good for bracing moorland walks, and a pleasant coast. Even in the vacation season, there are no tourist jams.

The town of **Jedburgh** is best known for its **abbey**▶ and anyone planning to visit the four great Borders abbeys—Jedburgh, Dryburgh, Melrose and Kelso—should visit the Abbey Visitor Centre here, which admirably explains their role. Jedburgh Abbey holds the record for border raids—destroyed and rebuilt eight times in its 400-year working life. Its finest features are the two late Norman doorways and the excellent tracery window in the north transept. Also in the town are Mary, Queen of Scots House and the Castle Jail Museum.

Selkirk is a tweed-manufacturing town and a good base. **Bowhill House** is 4 miles west, set in the high ground between two tributaries of the Tweed. Its many magnificent works of art include the last Leonardo da Vinci in private hands in Britain. The house is surrounded by beautiful grounds; hidden in the woods is an adventure playground no child will forget.

Just outside Innerleithen, 6 miles east of Peebles, is **Traquair House**▶▶, one of Scotland's oldest inhabited houses. Its forbidding outline is softened by the pale harling of its walls but it remains dark and chilly inside. In the gardens is an excellent maze that children will love. **Peebles**, a pleasant town set on the River Tweed, was the home of the writer John Buchan (1875–1940), most famous for his tales of spy-hunter Richard Hannay.

In **Galashiels** is **Abbotsford**▶, the imposing turreted mansion that the great novelist Sir Walter Scott built

Children's playthings on display in Traquair House

himself on the banks of the Tweed. It is still inhabited by his descendants and houses his extraordinary collection of assorted Scottish curiosities.

Melrose is an appealing town. Close by the compact main square stands **Melrose Abbey►**, its remains being the finest example of the golden age of Scottish ecclesiastical architecture. Its soft pink stone is warm, forgiving and kind, a magical atmosphere pervades the site. Robert the Bruce's heart is said to be buried here.

Dryburgh Abbey►►, set peacefully in an exquisite bend of the graceful River Tweed near St. Boswells, is the most moving of the four Borders abbeys. Large sections stand astonishingly well preserved, especially the cloisters. If you walk nowhere else, walk here; it's the best way to enjoy the peace and tranquillity of Scotland's serenest ruin. Leave your car and cross the Tweed by the footbridge.

A little way northeast is **Smailholm Tower►**, a classic pele tower (see panel), with a display of dolls and costumed figures. **Mellerstain House►►** is found 6 miles northwest of Kelso. This breathtaking Georgian house, built by William and Robert Adam in the mid-18th century

Jedburgh Abbey, sacked and rebuilt many times

Pele towers
The word pele or peel is derived from the Latin "palus" or palisade and was the name given to the tower houses built around the Scotland-England border against the raiding enemy. Smailholm Tower, near St. Boswells, is a well-preserved example from the 16th century. Then it housed a continuous day and night watch; now it stands square and stern and stark on a moorland crag, overhanging a sullen pool. The 15th-century towerhouse at Cranshaws in the Lammermuir Hills features in Scott's *The Bride of Lammermuir*.

(see panel page 51), is the perfect example of the Adams' skill in combining stateliness with domestic ease and comfort. Inside, the large, wide and light rooms, in their pale Adam colors, are as perfect as the day they were finished. A little museum contains a wonderful portrait of Bonnie Prince Charlie disguised as Flora MacDonald's Irish maid, Betty Burke (see page 246).

Kelso is a proud town but the abbey ruins are the least captivating of the Borders abbeys, the formidable square tower strongly resembling a fortress. To the west of Kelso stands **Floors Castle►►**, its Adam and Playfair exterior one of the stateliest of all the Border palaces. On a sunny day its pinnacled façade gleams above its terraced riverside grounds. Only the hall retains its original Adam interior but in the state rooms are many treasures. The 19th-century Gothick bird room is a popular curiosity.

The coast at **St. Abb's Head►** (see Walks, page 214) is a prime site for naturalists and birdwatchers.

Common ridings
These ceremonies take place annually in several Borders towns in recollection of the violent battles of the past. Horseriders in Selkirk, for instance, carrying symbols of the independence of their town, gallop over the moors to commemorate the Battle of Flodden Field.

The Falls of Clyde, in a gorge at New Lanark

▶ **The Clyde Valley** 210C3

Deep in the wooded Clyde Valley near Lanark (see Walks, page 214) is the 18th-century model mill town of **New Lanark▶▶**. It is linked with such key figures of the Industrial Revolution as the inventor Richard Arkwright and Robert Owen (1771–1858), the social reformer, who attempted through enlightened programs to create a caring industrial community here. His Nursery building, the Institute for the Formation of Character, the school and apartments housing the workers have all been restored and a thriving community is living here again. One of the mill buildings houses an award-winning visitor center that operates a history "ride" specifically tailored for children.

Some 5 miles west of Lanark, **Craignethan Castle▶▶** is a fine example of a 16th-century stronghold. The most exciting feature is the caponier, a large vaulted gallery built onto the floor of the moat providing efficient protection from artillery fire (though it nearly suffocated the defenders in gunpowder smoke); this one is thought to be the earliest example in Britain.

Bothwell▶▶, just southeast of Glasgow, boasts a pretty 14th-century church and a monument, by the bridge, that commemorates the defeat of the Covenanters (see panel) at the battle of 1679. However, the town is chiefly renowned for its 13th-century castle. Set high above the Clyde, its redstone outer walls studded with round towers, it always held a strategic role. It was much damaged in the Wars of Independence.

▶ Dumfries and Galloway 210B3

The western hills are wilder and more expansive than the better-known Borders District to the east. The character of the region is also more solemn, though it's enlivened by some interesting archaeological sites, some haunting ruins and some splendid castles. While much of the countryside inland is humdrum, the southern coast is a pleasant place to wander around, with an occasional surprising view of the English Lake District (best from the top of Criffell, south of Dumfries). The area is never crowded; some of the wildest parts of the Southern Uplands are in Galloway Forest Park (parts of which are tediously blanketed in evergreen plantations) and some of the Lowlands' most beautiful countryside is in the hills and valleys of the Rivers Nith, Annan and Esk, to the north and east of the gray stone town of Dumfries.

Standing beside the Solway Firth 9 miles south of Dumfries is **Caerlaverock Castle**▶▶. Its unusual triangular plan, its full moat and the pleasing green serenity of its site make this, "the lark's nest" castle, one of the most memorable in the country. It has been much fought over and the outer walls were beseiged by King Edward I in 1300 less than a decade after the foundations had been laid. The interior bears a very fine Renaissance façade added by the enlightened Lord Nithsdale, head of the Maxwell clan, in the 17th century. Not far away, at Ruthwell is the particularly fine carved Anglo-Saxon **Ruthwell Cross**▶. Over 16 ft. high and dated to the 7th century, it is one of the most important monuments of the Dark Ages.

Threave Castle and Threave Gardens (NTS)▶▶, a grim castle and a delightful garden, lie a few miles apart near Castle Douglas, 10 miles northeast of Kirkcudbright. Threave castle was built by Archibald the Grim, who boasted how the awful gallows' knob that sticks out over the entrance "never wanted a tassel." Threave Castle was a 14th-century stronghold of the notorious Black Douglases, so called because of their merciless pillaging, and was besieged unsuccessfully by the royal forces of James II in 1455.

Curling
For at least 350 years this team game, played on ice, has been enjoyed all over Scotland. The curling stones are made from granite and have handles sunken into the top. The object is to slide the stones along the ice into a tee, the team with the most stones at the center of the tee being the winner. The best stones are reputed to be from Ailsa Craig, a 1,100-ft. high volcanic plug of a rock 10 miles off Girvan that persistently pops up into view as you drive around the Ayrshire coast.

221

Threave Castle, lonely on an island in the River Dee

Dulce Cor
The beautiful ruined red walls of Sweetheart Abbey, south of Dumfries on the A710, have a romantic tale to tell. The abbey was founded in 1273 by Lady Dervorgilla after her husband John Balliol was killed by Robert the Bruce (she also founded Balliol College, Oxford, in his honor). She kept her husband's embalmed heart close to her until her death at the age of 90. Both were then interred in the church, which became known as Dulce Cor ("sweet heart").

The nearby (but separately administered) Threave Gardens are where the National Trust for Scotland trains its budding young gardeners. Every type of terrain and condition they are likely to encounter is recreated here, from rose to heather garden, from rock to wood; there are herbaceous borders, a walled garden and fabulous glasshouses in which exotic flowers and fruits grow. In spring there is a display of some 200 types of daffodil.

The town of **Kirkcudbright▶** is set sweetly on the River Dee around MacLellan's Castle. With its typical pastel-painted housefronts, it has long been beloved of Scottish artists ; E.A. Hornel was a member of the artists' colony founded here in the early years of this century. There are several art galleries in the town today. It is a tranquil place to spend a day wandering around. Visit the ancient toll-booth, with its curious and beautiful spire, or the Stewartry Museum with its many local antiquities and curios; a display explains the strange and ancient Scottish pastime of curling (see panel, page 221). In Gatehouse of Fleet, 8 miles northwest, is the **Mill on the Fleet▶▶**, a visitor center based on a restored 18th-century cotton mill that portrays the town's industrial past.

Whithorn, 18 miles south of Newton Stewart, is one of the oldest Christian centers in Britain; here, in 397, St. Ninian built the first Christian church in Scotland.

The most southwestern corner of this region is the strange spit of land known as the Rhinns of Galloway (from which there are views of the Mourne Mountains in Northern Ireland). Here is the **Logan Botanic Garden▶**, where plants from the temperate regions of the southern hemisphere thrive in a walled garden. **Castle Kennedy Gardens▶** near Stranraer, were laid out on a grand scale by 18th-century Lord Stair, with ruins, lakes and wooded walks. It is at its most majestic when the rhododendrons and azaleas are in bloom in early summer.

In the northern part of the Dumfries and Galloway District, set beside the River Nith near Thornhill, is **Drumlanrig▶▶**. No building looks more solid or more imposingly rooted in Scotland than this pink 17th-century palace. Standing proud upon its sculpted grassy mound, it dominates even the distant hills. Within its massive walls are the region's finest collections of old masters, including a Rembrandt, and outstanding collections of exquisite French furniture of the 18th century. A number of rural craftsmen, with work for sale, operate in the grounds.

Drumlanrig Castle, ringed by forests and hills

The Castle and Princes Street seen from Calton Hill

▶▶▶ Edinburgh   211C4

The capital of Scotland is an outstanding city. It is rich in open spaces, museums, beautiful buildings and elegant streets, all lit by the piercingly clear Lothian light. The dark courts, cobbled streets and steep steps of the medieval Old Town contrast with the gracious squares, circuses and crescents of the Georgian New Town. Edinburgh is at its most exhilarating during the renowned International Festival and Festival Fringe in August.

The **Royal Mile▶▶** is the original and chief street of the city. At its western end lies the **castle▶▶** with its many attractions; at the other end are the Abbey and **Palace of Holyroodhouse▶**, the official Scottish residence of the Queen (open to the public when the Royal Family is not here). The Royal Mile is the heart of the Old Town; many of the city's most historic landmarks are on it and there are numerous museums and houses to visit (see panel).

St. Giles' Cathedral▶, the High Kirk of Edinburgh, was originally built in the traditional shape of a cross though later additions have given it an unusual square design. **Canongate Kirk▶** is a dignified example of a Presbyterian church, with typical white-painted walls and wooden box pews. **The Royal Museum of Scotland▶▶** on Chambers Street has decorative art and archaeology galleries, a natural history section, a geology department and (most popular with the young) technology galleries. In the churchyard of **Greyfriars Kirk▶** is the flat tomb on which the National Covenant was signed in 1638 (see page 220) amid such excitement that when the ink ran out men wrote their names in blood. **The Grassmarket▶▶** is for many the pleasantest part of the Old Town, with its plentiful antique shops and bistros.

The Mound is a causeway between the Old and New Towns. There are views across to chilly **Calton Hill▶▶** where the **National Monument▶** stands, modelled on the Parthenon in Greece to commemorate the Scots who fell in the Napoleonic Wars. Though never completed, it's

The National Gallery
The collection includes Rembrandt's self-portrait at the age of 51, Poussin's sequence of "The Seven Sacraments" (now set in a room whose details are taken from the pictures), Velasquez's "Old Woman Cooking Eggs," Raphael's "Bridgewater Madonna," El Greco's "Saviour of the World," and many works by Scotland's own painters. "The Reverend Robert Walker Skating on Duddingston Loch" by Sir Henry Raeburn (1756–1823) is one of Scotland's favorite paintings. Graceful, pretty and amusing, it has a natural power beyond its apparent charm.

The Royal Mile: some museums and houses to visit
The Camera Obscura, near the castle in the Outlook Tower, gives a beautiful "living image" of the city projected via lenses (best on a bright day). Opposite, *The Scotch Whisky Heritage Centre* tells all there is to know about whisky and whisky-making. *Gladstone's Land* (NTS), on the Lawnmarket, is a re-creation of a typical Old Town, six-story tenement house. *Lady Stair's House* contains memorabilia of Scottish writers, including Robert Burns, Sir Walter Scott and Robert Louis Stevenson. *The People's Story* tells the story of ordinary folk from the 18th century on. *John Knox House* displays interesting artifacts from the life of this pivotal figure of the Scottish Reformation. Opposite is the absorbing *Museum of Childhood*. *Huntly House*, a striking 16th-century mansion, houses the city's excellent museum of its own history.

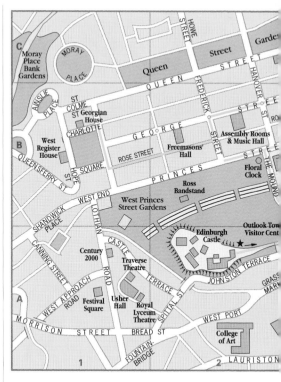

evidence of the 18th-century boast that Edinburgh had become the Athens of the North. Beside the Mound is the **National Gallery►►►**, a classical building housing the national art collection (see panel, page 223).

Princes Street► is the principal shopping street. Running along one side are Princes Street Gardens; the Scott Monument is the most striking, if endearingly over-the-top, landmark, covered with statuettes depicting characters from Sir Walter Scott's novels and poems.

In Queen Street, in the New Town, a distinctive red-brick Venetian palace houses two exceptional museums, the **National Portrait Gallery►** and the **Museum of Antiquities►**. There is not one second-rate picture in the portrait gallery, and no shortage of famous subjects. Especially striking is the wonderful Allan Ramsay portrait of the great 18th-century Edinburgh philosopher David Hume. The antiquities gallery houses major prehistoric, Viking and Roman collections. In 1791 Robert Adam was commissioned to design one superb square to enhance the quality of the New Town. Grand, spacious and elegant, his **Charlotte Square►** is the quintessence of the New Town. Number 7, the **Georgian House** (NTS), has been restored as a typical Georgian New Town home.

The **Royal Botanic Garden►**, beyond the New Town, has superb tropical greenhouses. Good walks are to be had on **Arthur's Seat**, a volcanic hill in Holyrood Park, and along the **Water of Leith**, to the west of the New Town.

EDINBURGH

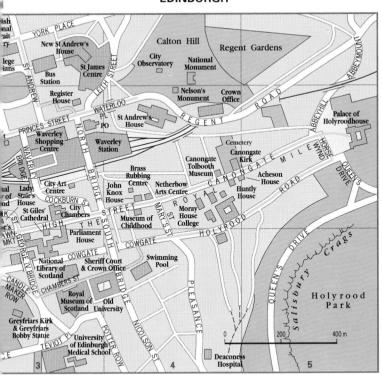

Walk From the Castle to Charlotte Square

Start at the Castle►►, then enter the Royal Mile►► at Lawnmarket to visit the Scotch Whisky Heritage Centre►, Camera Obscura►, and Gladstone's Land► (NTS). Continue along High Street past Parliament House, the Tron Kirk, the High Kirk of St. Giles► and the City Chambers. Then go on past the Museum of Childhood► and John Knox House along Canongate, to the People's Story Museum►, Huntly House, the Canongate Kirk► and its graveyard, to the Palace of Holyroodhouse►.

Return up Holyrood Road and into the Cowgate to pass the University, the Royal Museum of Scotland►►, Greyfriars Church► (and statue of the loyal little dog, Greyfriars Bobby) and into the Grassmarket►►. Turn up Victoria Street, left down Bank Street to Lady Stair's House► and then down The Mound to the National Gallery►►► and the Royal Scottish Academy (catch the views toward the National Monument on Calton Hill). Turn right into Princes Street► to the Scott Monument, across and into St. Andrew Square and Queen Street for the National Portrait Gallery► and Museum of Antiquities►.

Follow George Street as far as Frederick Street, turn left then right into Rose Street and into Robert Adam's Charlotte Square► to visit the Georgian House (NTS).

The Cramond ferry leaving the Dalmeny side of the river

▶▶   **The Firth of Forth**   *211D4*

The Firth of Forth is a wide tidal inlet that bites deep into the east coast of the country. From a first glance at a map it appears to have almost severed Scotland into two. It has functioned more as a trading canal than as a frontier moat. The long tidal shores are dotted with merchant towns whose markets and privileges are established in ancient royal charters. The old local adage says that a farm by the Forth is better than an earldom in the north—expressing the realities of this land that formed the heartland of the medieval kingdom of Scotland.

Four miles west of the Forth rail and road bridges is **Hopetoun House▶**, the beautiful stately home of the Marquis of Linlithgow. Begun in 1699 by Sir William Bruce and completed by William Adam and his sons, it houses a sumptuous collection of paintings, tapestry and furniture. An equal distance east of the bridges, near South Queensferry, is **Dalmeny▶**, a large 19th-century house set in a fine park. It's home to one of Britain's outstanding Rothschild Mentmore collections of 17th-century French furniture, tapestry and Sèvres porcelain. Dalmeny can be reached on foot along the estuary from Cramond, a lovely walk. **Cramond▶** is a pretty village of whitewashed cottages and old mills at the mouth of the River Almond, on the outskirts of Edinburgh. A little ferry takes you across to the Dalmeny estates and there are delightful walks up the riverbank.

Farther west, still on the southern side of the Firth, **Linlithgow Palace▶▶** stands above the town of Linlithgow. At the time of Mary, Queen of Scots' birth here in 1542 it was a magnificent structure but a fire in 1746 left it a ruin. Its enormous roofless red body survives and there is a fine octagonal fountain in the courtyard, a vast Great Hall and a swath of turf around the outer walls on which to picnic.

Across the Firth, on the western edge of Fife, the small coastal town of **Culross▶▶▶** (pronounced *Coo*-ross) is set in an unpromising landscape of coal mines with a

The Forth bridges
The Forth rail bridge, built between 1882 and 1889 and illuminated since its centenary, still wins the admiration of young engineers. For most of its life it was the longest bridge in the world. A little west is the fabulous modern suspension road bridge (1964), much lighter and a superb feat of modern engineering. A visitor center at South Queensferry explains the structures.

distant view of the Grangemouth refinery. Persevere, however, for Culross is one of the jewels of the Scottish National Trust. This perfectly preserved example of an early 17th-century trading burgh made its way in the world by digging coal from under the Forth, smelting iron to be hammered out into girdles and boiling up sea water to extract salt. The cobbled streets are lined with traditional corbelled houses, roofed with the distinctive terracotta pantiles of Fife. You can inspect three period interiors: start at the town's Tolbooth where free video shows on local history are shown alongside the jail chamber in the basement. Next door is the restored palace of Sir George Bruce, the local entrepreneurial landowner, with its painted ceilings, tiled kitchen and panelled rooms. Bishop Leighton's Study, also carefully restored, is the traditional name for the tall corbelled townhouse that overlooks the Mercat Cross. From there a short walk up steep Kirk Street leads to the slight ruins of a Cistercian monastery standing immediately beside the old abbey chapel, which has functioned, with later additions, as the parish church since the Reformation.

Dunfermline Abbey▶▶ stands above the wooded glen of Pittencrieff Park in Dunfermline. The abbey was founded as a Benedictine house in the 11th century. Its tower and eastern end were rebuilt in the 19th century to serve as a parish church, but the sturdy 12th-century nave with its solid pale stone columns, strong round arches and the zigzag chevrons so characteristic of the Romanesque is more interesting. The visitor center has a good range of display material.

A new attraction at North Queensferry is Deep Sea World. In summer, boat trips can be taken from South Queensferry, by the Forth bridges, to Inchcolm Island, to see the well-preserved abbey and a colony of seals.

See page 230 for the Firth of Forth fishing villages of the East Neuk of Fife.

Dunfermline Abbey, burial place of King Robert the Bruce

The Forth railroad bridge at dusk

Royal Tennis
The 16th-century Falkland Palace (NTS), inland from Kirkcaldy, was a favorite hunting seat of the Scottish kings until James VI died in 1625. The royal tennis court was built in 1539 and is still in use. Sir Walter Scott used the palace as the setting for part of his novel *The Fair Maid of Perth*. which was made into an opera by Bizet.

For a different perspective
To see another side of Glasgow, visit The Barras, the extensive and world-famous weekend flea market.. It was established 100 years ago and now has 800 stalls under cover. With street musicians, cafés and even a crèche, it makes for lively entertainment, even if you don't find a bargain.

Shipbuilding yards on the Clyde

▶▶▶ Glasgow   210C3

Glasgow's skyline of chimneys, factories and high-rises offers a prospect of almost grotesque beauty. These industrial outskirts are a potent reminder of Scotland's 19th-century industrial core but the middle of Glasgow is today a place of captivating charm and a vibrant, entertaining center. The city's merchant dynasties have bequeathed it an extraordinary legacy of art and architecture—and most of the museums and galleries are free. The grid plan of the streets makes it easy to explore.

The city has three distinct areas: the original medieval center, the Merchant City and the West End. The **cathedral▶**, a dark-hued, heavy Gothic glory begun in the 13th century, is one of the two surviving buildings of the medieval town, on the eastern side of the city. St. Mungo (or Kentigern) founded a missionary chapel here in the 6th century, around which the trading burgh of Glasgow later grew. Opposite the cathedral, the unique **St. Mungo's Museum▶** explores the religions of the world. In High Street, is **Provand's Lordship**, built in 1471 for a canon of the cathedral and now displaying household articles.

The Merchant City district has its origins in the heyday of the "tobacco lords." Glasgow was well placed for trade with the New World and the 18th century saw a period of glory as an international trading city. It was the tobacco lords who laid the foundations for later industrial development. By the 19th century Glasgow was one of the world's greatest ship-building centers and, in an expression of bursting civic pride, money was poured into the Merchant City district to create some of the best Victorian streets in Britain. The great rectangular **George Square▶** is the center of Glasgow today, flanked on one side by the splendidly overblown façade of the **City Chambers▶▶**, built 1883–8; be sure to take the free guided tour round the marbled interior. Immediately to the north is Queen Street Station; Central Station, with its even more impressive 19th-century interior, is just a few blocks west. **Trades House** with its Adam façade dates from 1791, while **Hutchesons' Hall** and **Stirling Library** are early 19th-century. Glasgow Green is one of many city parks and here is the **People's Palace▶**, an excellent museum devoted to the social history of Glasgow, and its huge Winter Gardens conservatory. Nearby is the old Templeton's carpet factory (1889), an amazing replica of the Doge's Palace in Venice.

In the leafy area of the West End, with its fine early 19th-century townhouses around Glasgow University, is the **Art Gallery and Museum▶▶**, an enormous Victorian red sandstone building in Kelvingrove Park. It holds works of art from neolithic weapons to Cubist paintings; there is a strong emphasis on 17th-century Dutch and Flemish works. In Kelvin Hall, opposite, is an exciting **Transport Museum▶▶**, with reconstructed subway stations and shops, old trams, cars and motorcycles. The **Hunterian Art Gallery▶▶** is renowned for its collection of works of James McNeill Whistler (1834–1903). Also strongly represented is 19th- and 20th-century Scottish art, including works of the Scottish colorists such as S.J. Peploe and of the "Glasgow Boys," a group of painters led by W. McGregor, who advocated realism in art instead of Victorian romanticism. The Mackintosh Wing is an

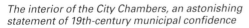
The interior of the City Chambers, an astonishing statement of 19th-century municipal confidence

Charles Rennie Mackintosh (1868–1928)
Mackintosh was prominent in the Arts and Crafts Movement and was the first Scottish architect since the 18th century to achieve international fame. While his stained glass and metalwork used the art nouveau motifs of intertwining tendrils, his buildings have a taut quality of austere, geometric simplicity; his furniture design is typified by the tall, starkly simple ladder-chair. The Glasgow School of Art (1896–1909) is his masterpiece, designed when he was only 28; other notable buildings in Glasgow include the Scotland Street School and the Willow Tea Rooms (now serving tea again).

elegant re-creation of the nearby house once occupied and furnished by Glasgow architect Charles Rennie Mackintosh (see panel). Within the Botanic Gardens is a beautiful 19th-century glasshouse, **Kibble Palace**▶▶, where tree ferns grow amid white staturary.

The **Glasgow School of Art**▶▶, in Renfrew Street, is the finest completed example of Mackintosh's vision. It houses a comprehensive collection of his paintings and his designs for furniture, metalwork, light fittings, and stained glass (good guided tours, daily). **The Tenement House**▶▶ (NTS) on nearby Buccleuch Street is the ordinary city apartment of a Miss Agnes Toward, preserved as she left it. The simple dignity of the four-roomed apartment and her belongings tell a visitor more about the realities of a Scottish life than two dozen ducal palaces.

A short drive but of a totally different atmosphere from the city center, is a fantastically light, glass-walled building constructed in 1983 in the grounds of Pollock House. It houses the extraordinary art collection of shipping magnate Sir William Burrell. Though it's vast, the **Burrell Collection**▶▶▶ is one that you will want to visit and revisit. Everything is of the best, be it the Egyptian alabaster, the Chinese ceramics or jade, the Persian rugs, the medieval illuminated manuscripts, stained glass or carved doorways.

The old Templeton's carpet factory, to be seen from Glasgow Green

St. Andrews, seen from the top of St. Rule's Tower

▶▶▶ St. Andrews   211D4

Scotland's oldest university, its first golf course and the ruins of its principal pre-Reformation cathedral mingle with the everyday business of a old Fife market town and summer resort. It was already a holy place for the southern Picts when a shrine to St. Andrew, patron saint of Scotland, was established on the eastern clifftops in the 8th century. Within a century St. Andrews had become the administrative center of Christianity in Scotland. The top of 12th-century St. Rule's church tower gives a bird's eye view over the enormous ruined nave of the adjoining 14th-century **cathedral▶▶** and of the town's little harbor with its long pier, known as a mole. Westward along the coast are the ruins of the bishop's **castle▶** with its bottle dungeon and 16th-century mine and counter mine. A visitor center interprets its role. Below the Martyrs' Memorial, the handsome **Royal and Ancient Club House** (home of the ruling body for golf the world over) overlooks the oldest course in the world and the British Golf Museum. Nearby a Sea World Marine park stands by the long West Sands. In the three converging streets that comprise the "auld grey toun" are lesser but impressive buildings such as the university's 15th- and 16th-century colleges and the West Port gate, all among elegant townhouses and secret "wynds," or alleyways.

The East Neuk A road south leads to **Anstruther▶**, one of several pretty old fishing villages dotted along the southern coast of Fife's East Neuk. Here is the Scottish Fisheries Museum and an aquarium. Boat trips go out in summer to the Isle of May. Fishermen's cottages in **Crail▶▶** are now home to artists and vacationers. To see a fishing fleet in action go to the harbor at **Pittenweem▶**; here St. Fillan, a 7th-century missionary, lived in a cave that is still used for the occasional church service. Flemish gables reflect former trading links with the Low Countries. Inland is **Kellie Castle▶▶** (NTS), a good example of the 16th-century round tower houses typical of the Lowlands; another is **Scotstarvit Tower▶** (NTS), near Ceres. Also in the vicinity is the **Hill of Tarvit Mansion House** (NTS), rebuilt by Sir Robert Lorimer.

▶▶ **Stirling**   *210D3*

Stirling Castle▶▶ stands in a strategically commanding
position on a volcanic crag, the symbolic key to Scotland.
For centuries the Old Bridge was the only "gateway to the
Highlands," and even today when the M9 highway connects highland and lowland, Stirling is still at the geographical and historical center of the country.

The Wallace Monument and its visitor center, on the
northeastern edge of the town, commemorate Scotland's
first freedom fighter, William Wallace; Wallace rose from
obscurity to lead the national resistance to the advances of
the English king, Edward I, winning a major victory at the
Battle of Stirling in 1297. On the other side of town, the
Bannockburn Heritage Centre tells the story of the most
famous battle in Scottish history (see panel). Midway
between them on the banks of the Forth are the restored
Gothic ruins of Cambuskenneth Priory. Walk up to the old
town to see the Church of Holy Rood where in 1543 Mary,
Queen of Scots was crowned at the age of nine months.
The Guildhall, the shell of Mar's Wark—built in 1570 as the
townhouse of the 1st Earl of Mar, Regent of Scotland—as
well as Argyll's Lodging, are all notable buildings in this
vicinity. Within the gray castle walls are 18th-century
artillery batteries, gardens, a royal chapel and the Renaissance palace of the Stewart Kings. Also here is the Argyll
and Sutherland Highlanders regimental museum. In summer, pageants and plays recapture bygone splendors.

Dunblane▶ is a small residential town beside the
meandering Allan River and the A9 divided highway. It has
one of Scotland's finer Gothic cathedrals; the tower is
12th-century but the splendid interior, one long soaring
207-ft. nave, is mid-13th-century. The town is a good base
for touring the Ochil Hills to the east. At the foot of the
Ochils near Dollar, 10 miles east of Stirling, **Castle
Campbell**▶ (NTS), built at the end of the 15th century,
stands perched on a huge crag. Do take the short trail
around its base through Dollar Glen, part of it hewn out of
rock, over catwalks and past cascades and drippy ferns. A
little west of Dunblane, **Doune** is worth a visit for a fine
14th-century royal **fortress**▶ and motor museum.

Robert the Bruce
The Battle of Bannockburn
was one of the most deci-
sive in Scottish history. For
several years Robert the
Bruce (1274–1329) had
been successfully waging a
guerilla war against the
English—and those of the
Scottish nobility whom he
had alienated. In 1314 he
was forced into a pitched
battle over the vital control
of Stirling Castle, with a
mere 5,000 men but great
cunning, he destroyed an
English force of some
20,000. Stirling surrendered
and Edward II fled to
Dunbar; Scotland later won
independence for 400 years
and Bruce was acknowl-
edged as king of Scotland.

231

Castle Campbell, a stronghold of the Campbell clan

▶▶▶ The Trossachs 210D2

The Trossachs is an area of rugged hills, tumbling burns (or streams) and picturesque lochs. It may lack the drama of the true Highlands but its accessibility from central Scotland has made it popular and it is well geared to visitors. Strictly speaking, the Trossachs is a narrow strip of country between Loch Katrine and Loch Achray, but in effect it's considered to stretch west from the busy resort town of Callander to the shores of Loch Lomond, with the somewhat commercialized Aberfoyle as its heart. It is undeniably beautiful but is also one of the most visited areas in Scotland, and in summer there are just too many buses and tourists here for those who prefer more lonesome parts.

The area became fashionable with the 18th-century Romantics in their cult of the picturesque—it was wild, but not too wild, and it was also easy to reach. Sir Walter Scott also helped to popularize the area, using the Trossachs as the setting for his poem *Lady of the Lake* and his novel *Rob Roy*. For this was the territory of Rob Roy's Clan Gregor, a near-criminal bend touched by a spirit of romantic lawlessness (see panel). The Trossachs was also the favorite sketching ground of the Glasgow Boys (see page 228).

The 23-mile long **Loch Lomond▶**, Scotland's largest inland loch (in terms of surface area), stretches from the suburbs of Glasgow to the fringes of the Highlands. It is surrounded by a dramatic variety of empty hills, rocky shores and wooded farmland but because it's the nearest Highland loch to the Clydeside conurbation, traffic along the road up its western shore is sometimes so busy that it is hard to enjoy its beauty.

There are several pleasant summer boat trips (but get there early, to avoid lines): along the length of Loch Katrine on the SS *Walter Scott*; on Loch Lomond from Balloch, Ardlui and Tarbet, on the western shore, and from Balmaha or the Inversnaid Hotel pier on the quieter eastern shore; a more modest excursion goes out to the ruins of Inchmahome Priory on an island in the Lake of Menteith. Activities such as pony trekking, cycling, fishing and golfing are easily available. Walkers can choose between numerous forest trails or ambitious hill walks up Ben Ledi (2,874 ft.) or Ben Venue (2,392 ft.).

Still waters: Loch Ard

Rob Roy MacGregor
Robert MacGregor, known for his red hair as Rob Roy (Red Robert) was a colorful and free-booting cattle thief whose exploits frequently involved robbing the rich for the benefit of the poor. He was forced to become an outlaw in about 1712, but having successfully outwitted all attempts to bring him to heel, he gradually returned to living openly among his own people. In 1725 he was given a formal pardon. The full story of this Scottish folk hero is told at the Rob Roy and Trossachs Visitor Centre in Callander.

■ The Highland clans in their 15th-century heyday formed a tribal system strong enough to threaten the authority of the Stewart monarchs. The aftermath of the last Jacobite rebellion of 1745 brought about the final dismantling of their distinctive way of life. However, the dress and tartan of the Highlands of former times then became fashionable—and the scene was set for the once outlawed cloth of a tribal minority to become the most potent symbol for the whole of Scotland.....■

How to recognize a fellow clansman
Contemporary evidence from the Battle of Culloden indicates a wide variety of tartans worn even by members of the same clan. The government forces were identifiable by the red or yellow tied badges on their bonnets, while the Jacobites had their famous "white cockades," inspired by the wild white rose said to have been plucked by Charles as a symbol for the campaign. In fact, the British army was the first to define uniform tartans in the 18th century.

233

Life beyond the Highland Line In Gaelic the word "clann" means family. By the 13th century, clans had evolved into self-governing tribal units at whose head was a chief or "father" to whom lesser chieftains and ordinary clansmen gave allegiance. The clan, at least in earlier times, counted its wealth in cattle. Consequently, cattle-raiding was common, as were territorial disputes. However, not all of the clan's preoccupations were warlike. The more powerful chiefs kept extensive retinues, an important member being the clan bard, who was official record keeper as well as composer. By the 18th century, better communications meant that the clans came more into contact with southern or Saxon—hence "sasunnach"—ways. Some chiefs even sent their children to school in the Lowlands and developed a taste for fine wines or fashionable clothes. Thus the system was already in decline before the shock of Culloden.

The dress of the clans The idea of a "clan tartan" was essentially a marketing device of 19th-century textile manufacturers. Tartan was banned after Culloden, though the Highland regiments of the British army were still permitted to wear it. Later, the fashion industry used the military as a source of inspiration and tartan became very fashionable. Then the visit of King George IV to Scotland in 1822 created an excuse for the new landowners and clan chiefs of Scotland to play act and dress up in tartan costumes. The cloth has remained popular ever since, creating its own mythology and conventions.

The Black Watch
One of General Wade's ways of policing the Highlands (see page 244) was to recruit local Highlanders. Six independent companies first enlisted in 1725 and from these was formed the 43rd, later the 42nd or Black Watch Regiment. By creating fighting units of this type, the martial spirit of the Highlands was harnessed for Britain's imperial wars of the 19th century.

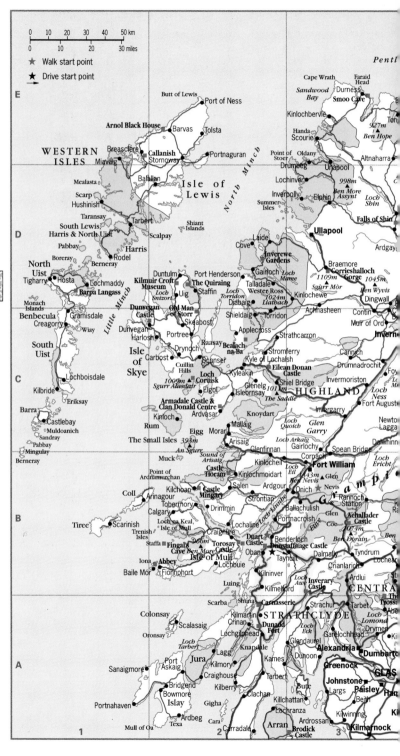

NORTHERN SCOTLAND

★ Walk start point

★ Drive start point

0 10 20 30 40 50 km
0 10 20 30 miles

Pentl

E

Butt of Lewis

Port of Ness

Cape Wrath Faraid Head

Arnol Black House

Barvas Tolsta

Sandwood Bay Durness

Smoo Cave

Breasclete **Callanish**
Stornoway

Kinlochbervie

927m ▲ Ben Hope

Ton

WESTERN ISLES Miavaig

Portnaguran

Handa Scourie Oldany Altnaharra

Point of Stoer

Isle of Lewis

North Minch

Mealasta Balallan

Drumbeg Unapool

Scarp
Hushinish

998m ▲ Ben More Assynt Loch Shin

Taransay

Shiant Islands

Lochinver Elphin

Inverpolly

Falls of Shin

Tarbert

Scalpay

Summer Isles

Ullapool

D

South Lewis, Harris & North Uist

Pabbay

Laide

Cove

Ardgay

Harris

Boreray Rodel

Berneray

Inverewe Gardens

Braemore **Corrieshalloch Gorge**

1109m ▲ 1045m

North Uist
Tighary Hosta

Duntulm

Port Henderson Gairloch Loch Maree

Ben Wyvis

Lochmaddy

Kilmuir Croft Museum

The Quiraing

Talladale Sgurr Mòr

Dingwall

Contin

Barpa Langass

Uig Staffin

Wester Ross

Kinlochewe

Monach Islands

Loch Snizort

Diabaig

1024m ▲ Liathach

Achnasheen

Muir of Ord

Benbecula Gramisdale

Dunvegan Castle

Old Man of Storr

Loch Torridon

Torridon

Cannich

Inver

Creagorry Wiay

Skeabost

Shieldaig

Strathcarron

Drumnadrochit

Dunvegan
Harlosh

Portree

Applecross

Stromferry

Eilean Donan Castle

South Uist

Carbost Drynoch

Raasay

Bealach-na-Ba

Kyle of Lochalsh

Invermoriston

Lochboisdale

Sconser

Stromeferry

Shiel Bridge **HIGHLAND**

Loch Ness

Kilbride Eriksay

Isle of Skye

Cuillin Hills

Loch Coruisk

Kyleakin

Glenelg

1011m The Saddle

Invergarry Fort August

Barra

1009m ▲ Sgurr Alasdair

Elgol

Isleornsay

Knoydart

Newto
Lagga

Castlebay

Muldoanich
Sandray

Armadale Castle & Clan Donald Centre

Ardvasar

Loch Quoich

Glen Garry

Dalwhin

Pabbay Mingulay

Kinloch

Mallaig

Loch Arkaig Gairlochy

Spean Bridge

Berneray

Rum

Eigg Morar

Arisaig

Glenfinnan

Corpach

Loch Ericht

The Small Isles 393m
An Sgurr

Sound of Arisaig

Kinlocheil

Loch Eil 1343m ▲ Ben Nevis

Fort William Glen Nevis

Castle Tioram

Kinlochmoidart

Ardgour Onich ★

A

Muck

Point of Ardnamurchan

Kilchoan **Castle Mingary**

Salen Strontian

Ballachulish

Rannoch Station

R

Coll Arinagour

Tobermory

Drimmin

Lochaline

Portnacroish

Achallader Castle

Glen Coe

Kes

Calgary

Loch na Keal, Isle of Mull

Craignure

Benderloch Connel 1074m ▲ Ben Dorain Ben

Tiree Scarinish

Trenish Isles

Duart Castle

Dunstaffnage Castle

Staffa **Fingal's Cave** 966m ▲ Ben More

Torosay Castle

Oban

Dalmally Tyndrum

Iona **Abbey**

Isle of Mull

Taynuilt

Crianlarich Lochea

Baile Mòr Fionnphort

Lochbuie

Kilninver

Loch Awe

Inverary Castle

Ardlui

St

Luing

Kilmelford

Strachur

Loch Lomond

CENTRA

The Trossa

Abe

Scarba Shuna

Carnasserie

Kilmartin **Dunadd Fort**

STRATHCLYDE

Tarbet

Drymen

Ki

Colonsay

Scalasaig

Crinan

Loch Eck

Glendaruel

Alexandria

Ki

Oronsay

Loch Tarbert

Lochgilphead

Dunoon

Garelochhead

Greenock

Dumbarto

Lagg

Knapdale

Kames

Johnstone **Paisley**

Han

Sanaigmore

Port Askaig

Jura Kilmory

Tarbert

Bute

Largs

GLAS

Bridgend

Craighouse

Kilberry

Clachan

Killchattan

Kilwinning

Ki

Islay Bowmore

Gigha

Lochranza

Ardrossan

Portnahaven

Ardbeg Cara

Arran

Kilmarnock

Mull of Oa Texa

Carradale

Brodick Castle

A

1 **2** **3**

234

NORTHERN SCOTLAND

SHETLAND Muckle Flugga

Stromness · Mainland · Houton
Hoy
Old Man of Hoy · Lyness
ORKNEY
Haroldswick · Unst
Uyeasound
Gutcher
West · Fetlar
Sandwick
Isbister
Hillswick · Yell
Burravoe
Sullom Voe · Toft
Out Skerries
Muckle · Brae
Papa · Roe · Whalsay
Stour
Sandness · Voe
Mainland
Catfirth
Walls · Lerwick
Vaila · Isle of Noss
Scalloway · Bressay
West
Burra
Shetland
Sandwick · Mousa
Tolob
Jarlshof · Sumburgh
Head

Stromness · Mainland · Houton
Dunnet · Burwick
Head · Duncansby
Scrabster · Head
Thurso · John O'Groats
Melvich
Wick
Grey Cairns of
Camster
Hill O'Many Stones
Latherton
Kinbrace
Helmsdale

Helmsdale

Brora
Invergordon
Tarbat
Ness
Portmahomack
Balintore
Burghead · Lossiemouth
Findhorn · Cullen · Portsoy · Rosehearty · **Fraserburgh**
Forres · **Elgin** · Buckie · Macduff
Nairn · Pluscarden · Keith · Banff · New · Rattray
Cawdor Castle · Abbey · Aberdhirder · Pitsligo · Head
Ardersier · Rothes · Turriff · Mintlaw · **Peterhead**
Culloden · Fetness · Aberlour · Dufftown · Huntly
Battlefield · Dava · Cruden Bay
Tomatin · Oldmeldrum · Ellon · Newburgh
Landmark · Nethy · Cabrach · Rhynie
or Centre · Bridge · Tomintoul · Mossat · Inverurie
Strathspey · Glenbuchat · Kildrummy · Kintore · Dyce
Steam Railway · Strathdon · Craigievar · Lumphanan · **Aberdeen**
Coylumbridge · Corgarff · Castle · Petercutter
Highland Wildlife Park · Balmoral · Aboyne · Banchory · Drum Castle
Aviemore · Castle · Ballater · Crathes Castle
Kingussie · Braemar · Strachan
Lin O'Dee · **Stonehaven**

GRAMPIAN

Mountains

Deeside &
Lochnagar · Clova · Fettercairn · Inverbervie
Blair Castle · Spittal of · Edzell Castle · Laurencekirk
Killiecrankie · Glenshee
Pitlochry · Kirkmichael · Brechin
Aberfeldy · Kirriemuir · **Montrose**
Kenmore · Blairgowrie · **Forfar** · Friockheim
Dunkeld · Alyth · Glamis · Inverkeilor
Caputh · Castle · **Arbroath**
Coupar Angus · **Dundee** · Carnoustie
Muirhead
Methven · Scone Palace · Newport-on-Tay
Crieff · **Perth** · M85 · Leuchars
Bridge · Elcho
of Earn · Castle
Gleneagles Hotel · **ORKNEY**
Campbell · Falkland
Castle · Palace · Loch
M90 · Leven
Alloa
Dunfermline
M9
EDINBURGH
Cumbernauld
M8 · **Livingstone**
Bathbridge
Motherwell · Peniculk
Wishaw · West Linton
Dolphinton
Lanark
Peebles

TAYSIDE

Firth of Tay

ORKNEY
Papa · North
Westray · Ronaldsay
Westray
The
North Sound
Westray
Firth · Rapness · Sanday
Rousay · Eday · Kettlestoft
Backaland
Birsay · Whitehall
Mainland · Redland · Stronsay
Skara Brae · Auskerry
Maes Howe · Finstown · Shapinsay
Ring of Brodgar
Stromness · Kirkwall
Old Man of Hoy · Houton · St Mary's
Hoy · Burray
Lyness · St Margaret's Hope
South
Ronaldsay
Burwick **5**

Northern Scotland The Highlands and Islands, with their awesome mountain and coastal scenery, have contributed much of what is now considered typical of Scotland. Malt whisky, bagpipes, tartans, clans, kilts and Highland flings were all distinctive aspects of Highland culture that today are considered essentially Scottish. This would have amazed any 17th-century Scot, for one of the key facts of Scottish history was the marked division between the northern Highlands and the main body of Scotland. The Highlands and the Lowlands were as different as chalk and cheese, and held each other in mutual scorn.

The water of life—pure single malt Scotch whisky

The great divide Though they might have traded cattle for corn at market towns, Highlanders and Lowlanders otherwise kept their distance. The Highlanders were Gaelic-speaking with a highly developed oral culture of bards, oaths and undying loyalty to kinship groups; the Lowlanders were English-speaking, literate and fond of lawsuits. The Highlanders were semi-nomads who counted their wealth in cattle and avoided towns, whereas the Lowlanders were firmly rooted in the farms and well-established towns that were evenly scattered over the coastal plains.The Highland Boundary Fault, running from southwest straight across to northeast Scotland, was not merely a geological divide: it was a linguistic, social, military, legal and economic boundary.

A war-torn territory Though the Highlands brought limited rewards back to the central government in Edinburgh, they provided a vital resource in times of danger. The mountain valleys could be relied upon to produce hardened troops for any military adventure that offered loot. The region also served as a bulwark against foreign

236

BEST PLACES TO GO
Coastal towns *Highland*
Portree (Skye), Dornoch,
Ullapool.
Orkney Stromness.
Strathclyde Inveraray,
Oban.
Coastal features *Highland*
Cape Wrath, Handa Island,
Stacks of Duncansby.
Orkney Old Man of Hoy.
Strathclyde Loch Etive.
Castles *Grampian* Crathes.
Highland Dunvegan (Skye),
Eilean Donan.
Strathclyde Duart (Mull),
Kilchurn.
Palatial interiors *Grampian*
Haddo.
Highland Cawdor.
Strathclyde Inveraray.
Tayside Blair.
Mountain walking
Cairngorms, Cuillins (Skye),
Fort William area, Glen
Coe, Torridon.
Prehistoric monuments
Hebrides Callanish Circle
(Lewis).
Orkney and Shetland Maes
Howe, Ring of Brogar,
Skara Brae, Jarlshof,
Mousa Broch.
**Traditional folk architec-
ture** *Hebrides* Arnol Black
House (Lewis).
Highland Kilmuir Croft
Museum (Skye), Kingussie
Folk Museum.
Island escapes *Hebrides*
Barra.
Highland Raasay, Rum.
Strathclyde Jura.
Christian architecture
Grampian St. Machars
Aberdeen, Elgin Cathedral.
Orkney St. Magnus
Kirkwall.
Strathclyde Isle of Iona.
Gardens *Grampian*
Crathes.
Highland Inverewe.
Strathclyde Crarae.

conquest, most graphically in the 14th century when the English occupied the Lowland towns for a generation but could make no effective headway into the Highlands. Even after the Act of Union between England and Scotland in 1707, the Highlands continued to supply manpower for Britain's imperial adventures, and to this day there is a tradition of military service.

Jacobite rebellions broke out in 1715 and 1719 as part of a long history of dissidence, but this time the south responded differently. General Wade was commissioned to build and design a string of strategic forts and fortified barracks for the military occupation of the Highlands, all linked by roads and elegant bridges. Several examples survive in the old county of Inverness-shire, in what is now known as **Highland** region. The Jacobite rising led by Bonnie Prince Charlie in 1745 (see page 246) had catastrophic effects, for the Hanoverian victory at Culloden Moor near **Inverness** was followed by the deliberate destruction of the military basis of Highland society. The legal powers of the clan chiefs were destroyed, the kilt and weapons were forbidden, and a series of ruthless judicial commissions brought the gallows to every glen. This was followed, a generation later, by an economic crisis resulting in the Clearances—wholesale eviction of the tenant farmers to make space for sheep pastures (often run by English-speaking farmers from the Lowlands), particularly in **Sutherland** and the **Black Isle**, the **West Highlands** and the **Hebrides**.

The heritage The rude stone castles of the Highland chiefs decayed into romantic ruin while the turf and stone round huts of the tenant crofters were reduced to lumps in the pasture. They were replaced by neat stone farmhouses, crisp neo-classical manses for the influential clergy and the light plain halls of their Presbyterian churches. Ironically, at the same time as the Highland crofters were being packed off in emigrant boats, the fashion for all things Highland got into full swing, intensified by Queen Victoria's patronage of **Deeside**. In the late 19th century a series of enormous and exclusive sporting estates were created for the summer recreation of Britain's wealthy, notably in **Tayside**, **Grampian**, **Sutherland** and **Wester Ross**. A series of wonderfully excessive Gothic Baronial lodges, hotels and palaces still are the dominant architectural note of the Highlands, softened by modern bungalows and the older, stone-built dormer-windowed house still seen all over the Highlands and Islands. The influx of English speakers helped make the Gaelic tongue obsolete, and, though still widespread in the crofting population of the **Western Isles**, it is now rarerly heard on the mainland.

Quoth God to the Highlander, "What will you do now?"

"I will down to the Lowland, Lord, and there steal a cow."
Anon

237

"HAD'S A DH'FHÀSAS FLÙR AIR MACHAIR MAIRIDH CLIÙ NA H-AINNIR CHAOIMH.
"THE PRESERVER OF PRINCE CHARLES EDWARD STUART WILL BE MENTIONED IN HISTORY, AND IF COURAGE AND FIDELITY BE VIRTUES, MENTIONED WITH HONOUR"
JOHNSON

Walks

Beinn Lora, Strathclyde   234B2
Forestry Commission parking lot just south of Benderloch village (north of Oban). Beinn Lora is a 1,010-ft. high hill with magnificent views of Loch Linnhe. Follow a path climbing through the forest; follow signs and eventually skirt an area of boggy pools; the summit then comes into view. Return the same way. (2½ hours)

Findlater Castle, Grampian   235D4
From Cullen harbor follow the shore-level road eastward; this dwindles to a coastal path. On a clear day the Caithness and Sutherland coastline can be seen across the Firth. Walk onto the 15th-century ruins of Findlater Castle, perched on the cliff. Either return the same way or follow the coast on through the old fishing village of Sandend and then onto Portsoy, with its attractive harbor. Frequent buses return to Cullen from Sandend or Portsoy. (2½ to 4 hours)

Duncansby Head, Highland   235E4
Parking lot at Duncansby Head light-house. From the very northeastern-most tip of the British mainland a fine coastal path heads south to the Stacks of Duncansby, a trio of natural pillars cut off from the mainland by erosion from the sea. Return the same way. (1½ hours)

Glen Nevis, Highland   234B3
Parking lot at end of road in Glen Nevis, southeast of Fort William. There is a waterfall by the parking lot. The path leads into a splendid gorge before entering more open terrain, passing further waterfalls and reaching ruins at Steall. Return the same way. (2 hours)

Kenmore, Tayside   235B4
Start in Kenmore village square (east end of Loch Tay). Take the road north-west, cross the River Tay, then immediately take a riverside path on the right; later, turn right on a road, then left on a rising forest track, which soon levels out; 45 minutes' walking leads to a well-marked vantage point for views over the loch and over Taymouth Castle; return to the last track junction you reach and turn right to go downhill to Kenmore. (2½ hours)

The stacks at Duncansby Head

 Aberdeen 235C5

The "Granite City" is the third largest in Scotland, but although the oil boom years of the 1970s have given rise to handsome new buildings on the waterfront and huge oil-rig vessels in the harbor, the town has managed to retain its Georgian roots and its 19th-century dignity. A major port, it has long been a bustling center of commerce, and the grand sweep of Union Street reflects the city's rich history. Elegant floral displays soften the imposing Victorian buildings and the silver granite squares and terraces.

St. Machar's Cathedral▶ was founded in 1131; the main part was built in the mid-15th century. It dominates the part of the city known as **Old Aberdeen**, a calm haven of cobbled streets and houses that date from 1500. In this area too is **King's College**, founded 1500–5 and part of the university, as well as the Cruickshank Botanic Gardens and Seaton Park. Farther out, the **Brig O'Balgownie** across the River Don is the oldest medieval bridge in Scotland.

Central Aberdeen is more formal, with straight rows of granite townhouses and spacious streets. Its numerous university buildings, markets and museums are dotted in and around Broad Street and Union Street. The **Tolbooth**, on the corner of Broad Street, is the town jail, built in 1627. You can tour the ancient cells by appointment.

Provost Ross's House (NTS) traces the city's history of fishing, ship-building and its North Sea oil and gas industry; **Provost Skene's House** is furnished in 17th-century style as a museum of local social life. **James Dun's House** has changing exhibitions that appeal to families and **Satrosphere** is a "hands-on" science and technology center. The city library, **St. Mark's Church** and **His Majesty's Theatre** are known collectively as "Education, Salvation and Damnation." The **Art Gallery and Museum**▶ has works by Romney, Reynolds, James McBey, Augustus John and Scottish impressionist William McTaggart among others. The **Duthie Park Winter Gardens** are the largest glassed gardens in Europe, a tropical paradise. Early risers can catch a glimpse of Aberdeen's **fish market and auction**, which begins at around 4:30AM, when the fishermen unload their catch.

Haddo House▶ (NTS) is a half-hour's drive north, near Pitmedden, a handsome house designed by William Adam in 1731 and still relatively unchanged.

In the tropical hot houses of Duthie Park

The Buchan coast
Aberdeen is the gateway to some of the country's most unspoiled coastline. Northward to Cruden Bay and onto the busy fishing ports of Peterhead (the biggest whitefish port in Western Europe) and Fraserburgh stretch glorious miles of untouched sandy beaches. Along the north-facing coast of this far corner of Scotland little fishing villages such as Pennan and Gardenstown, west of Rosehearty, hide under spectacular cliffs.

The River Dee near Braemar

Highland Games
Athletes compete at these traditional Highland gatherings, held all over Scotland in summer, in events such as putting the stone and tossing the caber (Braemar's weighs in at 132 pounds, claims to be the longest, at 19 ¾ ft., and has been thrown successfully—i.e., absolutely straight— less than five times); there are also bagpipe and dancing competitions. Tradition has it that the games originated in martial contests held by King Malcolm Canmore back in the 11th century, to find the toughest men to fight the Normans.

▶▶▶ **Deeside**   *235C4*

The River Dee drains the eastern slopes of the Cairngorms and flows almost 80 miles due east to Aberdeen and the North Sea, passing on its way through a classic Scottish landscape of blue hills and purply heather moors, deep green woods of larch, juniper and birch, rocky riverbeds and rippling waters.

The village of **Braemar**, 1,083 ft. up and circled by layers of hills, is at the heart of the most beautiful stretch of the Dee and a popular summer vacation area. Braemar is famous for its round-towered, L-plan castle, built as a hunting lodge by the 2nd Earl of Mar in 1628 and buffeted by the Jacobites in 1689, and for the Braemar Gathering held on the first Saturday in September. The Royal Family usually pays a visit to these Highland Games (see panel), which may account for the crowds of around 50,000 people. To the west of the village, at the head of the valley just beyond Inverey, is the **Linn o' Dee▶**, where the river waters cascade down into a series of rocky pools. The minor road from Braemar to this beauty spot, often reproduced in Victorian engravings and contemporary postcards, is an attractive drive. From the road, you can set off for some beautiful walks in the Mar Forest and the foothills of Ben Macdhui (4,301 ft.).

Balmoral Castle, some 9 miles east of Braemar, was bought by Queen Victoria and her husband Prince Albert in 1852. The old castle was too small and today's mansion, typically Scottish Baronial in style, was commissioned by Prince Albert. The Royal Family still spend vacations here; the grounds and exhibitions are open to the public May 1 through July 31. The peak of Lochnagar (3,786 ft.), which towers over Balmoral, was featured in Prince Charles' first book, *The Old Man of Lochnagar*, an illustrated children's story written to amuse his younger brothers. Across the main road is the granite Crathie Church, attended by members of the Royal Family when staying in Balmoral. Queen Victoria's favorite dram was Lochnagar malt whisky; the Royal Lochnagar Distillery today has a visitor center and shop and offers visitors a tour of the distillery.

Continuing east along the banks of the boulder-strewn Dee, the A93 passes through the granite village of **Ballater**, built at the end of the 18th century to accommodate visitors taking the spa waters of nearby Pannanich Wells. With its hotels and guesthouses, it makes a good base for walking around on the hills of Craigendarroch, Craig Coillich and Glen Muick.

The main road stays close to the river, pausing at **Aboyne**, a town neatly planned around a large level green where the Highland Gathering takes place in September. The valley then opens out to **Banchory**, where the Water of Feugh joins the Dee from the Forest of Birse. Watch the salmon leaping up the rapids from the Bridge of Feugh. Like most of these Deeside resorts, Banchory has a golf course.

North from Banchory about 15 miles, near Kemnay, **Castle Fraser▶** (NTS) is a massive Z-plan castle. It is an excellent example of the Scottish baronial style, notable for its turrets,

East along the Dee from Banchory, **Crathes Castle▶▶** (NTS) is a celebrated L-shaped tower house dating to 1553, one of the finest Jacobean houses in the country. Inside, the Room of the Nine Nobles, the Room of the Muses and the Room of the Green Lady are renowned for their remarkable, highly decorative ceilings. The ghost of the Green Lady, carrying a baby and, of course, dressed in green, is thought to haunt certain rooms. The grounds too are special, a labyrinth of color enclosed within the dark green walls of a 300-year-old yew hedge. Don't look at the plan, just be lured on by the skillfully contrived arches, avenues and enticing prospects.

About 6 miles down the glen, in the midst of a surviving parcel of the Caledonian Forest called the Old Wood of Drum, stands **Drum Castle▶** (NTS). A cold, solid 13th-century keep, thick-walled and 66 ft. high, adjoins a crow-stepped gabled Jacobean mansion. It houses a collection of portraits, silver and furniture and has fine grounds with a café and adventure playground.

Raising the Old Pretender's standard
Only the Highland chiefs were able to raise the men needed to fight the cause of Britain's exiled Stuart king. When George of Hanover became king of Britain in 1714, it was in Braemar, on the spot where the Invercauld Arms Hotel now stands, that the 6th Earl of Mar raised the standard in 1715 to launch the Jacobite Rising, proclaiming the Old Pretender, James VIII and III as king.

The Loch Ness monster
Mystery surrounds the Loch Ness monster, a supposedly dinosaur-like beast alleged to live in the depths of the lake. This legend gives a hypnotic lure to the surface waters of the loch, making even hardened skeptics pause a little longer than planned—just in case. The Loch Ness Monster Exhibition at Drumnadrochit has photographs of "Nessie," together with scientific explanations and demonstrations of the latest techniques being used to solve the mystery.

Inverness   234C3

Now as ever the Capital of the Highlands, Inverness has a strategic position, at the head of the Great Glen. Its full but often violent history has left it with few historic buildings. The city museum has a good, original collection.

Less than 6 miles out of town, the vast depressing Drummossie moor, renamed **Culloden**, witnessed the last battle fought on British soil, on April 18, 1746. This was the last gasp of Prince Charles Edward Stuart's attempt to gain the throne from the Hanoverian George II (see page 246). There is a good visitor center (NTS). A mile south stand the prehistoric **Clava Cairns** and standing stones.

Cawdor Castle►, a little to the east, was built by the Thanes of Cawdor in the 14th century. The original keep remains and inside are fine Jacobean rooms. At the entrance to the Inverness and Beauly Firth sits vast **Fort George►**, built between 1748 and 1769 in demonstration of the government's intent to keep the Jacobites at bay.

The largest loch in Scotland in terms of volume of water, **Loch Ness**'s reputation relies more on the "Nessie" legend (see panel) than its beauty. Good views can be had from **Urquhart Castle**, its ruins set on a rocky cliff.

Visit Beauly for the remains of its 13th-century priory and for Campbells, a good tweed, tartan and woolen shop. Strathpeffer is a Victorian spa town with several old hotels; walk from here to the Rogie Falls. The **Black Isle►** is in fact a broad, fertile peninsula whose shores are the haunt of wading birds. In Cromarty look at the old port, the lighthouse and **Cromarty Courthouse►**, a most illuminating visitor center. In Rosemarkie see the Pictish stone in the churchyard and Groam House Museum. In nearby Fortrose visit the Gothic cathedral ruins.

Loch Ness, seen near Drumnadrochit

LOCH NESS AND THE BLACK ISLE

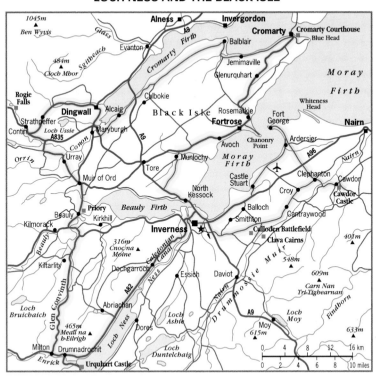

Drive Loch Ness and the Black Isle

A tour through varied mountain and coastal landscape 130 miles.

Leave Inverness on the A9 southeast, turn onto the B9006 to see **Culloden battlefield** and visitor center (NTS), and nearby **Clava Cairns** prehistoric stones. Continue to **Cawdor Castle►**, scene of the murder of Duncan in Shakespeare's *Macbeth*. Turn back and take the narrow B9006 to **Fort George►** with its regimental museum of the Queen's Own Highlanders. Follow the east coast of the **Moray Firth** into Inverness and out again on the A82 along the northern shore of **Loch Ness** to ruined **Urquhart Castle** and the Nessie Exhibition in **Drumnadrochit**.

From here take the road back north over the hills to the remains of **Beauly Priory**. At Muir of Ord take the A832 north-west to reach **Strathpeffer**. Head east to **Dingwall** and follow the Black Isle shore to reach the old seaport of **Cromarty**. Go south along the A832 to the charming little resorts of **Rosemarkie** and nearby **Fortrose**. Continue southwest to rejoin the A9 and cross over Moray Firth on the new Kessock suspension bridge back into Inverness.

A sgian dubh, Gaelic dagger, in Inverness Museum and Art Gallery

▶▶▶ Lochaber   *234C3*

This is the region once known as the West Highlands, an area of archetypal highland landscape—bleak moorlands set against soft valley meadows and the long reach of still lochs. It is the land of the Camerons and the Macdonnels, clans who provided the core support for the '45 Rebellion (see page 246) and who, a year later, dumped the Jacobite treasure into Loch Arkaig rather than see it in the hands of the Hanoverians.

At the southern end of Loch Ness (see page 244) the little town of **Fort Augustus** sits around the Caledonian Canal, a splendid waterway, with several staircase locks, designed by Thomas Telford. By linking the lochs of the Great Glen the canal joins Fort William at Loch Linnhe with Inverness on the Moray Firth. Fort Augustus has long since lost the fort built by General Wade (see panel); in its place is a Benedictine monastery and school.

The resort and aluminum smelting town of **Fort William** stands in the shadow of **Ben Nevis▶**, Britain's highest mountain at 4,419 ft. It is not the best in the Highlands for walking but if you do wish to climb it, allow five hours to get to the top and three hours to pick your way back down (it looks deceptively small because it lacks a definitive peak). It is of course essential to be properly equipped and take all safety precautions. Fort William is a modern, commercialized place, but makes a convenient base. Its story began in 1655 when General Monk built an earth-work fort here; this was replaced by General Wade's stone construction in the reign of William III; it was pulled down in the 19th century. The West Highland Museum in Cameron Square provides a good introduction to the region and its natural history.

South from Fort William the main road passes through **Glen Coe▶▶**, the scene, in the early hours of February 13, 1692, of Scotland's most infamous massacre. Acting under government orders, members of the Campbell militia who were billeted on members of the MacDonald clan, turned on their hosts—breaking the strict code of hospitality that existed between clans—and indiscriminately massacred them. An act, so the government thought,

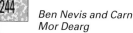

244

Ben Nevis and Carn Mor Dearg

The Caledonian Canal at Fort Augustus

Fishing boats in Mallaig harbor: the catch, much of it large shrimp, is auctioned on the quay

that would dissuade anyone from harboring doubts about the legitimacy of Queen Mary on the throne instead of her brother James VII (James II to the English). There is a visitor center near the foot of the glen.

West of Fort William, at the head of Loch Shiel, the **Glenfinnan monument►** (NTS) marks the spot where the Young Pretender, Prince Charles Edward (see page 246), raised his standard on August 19, 1745 and launched the campaign to see his father recognized as rightful king.

The songwriter's "Road to the Isles" from Fort William leads to **Arisaig and Mallaig►►** past the coral sandy beaches that featured in the movie *Local Hero*. Inland are the dark waters of Loch Morar, the deepest freshwater stretch of water in Britain, with its own lesser-known monster, Morag. On the wooded islands in the loch, the Jesuits maintained a secret seminary to keep the Roman Catholic faith alive. The busy fishing port of Mallaig is the departure point for ferries to the Inner Isles of Eigg, Muck, Rhum, Canna, Soay and Armadale on Skye (see pages 254–5). All the islands are easy day-trips; only the Skye boat takes cars.

To the south is the untamed **Ardnamurchan** peninsula, whose far point is the westernmost part of the British mainland. Isolated on a tide-washed island in Loch Moidart stands the gaunt, empty keep of **Castle Tioram►**, last used by the Macdonald chief of Clan Ranald, who burned it after the 1715 uprising failed, rather than let the Campbells take possession. A short walk from the hotel bar in the village of Kilchoan, **Castle Mingary►** stands in one of the most impressive locations on the peninsula's southern shore, looking across the sound of Mull to Tobermory.

The small Highland village of **Lochaline►**, where ferries depart for Mull, sits on the picturesque Morvern peninsula, overlooking the tidal inlet of Loch Aline. The strong square keep of 14th-century Ardtornish Castle was one of the chief bases of the Lord of the Isles (see panel, page 254).

The West Highland Line
The railroad that runs from Glasgow to Mallaig can justly claim to be British Rail's most scenic route. The construction of the line between Fort William and Mallaig in particular involved some spectacular feats of engineering, with gradients of up to 1 in 48, numerous rock cuttings and dramatic bridges, viaducts and tunnels. Some services are steam-hauled.

The monument to the '45 at Glenfinnan

The West Highland Way
This 95-mile long-distance footpath starts from Milngavie, just north of Glasgow, and heads north of the eastern side of Loch Lomond, passing Rannoch Moor, Glen Coe, Lochaber and Ben Nevis to reach Fort William. As you get farther north, the scenery is more and more magnificent. It is never really steep but be prepared for plenty of up-and-down sections.

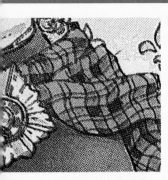

■ **Seen by contemporary opponents as a political and military threat to 18th-century Britain's stability, the Jacobites and their hopeless quest to restore a Catholic monarch to the British throne was soon turned into a romantic lost cause. At its head was the most romantic figure of all: Italian-born Prince Charles Edward Louis Philip Casimir Stuart, know variously as the Young Pretender, the Young Chevalier and, most familiarly, as Bonnie Prince Charlie. He was in Scotland for only 14 months....■**

"Charles was the candle who lighted the bonfire, but they [his Highland supporters] were the timber that filled a dark sky with their splendid ardour."
Eric Linklater, in *The Prince In The Heather*

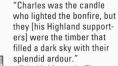

Charles set off from St. Nazaire on his escapade with the blessing of a French government eager to see Britain destabilized. When the handsome young man landed on the island of Eriskay in the Outer Hebrides, the local MacDonald chief told him to go home. Charles romantically replied that he had come home and, undaunted, went on to raise his standard at Glenfinnan in August 1745.

A persuasive personality The fatal charm of the Stuarts managed to persuade about one sixth of the estimated 30,000 fighting men in the Highlands of Scotland to take up arms in his cause. The campaign met with early successes but was finally halted on Culloden Moor in April 1746. There the Jacobites were blown away by the superior artillery of the British army. Charles went into hiding and the government forces (which comprised a number of Scottish regiments) went on to commit numerous atrocities in its efforts to destroy the Highland way of life. This policy was implemented by a far-off government in Westminster, who perceived the Highlands as a hotbed of potential Jacobites, where clan chiefs were able to call on, in effect, private armies.

The romance of a lost cause From these bare facts sprang the legend of an irresistibly handsome young man on a lost cause. With the real threat out of the way, the Jacobites were soon reinterpreted in song and story. Bonnie Prince Charlie became the figurehead of Jacobite mythology and has been on shortbread boxes ever since. Flora Macdonald—whose dealings with the Prince covered only a few days and who had to be persuaded to have anything to do with the business at all—was quickly fêted as a romantic heroine. The notion that the Prince was never betrayed by a sympathetic Scottish people is a still current tale. In reality his supporters had to keep him well out of the way. But none of this matters. With Bonnie Prince Charlie, the romance is all.

"Over the sea to Skye"
"Carry the lad born to be King over the sea to Skye" is perhaps the best-known line from the corpus of Jacobite songs, and alludes to the perilous voyage from Benbecula to Skye which Charles took while disguised as Betty Burke, Flora Macdonald's maid. "The Skye Boat Song," however, is a Victorian fake: its famous lyrics date from 1884 and most of the tune from 1879.

IN LOVING MEMORY OF PRINCE CHARLES EDWARD STUART (Bonnie Prince Charlie) GLENFINNAN A.D. 1745 R.I.P.

►► **Mull** *234B2*

The beautiful "isle-of-the-cool-high-bends," 24 miles long and 26 miles wide, has many aspects—fierce rocky cliffs, sheltered sandy beaches, quiet fishing coves, bleak moors, lone grey castles and lofty mountains—but is dominated by treeless green terraces of grazing land skilfully managed by crofts and small farms.

Duart Castle, perched above the narrow Sound of Mull 3 miles from Craignure, has its origins in the 13th century. It has been restored as the summer home of the chief of Clan Maclean. **Torosay Castle**, just outside Craignure, is a 19th-century baronial building (designed by David Bryce) well worth a visit, especially for its terraced grounds laid out by Robert Lorimer. A narrow gauge railroad runs between the castle and Craignure .

Tobermory►, named after a holy well dedicated to Our Lady, is the island's main town, its arc of brightly painted houses encircling a bay popular with sailboat owners.

The Holy Island of **Iona►►►**, the "Cradle of Christianity," is served by ferry from Fionnphort on the western tip of the Ross of Mull or by boat excursions

Ancient burial place of kings
St. Oran's Cemetery on Iona is the oldest Christian cemetery in Scotland. Here are buried 48 Scottish kings, including Kenneth MacAlpin, who first united the Scots and Picts in 843, and Duncan, murdered by Macbeth in 1040. Eight Norwegian kings also found their final resting place here, a reflection of the several hundred years of Norse occupation of Scotland from the 9th century on.

247

Near Aridhglas, Ross of Mull: lone standing stones may well be seen in the remoter parts of the country

from Oban. No cars are allowed on the island but all sights can be easily reached on foot. In AD563 St Columba and 12 companions landed here from Ireland and established a monastery as a base for numerous missionary journeys among the pagan Picts. It became the mother house of the Celtic church in Scotland and England. This era of great spiritual and creative achievement ended, however, with the Norse raid of 803 which killed 68 monks and persuaded those left alive to return to Ireland. Nothing of their monastery remains, but an astonishing collection of early Christian stone carvings recalls this heroic period. The existing abbey buildings all date from the second foundation in the early 13th century, when a Benedictine monastery and nunnery were established. The island's sense of peace is a source of spiritual refreshment for many visitors.

Fingal's Cave, Staffa
The cathedral-like cave that inspired Mendelssohn's *Hebrides Overture* is one of several on this tiny uninhabited island north of Iona. Smooth columns of black basalt, the result of volcanic action, rise out of the sea in what is known in Gaelic as An Uamh Ehinn, "the musical cave," because of the echoing sounds that the sea makes within it. Boat trips leave from Oban in summer.

The Crinan Canal
In 1793 work started on the construction of this short 9-mile canal that would link Loch Fyne with the Sound of Jura, saving ships the long, hazardous journey round the Mull of Kintyre. The chief engineer, Scotsman John Rennie, met with financial and engineering problems (Thomas Telford was also called upon for his expertise) and it was never a commercial success. However, it passes via 15 locks through a beautiful landscape of wooded mountains and its basin at Crinan is now popular with yachtsmen.

▶ **Oban and mid Argyll**   234B2

Oban is a popular family resort, accessible by bus and train from Glasgow. The harbor bustles with fishing vessels and ferries for the islands of Mull, Coll, Tiree, Colonsay and the Outer Hebrides. Promenade along the seafront, browse in the woolen mills, then stroll along to Dunollie Castle where the Lords of Lorne used to preside. McCraig's Tower, an unfinished folly modelled on Rome's Colosseum, overlooks the town with fine views across to the Inner Hebrides. Oban is not known for reliable weather but there are a number of indoor attractions to enjoy when it rains, such as a glassworks, pottery, toy and model display and the distillery, best known for its 12-year-old malt whisky. Just east of the town is the Oban Rare Breeds Farm. The road north passes the 13th-century MacDougall fortress of Dunstaffnage on its way to the Sea Life Centre on the shore of Loch Creran.

Just north of the village of Taynuilt is the **Bonawe Iron Furnace**▶. Here you can see the restored remains of a charcoal furnace, founded in 1753, that used local wood for iron smelting. At **Cruachan hydro-electric power station**▶ a minibus takes visitors deep into the mountain to see the great turbine hall. The village of Lochawe sits at the head of Loch Awe, the longest loch in Scotland, famous for its fishing. In summer the steamer *Lady Rowena* threads through the romantic burial islands of the MacNaughtons on Innis Fraoch and the MacArthurs on Innishail. The gaunt ruins of Kilchurn Castle, the original fortress home of the Campbells of Breadalbane, stands at the head of Kinloch Awe.

Inveraray▶, at the head of Loch Fyne, is a supremely elegant 18th-century town noted for its bridges, fishing harbor, gibbet pier, judges' lodgings and central double church. Its chief attraction is the Jail with its tableaus of jailers and wretched inmates. **Inveraray Castle**▶▶, home of the Campbell Dukes of Argyll, is a heavy gray stone castellated mansion, but it has delightful 18th-century interiors and is stuffed with Highland weapons, portraits and memorabilia. Walk through the grounds to the

A "Cal Mac" ferry arrives in Oban from the islands

summit of Duniquaich for a panoramic view over the area.

Crinan► is a tiny place at the western end of the Crinan Canal (see panel), its handful of houses and a hotel overlooking the yachting activity in the old basin. The hamlet of Kilmartin►► is surrounded by notable prehistoric sites including Bronze Age burial cairns and the Templewood stone circle; in the churchyard is a fine collection of medieval carved stones and in the church itself a good Celtic cross. Dunadd Hillfort was the capital of the early Scots kingdom of Dalriada. On its rocky top are carved a footprint and a boar.

Across the Sound of Jura lies Jura►►, the rugged, barely populated island, home of red deer, where George Orwell wrote *1984*. Next door, is the lovely, peaty isle of Islay►►, where no fewer than eight distilleries still operate (ferries from Kennacraig on the Kintyre peninsula).

The dazzling interior décor of Inveraray Castle

A carved stone at Kilmartin

The dawn of history
Grey recumbent tombs of the dead in desert places, Standing stones on the vacant wine-red moor, Hills of sheep, and the homes of the silent vanquished races, And winds, austere and pure.
   From "Blows the wind today" by **R.L. Stevenson** (1850–94)

Drive Mid Argyll

This tour takes in the beautiful sea loch of Loch Etive, the dramatic Pass of Brander and the shores of Loch Fyne, with its fine Inveraray Castle. Return through an area studded with prehistoric remains on a road past many sea lochs with views of the Inner Hebridean islands (approx.100 miles). There is an optional detour of approx. 40 miles down the Knapdale peninsula.

Leave **Oban►** going north on the A85 to pass Connel Bridge. Continue to Taynuilt for **Bonawe Iron Furnace►** and then on the A85 through a narrow treeless defile, the Pass of Brander, to **Lochawe**. Take the A819 south to **Inveraray►** with its splendid

castle►► and then turn south on the A83, skirting the shores of Loch Fyne and passing Auchindrain open-air museum and Crarae Glen woodland gardens. Reach the market town of **Lochgilphead** and turn north up the A816. A detour may be taken on the B841 to **Crinan►** at the end of the Crinan Canal and then south to Castle Sween and **Kilmory Knap** for its medieval carved stones.

Continue north on the A816 to **Dunadd Fort** and **Kilmartin►**, center for some absorbing prehistoric sites. Pass **Carnasserie Castle** at the west end of Loch Awe and, twisting in and out of view of the Firth of Lorne, return to Oban.

▶▶ Orkney and Shetland 235A5/235E5

These two northern archipelagos have such a different cultural atmosphere from the rest of Scotland that many visitors feel they have arrived in another country. For 600 years they were under Norse rule and even when this domination officially ended, in the 15th century, it was another 200 years before the Scottish throne became strong enough to exert any real authority over these remote islands. Both groups of islands are astonishingly bleak and treeless and initially seem almost featureless, but both have splendid cliff and sea loch scenery and rare birdlife. Despite boasting what is arguably the finest collection of prehistoric sites in Britain, they receive comparatively few visitors.

Wildlife
Both island groups are renowned for their seabird colonies, which are among the most important in the world. On Shetland, visit the Island of Noss, accessible by small ferry (weather permitting). Here and at Hermaness on the north of Unst you get wonderful views of puffins, gannets, guillemots, razorbills and many more species. As you explore the island, watch out for great skuas, arctic skuas and whimbrels, which nest on the moorland. On Orkney, visit Yesnaby Cliffs on Mainland, both for their seabirds and for the rare and miniature Scottish primrose.

Precarious cliffs at Yesnaby, Orkney

Orkney Islands In Kirkwall on Mainland the unaltered pre-Reformation **Cathedral of St. Magnus**▶▶ stands in proud dominance over the town. It was begun in the 12th century and the massive round pillars and arches of the arcades date from this time. In one of the pillars two skeletons were discovered early this century, one of which may be St. Magnus himself. In the cathedral precincts are the ruins of the Bishop's Palace and Earl's Palace and **Tankerness House Museum**, a 16th-century townhouse turned into a museum of Orkney. Around the precincts wind streets of crowstepped gabled houses, brightly painted.

Skara Brae▶▶▶, also on Mainland, is an entire neolithic settlement that lay perfectly preserved in sand dunes for 4,000 years until a storm first uncovered a corner of it in 1850. Inside the houses are beds, hearths, dressers, closets, even fish tanks. The inhabitants left pots, jewelry, clothes and tools, which are displayed in the museum. The Ring of Brogar▶▶ is a wide circle of stones. When first constructed it was surely one of the most magnificent stone circles ever built by neolithic man. The scale is quite breathtaking and although only some of the stones remain the original majesty is well preserved. Many of the stones reach a height of 14¾ ft. Nearby, **Maes Howe**▶▶ is the finest chambered cairn, or burial chamber, in Europe, both for size and preservation. It was built around

2700BC and so had been standing for at least a century before the first circle was marked out at Stonehenge in Wiltshire. It remained intact for nearly 4,000 years until the Vikings plundered it; their rude Norse inscriptions can still be seen on the walls.

The **Pier Arts Centre▶** is a delightful little gallery in the ferry port of Stromness. It has the best collection of modern British art in the north of Scotland. The masterpieces of Ben Nicholson and Barbara Hepworth admirably complement the island's ancient remains.

The famous **Old Man of Hoy▶▶** is an enormous stack of rock rearing a tremendous 443 ft. out of the sea off the island of Hoy. Like most of Orkney's cliff scenery, it is best seen from a boat (or the ferry from Scrabster).

Shetland Islands This is the most northerly part of Great Britain (Shetland is about 60 miles north of Orkney) and the beauty of midsummer nights when there is little or no darkness has to be seen to be believed. The main industries are crofting, fishing and knitting. The fine wool of the Shetland sheep is knitted up in traditional, distinctive colors and patterns, often known as Fair Isle.

Some people travel to Shetland just to see **Mousa Broch▶▶▶**, on a little island to the southeast of Mainland. The Iron Age fortress tower still stands over 39 ft. high, all its distinctive features wonderfully preserved. Interestingly, when Shetland was covered with brochs (see panel), Mousa was acknowledged to be the smallest and meanest of them all. **Clickhimin▶**, near Lerwick, is another well-preserved broch.

On the southernmost tip of Mainland is **Jarlshof▶▶▶**, one of the most remarkable prehistoric sites in Europe. Impressive remains, standing several feet high, can be seen of the Bronze Age courtyard settlements, the Iron Age "wheelhouses" (see panel) that succeeded them and the longhouses of the Viking settlers who came next. There is also a 16th-century laird's house, home of Earl of Orkney Patrick Stewart and linked with Walter Scott's novel *The Pirate*. The same earl, renowned for his cruelty, built **Scalloway Castle**. The **Shetland Museum** in Lerwick tells the islands' story.

Brochs and wheelhouses
Brochs are round towers, shaped like modern cooling towers, that are found only in the north of Scotland, the Outer Hebrides and Orkney and Shetland. Built by the Picts during the 1st and 2nd centuries BC as defensive structures, they typically have double, stone walls with an inner staircase between, giving access to upper galleries. In the middle was a courtyard. Wheelhouses were a specialty of prehistoric Scotland, round buildings with a thick outer wall and a slab or corbelled roof. A number of inner walls ran in from the outer wall to a central area, like spokes of a wheel, forming "rooms."

An Iron Age wheelhouse at Jarlshof, Shetland

Loch Tay, noted for its salmon fishing

►► **Perthshire** 235B4

More or less at the center of Scotland and rich in historical associations, Perthshire (now, with the addition of Angus, labeled Tayside Region) is a county of contrasts. As you travel north the lush farmland of the south is slowly transformed into the rounded heather-covered slopes of the Grampian Mountains. Cut through with great lochs, it is bound into one region by the silver waters of the Tay.

The town of **Perth►** enjoys a pleasant position beside the River Tay and its road and railroad network makes it a good base. Despite its Tay bridges, its Georgian terraces and the Millais paintings in the city art gallery, it does not quite live up to the expectations set by its long history. **Branklyn Garden►** (NTS) is small but delightful collection of rhododendrons, shrubs and alpines. Balhousie Castle houses the regimental museum of the Black Watch. **Nearby attractions►►** include the ruined pre-Reformation nave of Dunkeld Cathedral, the painted wooden ceilings of Huntingtower Castle (once known as Ruthven, where James VI met treachery at the hands of local lords), the 10th-century round tower at Abernethy and the world's highest beech hedge at Meikleour.

Just 2 miles upriver from Perth is **Scone Palace►►►** (pronounced "Skoon"), one of Scotland's great treasure houses. Scone was the coronation place of all the Scottish kings until the time of James I, the seat of Pictish government and the site of the famous Stone of Scone (see panel). The present palace was built over the foundations of the ancient abbey by Wyatt at the onset of the fashion for Gothick in the first decade of the 19th century. Its state rooms display the many treasures from England and France that were assembled by the Earls of Mansfield, but it is chiefly loved for its lived-in, family atmosphere.

The Stone of Scone
Also known as the Stone of Destiny, this is believed to be a druidic talisman, consecrated by St. Columba at Iona, that was used in the investiture of the Dalriadic princes. It was brought here in the 9th century by Kenneth MacAlpin, the man who united Scotland after his defeat of the Picts at Scone. In 1296 it was removed by King Edward I of England and placed under the coronation chair in London's Westminster Abbey—except for a brief period in the 1950s when it was sensationally stolen and mysteriously reappeared in Arbroath Abbey.

Pitlochry is a Highland resort town, in a beautiful setting of loch, river, mountain and wood. It was created in the Victorian era when the railroad station and the Hydro, the large (and originally strictly teetotal) hotel, offered healthy walking breaks, away from the smog and sin of the big cities. It boasts a respected Festival Theatre with a broad summer programme. Local beauty spots include the Queen's View up Loch Tummel and Loch Rannoch, beneath volcano-shaped Schiehallion (3,490 ft.). Just outside town is the site of the Battle of Killiecrankie (an early Jacobite victory) with its visitor center (NTS).

To the northwest is **Blair Castle►►►**, its white walls and turrets surrounded by the rugged beauty of the Atholl Hills. The province of Atholl has been ruled from this towerhouse since the 13th century. The castle is famous as the seat of the only duke to be permitted a private army, the 100-strong Atholl Highlanders, who are recruited from tenants and neighbors. They parade on the last Sunday of May; the tunics, worn with a distinctive white bow tie, enliven many a Highland Ball throughout the year. The castle has many rooms open to the public, packed with treasures, including some rare surviving examples of 17th-century Scottish furniture. In the quaint 18th-century village outside the castle gates there is a local folk museum. A 3-mile track leads to the gorge, bridges and waterfall of Bruar.

Each loch in Scotland has its own marked character but the serpentine twist of the 14-mile long **Loch Tay►►**, overlooked to its north by the 3,983 ft. summit of Ben Lawers, has a serenity totally out of keeping with the bloody clan feuds that went on around its shores. At its western end the village of **Killin** is noted for the **Falls of Dochart►**. Between the village and Loch Tay are the ruins of Finlarig, the murderous stronghold of Black Duncan of the Cowl, who was the acquisitive chief of the local Campbells. His wealthy descendants built the elegant bridge and model village of **Kenmore**, at the east end of the loch. The market town of **Aberfeldy**, 7 miles east, with its monumental Wade bridge (see panel, page 244), is a popular base for summer visitors. You can walk to such nearby attractions as Castle Menzies, a classic 16th-century Z-plan tower house, and the old Kirk of Weem with its pair of Celtic crosses.

Scone Palace: the bedroom used by Queen Victoria

Highland genealogy
Beware of trying to follow too closely the tangled web of Highland genealogies. Despite fearsome blood feuds, practically all the great chiefs and nobles were, and are, interrelated. This allowed any one family to keep a finger in a number of pies, which was the best way to survive the mercurial and murderous politics of Scotland. The Murrays are a fine example: during the '45 Rebellion John Murray, the 1st Duke of Atholl remained a fervent Hanoverian while his son George was in effective command of the Jacobite army.

253

Perth city's coat of arms, on a lamppost

▶▶▶ **Skye** 234C2

The most startlingly magnificent of the Hebridean islands, Skye is also the closest to the mainland. A bridge currently under construction will link it by road to the mainland, due to be completed in 1995. Until then it is a ferry journey of just five minutes from Kyle of Lochalsh to Kyleakin or a half-hour from Mallaig to Armadale. It is an island of extremely irregular shape, a sort of smudged handprint some 50 miles from end to end and varying from 4 through 25 miles in width. It consists of a central nexus—on which are **Portree**, the bustling capital (and hub of the island's bus network), and the Cuillin Hills; a number of long peninsular fingers stretch out from there, intersected by sea lochs. The landscape changes with disorienting ease from Alpine peaks, to rolling farmland, bleak moorland, wooded valleys, coves of white coral sand and cliffs dotted with secret caves.

Close to the ferry terminal at Armadale, the restored ruins of the 19th-century castellated mansion of Armadale now house the **Clan Donald Centre**▶. Displays and videos tell the story of the clan and its progenitor, Somerled, the first Lord of the Isles (see panel).

The central chain of mountain peaks, the **Cuillins**▶▶, their jagged silhouette seldom seen without at least a wisp of cloud, provides some of the most splendid scenery and demanding climbing in Britain. Rising to 3,310 ft., they enclose Loch Coruisk, a great pool of water locked in an amphitheater of crags of the blackest gabbro; it's a scene of overpowering desolation and grandeur. You can reach it by boat trip from Elgol, or in a full day's walk from Elgol or Sligachan (it's not a walk, however, for the faint-hearted).

The **Skye Heritage Centre**▶ tells the island's story from the point of view of the ordinary people rather than the landowners. At Skeabost, a little way northwest of Portree, are the ruins of the tiny **Columban Chapel**▶, one of a number of the earliest Celtic churches known to have been built here.

The path to Moonen bay and cliffs

254

Lords of the Isles
The lordship of the Isles was an independent state that controlled the islands and much of the west coast of Scotland in the medieval period. The founder was Somerled, the great progenitor of clan Macdonald, who used the conflict between his Norse overlords and the Scots kings to establish a near autonomous state in the 12th century. When Norse overlordship had ended, the Macdonald chiefs agreed to accept the rule of one of their number, Donald of Islay, as Lord of the Isles. Eventually James IV managed to annex the title in 1493 (one still borne by the heir apparent to the British throne).

An old croft house, traditionally maintained

Farther west, **Dunvegan Castle**►► has been home to the MacLeods of Skye since the 12th century. Striking a magnificent attitude on this remote shore of the island, it contains treasures sacred to the clan such as the fairy flag, which when waved has the power to save the clan. Legend says it will only work three times, and it's already been used twice, with miraculous results. Close by is **Kilmuir Churchyard and Croft Museum**►. In the churchyard lie the remains of Flora MacDonald, Hebridean heroine of the '45 Rebellion (see panel, page 246), beneath an imposing Celtic cross. The croft museum uses four thatched cottages to recreate aspects of the simple yet heroic self-sufficiency of the island's crofters.

North of Portree, the **Old Man of Storr**► is another of the geological wonders of Skye—a precariously balanced rock needle. The scene of weird desolation is accentuated by the wind sobbing in the gullies. **The Quiraing**►► is one of the strangest and most fascinating hills in Scotland. Seldom seen without its raven guardians swirling around, it is a confused mass of cliffs, scree slopes and towering pinnacles.

On a wind-blown promontory at the northern end of the Trotternish peninsula stand the ruins of **Duntulm Castle**►, a fortress built by the Macdonalds of Sleat when they were battling with the MacLeods of Dunvegan for the control of this region (see panel, Lords of the Isles). From Sconser a little ferry goes across to the tranquil island of **Raasay**►►. A track follows its long spine of hills to end at the silhouetted ruins of medieval Brochel Castle.

Across the Cuillin Sound south of Skye lie the **Inner Isles**, Rum, Eigg, Muck and Canna, served by ferries from Mallaig on the mainland and Armadale on Skye. Each has limited accommodation. **Rum**►► is the largest of the group and has a volcanic mountain cluster, the highest peak being Askival (2,657 ft.). Owned by Scottish Natural Heritage, it's a haven for nature lovers.

Might is right?
The 1882 Battle of the Braes was a half-heroic, half-comical affair. A group of bailiffs who were attempting to evict crofters from the coastal strip just south of Portree were beaten off by a fierce band of Hebridean housewives armed with stone-weighted stockings. The English government, used to sending gunboats all over the world to force their way, promptly sent one up to Skye but backed down in the face of universal hostility. Instead they sent a Commission whose report paved the way for the enlightened Crofting Acts.

The valley of the River Spey near Newtonmore

Gordonstoun School
The school, near Elgin, is famous nowadays as the establishment where the Queen's three sons were educated, but its buildings have had a local notoriety since the 17th century, when they served as the residence of Sir Robert Gordon. Known as the Warlock Laird, he laid out the school's famous round square so that his diabolic familiars could never corner him. His accomplice, the local minister, was not so lucky and was found one morning horribly shred by giant claws outside the kirk.

▶ **Spey Valley**   235C

One of the broad classifications of single malt whiskies is the Speyside malts which take their name from the River Spey. It rises in the Monadliath (literally "the gray moors") and runs northeast, eventually spreading through the wildlife-rich Insh Marshes with the Cairngorms as a spectacular backdrop. Beyond Grantown-on-Spey it reaches the whisky distilling area stretching all the way to the Moray coast. The typical Strathspey view features a pleasing mix of woods and farmlands backed by moorland slopes and, inevitably, a plume of white steam jetting up from yet another distillery tucked into the landscape. Visit Glenfiddich at Dufftown for a wide-ranging and entertaining interpretation of malt whisky, though there are plenty of other famous names, many of which have visitor centers, some on the marked Malt Whisky Trail.

The resort town of **Aviemore** is a rather unattractive creation of the 1960s but it's a popular base for hill walking in the Cairngorm Mountains in summer and skiing on them in winter. Cairn Gorm itself rises to 4,084 ft.; take the ski lift (it operates all year round) for a wonderful view. Other activities might include a visit to the osprey reserve at Loch Garten, a ride on the Strathspey Steam Railway from Aviemore to Boat of Garten (good walks at either end) or a visit to the Landmark Highland Heritage visitor center. There are facilities for indoor sports, a swimming pool, ice-skating rink, movie theater and discos. South along the A9 toward Kingussie is the Highland Wildlife Park.

Kingussie▶, pronounced "Kinusie," is a pleasing town of just one main street, with plenty of beautiful walks nearby. If you visit only one highland history museum in Scotland, visit the **Highland Folk Museum▶▶** here. It is divided into indoor and outdoor exhibitions and includes a "black house" from the Outer Hebridean island of Lewis, a clack mill, a salmon smokehouse and

ascinating exhibits from farming and domestic life. On
natural escarpment the other side of the Spey and
he A9 stands the gaunt roofless ruin of the Ruthven
Barracks, a sister to the one in Glenelg (see page 258).
They were built to police the main Highland trade routes
after the 1715 rebellion was suppressed, but a generation
ater, in 1746, they were blown up by retreating
Jacobites.

Elgin, the administrative center of Moray, is the largest
own in the favored Laigh of Moray. (Laigh means a shel-
ered low-lying area and, in this case, refers to its
position in the "rain shadow" of the Grampians.) Elgin's
cathedral, "the lantern of the North," founded in 1224,
was burned in 1390 by the villainous Wolf of Badenoch.
Though subsequently rebuilt, it is now a picturesque ruin.
The local museum features a display on Britain's oldest
dinosaurs, found nearby. East of the town is the attractive
community of Fochabers, with plenty of antique shops to
attract browsers. On the coast, the otherwise rather
workaday town of Buckie is enhanced by an interpretation
of the development of the northeast fishery, the Buckie
Drifter.

Pluscarden Abbey▶ lies in a fertile valley about 6 miles
southwest of Elgin. Its atmosphere is potent, with Benedictine monks going to and fro amid the Gothic ruins.
Originally founded by Alexander II in the early 13th century, the abbey was badly damaged by the endemic warfare
of the region and fell into further decay after the
Reformation. It was partly restored by the Marquis of
Bute in the 19th century and in 1943 was bestowed by his
son on a Benedictine community from Prinknash in
Gloucestershire. The monks moved in five years later and
are now rebuilding it.

The pretty coastal village of **Findhorn▶**, due north from
Forres, made headline news in the early 1960s with tales
of its hippie community. This developed into the Findhorn
Foundation, a center for mystic thought and learning with
some 200 community members.

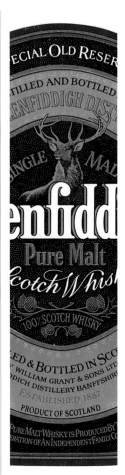

The copper stills at Glenfiddich Distillery

The Speyside Way
The 47-mile long-distance
path starts at Spey Bay
where the River Spey flows
into the North Sea and
offers fairly easy walking
as far as Ballindalloch
before tackling the more
challenging section
through the hills to
Tomintoul. The countryside
is varied and the path
passes near several
whisky distilleries.

▶▶ Sutherland, Caithness and Wester Ross   *234C2*

The northernmost reach of mainland Scotland is often referred to as the last great wilderness of Europe. The eastern coast, a fertile strip backed by low brown moorland, could hardly be in greater contrast to the green-gray mountains that overlook the long, intruding sea lochs of the west coast of Ross.

In a remote and picturesque situation on the Sound of Sleat, **Glenelg▶** was once on the main cattle-droving route to Skye. Here are to be found the two best-preserved brochs (see panel, page 251) in mainland Scotland, a handsome, ruined Hanoverian barrack block and Sandaig Bay, site of Gavin Maxwell's otter refuge of "Camusfearna" so vividly described in *Ring of Bright Water*. In summer you can take a ferry across the surging Kylerhea tidal stream to Skye.

Picture-postcard scene: a piper at Eilean Donan Castle

North, across Loch Duich, the stunning **Eilean Donan Castle▶▶** stands on an islet at the meeting of three lochs. It is an ancient Iron Age site but the castle, a Mackenzie fortress, was entirely rebuilt early this century by Colonel Macrae who saw its original appearance in a dream. On the northern shores of this peninsula are the stonebuilt houses and palm trees of the delightful seaside village of **Plockton▶**. West of Lochcarron, the adventurous should take an exhilaratingly twisty road (certainly not one for timid drivers), over **Bealach Na Ba (The Pass of the Cattle)▶** The glacier-scarred rocks on the summit of this pass offer a very fine view over Skye, especially at sunset. The road leads down to the remote coastal village of **Applecross**. A carved Celtic cross beside the kirk marks the site of the once influential 7th-century monastery of St. Maelrubha.

Torridon▶▶ lies at the end of one of Wester Ross's wildest glens. The road along the southern shores of Upper Loch Torridon offers magnificent views of Beinn Alligin (3,232 ft.). A National Trust for Scotland countryside center in Torridon has a deer museum and an audiovisual presentation on local wildlife. Farther north, in one of the most beautiful corners of the west coast, lies the spectacular, world-famous **Inverewe Garden▶▶▶** (NTS), a collection of 2,500 species of tender and hardy shrubs and trees flourishing in the warmth of the Gulf Stream.

The Sutherland Clearances
Dominating the skyline around the village of Golspie is a statue of the 1st Duke of Sutherland. He is the infamous Leviathan of Wealth who between 1810 and 1820 evicted 15,000 of his tenants from their self-sufficient crofts in order to turn their small plots into profitable sheep pasture.

Dornoch's claims to fame
Besides having the third oldest golf links in the world, considered as far back as 1630 to be superior to those of St. Andrews, Dornoch also claims the best sunshine record in northern Scotland and the dubious distinction of being the last place in Scotland to burn a witch. The Witch's Stone by the 17th hole of the golf links commemorates the country's last judicial execution for witchcraft, in 1722.

Inverewe Garden, on the shores of Loch Ewe

In the far north, you can take a ferry and minibus from Durness to **Cape Wrath▶▶** to see some stupendous coastal scenery. Britain's highest mainland cliffs are nearby Clo Mor, east of Cape Wrath. Just outside Durness itself is the Smoo Cave, which is in fact three vast caves in the limestone cliffs, with a waterfall. A boat trip can be taken right into the second and third caves.

Few people who come this far north fail to visit Britain's most northern point, **John O'Groats**, named after the Dutchman Jan de Groot. It's basically an untidy collection of tourist shacks, as disappointing to many visitors as is Britain's southernmost extremity, Land's End. Persevere instead to nearby Duncansby Head (see Walks, page 238): the three dramatic offshore stacks rise to over 197 ft., the wind blows off the wild North Sea in fiery gusts and the adventurous spirit feels true delight.

South of Wick, near the village of Lybster, are two impressive ancient relics, the **Hill O' Many Stones** and the **Grey Cairns of Camster▶▶**. The former is a curious and attractive arrangement of 22 rows of stones in a fan shape, the latter two excellently preserved neolithic burial chambers. If you do not mind the idea of crawling into someone's grave, you can enter one of the most handsome in the country, 197 ft. long and 59 ft. wide with separate chambers inside.

North of Dornoch the fairytale towers of **Dunrobin Castle▶▶** stand on a coastal escarpment, the former seat of the Earls and Dukes of Sutherland, the largest landowners in Britain. Despite its fanciful 19th-century exterior, it is an ancient fortress with a medieval keep as its core. The collection of paintings inside includes a Reynolds and two Canalettos. **Dornoch▶▶** is a secluded and ancient royal burgh, a pretty little sandstone town with miles of safe sandy beaches. The small cathedral of the Bishops of Caithness dates from the 12th century. The town is also renowned for its golf links.

Generating power
Standing on the clifftops 10 miles west of Thurso, the giant golf-ball shape of Dounreay nuclear power station can be seen for miles around. Elsewhere the waters of Scotland's mountains and reservoirs are harnessed to produce electricity: the great pipes of the hydro-electric plant at Kinlochleven can be seen on the hillsides south of Fort William and those of the Tay-Tummel system around Glen Affric. The pumped storage plant at Ben Cruachan in Argyll has a visitor center.

Wildlife
The flow or marsh country of Caithness and Sutherland is a vast stretch of plantations. It is home during the summer months to greenshanks, dunlins, golden plovers and other wading birds. Dunnet Bay, near Wick, is an excellent birdwatching spot in winter. Look for great northern divers, long-tailed ducks and scoters. The flora of the arctic species mingles with mountain species, almost at sea level. Handa Island off Scourie, is another wonderful site for breeding seabirds. A private ferry often runs from Tarbert.

Scarista Bay, Harris

The Lewis Chessmen
The wild, sparsely populated lands on the western extremity of Lewis present some of the most magnificent scenery and the most perfect white sand beaches. This is the home of the extraordinary Lewis chessmen, dating from the 12th century. Their chance discovery last century caused a storm of controversy; their workmanship and artistry were of a standard many found hard to credit.

▶▶▶ The Western Isles 234D1

Sail west across the Minch and you reach the Outer Hebrides, or Western Isles. For the most part the eastern side of the archipelago is barren, rocky and steep. Its west coast is all silver-white beaches, long and empty and backed by the "machair," fertile peaty grassland enriched by white shell-sand—an almost unique habitat that supports a rich wildlife. Between the two lie watery, peaty and totally treeless moors.

The Western Isles change their religion with their latitude: strict Presbyterianism in Lewis, Harris, Berneray and North Uist; Roman Catholicism in South Uist, Eriskay and Barra; with Benbecula in between a mixture of the two. The difference is readily apparent: strict observation of the Sabbath in the northern islands means people go out only to attend church services and shops and bars are closed, whereas Sundays in the south are more lively and relaxed. Even the houses on the southern islands have a brighter look, often with colored roofs and painted walls.

It is a perfect place to get away from it all. The people are exceptionally friendly and welcome visitors, but you will not find organized facilities. The few "sights" are mostly archaeological; what visitors will remember is the empty beaches, the lochs, the hills, the wildlife, the pure quality of the light and the way of life.

Lewis and Harris Lewis and Harris are in fact one island, linked to the mainland and Skye by ferries from Stornoway and Tarbert. The world-famous Harris tweed is still produced here. The stone circle of **Callanish▶▶▶** is one of the most haunting and eloquent places in Britain. An open-air temple of the Bronze Age that seems to have related particularly to the moon, it is tucked onto a broad peninsula on the west coast of Lewis that protrudes into the sheltered waters of Loch Roag. The inner circle of 13 stones surrounds a central 16-ft., 5 ton menhir. In the central cairn, remains of a human cremation were discovered when the 5-ft. high banks of peat were removed in 1860. **Rodel Church▶▶**, a bold attractive cruciform dating from

1500, stands on the southern tip of Harris. The cold bleak interior preserves a number of carvings.

North and South Uist On the road south from Lochmaddy is the finest chambered cairn in the Hebrides, **Barpa Langass►**. A huge pile of stones sits on the side of the hill, Ben Langass; a little tunnel leads into the communal burial chamber built by Bronze Age Beaker people.

The northwest coast of North Uist has several beautiful coves and beaches; the one near Hosta is, on a clear day, the best place to see **St Kilda**, the most remote and evocative of the Hebrides 45 miles out in the Atlantic. Nearby **Balranald nature reserve►** offers a guided walk across the flower- and bird-rich machair.

North Uist, Benbecula and South Uist are linked by a causeway. Near the top of South Uist the road passes Hew Lorimer's granite statue of Our Lady of the Isles serenely looking out to sea. At Milton a cairn stands on the site of the birthplace of Jacobite heroine Flora Macdonald (1722). At the island's southern tip a ferry goes to tiny **Eriskay**, celebrated in the Gaelic melody, the Eriskay Love Lilt. It was here that Bonnie Prince Charlie first set foot in Scotland on his way from France and here that the whisky-laden SS *Politician* went down, inspiration for Compton Mackenzie's novel *Whisky Galore*.

Barra►► is a microcosm of all the Outer Hebrides with its rocky coastline on the east, sandy bays and machair on the west. Small-scale farming is still the main occupation and Gaelic is still spoken. Ferries connect Castlebay with South Uist and the mainland.

Harris wool, here being sold locally; the tweed is sold worldwide

261

The standing stones at Callanish on the Isle of Lewis

Croft houses old and new
The Arnol Black House on the west coast of Lewis is a traditional crofter's house that gives a fascinating insight into the way of life that was common only 20 years ago. Inside the thick stone walls a peat fire smoulders in the middle of the floor, the smoke filtering out through the oat straw thatch held down by stone-weighted strands of rope. Many of these old croft houses can still be seen, some left in ruin, some given new roofs. The modern houses that replace them are similarly low buildings, usually with dormer windows.

Highland land use

■ **Mountains, lochs and glens make a magnificent landscape but a harsh environment in which to live and work. Traditionally the Highlands supported a sophisticated, martial society with its own code of ethical conduct and unbreakable social responsibilities. This was wilfully destroyed in the mid-18th century and within a generation the infamous Clearances began, when the people were driven from the land....■**

Prophet of doom
The 17th-century poet Brahan Seer, born on Lewis in the Outer Hebrides, described how the glens would be emptied of their people by sheep, how the sheep would in turn be displaced by deer before the coming of the black rain that would clear all life from the land. The "black rain" has been widely identified with fall-out from a nuclear war or a disaster at the Dounreay nuclear reactor. Too many of his prophecies have been fulfilled for his dark vision of the future of the Highlands not to cast a chill of apprehension.

Mass evictions and emigrations have left the landscape dotted with ruined crofters' houses

The rule of the Highland chieftain Up until the defeat of the Jacobite clans at Culloden Moor in 1746, the Highlands were divided into small communities by the dramatic landscape of mountains and sealochs. It was primarily a cattle-breeding society that traded for grain grown in the Lowlands. The Highland cattle, small herds of sheep, goats and chickens were highly mobile and every community required a strongly motivated fighting force to protect its wealth from "lifting." This was the economic basis of the closely knit and intensely martial Highland clans. There was a long tradition of paternalistic care, but it was a feudal society for the simple harsh reason that a hundred strong men in times of crisis were of much greater use than a money rent.

The changing tide After the battle of Culloden, the victorious Hanoverian government, frightened by the partial success of the Highland army that rallied to Bonnie Prince Charlie, determined to control this militant society. They banned firearms, the martial kilt and the strong legal powers of the clan chiefs—and they were undeniably thorough. Within a few years the Highlands were at peace and money rents began to replace feudal tenures. For a few glorious decades everything seemed rosy—the potato provided a new cheap staple crop for the poor, corn prices stayed down and livestock prices soared. Capitalists built iron foundries, fishing harbors, piers, linen and woollen mills, partly financed by enormous profits made by gathering kelp. The population quickly doubled but the plots of farming land became ever smaller.

The Clearances The end of the Napoleonic wars brought a violent depression with the total collapse of fish, cattle and kelp prices and the near extinction of rural industries. Only sheep brought in a handsome profit. Sheep farming, however, was incompatible with thousands of tenants packed into the glens and coastal strips and many people began to be evicted from their land to make room for sheep paddocks. They were moved south to the slums of the industrial cities or packed off to Canada, Australia, New Zealand and the U.S. Gladstone's Crofting Act of 1886 gave the surviving tenants a guaranteed claim on their smallholdings and allowed strong communities to survive in the Hebrides, but many big estates turned over to deer hunting and grouse shooting. With forestry, fish farming and tourism, this still plays a major part in the Highlands' economy.

TRAVEL FACTS

Arriving

By Air London has four airports. The largest is **Heathrow** (in fact the largest in the world). Airbuses and underground trains connect to central London; the Underground is cheaper and generally quicker, but neither runs all night. Daytime taxis to the center cost £30. The next largest airport, **Gatwick**, is generally more manageable than Heathrow; access to London is much better too, with a direct rail link to Victoria Station. **Luton** (north of London) has a bus link to the railroad station, and **Stansted** has trains to London Liverpool Street. **Birmingham, Edinburgh, Glasgow, Leeds/Bradford** and **Manchester** also serve international flights.

By Boat Numerous ports have cross-Channel services to the rest of Europe. Dover in east Kent (71 miles from London) is the main cross-Channel port connecting with Belgium and France; if you get stuck here for the night, there are plenty of Bed and Breakfast establishments along the main roads (ask any taxi driver to direct you to one).

By Rail Direct services via the Eurotunnel run from the European mainland.

Camping

Campsites are abundant in Britain, ranging from small fields with just a single cold tap by way of facilities to large-scale sites with showers and stores. Useful sources of information include the *Freedom* brochures published by the English Tourist Board (for a free copy tel: 0452 413041) and the list published by the Camping and Caravanning Club (East Grinstead House, East Grinstead, West Sussex RH19 1UA, tel: 0203 694995). Tourist information centers can help with lists of local sites.

If you want to try camping in the wilds, be aware of all that the British climate can throw at you, and remember that even open moorland is owned by someone—try to find the owner to ask permission first if possible.

Children

Many **hotels**, particularly larger ones, provide babysitting services, and baby-listening devices are often available. Inquire when making your reservation about child discounts, and if there are any special facilities; British hoteliers are generally not too good about entertaining the youngest travelers—toy boxes, children's books, emergency medical supplies and interesting children's meals are in short supply. Some establishments operate a "no children" rule.

Child **discounts** are offered for many admission fees. On the rail network, up to two children under five years of age may travel free with each fare-paying passenger, while children of five and over and under 16 travel at half the full price. Anyone traveling by train with children should invest in a Family Railcard: up to four under-16-year-olds travel anywhere in the country for £1 and up to four

FOR TRAVEL DETAILS
London Heathrow tel: 081-759 4321
London Gatwick, tel: 0293 535353
European Rail Travel Centre, Victoria Station, tel: 071-834 2345

accompanying adults have a discount of either a third or a quarter.

Currently the law in **pubs** is that children under 14 are not allowed in the bar area. Some pubs allow accompanied children onto the premises (in the restaurant, for instance) and in the garden, but practice varies enormously and the licensing laws are likely to be reformed. You have to be 18 or over to buy or consume alcohol in a pub.

Theme parks and safari parks include Alton Towers (Staffordshire), Camelot Theme Park (Preston, Lancashire), Chessington's World of Adventures (Surrey), Knowsley Safari Park (Prescot, Merseyside), Lightwater Valley (Ripon, North Yorkshire), Lions of Longleat Safari Park (Warminster, Wiltshire), Thorpe Park (Chertsey, Surrey), West Midland Safari and Leisure Park (Bewdley, Hereford and Worcester)

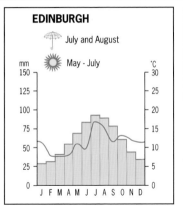

EDINBURGH

☂ July and August

☀ May - July

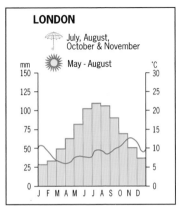

LONDON

☂ July, August,
October & November

☀ May - August

November since records began"). In short, the British climate is a fascinatingly fickle beast: the seasons are distinctive but fuse into each other; brilliant mornings often cloud over as they proceed. No wonder the umbrella seems like part of the national costume. Be prepared for sudden changes in temperature: bring rainproof footwear and clothing.

The prevailing wind comes from the west, bringing most rain to western Britain; a rain-shadow effect causes eastern areas to have considerably lower rainfall. The south coast gets less rain than the far north, and the climate tends to get warmer the farther south you go. In mid-June it stays light until 10PM (later in northern Scotland); but in winter it gets dark early, and the very far north stays gloomy all day.

Travel in spring and you could

and Woburn Wild Animal Kingdom and Leisure Park (Woburn, Bedfordshire).

London, the South Coast (Devon, Dorset and Sussex in particular), the North Yorkshire coast and Cornwall are among the most appealing **areas** for families; older children may also enjoy the Lake District, Exmoor, Pembrokeshire, York, Edinburgh and the Scottish Highlands.

The Family Holiday Guide *Children Welcome* lists places to stay and visit for those traveling with children.

Climate and seasonal considerations
Britain is a temperate country—the weather is seldom extremely hot or extremely cold and there is no prolonged rainy or dry season—yet every year seems to break some meteorological record ("the coldest May this century"; "the driest

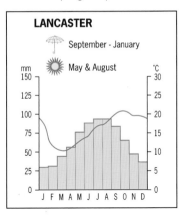

LANCASTER

☂ September - January

☀ May & August

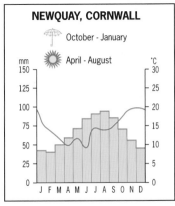

NEWQUAY, CORNWALL

☂ October - January

☀ April - August

encounter blustery squalls or fragrant whiffs of nature reawakening in benign sunshine; May and June are excellent times to travel, with the long daylight hours and comparatively uncrowded roads and sights (except at Bank Holiday weekends). Oxford and Cambridge colleges are mostly closed in the weeks running up to examination time in late May and early June.

Summer school holidays make late July and all of August extremely busy in many areas, including national parks and coastal areas—Devon, Cornwall, the Lake District, the South Coast, the Scottish Highlands (also infested with midges over this period) and Snowdonia are among the most crowded regions. Some historic cities fill almost to capacity, York, Chester and Canterbury among them. But other places are still quite manageable, including the Welsh borderlands, Eastern England, East Anglia and the Scottish borders. September can have fine late summer weather; if you aren't traveling with school-age kids, this is a good time to visit.

Visitor numbers drop appreciably along with the temperature in October and November (the West Country stays reasonably mild), but Christmas is busier, with many hotels offering special Christmas break deals. Many attractions close between October or November and Easter (including most National Trust properties). Scottish winters get enough snow for skiing to be feasible in places, notably the Cairngorms.

During the grouse-shooting season (August 12 to December 10) and deer-stalking season (July 1 to February 15) access is barred to many tracts of open land in Scotland.

Crime
Violent crime is still very rare in Britain and city centers are mostly quite safe, but minor offenses against property have risen over recent years, particularly in some inner city areas. Even in remote countryside, it is wise to be on guard against car theft, and keep all valuables are locked out of sight. Be extra vigilant of your belongings at airports and major railroad stations: do not let them out of your sight. Because of the spate of terrorist bombs, unattended parcels are likely to be removed.

Customs
Note the distinction between **duty-free** and **duty-paid** allowances; duty-free goods (bought at duty-free shops in airports, ferry terminals on ferries and on airplanes, even those in the E.C.) have had no duty paid on them and do not entitle you to the higher allowances now set for duty-paid goods bought in the E.C. The countries of the E.C. are Belgium, Greece, the Netherlands, Denmark, Italy, Portugal, France, the Irish Republic, Spain (not the Canary Islands), Germany, Luxembourg and the United Kingdom (not the Channel Islands).

Disabled visitors
The English Tourist Board grades hotel, farmhouse, inn and guesthouse accommodation according to suitability for disabled visitors from Category 3 (suitable for a wheelchair user who is also able to walk short distances and up at least three steps) to Category 1 (accessible for a wheelchair-user traveling alone). You can get help finding suitable accommodation from the Holiday Care Service, 2 Old Bank

A clock in Chester commemorates Queen Victoria's diamond jubilee

DUTY FREE ALLOWANCES

Duty-free allowances (for goods bought in or outside the EC) and duty-paid allowances for goods bought outside the EC.

Cigarettes	200
or cigarillos	100
or cigars	50
or tobacco	250g
Still table wine	2 liters
Spirits, strong liquor over 22% volume	1 liter
or fortified or sparkling wine, other liquor	2 liters
or additional still table wine allowance	2 liters
Perfume	60cc/ml
Toilet water	250cc/mll
All other goods including gifts and souvenirs	£36 worth

Chambers, Station Road, Horley, Surrey RH6 9HW, tel: 0293 774535, and from the Royal Association for Disability and Rehabilitation (RADAR), 25 Mortimer Street, London W1N 8AB tel: 071-637 5400; RADAR publishes annually *Holidays in the British Isles—A guide for Disabled People* as well as *The Countryside and Wildlife for Disabled People.*

Some hotel chains have bedrooms adapted for use by the disabled; these include Crest, Holiday Inn, Novotel, Swallow and Forte.

Toilets for wheelchair-users are provided in many museums and tourist sites but Britain still has some way to go; a special key and booklet showing toilets for the disabled are available from RADAR.

Wheelchair-users planning train travel should first contact British Rail (tel: 071-928 5151) so that arrangements can be made for boarding and seating. Local disability associations can help with recommending accommodation and places to visit; RADAR has contact addresses and telephone numbers.

Driving

Driving in Britain can be a delightful way to see the country, or a diabolically frustrating experience. In many remote country areas it is the only feasible way of getting around; for village-to-village wandering (such as the Cotswolds, the Weald and Constable Country), where local public transportation is limited, the car really comes into its own. The huge network of narrow, crooked lanes (many very ancient indeed) is a particular feature. Rural tourist areas such as the Lake District and the Cornish coastal towns and villages can get so busy in summer that finding somewhere to park requires ingenuity; consider using local buses (if there are any) or finding a footpath (often possible by using coastal paths).

Breakdown Car rental companies normally provide coverage with one or other of the major motoring organizations in Britain, the A.A. or the R.A.C. On major highways, there are emergency telephones at the side of the hard shoulder every mile. Arrows

267

GUIDE LEVELS

Guide levels for duty-paid goods bought in the EC.
You can bring in any amount of goods, but beyond these guide limits you have to be able to show the items are for your own personal use (this includes gifts); if you are receiving any payment in return for these goods (including payment of your travel expenses) you will be liable for duty.

Cigarettes	800
Cigarillos	400
Cigars	200
Tobacco	1kg
Spirits	10 liters
Intermediate products (sherry, port etc)	20 liters
Wine (of which not more than 60 liters to be sparkling wine)	90 liters

on posts indicate the direction of the nearest one.

Car rental Large firms with numerous branches and desks at airports include Avis tel: 081-848 8733, Europcar Godfrey Davis tel: 081-950 5050 and Hertz tel: 081-679 1799. These may not be the cheapest; telephone around for the best deal.

Licenses (permits) Australian, Canadian, Irish, New Zealand and US driving licenses or permits are acceptable. Holders of permits written in a foreign language are advised to obtain an official translation from an embassy or recognized automobile association, or an international driving licence before they leave their country. Car rental firms all require you to have held your license or permit for at least a year.

Motorways These link most major cities; service areas are indicated well in advance. On some motorway stretches, however, there aren't many stopping-places, e.g., the M25 (London's busy orbital route), the M11, M20 and M40.

Parking restrictions Never park on a double yellow line; parking on single yellow lines is generally permitted on Sundays and at other times as displayed. Wheel clamps are increasingly used to combat illegal parking and the fee/fine to release your car is hefty.

Ramblers dressed wisely for winter

Traffic regulations Traffic drives on the left (it goes clockwise at traffic circles, which crop up frequently at intersections). Speed-limit and destination signs use miles (one kilometer is roughly ⅝ of a mile). Speed limits for cars are 70mph for motorways and dual carriageways, 60mph for other roads, and 30mph in built-up areas unless otherwise indicated. Front-seat passengers and drivers must wear seatbelts; rear-seat passengers must wear seatbelts if the vehicle has them. Drivers must be at least 17 years of age.

Electricity
The current in Britain is 240 volts, alternate current. Plugs have three square pins.

Embassies and consulates in London
Australia Australia House, Strand, WC2, tel: 071-438 8000 or 071-379 4334
Canada 38 Grosvenor Street, W1, tel: 071-258 6600
Eire 17 Grosvenor Place, SW1, tel: 071-235 2171
New Zealand New Zealand House, Haymarket, SW1, tel: 071-930 8422
USA 24 Grosvenor Square, W1, tel: 071-499 9000

Health
Most visitors receive free treatment under the National Health Service. However, visitors from countries which do not have a reciprocal agreement with Britain may find they are charged. Accident victims must be admitted through emergency rooms in hospitals. Local doctors (G.P.s) will see visitors; ask at your hotel or at a pharmacy for details. If you take medication, make a note of the medicines you use. A charge is made for dental treatment.

Hitchhiking
Hitchhiking is not illegal in Britain, although the occasional report of violent crime associated with hitching keeps many people from doing it. It is illegal to stand on the hard shoulder of motorways; however, hitchhikers may wait near traffic circles by motorway feeder roads.

Holidays

Summer school holidays generally last from late July to early September; the country virtually closes down from Christmas Day to New Year's.

Jan 1 New Year's Day
Jan 2 New Year's Day (Scotland only)
Late March to early April Good Friday, followed three days later by Easter Monday
First Monday in May May Day Bank Holiday
Last Monday in May Spring Bank Holiday (Whitsun)
First Monday in August Bank Holiday (Scotland only)
Last Monday in August Bank Holiday (England and Wales only)
December 25 Christmas Day
December 26 Boxing Day

Insurance

Travel insurance should cover for accident or illness, for loss of valuables, for injury or death while driving, and for trip cancellation. You may be covered for personal items through your homeowner's insurance. Be sure to leave the original policy details at home and take only a photocopy on your travels. Shop around for the best buy: prices and what is covered vary enormously.

Language

Welsh words and phrases Welsh is still spoken in many areas of Wales and, although English is also universally spoken and understood (and signs are normally bilingual), attempts at a few words are always appreciated. Given a few rules, pronunciation is surprisingly easy: *u* as in wh*ee*l; *y* as in t*i*n or t*u*m; *f* as in *v*an; ff as in *f*un; *th* as in *th*ought; *dd* as in *th*en; *ch* as in lo*ch*; and for *ll*, put the side of your tongue against your teeth and blow.

Useful phrases

Diolch (yn fawr)	thank you (very much)
os gwelwch yn dda	please
esgusodwch fi	excuse me
ble mae("r). . ?	where is/are (the)?
sut (or shwt) mae?	how are you?

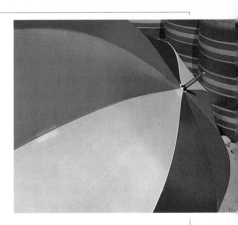

Beach umbrellas and windshields may be handy for a day at the sea

da iawn, diolch	very well, thanks
gwesty	hotel
traeth	beach
toiledau/tai bach	toilets
ar agor	open
ar gau	closed
Hoffwn. . .	I would like. . .
Bore da	good morning
Prynhawn da	good afternoon
Nos da	good night
Mae'n ddrwg gen	I'm sorry
Fedra' i ddim siarad Cymraeg	I can't speak Welsh
Y dref	the town
Y pentref	the village
Pa ffordd?	which way?
Cyfeiriadau	directions
Gwybodaeth	information
Bwrdd Croeso	Tourist Board

Lost property

Items are often handed into police stations; they pass on information about lost items to other branches. To make life easier for you and the police, make sure your address in Britain is shown on all your valuables. For items lost while on public transportation, contact the bus station, train station or airport involved.

The London Regional Transport Lost Property Office is at 200 Baker Street, NW1, tel: 071-486 2496 (recorded message).

Maps

The Automobile Association (A.A.) publishes a comprehensive road atlas of Great Britain and an atlas of town plans.

Britain has been mapped accurately, down to the last garden fence, by the Ordnance Survey (O.S.). If you intend to spend some time exploring a region, invest in the pink-covered O.S. Landranger maps, 1:50,000 scale (2cm to the km): contours show relief, and footpaths are mapped. For hiking, the green-covered O.S. Pathfinder maps, 1:25,000 scale (4cm to the km), showing field boundaries, are best; for some of the most popular walking areas (including many national parks) the yellow-covered O.S. Outdoor Leisure 1:25,000 scale maps are published, giving more tourist information. O.S. maps are widely available; a full selection is available at Edward Stanford Ltd, 12–14 Long Acre, London WC2, tel: 071-836 1321.

Media

Newspapers Britain is sometimes said to have the best and the worst newspapers in the world. The style contrasts between the "quality" broadsheets (the *Independent*, *Guardian, Times, Financial Times* and *Daily Telegraph*) and the more widely selling "popular" tabloids (the *Daily Mail, Daily Express, Sun, Mirror, Star* and *Sport*). For London, the weekly *Time Out* gives the lowdown on eating places and entertainment. There are several regional dailies.

Television There are four channels: the government-funded BBC1 and BBC2, and the commercial channels ITV and Channel 4. Many hotels now have cable and satellite TV, giving access to foreign stations.

Radio There are five BBC radio stations, Radio 1 (pop music), Radio 2 (light music), Radio 3 (classical music), Radio 4 (news, drama and general interest) and Radio 5 (sport and programs for younger listeners). Classic FM, broadcasting lighter classical music, is the most popular independent radio station. There are also numerous local stations. Frequencies can be found in newspapers and the weekly *Radio Times* and *TV Times* magazines.

Money matters

Credit cards are widely accepted, at nearly all gas pumps, most restaurants and many stores. Travelers' checks (try to get £ sterling ones) and Eurocheques are a safe way of carrying money. The pound (£) is divided into 100 pence (p). Denominations are 1p, 2p, 5p, 10p, 20p, 50p and £1 coins, then £5, £10, £20 and £50 notes. Banks in Scotland issue their own banknotes; they are legal currency throughout the U.K.

VAT refunds For purchases over £50, Value Added Tax is refundable to foreign visitors when they leave the country; ask for a form when you make your purchase.

Tipping Generally, tip 10–15 percent in a restaurant if service has not already been added (if in doubt, ask whether service is included), or not at all if you think the meal and/or service was not up to scratch; total payment boxes on credit card slips are often left empty, leaving you to add a tip (whatever you decide, remember to fill it in!). Taxi-drivers expect 10 percent; minicab drivers (whom you order by telephone and are told a price before you travel) generally do not expect anything. Porters in luxury hotels expect £1. Hairdressers and barbers can be tipped 10 percent.

Opening hours

Standard office hours are Monday to Friday, 9AM to 5PM; stores generally stay open until 5:30 or 6PM, and operate 9AM to 5:30PM on Saturdays. In central London and certain other cities many stores are open until late in the evening on Thursdays.

Banks are open Monday to Friday; most close at 4:30PM; a few stay open on Saturday mornings.

Pubs may stay open from 11AM to 11PM, but in England and Wales they often shut in the afternoons; on Sundays pubs in England and Wales open from 12 noon to 3PM and 7 to 10:30PM, while Scottish pubs open mostly from 12:30 to 2:30PM and 6:30 to 11PM. The law may soon be change to allow Sunday afternoon opening.

Sundays in England and Wales are still regulated by the anachronistic Sunday trading laws, which have become absurdly complex—to the point that it is illegal to buy a Bible on a Sunday but legal to buy pornography. Similarly, a "fish and chip" shop cannot open on a Sunday, but a Chinese take-out restaurant can sell "fish and chips"! In practice the laws are often flouted, and recently the big supermarkets and a few main stores have gambled on Sunday opening. This "day of rest" remains quiet, however—regional town centers and even London's Oxford Street look pretty dead then; theaters generally make a habit of staying closed on Sundays too.

A London "bobby" on the beat

Organized tours

Tourist information centers stock information on privately run excursion buses. Day tours can be a good way of seeing the sights, particularly for those with a crowded itinerary. Tour buses frequently circuit the sights of Oxford, Stratford-upon-Avon, Windsor, Bath, Cambridge and certain other historic centers.

In London Special narrated **sightseeing buses** tour the center; the Original London Sightseeing Tour

makes a 1½-hour round trip (join it at Piccadilly Circus, Victoria or Baker Street), while the London Plus tour enables the user to get on and off at will over a two-day period. Tickets for both are available on the buses or at a discount rate from the Piccadilly Circus travel information center. The **Riverbus** service makes a speedy trip along the Thames. **Canal trips** are offered from Camden Lock to Little Venice by Jenny Wren Cruises (tel: 071-485 4433) and from Little Venice to Camden Lock by Jason's Trip (071-286 3428). Special interest **walking tours** are given daily by Citisights of London (081-806 4325), City Walks of London (071-700 6931), Original London Walks (071-624 3978), Perfect London Walks (071-624 3978) and Tourguides (071-839 2498). Walks last about two hours, usually starting from a subway station; reservation is not necessary.

Pharmacies

Usually called chemists, these have a range of medicines you can buy without a doctor's prescription. Opening time times for chemists vary; details of locations of the chemist on call are posted in the windows.

Places of worship

The established churches in Britain are Protestant but there are numerous Roman Catholic churches. In London, all major religions are represented. Denominational headquarters include **Westminster Abbey** (Church of England), Deans Yard, SW1, tel: 071-222 5152, **Westminster Cathedral** (Roman Catholic), Victoria Street, SW1, tel: 071-834 7452, **United Synagogue**, Upper Woburn Place, WC1, tel: 071-387 4300, **Methodist Central Hall**, Storeys Gate, SW1, tel: 071-222 8010, **London Central Mosque**, 146 Park Road, NW8, tel: 071-724 3363.

Police

Telephone 999 for emergencies only; police stations are listed in the Phone Book under "Police."

Traffic wardens (black and yellow uniforms) deal with everyday parking matters and sometimes direct traffic.

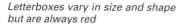

Letterboxes vary in size and shape but are always red

Post offices

Main post offices open from 9AM to 5:30PM, Monday to Friday and 9AM to 12:30PM on Saturday. Many newsagents and corner shops sell stamps in booklets. Domestic letters bearing first-class stamps generally take a day less than those with second-class ones. First-class letter rate is the same as the rate for E.C. countries. Postcards and letters are charged at the same rate.

Public transportation

Air travel There are over 30 regional airports in England, Scotland and Wales. British Airways guarantee a place on the next available flight for Shuttle services between London Heathrow, Manchester, Edinburgh and Glasgow; a seat on a British Midland flight will normally be available on the same day that you buy your ticket. For reservations ring British Airways tel: 081-897 4000, British Midland tel: 081-589 5599. Off-peak, standby and advance ticket discounts are available.

Buses Generally speaking, services in rural areas are infrequent. An exception is the Isle of Wight, where bus services are excellent.

Motorcoach Long-distance buses and coaches serve the towns the rail-roads cannot reach; fares are lower than rail, but the trip may not be as comfortable. The main London terminus is Victoria Coach Station, Buckingham Palace Road (near Victoria railroad station), SW1 tel: 071-730 3499 (reservations), 071-730 0202 (National Express services), 071-823 6567 (for a list of other telephone numbers).

Rail The national network is maintained and run by British Rail. At the time of publication of this guide, the privatization of large sections of it was imminent; we wait to see the effect this has on efficiency, timing, ticketing and fares. Grumbling about the railways, in the land where they were invented, is a favorite British pastime; in fact rail is a comfortable, though not particularly cheap, way of seeing the country, although there can be delays and cancellations. Beware of weekend engineering works: regional maps showing affected services for each weekend ahead may be posted at stations. Special bus services fill in for the closed sections of line, but they add significantly to the journey time.

Railroad tickets are subject to numerous special deals; day return or saver tickets (return within a given period) are much cheaper than two single tickets for the same journey, but are subject to time restrictions (typically not to be used before 9am); Saver tickets are more expensive on Fridays and certain other days. Apex tickets give discounts for booking seven days or more in advance on InterCity (long-distance) journeys. BritRail passes, which are only available abroad, will save money for those intending to make more than one long train journey. Young Persons' Railcards (for under-24s) and Senior Citizens' Railcards (for over-60s) give one-third off the full ticket price. Bicycles are carried free of charge on most services.

Apart from the London–Scotland and London–Cornwall lines at peak periods, it is seldom necessary to reserve. First-class travel is available. Train information can be obtained by telephone: look in the telephone directory under "British Rail."

Season tickets
Those intending to visit a number of stately homes and castles should consider taking out a season ticket for the **National Trust** (N.T.) and **National Trust for Scotland** (N.T.S.) (see panel, page 103; note that membership in the N.T. entitles you to entry to N.T.S. properties, and vice versa) and/or **English Heritage** (E.H.), **Cadw** (for Wales), **Historic Scotland** (H.S.) (see panel, page 124). Membership is available in all of these at any staffed property.

Senior citizens
Anyone aged 60 or over is entitled to a Senior Citizen's Railcard and can get discounts for numerous admissions.

Student and youth travel
Youth hostels These offer bargain basement accommodation; Britain is the birthplace of the Youth Hostels Association (Y.H.A.) and has an excellent network of hostels ranging from primitive converted primary schools to manor houses and medieval castles. These can be better places for meeting people than guesthouses and hotels, especially the smaller and more personal youth hostels; some have stunning locations, such as in the Lake District, Snowdonia and the Scottish Highlands. There is no upward age restriction. Accommodation is simple, usually in dormitories, although some hostels have family rooms; food is served at most hostels, at set times, although it is always possible to bring and cook your own. Few establishments allow hostellers to stay in during the day; at peak times and on weekends you should reserve ahead. You must join the Y.H.A. (unless you hold a youth hostel card from another country) in order to stay; membership can be taken out at any hostel.

The central London information outlet is the Y.H.A. shop and Y.H.A. travel, both at 14 Southampton Street, WC2, tel: 071-836 1036. The Scottish Y.H.A. is based at 7 Glebe Crescent, Stirling FK8 2JA, tel: 0786 451181.

International student cards These useful IDs help you gain reduced

The familiar red British telephone box is almost a thing of the past. A few have been retained—some pre-war specimens were listed as architecturally important structures, and rather more were kept on in landmark preservation areas. But now the utilitarian British Telecom steel model (considerably more reliable than its predecessor) is here to stay.

admission fees to tourist sights and places of entertainment. Young Persons' **railcards** give a third off the price of under-24s rail tickets.

Telephones
In emergencies tel: 999 (police, fire and ambulance); calls are free.
Operator tel: 100 (free).
Directory inquiries tel: 192 (free from pay phones only).
Calls on numbers prefixed 0800 are free.

Note that during the time this book is in print, all area codes will be given an extra digit.

To make a call from a public telephone, put the money in before dialing (if you put in large denomination coins, beware: you will not get change), and collect any unspent coins when you hang up. Phone cards can be bought from newsagents and corner shops. Mercury phonecards enable calls to be made using the Mercury network to any British Telecom number.

The dial tone is a continuous purr, the ringing tone is a repeated brr-brr, and a repeated single tone tells you the line is busy; a continuous tone means the number dialled is unobtainable.

To call abroad, dial 010 followed by the country's code, followed by the local number minus the initial 0.

Australia 61	New Zealand 64
Canada 1	U.S.A. 1
Eire 353	

Time
When it is 12 noon in Britain between the last Sunday in October and the last Saturday in March it is 8–10PM in Australia, 4–8:30AM in Canada, 12 noon in Eire, midnight in New Zealand and 4–7AM in U.S.A.

CONVERSION CHARTS

FROM	TO	MULTIPLY BY
Inches	Centimeters	2.54
Centimeters	Inches	0.3937
Feet	Meters	0.3048
Meters	Feet	3.2810
Yards	Meters	0.9144
Meters	Yards	1.0940
Miles	Kilometers	1.6090
Kilometers	Miles	0.6214
Acres	Hectares	0.4047
Hectares	Acres	2.4710
U.S. Gallons	Liters	3.7854
Liters	U.S. Gallons	0.2642
Ounces	Grams	28.35
Grams	Ounces	0.0353
Pounds	Grams	453.6
Grams	Pounds	0.0022
Pounds	Kilograms	0.4536
Kilograms	Pounds	2.205
U.S. Tons	Tonnes	0.9072
Tonnes	U.S. Tons	1.1023

MEN'S SUITS

UK	36	38	40	42	44	46	48
Rest of Europe	46	48	50	52	54	56	58
US	36	38	40	42	44	46	48

DRESS SIZES

UK	8	10	12	14	16	18
France	36	38	40	42	44	46
Italy	38	40	42	44	46	48
Rest of Europe	34	36	38	40	42	44
US	6	8	10	12	14	16

MEN'S SHIRTS

UK	14	14.5	15	15.5	16	16.5	17
Rest of Europe	36	37	38	39/40	41	42	43
US	14	14.5	15	15.5	16	16.5	17

MEN'S SHOES

UK	7	7.5	8.5	9.5	10.5	11
Rest of Europe	41	42	43	44	45	46
US	8	8.5	9.5	10.5	11.5	12

WOMEN'S SHOES

UK	4.5	5	5.5	6	6.5	7
Rest of Europe	38	38	39	39	40	41
US	6	6.5	7	7.5	8	8.5

The rest of the year, clocks go forward one hour to British Summer Time.

Toilets
Normally marked "W.C." or "Toilets," these are divided into "Men" or "Gents" and "Women" or "Ladies." Paper should always be provided and with a few exceptions, such as main London railroad stations, entry is free. Public lavatories, or "loos," are usually in fair supply. Restaurants and pubs generally won't let non-customers use their toilets.

Tourist offices
There are over 800 tourist information centers in Britain, run by regional tourist boards for England, Wales and Scotland: most are well-marked (look for the *i* sign). Many offer hotel reservation services. Additionally, national parks have numerous visitor centers with excellent local information.

Walking and hiking
Britain has lots to offer the walker, ranging from easily managed marked trails to challenging mountain terrain. England and Wales are served by a unique network of public rights of way, which crisscross private land but are open to walkers; Scotland has an informal rule tolerating access to open land except in the shooting seasons. Public footpaths (marked with yellow arrows) are for walkers only; public bridleways (marked in blue) are open to horseback riders and cyclists too. National trails (official long-distance paths) are indicated with acorn motifs. Some walks are suggested in this guide: farther routes, with excellent O.S. maps, are described in detail in the AA/Ordnance Survey Leisure Guides. Guided walks are offered by numerous bodies, including national park authorities (contact information offices for details). If you prefer to branch out on your own and devise your own walks, you need a good map (see Maps), and proper equipment: do not underestimate the perils of the mountains (see page 168).

HOTELS AND RESTAURANTS

HOTELS AND RESTAURANTS

ACCOMMODATIONS

Tourist information centers can help with local accommodations lists, and many provide a reservation service. Bed and Breakfast ("B&B") is ubiquitous and often an excellent value: typically it consists of a room in a private house (some have separate bathrooms) and use of a living room.

Regional tourist boards publish lists of farmhouses, inns and guesthouses offering B&B (including the English Tourist Board's book *Where to Stay*). Country house hotels give you the chance to stay in period country homes; many are privately run by families. Many pubs have a few rooms for overnight visitors (some are included under Restaurants, pages 281–4). Generally, supply outstrips demand: provided you are prepared to drive to the next town, you will always find a bed, although be warned that the most popular resort towns and the Scottish Highlands can get very busy in season.

The following recommended hotels and inns are divided into three price categories, based on bed and breakfast for one person sharing a double- or twin-bedded room:
budget (£): you are likely to pay under £30.
moderate (££): you are likely to pay £30–£50.
expensive (£££): you are likely to pay over £50.

LONDON
Chelsea, Knightsbridge and Victoria

Basil Street (£££) 8 Basil Street, SW3 1AH (tel: 071-581 3311). Formal, old-fashioned yet stylish.
Draycott (£££) 24–6 Cadogan Gardens SW3 (tel: 071-730 6466). Fashionably elegant; quiet garden; close to Sloane Square.
Ebury Court (££) 24–32 Ebury Street SW1W 0LU (tel: 071-730 8147). Bedrooms neither commodious nor luxurious, but plenty of personalized charm.
Elizabeth (£) 37 Eccleston Square SW1 (tel: 071-828 6812). Worthy small hotel in Victoria overlooking private gardens.

Bayswater, Kensington and Hyde Park

Garden Court (£) 30 Kensington Gardens Square W2 (tel: 071-229 2553). Well-established, popular and excellent value small hotel on a leafy Bayswater square.
Gore (£££) 189 Queen's Gate SW7 5EX (tel: 071-584 6601). Imaginatively furnished with antiques; near the Royal Albert Hall.
Holland Park (£) 6 Ladbroke Terrace W11 (tel: 071-792 0216). Quietly situated, with views over immaculate garden, near Notting Hill.
Parkwood (££) 4 Stanhope Place W2 (tel: 071-262 9484). Pretty hotel in quiet street fronting onto Hyde Park; popular with families.
Rushmore (£) 11 Trebovir Road SW5 (tel: 071-370 6505). One of the best in Earl's Court; ravishing interior design includes *trompe-l'oeil* paintings.
Vicarage Court (£) 10 Vicarage Gate W8 (tel: 071-229 4030). Small hotel in pretty Church Street area; old-fashioned feel of rural vicarage.

Marylebone and Regent's Park

Dorset Square (£££) 39–40 Dorset Square NW1 (071-723 7874). Comfortable Regency house on a square where M.C.C. (Marylebone Cricket Club) once played.
Durrants (££) George Street, W1H 6BJ (tel: 071-935 8131). Traditional and unmistakably English in the best sense; a former 18th-century coaching inn.
Gresham (££) 116 Sussex Gardens W2 (tel: 071-402 2920). One of the best in Paddington area; luxurious rooms, friendly service.

Bloomsbury, Covent Garden and Soho

Fielding (££) 4 Broad Court, Bow Street WC2B 5QZ (tel: 071-836 8305). Cheerful Georgian building in the heart of Covent Garden.
Thanet (£) 8 Bedford Place, Russell Square WC1 (tel: 071-636 2869). Budget hotel close to British Museum; clean, fresh décor; excellent breakfast menu.

Beyond the center

New Barbican (££) Central Street EC1 (tel: 071-251 1565). Large, modern, friendly hotel, well placed for Barbican arts complex and the City.
Sandringham (£) 3 Holford Road NW3 (tel: 071-435 1569). Small, friendly hotel with garden, on edge of Hampstead Heath.
Tower Thistle (£££) St Katharine's Way E1 (tel: 071-481 2575). Modern hotel very convenient for City; fine views of Tower Bridge.

THE WEST COUNTRY
Bath, Avon

Paradise House (£) 86–8 Holloway, BA2 4PX (tel: 0225 317723). Quietly located in an elevated position, minutes from the center.
Royal Crescent (£££) 16 Royal Crescent, BA1 2LS (tel: 0225 319090). In Bath's most famous street; the interior matches the splendor of the setting.
Somerset House (£) 35 Bathwick Hill, BA2 6LD (tel: 0225 466451). Homelike and friendly Regency house.

Bradford-on-Avon, Wiltshire

Bradford Old Windmill (£) Masons Lane, BA15 1QN (tel: 0225 866842). Converted windmill with entertaining knickknacks; vegetarian food.

Bristol, Avon

Avon Gorge (££) Sion Hill, Clifton, BS8 4LD (tel: 0272 738955). Dramatic views of Clifton Suspension Bridge, convenient for city center and M5.
Seeley's (£), 17–27 St Paul's Road, Clifton, BS18 1LX (tel: 0272 738544). Friendly family-run hotel.

Cornwall

Garrack (££) Burthallan Lane, St Ives, TR26 3AA (tel:

0736 796199).
Accomplished seaside hotel, well out of the central bustle.
Marina (£) Esplanade, Fowey, PL23 1HY (tel: 0726 833315). In the hub of an enchanting waterside town.
Portgaverne (££) Port Gaverne, nr Port Isaac, PL29 3SQ (tel: 0208 880244). Pleasant inn by a cove on an unspoiled coast.
Seafood Restaurant (££) Riverside, Padstow, PL28 8BY (tel: 0841 532485). Excellent restaurant with rooms looking out over the Camel Estuary; no lounge.
Talland Bay (£££) Talland, nr Looe, PL13 2JB (tel: 0503 72667). Restful and well kept; by a rocky cove, a short walk from Polperro.

Dartmoor, Devon
Bel Alp House (£££) Haytor, nr Bovey Tracy, TQ13 9XX (tel: 0364 661217). Secluded Edwardian house with spacious grounds and superb views; furnished with flair; good dinners.
Holne Chase (££) nr Ashburton, TQ13 7NS (tel: 0364 3471). Peacefully located by the River Dart; well-appointed rooms.
Oxenham Arms (££) South Zeal, nr Okehampton, EX20 2JT (tel: 0837 840244). Pleasant 15th-century inn in village street .

Dartmouth, Devon
Brookdale House (££) North Huish, South Brent, TQ10 9NR (tel: 054882 402). Civilized retreat in quiet countryside.

Dorset
Hams Plot (£) Beaminster, DT8 3LU (tel: 0308 862979). Regency house in small town with sleepy main square; pool, veranda, country and antique furnishings.
Plumber Manor (££) Hazelbury Bryan Road, Sturminster Newton, DT10 2AF (tel: 0258 72507). Jacobean manor; restaurant with 16 bedrooms.
Priory (££) Church Green, Wareham, BH20 4ND (tel: 0929 551666). An 800-year-old priory in a small town;

converted into a comfortable hotel, with riverside gardens.

Exeter, Devon
Woodhayes (££) Whimple, nr Exeter, EX5 2TD (tel: 0404 822237). Looks after guests well; an excellent base for south Devon.

Exmoor
Heddon's Gate (££) Heddon's Mouth, Parracombe, Barnstaple, Devon EX31 4PZ (tel: 0598 3313). Turn-of-the-century; finely set in wooded valley leading to small cove.
Royal Oak Inn (££) Winsford, nr Minehead, Somerset TA24 7JE (tel: 064385 455). Rambling, thatched village inn.
Tarr Steps (££) Hawkridge, Dulverton, Somerset TA22 9PY (tel: 064385 293). Old rectory by River Barle; ideal for country sports; equipment available.

Scilly, Isles of
Island Hotel: (£££) Tresco, TR24 0PU (tel: 0720 22883). Modern hotel; island a refreshing getaway.

SOUTHERN ENGLAND
Brighton, East Sussex
Courtlands (£) 19–27 The Drive, BN3 3JE (tel: 0273 731055). Quietly situated, within easy walking distance of town and seafront; swimming pool.
Grand Hotel (£££) King's Road, BN1 2FW (tel: 0273 321188). The grandest of the grand seafront hotels.
Adelaide (££) 51 Regency Square, BN1 2FF (tel: 0273 205286). Small hotel in elegant square facing on to the seafront.

Canterbury, Kent
County (££) High Street, CT4 7BX (tel: 0227 730080). In heart of city, traditional, long-established hotel.
Thruxted Oast (££) Mystole, Chartham, nr Canterbury CT4 7BX (tel: 0227 730080). Five converted oast houses (built for drying hops); rustic furnishings, open fire; country setting.

Dover, Kent
Wallett's Court (£) West

Cliffe, St Margaret's at Cliffe, nr Dover, CT15 6EW (tel: 0304 852424). Lone manor house with old-fashioned rooms in main house, newer ones in barn annex.

Isle of Wight
Albion (££) Freshwater Bay, PO40 9RA (tel: 0983 753631). Large hotel in prominent position on seashore and promenade; sunny balconies.
Seaview Hotel: (££) High Street, Seaview, PO34 5EX (tel: 0983 612711). First-class seaside hotel, ideal for families; nautical trappings.

Rye, East Sussex
Jeake's House (£) Mermaid Street, TN31 7ET (tel: 0797 222828). Gabled, part tile-hung 17th-century house in pretty cobbled street.

Weald
Old Cloth Hall (££) Cranbrook, Kent TN17 3NR (tel: 0580 712220). Private, half-timbered Tudor manor house, outside the town, with ten bedrooms.
Tanyard (££) Wierton Hill, Boughton Monchelsea, nr Maidstone, Kent ME17 4JT (tel: 0622 744705). Fine 14th-century, Wealden half-timbered house, in charming grounds; ultra-rural.

Windsor, Berkshire
Sir Christopher Wren's House (£££) Thames Street, SL4 1PX (tel: 0753 861354). Elegant hotel, fine riverside site.

HEART OF ENGLAND
Chiltern Hills
Beetle and Wedge (££) Moulsford-on-Thames, Oxfordshire OX10 9JF (tel: 0491 651381). Ideally placed for exploring the Thames Valley; by the river.

Cotswolds
Bibury Court (££) Bibury, nr Cirencester, Gloucestershire GL7 5NT (tel: 0285 740337). Old-world Jacobean mansion by River Coln, offering a relaxed and not over-manicured retreat.
Buckland Manor (£££) Buckland, nr Broadway, Hereford & Worcester

WR12 7LY (tel: 0386 852626). In a quiet backwater village beneath the escarpment: a medieval manor adjoining the church; supreme class, priced accordingly.
Collin House (££) Collin Lane, Broadway, Hereford & Worcester WR1 7PB (tel: 0386 858354). Exemplary country house hotel, quietly set behind main street.
Cotswold House (££) The Square, Chipping Campden, Gloucestershire GL55 6AN (tel: 0386 840330). Formal elegance; murals and antiques.
Painswick (££) Kemps Lane, Painswick, Gloucestershire GL6 6YB (tel: 0452 812160). Stylish former rectory in handsome small town.

Ludlow, Shropshire
Feathers (£££) Bullring, SY8 1AA (tel: 0584 875261). Famous half-timbered building which has functioned as a hotel since 1600s.
Old Rectory (£) Hopesay, nr Craven Arms, SY7 8HD (tel: 05887 245). Stone-built 17th-century house; relaxed; no smoking.

Malvern Hills
Hope End (££) nr Ledbury, Hereford & Worcester HR8 1JQ (tel: 0531 633613). A country house situated amid green, rolling hills; stylish décor; homegrown produce and accomplished cooking.

Oxford, Oxfordshire
Cotswold House (£) 363 Banbury Road, OX2 7PL (tel: 0865 310558). Well-run B&B 2 miles from city center; frequent buses; eating places nearby; no smoking.
Linton Lodge (£) Linton Road, OX2 6UJ (tel:0865 53461). Large hotel comprising several houses in a quiet residential area close to colleges and River Isis.
Randolph (£££) Beaumont Street, OX1 2LN (tel: 0865 247481). Large, comfortable and long-established hotel in city center.

Stratford-upon-Avon, Warwickshire
Dukes (££) Payton Street, CV37 6UA (tel: 0789 269300). Hospitable hotel in restored Georgian town villas close to center.
Shakespeare (£££) Chapel Street, CV37 6ER (tel: 0789 294771). 17th-century Forte hotel with labyrinthine interior; central location.
White Swan (££–£££) Rother Street, CV37 6NH (tel: 0789 297022). Half-timbered building with modern facilities close to town center and the Bard's birthplace.

EASTERN ENGLAND
Cambridge, Cambridgeshire
Arundel House (£) 53 Chesterton Road, CB4 3AN (tel: 0223 67701). Victorian terrace by Jesus Green; 10 minutes' walk to center.
Garden House (£££) Granta Place, Mill Lane, CB2 1RT (tel: 0223 63421). Modern hotel, nicely sited by river and within a short walk of the city center and colleges.
Gonville (££) Gonville Place, CB1 1LY (tel: 0223 66611). Traditional hotel in center, overlooking Parker's Piece park.

Constable Country
Maison Talbooth (£££) Stratford Road, Dedham, nr Colchester, Essex CO7 6HN (tel: 0206 322367). Top-notch, comfortable B&B.
Great House (££) Market Place, Lavenham, Suffolk CO10 9QZ (tel: 0787 247431). Georgian exterior belies an ancient timber-framed structure. Restaurant (French and English cuisine); four bedrooms.

Lincoln, Lincolnshire
D'Isney Place (££) Eastgate, LN2 4AA (tel: 0522 538881). Red-brick house begun in 1735, near cathedral; B&B.

North Norfolk coast
Cley Mill (£) Cley-next-the-sea, Holt, Norfolk NR25 7NN (tel: 0263 740209). Photogenic windmill by saltmarshes; homelike comforts.
Morston Hall (££) Morston, Holt, Norfolk NR25 7AA (tel: 0263 741041). By marshes, a 17th-century brick-and-flint house; only four bedrooms; excellent restaurant.

Norwich, Norfolk
Friendly (££) 2 Barnard Road, Bowthorpe, NR5 9JB (tel: 0603 741161). Friendly modern hotel on outskirts of city; pool and gymnasium.
Maid's Head (££) Tombland, NR3 1LB (tel: 0603 761111). Dating from 1272, England's oldest hotel in continuous use; the best bet in the city.

Southwold, Suffolk
Swan (££) Market Place, IP18 6EG (tel: 0502 722186). Traditional hotel; considerable standards of comfort.

Stamford, Lincolnshire
George (£££) 71 St Martins, PE9 2LB (tel: 0780 55171). Splendid coaching inn; elegant public rooms and a good restaurant.

WALES
Brecon Beacons
Abbey (£) Llanthony, nr Abergavenny, Gwent NP7 7NN (tel: 0873 890487). Eccentric and devoid of creature comforts, but spectacularly rich in character.
Gliffaes (££) nr Crickhowell, Powys NP8 1RH (tel: 0874 730371). Traditional family-run hotel, overlooking River Usk and set in parkland; good fishing near by.
Llangoed Hall (£££) Llyswen, Powys LD3 0YP (tel: 0874 754525). Stylishly Edwardian, rebuilt by Clough Williams Ellis (of Portmeirion fame); personal touches; classic cooking.

Gower, West Glamorgan
Fairyhill (££) Reynoldston, nr Swansea, SA3 1BS (tel: 0792 390139). Mansion in woodlands with own trout stream; restrained décor; local dishes on an ambitious menu.

Llandrindod Wells, Powys
Lake (££) Llangammarch Wells, LD4 4BS (tel: 05912 202). Established as a spa hotel in the 1890s; now a graceful rural retreat overlooking a small lake.

Pembrokeshire Coast, Dyfed
Cnapan (£) East Street, Newport, SA42 0WF (tel: 0239 820575). Homelike pink house in long village in

northern Pembrokeshire; imaginative health-food cooking.

Penally Abbey (££) Penally, nr Tenby, SA70 7PY (tel: 0834 843033). Georgian Gothic house, close to coast, high-ceilinged rooms, four-poster beds, ruined chapel; modern annex; French-influenced cooking.

Snowdonia, Gwynedd
Maes-y-Neuadd (£££) Talsarnau, nr Harlech, LL47 6YA (tel: 0766 780200). Ancient granite and slate building with splendid vistas; open fire.
Old Rectory (££) Llansanffraid Glan Conwy, nr Conwy, LL28 5LF (tel: 0492 580611). Fine views of mountains and Conwy Castle; gourmet dinners.
Portmeirion Hotel: (£££) **and village** (££) Portmeirion, LL48 6ER (tel: 0766 770228). Extraordinary Italianate village (see page 169); hotel fronts estuary and has lavish interior; also offers rooms in the "village."
St Tudno (££) Promenade, Llandudno, LL30 2LP (tel: 0492 874411). Bay-windowed hotel on handsome Victorian seafront; outstanding hospitality.
Sygun Fawr (£) Beddgelert, LL55 4NE (tel: 076686 258). Stone manor up steep lane from village; popular with climbers and walkers.

Wye Valley
Parva Farmhouse (£) Tintern, nr Chepstow, Gwent NP6 6SQ (tel: 0291 689411). Cozy without being cute.
Crown at Whitebrook (££) Whitebrook, Gwent NP5 4TX (tel: 0600 860254). Small country hotel with pretty bedrooms and comfortable lounge, in densely wooded valley near River Wye.

NORTHWEST ENGLAND
Chester, Cheshire
Green Bough (£) 60 Hoole Road, CH2 3NL (tel: 0244 326241). On tree-lined main road into center; personal service; antique beds (with modern bases).

Grosvenor (£££) Eastgate Street, CH1 1LT (tel: 0244 324024). Four-star luxury hotel at the heart of this historic city.

Lake District, Cumbria
Bridgefield House (££) Spark Bridge, nr Ulverston, LA12 8DA (tel: 022985 239). Secluded, small-scale country house hotel; imaginative cooking.
Howtown (£) Howtown, Ullswater, nr Penrith, CA10 2ND (tel: 07684 86514). On east shore; former farmhouse in tiny hamlet, handy for lake steamer service; not luxurious but excellent service and value.
Mill (££) Mungrisdale, nr Penrith, CA11 0XR (tel: 07687 79659). Cozy and informal, former mill cottage, in quiet rolling moors of northern fells (not the same establishment as the nearby Mill Inn).
Old Vicarage (££) Church Road, Witherslack, nr Grange-over-Sands, LA11 6RS (tel: 05395 52381). High standards of cooking and comfort; beneath Whitbarrow Scar.
Pheasant Inn (££) Bassenthwaite Lake, nr Cockermouth, CA13 9YE (tel: 07687 76234). Large, old, period inn with good restaurant; informal atmosphere; modern bedrooms.
Rothay Manor (£££) Rothay Bridge, Ambleside, LA22 0EH (tel: 05394 33605). Elegant Regency house; charming veranda; renowned cuisine; secluded site.
Seatoller House (£) Borrowdale, nr Keswick, LA12 5XN (tel: 07687 77218). Not for privacy seekers, but great for those who like a house-party atmosphere; simple bedrooms, farmhouse kitchen.
Sharrow Bay (£££) Ullswater, nr Penrith, CA10 2LZ (tel: 07684 86301). One of Lakeland's most celebrated hotels, highly rated for comfort and its cuisine.
Wasdale Head Inn (££) Wasdale Head, nr Gosforth, CA20 1EX (tel: 09467 26229). Long-established

haunt of walkers and climbers in spectacular isolated position.

Peak District
Callow Hall (££) Mappleton Road, nr Ashbourne, Derbyshire DE6 2AA (tel: 0335 43403). Grand country house outside Ashbourne.
Cavendish (££) Baslow, Derbyshire DE4 1SP (tel: 0246 582311). High-class comfort and in the best taste; a civilized retreat in the Chatsworth estate.
Riber Hall (££) nr Matlock, Derbyshire DE4 1SP (tel: 0629 582795). Elizabethan manor perched above Derwent Gorge; plenty of period character but with modern facilities too.

NORTHEAST ENGLAND
Durham
Newton Grange Royal County (££) Old Elvet, DH1 3JN (tel: 091-386 6821). Ample, comfortable hotel, extending onto river bank.
Three Tuns (££) New Elvet, DH1 3AQ (091–386 4326). Old-established, comfortable city center hotel.

Northumberland
Breamish House (££) Powburn, nr Alnwick, NE66 4LL (tel: 066578 266). Former hunting lodge; unpretentious and relaxed; commendable service and country cooking.
Royal (£) Priestpopple, Hexham, NE46 1PQ (tel: 0434 602270). Refurbished old coaching inn in town center; friendly service.

North York Moors,
Lastingham Grange (£££) Lastingham, YO6 6TH (tel: 07515 345). Old-fashioned and welcoming, in pleasantly tranquil village.
Mallyan Spout (££) Goathland, nr Whitby, YO22 2SDA (tel: 0947 86206). Village in fine walking country. Cottagey rooms.

York, North Yorkshire
Abbots Mews (££) 6 Marygate Lane, YO3 7DE (tel: 0904 634866). Just outside city walls, quietly located; converted coachman's cottage with small garden.

HOTELS AND RESTAURANTS

Cottage (£) 3 Clifton Green, YO3 6LH (tel: 0904 643711). Overlooking Clifton Green, 10 minutes' walk from city center; attractive, friendly.
Mount Royal (££) The Mount, YO2 2DA (tel: 0904 628856). Two early 19th-century houses made into one; antiques, plants and a welcoming atmosphere; dining room in modern extension. South of center.

Yorkshire Dales
Amerdale House (££) Arncliffe, nr Skipton, BD23 5QE (tel: 0756 770250). Beautifully set manor house in Littondale; friendly and run with flair.
Ashfield House (£) Grassington, nr Skipton, BD23 5AE (tel: 0756 752584). Small-scale hotel off the Square: rustic pine décor and a warm welcome; country cooking.
Burgoyne (££) Reeth, DL11 6SN (tel: 0748 84292). At top of green in an appealing Swaledale village; a comfy base for the northern Dales.
Miller's House (££) Middleham, Wensleydale, DL8 4NR (tel: 0969 22630). Off enchanting village square; elegant public rooms and individually furnished bedrooms; accomplished cooking.

SOUTHERN SCOTLAND
Borders
Medwyn House (£) Medwyn Road, West Linton, EH46 7HB (tel: 0968 60542). Attractive guesthouse, a former coaching inn in a village abutting the Pentland Hills near Edinburgh. Excellent value.
Cringletie House (££) Peebles, EH45 8PL (tel: 0721 730233). Romantic-looking country house, family-run.
Tweed Valley (££) Galashiels Road, Walkerburn, EH43 6AA (tel: 089687 636). Traditional comfort; elevated site above the River Tweed.

Dumfries and Galloway
Balcary Bay (££) Auchencairn, nr Kirkcudbright, DG7 1QZ (tel: 055664 217). Small, lone hotel by shore, overlooking

the Solway Firth and the Lake District mountains; ideal for cliff walks.
Knockinaam Lodge (££) Portpatrick, Rhinns of Galloway, DG9 9AD (tel: 077681 471). On the west coast, looking towards the Mountains of Morne in Ireland; well-equipped and spacious bedrooms.

Edinburgh, Lothian
Bruntsfield (££) 69/74 Bruntsfield Place EH10 4HH (tel: 031-229 1393). Family-owned hotel overlooking links; south of city center.
Caledonian (£££) Princes Street, EH1 2AB (tel: 031-225 2433). 90-year-old former railroad hotel affectionately known as "The Cally;" grand foyer, attractive rooms, friendly service.
Howard (£££) 32–6 Great King Street, EH3 6QH (tel: 031-557 3500). High-class comfort: a Georgian row in the New Town.
Rothesay (££) 8 Rothesay Place, EH3 7SL (tel: 031-225 4125). Reasonably priced, family-run hotel.
Roxburghe (£££) 38 Charlotte Square, EH2 4HG (tel: 031-225 3921). Fine example of Adam architecture minutes from Princes Street; range of bedrooms.
Scandic Crown (£££) 80 High Street, The Royal Mile, EH1 1TH (tel: 031-557 9797). In the heart of the Old Town, a promising newcomer; modern interior.

Firth of Forth, Lothian
Greywalls (£££) Gullane, Muirfield, EH31 2EG (tel: 0620 842144). Splendid house designed by Lutyens, overlooking golf links east of Edinburgh.

Glasgow, Strathclyde
Babbity Bowster (££) 16–18 Blackfriars Street, G1 7PE (tel: 041-552 5055). Small hotel with café-bar; jazz, folk music and poetry-reading site. In the old "Merchant City."
Ewington (££) 132 Queens Drive Queens Park, G42 8QW (tel: 041-423 1152). Well-equipped and friendly hotel in row overlooking

Queens Park.
One Devonshire Gardens (£££) 1 Devonshire Gardens, G12 0UX (tel: 041-334 9494). Supremely elegant hotel occupying a row of town-houses; mahogany, rich fabrics.

St Andrews, Fife
St Andrews Old Course (£££) Old Station Road, KY16 9SP (tel: 0334 74371). By the famous golf course and the sea; elegant, well-equipped and comfortable.
Scores (£) 76 The Scores, KY16 9BB (tel: 0334 72451). In two 1880s fashionable townhouses, overlooks seafront and convenient for Old Course.

Trossachs
Roman Camp (££–£££) Callander, FK17 8BG (tel: 0877 30003). Enlarged manor house on banks of River Teith.
Rowardennan (£) Rowardennan, by Drymen, G63 0AR (tel: 036087 273). On eastern shore of Loch Lomond, amid rugged scenery; warm and homelike.

NORTHERN SCOTLAND
Deeside, Grampian
Banchory Lodge (£££) Banchory, AB31 3HS (tel: 03302 2625). Refreshingly unpretentious, rambling Georgian house in secluded gardens; fresh flowers, antiques and bric-à-brac; hearty Scottish fare.
Kildrummy Castle (£££) Kildrummy, AB33 8RA (tel: 09755 71288). Victorian mansion by castle ruin; tapestries, oak panelling.

Inverness, Highland
Dunain House (££) nr Inverness, IV3 6JN (tel: 0463 230512). Friendly country house outside Inverness, with good country cooking.
Knockie Lodge (£££) White Bridge, IV1 2UP (tel: 04563 276). Memorably restful, with sheep and cattle for company; "lived in" rather than elegant; unpretentious and competent cooking.

Lochaber, Highland
Arisaig House (£££) Arisaig, PH39 4NR (tel: 06875 622). West coast views from its

eck; an austere exterior onceals an attractive interi- r. Imaginative *à la carte* enu, and helpful staff.
rdsheal House (£££) entallan, Glen Coe, PA38 BX (tel: 063174). Well laced for exploring Loch innhe and Glen Coe; fur- ished with flair by merican owners.

ban and mid Argyll, trathclyde

airds (£££ including dinner) ort Appin, Appin, PA38 DF (tel: 063173 236). Small otel north of Oban with tunning views of Loch innhe; unassuming from utside, but extremely wel- oming and comfortable.
sle of Eriska (£££) Eriska, edaig by Oban, PA37 1SD el: 063172 371). Idyllically et on an island connected y bridge to mainland; putt- g green, croquet lawn, lus books and games. retty rooms, antiques.

erthshire, Tayside

almunzie House (£) Spittal f Glenshee, Blairgowrie, H10 7QS (tel: 0250 85224). Turreted house in s own private glen; offers shing and golf; a favorite vith families.
iuinach House (££) By the irks, Urlar Road, berfeldy, PH15 2ET (tel: 887 820251). Edwardian ouse, off A826, inviting ounge with open fire and ooks; excellent cooking, omegrown produce.

hetland

urrastow House (£) Walls, E2 9PB (tel: 059571 307). emotely set on shore of a ake, this will appeal to hose seeking quiet and olitude; charmingly deco- ated rooms, excellent food.

kye, Highland

inloch Lodge (£) Isle rnsay, Sleat, IV43 8UY (tel: 4713 214/333). Peace and ranquillity in a friendly aelic atmosphere; small, ld hotel.
iewfield House (£) Portree, √51 9EU (tel: 0478 612217). nposing, old-fashioned ictorian house in exten- ve grounds.

Spey Valley and Cairngorms, Highland

Columba House (£) Manse Road, Kingussie, PH21 1JF (tel: 0540 661402). Converted 19th-century manse in elevated grounds; comfortable and relaxed; good home cooking.

Sutherland, Highland

Ceilidh Place (£) 14 West Argyll Street, Ullapool, IV26 2TY (tel: 0854 612103). Several cottages made into a local meeting-place: book- shop, coffee and wine bar, gallery and hotel; outgoing and friendly owners; simple bedrooms; vegetarian and fish emphasis to the menu.

RESTAURANTS

Roast beef and Yorkshire pudding, plus apple pie and custard as a dessert, is the quintessentially British dish; but the nation's gastronom- ic tastes are becoming increasingly cosmopolitan. Many hotels and restaur- ants offer French cuisine, while Indian and Chinese restaurants are the leading ethnic eateries. Fish and French fries (known as fish supper in Scotland) is the traditional, sustaining take- out food and is still very inexpensive. Pub meals are among the cheapest sit- down options (an elaborate bread, cheese, pickle and salad platter is known as a ploughman's lunch). In Scotland, high tea is often served in late afternoon and early evening—a hot dish, bread and butter, cake and/or scones, a pot of tea.

The following restaurants are divided into three price categories:
budget (£): a meal is likely to cost under £10 per head.
moderate (££): a meal is likely to cost £10–£20 per head.
expensive (£££): a meal is likely to cost over £30 per head.

LONDON

The range of restaurants in London is unlimited, both in type of cuisine and price category. The selection given below is restricted to those that count among London's most highly rated or memorable eating places and those that offer a typi- cally British meal. For fur- ther suggestions on where to eat, see page 59.

Alastair Little (££–£££) 49 Frith Street, W1 (tel: 071- 734 5183). Unassuming- looking Soho restaurant, minimalist décor, not luxu- rious; but high-quality dish- es with Asian and Mediterranean flavors.
Capital Hotel (££) Basil Street, Knightsbridge, SW3 (tel: 071-589 5171). Stylish cocktail bar and small din- ing-room; good value set lunches and dinners.
Fortnum and Mason (££) 181 Piccadilly (tel: 071- 7348040). The renowned top people's department store serves everything from Welsh Rarebit to top- quality roast beef; excellent place to sample that British institution, high tea.
Four Seasons, Inn on the Park (£££) Hamilton Place, Park Lane, W1 (tel: 071-499 0888). Refined and smooth- ly executed cooking.
Le Gavroche (£££) 43 Upper Brook Street, W1 (tel: 071- 408 0881). Superlative restaurant with a friendly atmosphere; set-menu options available.
Grill Room, Savoy (£££) Strand, WC2 (tel: 071-836 4343). Formal, supremely competent restaurant in one of Britain's grandest hotels.
Place Below (£) St Mary-le- Bow, Cheapside, EC2 (tel: 071-329 0789). Outstanding restaurant in crypt of Wren's church; home- made, superb quality vege- tarian dishes.
Le Soufflé, Inter- Continental (£££) 1 Hamilton Place, Hyde Park Corner, W1 (tel: 071-409 3131). Imaginative cooking; formal service.
Sweetings (££) 39 Queen Victoria Street EC4 (tel: 071- 248 3062). City institution with Edwardian atmosphere serving fresh fish and steamed puddings to City gents.

HOTELS AND RESTAURANTS

Terrace, Dorchester Hotel (£££) 53 Park Lane, W1 (tel: 071-629 8888). Renowned French cuisine.
Veronica's (££) 3 Hereford Road, W2 (tel: 071-229 5079). Historically researched English food; British wines and cheeses.
Wilson's (££) 236 Blythe Road, W14 (tel: 071-603 7267). High quality food with a Scottish bias in Shepherd's Bush. Reservations essential.

THE WEST COUNTRY
Bath
Canary (£) 3 Queen Street (tel: 0225 330280). Long-established teashop, with range of teas, snacks, bakery products and lunches.
Royal Crescent (£££); see Accommodations.
Tarts (£–££) 80 Pierrepont Place (tel: 0225 330280). Cellar restaurant with daily menu.

Bristol
Arnolfini (£) Narrow Quay, Prince Street (tel: 0272 279330). Organic-food café-bar in arts center in converted dockland warehouse.

Cornwall
Seafood Restaurant (££); see Accommodations.
Shipwrights Arms (£) Helford (tel: 032623 235). Quaint pub with garden by a sailboat-filled creek; bar food.
Portgaverne (£–££). Bar food, and excellent buffet outside winter months; see Accommodations.

Dartmoor
Castle Arms (£) Lydford, nr Okehampton (tel: 082282 242). Pretty inn adjacent to ruined castle and close to Lydford Gorge; appetizing pub food; simple bedrooms.
Gidleigh Park (£££) Chagford (tel: 0647 432367). Idyllic mock-Tudor hotel on the edge of the moor; not cheap, but cooking of international repute.
Oxenham Arms (£). Good-value pub food; see Accommodations.
Primrose Cottage (£) Lustleigh (tel: 06477 365). Thatched cottage offering sumptuous cream teas;

cakes and lunches too.
Dartmouth
Carved Angel (£££) 2 South Embankment (tel: 0803 832465). French regional and British cuisine, with personal touches. Something of a national institution.

Dorset
Three Horseshoes (£–££) Powerstock, nr Beaminster (tel: 030885 328). Pleasant inn in center of thatched village in hilly countryside; good fish dishes.

Exmoor
Anchor and **Ship** (£–££) Porlock Weir (tel: 0643 862507). Inn and hotel with same owners; casseroles and seafood platters; traditional pub games; good, simple bedrooms.
Rising Sun (£–££) Lynmouth (tel: 0598 532223). Old-world former smugglers' inn in a popular coastal village; oak-panelled restaurant and bar; attractive bedrooms.
Royal Oak Inn (£–££); see Accommodations.
Tea Shoppe (£) 3 High Street, Dunster (tel: 0643 821304). Choice tea shop; cream teas, cakes, lunches.

Salisbury
Michael Snell (£) 8 St Thomas's Square (tel: 0722 336037). Popular tearoom, patisserie; quiches, salads.

Wells
Cloister (£) Wells Cathedral (tel: 0749 76543). Unpretentious bistro in cathedral; tasty soups, quiches and salads.

SOUTHERN ENGLAND
Brighton
Browns (£–££) 3–4 Duke Street (tel: 0273 23501). Excellent value brasserie for snacks or full meals.
Topps (££) 17 Regency Square BN12FG (tel: 0273 729334). Cozy basement restaurant ("Bottoms") in Regency hotel; honest food.

Canterbury
Il Vaticano (£) 35 St Margaret Street (tel: 0227 765333). Authentic Italian pasta.

Eastbourne
Star (££) Alfriston, nr

Eastbourne (tel: 0323 870495). Famous old-world inn/hotel, run by Forte, in charming village. Soup and ploughman's lunch, hot dishes, Sunday buffet.

Hastings
Roser's (££) 64 Eversfield Place (tel: 0424 712218). Intimate restaurant; small French-inspired menu, excellent wines.

Isle of Wight
Seaview Hotel: (££); see Accommodations.

New Forest
Le Poussin (££) The Courtyard, Brookley Road, Brockenhurst (tel: 0590 23063). Delicious ingredients, offered simply and sympathetically.

Weald
Brown Trout (£–££) Lamberhurst (tel: 0892 890312). Pub near Scotney Castle; excellent seafood.
Griffin (£–££) Fletching (tel: 082572 2890). Unspoiled 16th-century village pub with hearty bar food.
Rose and Crown (£–££) Mayfield (tel: 0435 872200). Timber-built pub of considerable character with a wide ranging menu.
Thackeray's House (££) 85 London Road, Tunbridge Wells (tel: 0892 511921). Historic house, connections with novelist William Thackeray; accomplished, uncomplicated cooking.

Winchester
Wykeham Arms (£–££) 75 Kingsgate Street (tel: 0962 853834). Between the cathedral and Winchester College, open fires and cozy corners; interesting menu.

Windsor
Waterside (£££) River Cottage, Ferry Road, Bray (tel: 0628 20691). Splendid restaurant with rooms (outside Windsor); French and Mediterranean influences.

HEART OF ENGLAND
Chiltern Hills
Beetle and Wedge (££); see Accommodations.

Cotswolds
Bakers Arms (£–££) Broad

Campden, near Chipping Campden (tel: 0386 840515). Enticing old inn in classic Cotswold village; good food.

Feathers (££) Market Street, Woodstock (tel: 0993 812291). Gracious old hotel with daily menu. Close to Blenheim Palace.

Fleece (£–££) Bretforton, nr Evesham (tel: 0386 831173). Superb half-timbered pub owned by the National Trust; period furnishings and inglenook fireplaces.

Green Dragon (£–££) nr Cowley (tel: 0242 870271). Good pub food, plus real ales and cider.

Greenstocks (£–££) Cotswold House Hotel, The Square, Chipping Campden (tel: 0386 840330). Good-value lunches; more expensive dinners.

Lamb (££) Shipton-under-Wychwood (tel: 0993 830465). Inn offering a short set-price menu; local produce used in cooking.

Oakes (££–£££) 169 Slad Road, Stroud (tel: 0453 759950). Cozy former schoolhouse; simple interior; warm welcome; quality classic cooking with a refreshing lack of fussiness.

Redmond's (££–£££) Cleeve Hill, nr Cheltenham (tel: 0242 672017). Mainly British fare; first-class ingredients.

Hereford
Olde Salutation (£–££) Weobley, nr Hereford (tel: 0544 318433). Medieval inn in picturebook half-timbered village; good-value Sunday lunch.

Rhydspence (£–££) Whitney on Wye (tel: 04973 262). Quaint old inn; tempting main dishes and excellent desserts. Close to Hay-on-Wye and the Welsh border.

Ludlow
Hardwicks (£) 2 Quality Square (tel: 0584 6470). Wholesome daytime vegetarian eatery.

Malvern Hills
Hope End (££); see Accommodations.

Oxford
Browns (£–££) 5–11 Woodstock Road (tel: 0865

511995). Excellent value brasserie for snacks or full meals.

St Aldate's Coffee House (£) 94 St Aldate's (tel: 0865 245952). Inexpensive, self-service student haunt opposite Christ Church; cakes, snacks, light lunches.

Turf Tavern (£–££) Bath Place, off Holywell Street (tel: 0865 243235). Picturesque old pub with yard, in city center but well hidden in a tiny alley (on Walk page 127); good bar food; often crowded.

Le Manoir aux Quat' Saisons (£££) Great Milton (tel: 0844 278881). Cotswold mansion southeast of Oxford offering some of the finest and most inspired cooking in the land; less expensive high teas. Splendid accommodations.

Stratford-upon-Avon
Slug and Lettuce (£–££) 38 Guild Street (tel: 0789 299700). Appetizing fare on an enterprising pub-cum-bistro menu; good wines.

EASTERN ENGLAND
Cambridge
Browns (£–££) 23 Trumpington Street (tel: 0223 461655). Excellent value brasserie for snacks or full meals.

Midsummer House (££–£££) Midsummer Common (tel: 0223 69299). Worth seeking out: a short walk from the city center. Accomplished cooking; excellent wines and cheeses.

Waffles (£) 71 Castle Street (tel: 0223 312569). Waffles in all styles.

Constable Country
Great House (££); see Accommodations.

Le Tolbooth (££–£££) Dedham, Essex (tel: 0206 323150). Half-timbered, on banks of Stour; seasonal menu.

Marlborough Head (£–££) Dedham, Essex (tel: 0206 323250). Excellent stop-off for bar food.

Lincoln
Wig and Mitre (£–££) 29 Steep Hill (tel: 0522 535190). Brasserie-style inn dating

from the 14th century and close to the cathedral; good for inexpensive lunches and festive, drawn-out dinners.

Norwich
Adlard's (££–£££) 79 Upper Giles Street (tel: 0603 633522). Friendly service; fixed-price French menus; good value lunches.

Mange Tout (£) 22–4 White Lion Street (tel: 0603 617879). Bistro/coffee shop.

North Norfolk Coast
Lifeboat (£–££) Thornham (tel: 048526 236). Pleasant old pub by saltmarshes; settles, old lamps and antique weaponry constitute the décor. Sandwiches and tasty fish dishes.

Southwold
Crown (£–££) 90 High Street (tel: 0502 722275). Agreeable pub serving excellent fish dishes; tends to get crowded; reserve at busy times.

Stamford
George (£–££) ; see Accommodations.

WALES
Brecon Beacons
Bear (£–££) Crickhowell (tel: 0873 810408). Coaching inn dating from 15th century; imaginative food.

Walnut Tree (££–£££) Llandewi Skirrid, nr Abergavenny (tel: 0873 852797). Adapted Italian cuisine; pub-like bar and bistro, plus a restaurant.

Pembrokeshire
Cnapan (£–££); see Accommodations.

Snowdonia
Jodies (£–££) Menai Bridge, Anglesey (tel: 0248 714864). Wine bar by Menai Straits.

Tu-Hwnt i'r Bont (£) Llanrwst (tel: 0492 640138). Old-world, low-ceilinged tearoom; Welsh bara brith; cakes, salads.

Ty Gwyn (£–££) Betws-y-coed (tel: 0690 710383). Pleasant old coaching inn on edge of village; good food and accommodations.

Wye Valley
Crown at Whitebrook (££); see Accommodations.

HOTELS AND RESTAURANTS

NORTHWEST ENGLAND
Lake District
Britannia (£–££) Elterwater, nr Skelwith Bridge (tel: 05394 37210). Snug old pub by village green; restaurant attached. Accommodations.
Pheasant Inn (££); see Accommodations.
Sharrow Bay (£££); see Accommodations.
Sheila's Cottage (£–££) The Slack, Ambleside (tel: 05394 33079). High-quality tea-room and restaurant; a Lakeland institution.
Sun (£–££) Coniston (tel: 05394 41248). Home-cooked food offered in hotel.

Liverpool
Armadillo (£–££) 20-2 Matthew Street (tel: 051-236 4123). Popular and excellent value for lunch; more expensive dinners; opposite the Beatles' "Cavern."
Philharmonic (£) 36 Hope Street (tel: 051-709 1163). Outstanding example of a Victorian "gin palace," mahogany fittings, stained glass. Inexpensive bar food.

Manchester
Yang Sing (£) 34 Princess Street (tel: 061-236 2200). Popular Chinatown haunt.

Peak District
Fischer's (££–£££) Baslow Hall, Carver Road, Baslow (tel: 0246 583259). Smart hotel in Edwardian manor; innovative cuisine with Japanese touches; cheaper high teas and bistro meals.
Green Apple (£–££) Diamond Court, Water Street, Bakewell (tel: 0629 814404). Light lunches and more ambitious dinners.
Rose Cottage Café (£) Castleton (tel: 0433 20472). Daytime eatery, popular with hikers.

NORTHEAST ENGLAND
Northumberland
Olde Ship (£–££) Seahouses (tel: 0665 720200). Old inn in harborside setting, popular with fishermen; bar snacks, fish dishes, Sunday roasts; well-equipped bedrooms.
Warenford Lodge (£–££) Warenford (tel: 0668 213453). Situated off A1 between Alnwick and Belford; inventive pub food.

North York Moors
Fauconberg Arms (£–££) Coxwold (tel: 03476 214). Appealing pub in enchanting village; hearty fare.
Magpie Café (£–££) 14 Pier Road, Whitby (tel: 0747 602058). Whitby crab, Esk salmon and other fresh fish.

York
Betty's (£) 6–8 Helen's Square (tel: 0904 659142). Celebrated tearoom chain (branches in Harrogate, Ilkley and Northallerton; also own Taylors, 46 Stonegate).
St. Williams (£) 3 College Street (tel: 0904 634830). Self-service snacks and lunches by the Minster.

Yorkshire Dales
Kings Arms (£–££) Market Place, Askrigg (tel: 0969 50258). Village inn.
Royal Oak (£–££) Market Place, Settle (tel: 0729 822561). Good choice of *à la carte* and bar meals.
Tea Cottage (£) Bolton Abbey (tel: 075 671495). Pretty tearoom with garden.

SOUTHERN SCOTLAND
Borders
Burt's Hotel: (£–££) The Square, Melrose (tel: 089682 2285). Fine 18th-century inn in town center with fixed-price and *à la carte* menus.

Dumfries and Galloway
Knockinaam Lodge (££); see Accommodations.

Edinburgh
Caledonian (££) Princes Street (tel: 031-225 2433). "The Cally," splendid 90-year-old former railroad hotel; an old favorite.
Henderson's (£) 94 Hanover Street (tel: 031-225 2131). Healthy, organic buffet fare.
Kalpna (£) 2-3 St Patrick's Square (tel: 031-667 9890). Top-value Indian restaurant; vegetarian options.
Martin's (££) 70 Rose Street North Lane (tel: 031-225 3106). Unpretentious but accomplished cooking; light and airy décor; a firmly established favorite.

Falkland
Kind Kittock's Kitchen (£)

Cross Wynd (tel: 0337 57477). Good-value lunches and teas.

Glasgow
Babbity Bowster (£–££); see Accommodations.
Café Gandolfi (£–££) 64 Albion Street (tel: 041-552 6813). Bistro in panelled former pub; great variety.
Ubiquitous Chip (£–££) 12 Ashton Lane (tel: 041-334 5007). Ex-warehouse off Byres Road; choice ingredients (no French fries!), Scottish dishes and salads.
Willow Tea Rooms (£) 217 Sauciehall Street (tel: 041-332 0521). Faithfully restored Rennie Mackintosh tearoom

St Andrews
Brambles (£) 5 College Street (tel: 0334 75380). Self service student haunt; predominantly vegetarian.
Peat Inn (£££) Peat Inn, by Cupar (tel: 033 484 206). One of the best-known restaurants in Scotland, in rural location. French cuisine.

NORTHERN SCOTLAND
Perthshire
Killiecrankie (£–££) Pass of Killiecrankie, nr Pitlochry (tel: 0796 3220). Scottish game, meat and fish.
Nivingston House (££) Cleish (tel: 05775 850216). Low-ceilinged bar, open fire; fixed-price four-course menu; accommodations.

Speyside
Muckrach Lodge Hotel (£) Dulnain Bridge (tel: 047985 257). Light lunches; excellent sandwiches.

Skye
Ardvasar Hotel: (££) Ardvasar (tel: 04714 223). Short, daily-changing menus; Scottish lamb and venison from local estates.
Hotel Eilean Iarmain (£–££) Isle Ornsay (tel: 04713 332). Small inn by natural harbor looking over Sound of Sleat; home cooking; good wines.

Sutherland
Altnaharrie Inn (£££) Ullapool (tel: 085483 230). Former drovers' inn; simple charm; virtuoso dinners.
Ceilidh Place (£); see Accommodations.

284

Index

a

bey Dore 122
beydale Industrial Hamlet 21, 192
botsbury 77
botsford 36, 218–19
erdeen 239
erfeldy 253
erystwyth 159
oyne 241
commodations 276–81
am, Robert 51
a Force 178
edale 208
leburgh 146
riston 99
erford 79
oway 216
owick 199–200
arnun 67
on Towers 189
berley 20, 97
nerican Museum 65
glesey 154
glesey Abbey 17, 138
gus 215
struther 230
tony 71
oor Low 186
oroath 215, 216
hitecture
  domestic 30–1
  early and medieval 28, 29
  semi-detached houses 22
nside Knott 175
an 215
eton Manor 100
sts 38–9, 149
festivals 18
undel 97
hburton 73
ndown Forest 89, 92
nmolean 126
dley End House 143
sten, Jane 36, 77, 108
ebury 65
emore 256
oridge 85
ot St. Lawrence 147
36, 216
sgarth Falls 209

B

kewell 186
moral Castle 241
mburgh 199
nockburn Heritage Centre 231
nard Castle 209
nsley House Garden 118
ra 261
teman's 103
th 63, 65–6
ttle 99
achy Head 98–9
amish: North of England Open Air Museum 21, 192, 194
aulieu Abbey 101
aumaris 154
ddgellert 20, 167
ddfordshire 137
druthan Steps 69
nn Lora 238
voir Castle 137
n Nevis 244
rkeley Castle 119

Berkshire 89
Berwick-upon-Tweed 199
Betws-y-coed 167
Beverley 192, 194
Bewdley 115
Bewl Water 92
Bibury 119
Big Pit Mining Museum 20, 156
Bignor Roman Villa 97
Binham 142
Birmingham 111–12
Black Country 111–12
Black Country Museum 20
Black Isle 242
Blackpool 95, 176
Blaenau Ffestiniog 20, 167
Blair Castle 253
Blenheim Palace 30, 114
Blickling Hall 142
Blists Hill Open Air Museum 123
Bluebell Railway 90
Bodiam Castle 99
Bodmin Moor 67
Bodnant Gardens 17, 169
Bolderwood 101
Bonawe Iron Furnace 248
Bonnie Prince Charlie 246
Borders, The 217, 218–19
Boscastle 68
Bosham 96
Bothwell 220
Bourton-on-the-Water 120
Bowhill House 218
Bowood 120
Bradford 192, 194–5
Bradford on Avon 67
Braemar 240
Branklyn Garden 17, 252
Brechin 215
Brecon Beacons National Park 153, 155
Bridgewater Canal 128
Bridgnorth 114–15
Brighton 88, 90–1, 94, 95
Bristol 63, 72
British people 12–13
Broadstairs 91
Broadway 120
Brodick Castle 215
Brontë Parsonage Museum 198
Brontë sisters 36, 198
Buckfastleigh 73–4
Buckie 257
Buckinghamshire 113
Buckland Abbey 74
Bucklers Hard 101
Bude 68
Burford 120
Burghley House 147
Burnham Overy Staithe 142
Burnham Thorpe 142
Burns, Robert 36, 216
Burrell Collection 229
Buscot Park 118
buses and motorcoaches 272
Bute 215
Buttermere 175, 178
Buxton 187
Byland Abbey 202

C

Caerlaverock Castle 221
Caernarfon 167, 169
Caerphilly Castle 157
Calderdale 195
Caldey Island 165
Callander Crags 214
Callanish 260

Cambrian Mountains 159
Cambridge 137, 138–9
camping 264
canals 128–9
Canterbury 93
Cape Wrath 259
Cardiff 157
Carisbrooke Castle 100
Carlisle 176
Carreg Cennen Castle 155
Cartmel 179
Castell Coch 157
Castle Acre 140
Castle Bolton 209
Castle Drogo 73
Castle Howard 30, 195
Castle Kennedy Gardens 222
Castle Museum, York 206
Castle Rising 140
castles and manors 26–7
Castleton 186
Cawdor Castle 242
Centre for Alternative Technology 164
Cerne Abbas 76
Chalfont St. Giles 36, 116
Chalkpits Museum 20
Channel tunnel 98
Charleston Farmhouse 91
Charlestown 71
Chartwell 102–3
Chatham Dockyard 20, 96
Chatsworth House 17, 187
Chatterley Whitfield Mining Museum 21, 189
Chawton 36
Cheddar Gorge 64, 84–5
Chedworth Roman Villa 119
Chee Dale 175
Cheltenham 117
Chenies 116
Chepstow 171
Cheshire 174
Chesil Beach 77
Chester 177
Cheviot Hills 201
Chichester 96
Chichester Harbour 96
Chiddingstone 107
Chilham 93
Chiltern Hills 113, 115
Chipping Campden 120
Chipping Norton 120
churches and monasteries 28–9
Cinque Ports 34, 105
Cirencester 118
clans and tartans 233
Cley 142
climate 265–6
Clovelly 72
Clyde Valley 220
Coalbrookdale Furnace and Museum of Iron 123
Cockermouth 178
Coldharbour Mill 20
Colns 119
Constable, John 38, 148
conversion charts 274
Conwy 167, 169
Cook, Captain James 203
Cookham 39, 109
Corfe Castle 77
Cornwall 62
Corsham Court 65
Cotehele 71
Cotswold Wildlife Park 119
Cotswolds 113, 118–21
Coventry 112
Coxwold 36, 202
Cragside 201

Craignethan Castle 220
Crail 230
Cramond 226
Crathes Castle 17, 241
crime 266
Crinan Canal 248
Croft Castle 122
Cromarty 242
Cromford 21, 40, 186
Cromford Mill 21
Cuillins 254
Culbone 79
Culloden 242
Culross 226–7
Culzean Castle 216
Cumbria 173
customs regulations 266, 267

D

D-Day Museum 104
Dalby Forest 203
Dalmeny 226
Dan-yr-ogof Caves 155
Dark Peak 187
Dartmoor 37, 62
Dartmoor National Park 73–4
Dartmouth 74
Deal 98
Dedham 148
Deeside 240–1
Dent 209
Dentdale 209
Derbyshire 174
Derwent Water 178
Devon 62
Dickens, Charles 91, 104
Dinas Island 158
disabled visitors 266–7
Ditchling Beacon 92
Dolgellau 167
Dorchester 37, 75
Dornoch 258, 259
Dorset 63
Doune 231
Dounreay 259
Dove Cottage 36, 178
Dove Dale 186
Dover 88, 98
Down House 103
Drake, Sir Francis 80
Drewsteignton 73
driving 267–8
Drum Castle 241
Drumlanrig 222
Dryburgh Abbey 219
Dumfries and Galloway 212, 221–2
Dunblane 231
Duncansby Head 238, 259
Dunfermline Abbey 227
Dungeness 105
Dunkery Beacon 79
Dunrobin Castle 259
Dunstanburgh Castle 199
Dunster 79
Duntisbournes 119
Dunvegan Castle 255
Durham 196
Durham, County 192
Duxford Air Museum 138

E

East Anglia 136
Eastbourne 98
Eastwood 137
economy 14
Edinburgh 212–13, 223–5
Edzell 17, 215

INDEX

Eildon Hills 218
Eilean Donan Castle 258
Elan Valley 159
Elgar, Sir Edward 125
Elgin 257
Ely 140
English Heritage 124
English Marches 112–13
Erddig 159
Eskdale 178
Eton 109
events 18
Exeter 62, 78
Exmoor National Park 78–9

F

Fairford 119
Fal Estuary 71
Falkland Palace 227
Felbrigg 142
Fens 136
Finchcocks 103
Finchingfield 148
Findhorn 257
Findlater Castle 238
Fingal's Cave 247
Firth of Forth 226–7
Fishbourne Roman Palace 96, 97
Fishguard 165–6
Fitzwilliam Museum 138
Flatford Mill 148
Floors Castle 219
Fort William 244
Fortrose 242
Fountains Abbey 29, 197
Fowey 71

G

gardens 16–17
Gardens of the Rose 146
Gatehouse of Fleet 222
Geevor Tin Mine 20
Glamis Castle 215
Glasgow 228–9
Glasgow School of Art 229
Glastonbury 80
Glen Coe 244–5
Glen Nevis 238
Glendurgan 16, 72
Glenelg 258
Gloucester 117
Gloucestershire 113
Godshill 100
Gordonstoun 256
government 11
Gower 153, 162
Grasmere 175, 179
Grassington 208
Great Coxwell Tithe Barn 118
Great Malvern 125
Grey Cairns of Camster 259
Grey Mare's Tail 214
Grime's Graves 140
Grinton 207
Guisborough Priory 202

H

Haddo House 239
Haddon Hall 187
Hadleigh 148
Hadrian's Wall 193, 201
Hailes Abbey 120
Halifax 195
Hampshire 89
Hardknott Pass 178

Hardy, Thomas 37, 63, 75
Hardy's Birthplace 75
Harewood House 197
Harlech 167, 169
Harris 260–1
Hartland Quay 72
Harvington Hall 115
Hastings 99
Hatfield House 146
Hawes 209
Hawkshead 179
Haworth 36, 197, 198
Hay-on-Wye 155
health 268
Hebden Bridge 195
Helmsley 202
Henley-on-Thames 109
Heptonstall 195
Hereford 122
Herefordshire 112–13
Hertfordshire 137
Hesket Newmarket 178
Hever Castle 17, 102
Hexham 201
Hidcote Manor 120
High Force 208
Higher Bockhampton 75
Highland Folk Museum 256–7
Highlands 236–7, 262
history of Britain
    Industrial Revolution 40–1
    maritime history 34–5
    monarchs 32–3
    prehistoric Britain 24–5
hitch-hiking 268
Holkham Hall 142
Holy Island 193, 199
Hopetoun House 226
Houghton Hall 142
Hubberholme 208
Hughenden Manor 116
Hull 192
Hunterian Art Gallery 228–9
Hutton-le-Hole 202
Hythe 105

I

Ightham Mote 103
industrial museums 20–1
Ingleborough 209
Ingleton Waterfalls 193
inner cities 184–5
insurance 269
Inveraray 248–9
Inverewe Garden 258
Inverness 242
Iona 247
Ironbridge Gorge 20, 123
Islay 249
Isle of Man 176
Isle of Wight 89, 92, 100

J

Jamaica Inn 67
Jarlshof 251
Jedburgh 218
Jervaulx Abbey 209
John O'Groats 259
Johnson, Dr. 122
Jorvik Viking Centre 206
Jura 249

K

Kellie Castle 230
Kelso 219

Kendal 179
Kenilworth Castle 133
Kenmore 238, 253
Kent 88
Keswick 178
Kiftsgate Court Gardens 120
Kilmartin 249
Kilpeck Church 122
Kingley Vale 96
King's College Chapel 28
King's Lynn 140
Kingussie 256
Kirkcudbright 222
Knole 103

L

Lacock Abbey 67
Lake District 36, 39, 173, 174, 175, 178–81
Lancashire 173–4
Land's End 69
landscape 25, 144–5
language, Welsh 160–1, 269
Lanhydrock House 67
Lanreath 67
Laugharne 36
Launceston 67
Lavenham 148
Ledbury 125
Leeds 137
Leeds Castle 103
Leicester 137
Leicestershire 137
Lewes 91
Lewis and Harris 260–1
Lichfield 122
Lincoln 141
Lindisfarne Castle 199
Lingholm Gardens 178
Linlithgow Palace 226
Linn o'Dee 240
literary heritage 36–7
Little Moreton Hall 30, 189
Little Walsingham 142
Liverpool 174, 182
Lizard peninsula 64, 70
Llanberis 20, 167
Llandrindod Wells 162
Llandudno 95, 167
Llangollen, Vale of 163
Llechwedd Slate Caverns 20, 167
Llyn Idwal 158
Loch Awe 248
Loch Lomond 232
Loch Morar 245
Loch Ness 242
Loch Tay 253
Lochaber 244–5
Lochaline 245
Logan Botanic Garden 222
London
    accommodations 58, 276
    airports 264
    Apsley House 50
    art exhibitions 48
    Bethnal Green Museum of Childhood 49
    British Museum 45, 47
    Buckingham Palace 43, 53
    Cabinet War Rooms 49
    cemeteries 50
    Chiswick 46
    Chiswick House 46, 51
    churches 54
    City 45
    Commonwealth Institute 49

Courtauld Institute 47
Covent Garden 44, 47, 52
day-trips from 47
Design Museum 49
Docklands 46
Dr. Johnson's House 51
eating out 59, 281–2
embassies and consulates 268
Fenton House 51
Geffrye Museum 49
getting around 46
Greenwich 46, 47
Ham House 46, 51
Hampstead 46
Hampton Court 30, 51
historic houses 50–1
history 44, 45
Houses of Parliament 43
Imperial War Museum 49
Kensington Palace 50–1
Kenwood House 51
Kew 16, 51
Leighton House 51
London Dungeon 49
London Transport Museum 47
London Zoo 48
Madame Tussaud's 49
Museum of London 46, 49
Museum of the Moving Image 49
museums and art galleries 47–9
National Gallery 43, 47
National Maritime Museum 46, 47
National Portrait Gallery 47
Natural History Museum 48–9
nightlife and entertainment 55
Osterley Park 51
pubs 59
Regent's Park 45
Richmond 46
Royal Air Force Museum 49
St. Bartholomew the Great 46, 54
St. James's Park 43
St. Martin-in-the-Fields 43, 54
St. Paul's Cathedral 46, 54
Science Museum 49
shopping 56–7
Sir John Soane's Museum 50
Smithfield 46
Soho 44
Southwark Cathedral 54
Speakers' Corner 57
street markets 57
Syon House 31, 51
Tate Gallery 49
tours, organized 271
Tower Bridge 45, 53
Tower of London 45, 53
Trafalgar Square 42–3
Victoria and Albert Museum 49
Wallace Collection 48
Wembley Stadium 48
West End 42–3
Westminster Abbey 31, 44, 54
Westminster Cathedral 54
Whitehall 45

ng Man of Wilmington
99
ng Melford 148
ngleat 80
ver Broadheath 125
ver Slaughter 120
wry, L.S. 39, 183
dlow 124
ivingstone Park 92
worth Cove 64, 77
ndy Island 72
lford Gorge 64, 73
ne Hall 187
ne Regis 77

M

achynlleth 164
ackintosh, Charles
Rennie 229
es Howe 250–1
esllyn Woollen Mill
useum 21
aiden Castle 75
alham 208
allaig 245
alvern Hills 125
anchester 174, 183
apledurham 116
ps 269–70
see also Contents
atlock Bath 187
edia 270
ellerstain House 219
elrose 219
evagissey 71
dland Motor Museum
115
lford Haven 166
ton Abbas 76
ton, John 36, 116
ton Keynes 137
nsmere 146
nster Lovell 120
nterne Magna 76
el Fammau 158
narchy 11
onasteries 28–9
oney 270
onk's House 91
onmouth 171
onsal Dale 175, 186
ontgomery 166
ontrose 215
orecambe Bay 173
oretonhampstead 73
orwenstow 68
ount Grace Priory 202
ousa Broch 251
ousehole 69
ull 247
useum of the Lancashire
Textile Industry 21

N

ional character 13
tional Cycle Museum
141
tional Gallery of
Scotland 223, 224
tional Gardens Scheme
17
ional holidays 269
tional Lighthouse
Centre 70
tional Motor Museum
101
tional Museum of
Photography, Film and
Television 194
tional Museum of

Wales 157
National Railway Museum
206
National Tramway
Museum 187
National Trust 102, 145
National Waterways
Museum 117
National Wireless
Museum 100
Near Sawrey 178
Nedd, Hepste and Mellte
Waterfalls 155, 158
Nelson, Lord Horatio 35,
142
Nether Stowey 82
New Forest 101
New Lanark 214, 220
New Lanark Mills 21
New Mills 187
Nidderdale 208
Norfolk 136, 142
Norfolk Broads National
Park 141
North Bovey 73
North of England Open Air
Museum 21
North and South Downs
87–8
North and South Uist 261
North York Moors 192
North York Moors National
Park 202–3
North Yorkshire Moors
Railway 203
Northamptonshire 137
Northleach 119
Northumberland 192
Northumberland Coast
199–200
Northumberland National
Park 200–1
Norwich 143, 149
Nottingham 137
Nottinghamshire 137

O

Oban 248
Okehampton 74
Old Man of Hoy 251
Old Man of Storr 255
Old Radnor Church 163
Old Sarum 83
opening hours 270–1
Orkney Islands 250
Osborne House 100
Owletts 103
Oxford 126–7

P

Padstow 19, 68
pageantry and spectacle
18
Painswick 118, 119
Painswick Rococo Garden
17, 118
Paradise Silk Mill and
Museum 21
Parham House 97
Parracombe 78
Paul Corrin Musical
Collection 67
Peak Cavern 187
Peak National Park 174,
186–7
Peebles 218
Pembroke 165
Pembrokeshire 153

Pembrokeshire Coast
National Park 165–6
Penjerrick 16, 71
Pennines 191
Penrhyn Castle 169
Penshurst Place 102
Penwith 68, 69
Penzance 70
Perth 252
Perthshire 252–3
Peterborough 147
Petworth 101
Pevensey Castle 99
pharmacies 271
Pickering 203
Pistyll Rhayader 164
Pitlochry 252–3
Pittenweem 230
placenames 81
places of worship 271
Plas Newydd (Anglesey)
154
Plas Newydd (Llangollen)
164
Plockton 258
Pluscarden Abbey 257
Plymouth 80
Poldark Mine 20
Polesden Lacey 102
police 271
Polperro 71
Pontcysyllte Aqueduct 129
Port Isaac 68
Port Sunlight 188
Portloe 71
Portmeirion 169
Portsmouth 104
post offices 272
Postbridge 73
Potter, Beatrix 178
Power of Wales 167
Powis Castle 17, 166
Preseli Hills 166
Princetown 73
Prinknash Abbey 119
public transportation 272
pubs 15

Q

Quantock Hills 62, 82
Quarry Bank Mill 21, 189
Quebec House 103

R

Raasay 255
rail services 272
Ramsey Island 165
Ramsgate 91
Reeth 207, 208
restaurants 281–4
Ribblesdale 209
Richborough Castle 105
Richmond 208–9
Ridgeway Path 115
Rievaulx Abbey 202
Ring of Brogar 250
Ripon 197
Rob Roy 232
Robert the Bruce 231
Robin Hood's Bay 203
Rochester 96
Romney Marsh 105
Romsey 108
Rosemarkie 242
Ross-on-Wye 171
Royal Pavilion, Brighton 90
Rum 255
Runswick Bay 193, 203
Ruthwell Cross 221
Rye 104–5

S

Saffron Walden 143
St. Abb's Head 214, 219
St. Albans 146
St. Andrews 230
St. David's 165
St. Ives 39, 69
St. Just in Roseland 71
St. Michael's Mount 70
St. Neot 67
Salisbury 63, 82–3
Saltaire 194
Sandringham 142
Sandwich 105
Scarborough 203
Scilly, Isles of 83
Scone Palace 252
Scott, Sir Walter 36,
218–19, 232
Scottish Mining Museum
21
seaside resorts 94–5
season tickets (historic
houses) 273
Selborne 36
Selkirk 218
Selworthy 79
senior citizens 273
Seven Sisters 98, 99
Severn Valley Railway 115
Sezincote 120
Shakespeare, William 36,
131, 132
Shakespeare's Birthplace
131
Shaw, George Bernard
147
Shaw's Corner 147
Sheffield 21, 192
Shetland Islands 250, 251
Shobdon 122
shows and fêtes 18
Shrewsbury 130
Shropshire 112
Sissinghurst Garden 17
Skara Brae 250
Skegness 95
Skokholm 165
Skomer 165
Skye 254–5
Slimbridge 113, 119, 144
Smailholm Tower 219
Snowdon 168
Snowdon Mountain
Railway 167
Snowdonia National Park
153, 167–70
Snowshill 120
Solva 166
Somerset and Avon 62–3
South Downs 87–8
South Uist 261
South Shropshire Hills 130
South Wales valleys 156
Southampton 89
Southsea 104
Southwell 146
Southwold 146
Spalding 141
Spey Valley 256–7
sporting events 18
Staffordshire 174
Staithes 193, 203
Stamford 147
Standen 102
Stinsford 75
Stirling 231
Stoke-by-Nayland 148
Stoke-on-Trent 21, 189
Stokesay Castle 27, 124
Stonehenge 63, 84
Stonor House 116

INDEX

Stott Park Bobbin Mill 21, 179
Stourhead 16, 84
Stourport-on-Severn 115
Stratford-upon-Avon 36, 131–2
student/youth travel 273
Studley Royal 17, 197
Sudbury 148
Sudeley Castle 120
Surrey 89
Sussex 88–9
Swaledale 208–9
Sweetheart Abbey 222
Sygun Copper Mine 20, 167
Symonds Yat 158

T

Tarn Hows 179
Tarr Steps 79
tartans 233
Teesdale 208
telephones 273
Tenby 165
Tenement House 229
Tewkesbury 117
Thames Valley 109
Thaxted 148
Thirlmere 178
Thomas, Dylan 36, 160
Thornton Dale 202
Thorpeness 146
Threave Castle and Gardens 221–2
Three Peaks 209

time 273–4
Tintagel 62, 68
Tintern Abbey 171
tipping 270
Tissington 186
toilets 274
Tolpuddle 76
Torridon 258
Totnes 74
tourist offices 274
Traquair House 218
Trebah 16, 71
Trelissick 16
Trerice 69
Tresco 83
Tretower 155
Trewint 67
Trewithen 16
Tring Reservoir National Nature Reserve 115
Trossachs 232
Tunbridge Wells 107
Tyne and Wear 192

U

Ullswater 175, 178
United Kingdom 11
Upper Swaledale 193

V

Valle Crucis Abbey 163
Valley of Rocks 64, 78
Verulamium 146
Veryan 71

W

Waddesdon Manor 132
Wakehurst Place 17
Walberswick 146
Walker Art Gallery 182
walking and hiking 274
Walmer 98
Walpole St. Peter 140
Walsoken 140
Warkworth 200
Warwick 133
Warwickshire 113
Wast Water 178
Watercress Line 108
Watersmeet 78
Weald 87, 103, 107
Weald and Downland Open Air Museum 96–7
Wells 84
Wells-next-the-sea 142
Welsh Folk Museum 157
Welsh Slate Museum 20–1,167
Wensleydale 209
West Highland Line 245
West Highland Way 245
West Somerset Railway 82
West Wycombe 116
Western Isles 260–1
Westonbirt Arboretum 118
Weymouth 77
Wharfedale 208
Wheal Martyn 20
Whipsnade Wild Animal Park 116

Whitby 37, 202, 203
White Peak 186–7
Whithorn 222
Wicken Fen 140
Widecombe in the Moor 73
Wilmington, Long Man of 99
Wilton House 83
Wiltshire 63
Wimpole Hall 138
Winchcombe 120
Winchelsea 105
Winchester 89, 107–8
Windermere 179
Windsor 109
Windsor Castle 89, 109
Winkworth Arboretum 16
Wisley Garden 16–17
Woburn Abbey 147
Wookey Hole 85
Worcester 125
Wordsworth, William 36, 82, 178
Wren, Sir Christopher 54
Wye Valley 171
Wyre Forest 115

Y

Yarmouth, Isle of Wight 100
York 204–6
Yorkshire 191–2
Yorkshire Dales 192, 208
Yorkshire Dales National Park 208–9

Picture credits

The Automobile Association would like to thank the following for their assistance in the preparation of this book.
BRIDGEMAN ART LIBRARY 38a *Fitting Out, Mousehole Harbour, 1919* by Stanhope Alexander Forbes (1857–19 (Bradford Art Galleries and Museums/Bridgeman Art Library, London), 149a *Wood Scene, 1810* by John Cro (1768–1821) (By courtesy of the Board of Trustees of the V&A/Bridgeman Art Library London), 149b *Fishing Boats Yarmouth* by John Sell Cotman (1782–1842) (Christie's London/Bridgeman Art Library, London). BRITISH WAT WAYS BOARD 128a Buckby Locks. MARY EVANS PICTURE LIBRARY 32a Charles II, 32b Elizabeth I, 32c Henry V 33 Charles I, 39a J M W Turner, 40a Manchester 1870, 94b bathing machine at Brighton, 94c Hastings. J MORG 160a Royal National Eisteddfod of Wales, 161 Rhymney Valley. RITZ HOTEL 59b tea at the Ritz. ROYAL GEOGRA ICAL SOCIETY 21b map of Britain. SPECTRUM COLOUR LIBRARY (Spine) Queen's Head pub sign, Rye. T MANSELL COLLECTION 216a Robert Burns, 246b Charles Stuart. ANDY WILLIAMS PHOTO-LIBRARY (Cover) tage, Polperro.

All remaining pictures are held in the Association's own picture library (AA PHOTO LIBRARY) with contributions fro M ADELMAN 36a, 41, 227a, 238, 261a, 262b. M ALLWOOD-COPPIN 26–7, 130a, 130b. A BAKER 4, 20b, 64b, 6 112, 123c, 179, 198a, 198b, 198c, 208a, 212a, 230a, 230b, 231, 232, 236, 252, 256. P BAKER 26b, 44, 60, 63, 68, 75a, 75b, 77, 106b, 140, 173, 174, 186a, 187, 197a, 203a, 206a. J BEAZLEY 16a, 186c, 190, 193, 194a, 194b, 19 199, 200, 214, 216b, 217, 221, 222b, 237, 249a, 259. A W BESLEY 5b, 70c, 71a. M BIRKITT 5c, 28b, 65a, 84, 95a, 1 115, 131. E A BOWNESS 18a, 243. P & G BOWATER 229b. P BROWN 12b, 88b, 90, 91, 97a, 99, 104a, 105 BURCHILL 176a. I BURGUM 110a, 123a, 123b, 124b, 150, 152a, 152b, 155a, 156a, 157a, 157b, 162, 164a, 165a, 16 167, 168, 169a, 169b, 171b, 269. J CARNIE 233a, 245a, 245b, 253c, 258. D CORRANCE 225, 233b. D CROUCH 159a, 163, 164b, 222a. P DAVIES 146, 147. P EDEN 100b. R ELLIOTT 224, 226–7. P ENTICKNAP 108. R FLETCH 34b. D FORSS 15a, 30b, 50, 81b, 89, 92, 95b, 98, 102b, 103, 109a, 109b, 128b, 142a. S GIBSON PHOTOGRAPHY 2 220, 228, 229a. J GRAVELL 166. V GREAVES 132. S GREGORY 202a. A GRIERLY 18 A J HOPKINS 25, 82–3, 86, 171a. R JOHNSON 250, 251. A LAWSON 23, 69a, 70a, 70b, 74a, 74b, 116, 126–7, 144 McCRAE 125b. E MEACHER 5a. C MOLYNEUX 209a. R MORT 12a, 14a, 54b, 272. J MORRISON 192, 209b. R NE TON 21a, 37, 80a, 85, 143a, 158, 160b, 189, 206b. D NOBLE 17, 93, 104b, 106. K PATERSON 215, 249b. A PERK 156. J PERRIN 153. N RAY 19, 62, 67. G ROWATT 203. P SHARPE 3, 175, 178, 219, 240, 248. M SHORT 110b, 1 119. B SMITH 11a, 45, 56a, 59a. A SOUTER 10a, 24a, 72, 81a, 118b, 120, 136. F STEPHENSON 18b. R STRANGE 1 13b, 14b, 46, 48, 51, 57a, 57b. R SURMAN 28a, 113. M TAYLOR 223. T TEEGAN 79. T D TIMMS 27. M TRELAW 7a, 47, 54a, 58b, 96, 241, 271. P TRENCHARD 35b. R VICTOR 13a. W VOYSEY 16b, 22b, 34a, 35a, 38–9, 49, 53b, 82b, 87, 88a, 101a, 107b, 156b. R WEIR 6, 7b, 239, 244a, 254, 257, 260. L WHITWAM 10b, 30a, 40b, 129, 138a, 13 141, 143, 177, 182, 183a, 183b, 184a, 184–5, 185a, 186b, 188a, 188b, 188c, 195, 201, 204, 206c, 208b, 266, 268, 2 H WILLIAMS 24b, 29, 64a, 122a, 122b, 207. P WILSON 55, 56b, 58a. T WOODCOCK 9.

Contributors

Series advisor: Ingrid Morgan   **Designer:** KAG Design Ltd
Joint series editor: Susi Bailey   **Indexer:** Marie Lorimer
Copy editor: Sue Gordon   **Verifier:** Joy Nelson